Performing and Reforming Leaders

PERFORMING AND REFORMING LEADERS

Gender, Educational Restructuring, and Organizational Change

JILL BLACKMORE
and
JUDYTH SACHS

STATE UNIVERSITY OF NEW YORK PRESS

Published by
State University of New York Press, Albany

For information, address State University of New York Press,
194 Washington Avenue, Suite 305, Albany, NY 12210-2384

Production by Christine L. Hamel
Marketing by Michael Campochiaro

Library of Congress Cataloging-in-Publication Data

Blackmore, Jill.
    Performing and reforming leaders : gender, educational restructuring, and
organizational change / Jill Blackmore and Judyth Sachs.
      p. cm.
    Includes bibliographical references and index.
    ISBN-13: 978-0-7914-7031-2 (hardcover : alk. paper)
    ISBN-13: 978-0-7914-7032-9 (pbk. : alk. paper)
    1. Women educators. 2. Educational leadership. I. Sachs, Judyth, 1954– II. Title.

LB2837.B57 2007
371.20082—dc22
                                                                              2006013725

10 9 8 7 6 5 4 3 2 1

To Jesse,
the next generation

Contents

Acknowledgments

This text draws on the collective work of our colleagues in Australia, the United Kingdom, New Zealand, Canada, and the United States who have tracked and mapped the various trajectories of educational reform over the past decades. It also owes considerably to the policy analysis and activism of feminists in universities, schools, and vocational education. Finally, the research project could not have been completed without the input and hard work of three research fellows at Deakin University—Judy Bowly, Karen Tregenza, and Karin Barty. Academic research is increasingly reliant upon a group of educational outworkers, a group that is both casualized and feminized. And of course, as all families of academics understand, there is an implicit contract in terms of their continual and unflinching support of our labor, particularly at the point of production, the home.

Abbreviations

AAA	Affirmative Action Agency
ACE	Adult and Community Education
AQF	Australian Qualifications Framework
ARC	Australian Research Council
AVCC	Australian Vice-Chancellor's Committee
CAE	College of Advanced Education
CBT	Competency-Based Training
CSF	Curriculum Standards Framework
DEST	Department of Education Science and Technology
DETYA	Department of Education, Training, and Youth Affairs
DVC	Deputy Vice-Chancellor
EEO	Equal Employment Opportunity
EO	Equal Opportunity
ESL	English as a Second Language
MCEETYA	Ministerial Committee of Employment Education Training and Youth Affairs
NCVER	National Council for Vocational Education Research
NESB	Non-English-Speaking Background
OTM	Open Training Market
TAFE	Technical and Further Education
TESL	Teaching of English as a Second Language
Utech	Universities of technology
VC	Vice-Chancellor
VCAL	Victorian Certificate of Applied Learning
VET	Vocational Education and Training

INTRODUCTION

"Living at the Crossroads"

EDUCATIONAL RESTRUCTURING

This book is about the experience of women leaders in three Australian education sectors during a period of rapid change and significant educational restructuring over the past two decades.[1] Here we demonstrate the impact of globalization and the perceived shift to knowledge-based economies that since the 1980s have provided the major justification for radical educational reform in Australia and other Anglophone nation-states. For our purposes educational reform needs to be seen within the broader context of restructuring in economic and social relations among the individual, the state, and new modes of governance. In Australia during the 1990s, as previously in England and New Zealand, new public administrative and market-oriented reforms vocationalized education, linking it more tightly to the economy. Reform discourses promoted a seamlessness among schools, universities, and vocational education and deregulated education markets to encourage competition between public and private providers. This blurring of boundaries has in turn given rise to "institutional identity crises," as schools, technical and further education institutes (TAFE), and universities struggle to develop new profiles in order to maintain their legitimacy and existence in the eyes of key stakeholders and the community as well as their distinctive contribution to education.

As education is now a key commodity in postindustrial knowledge-based economies, the status of educators as professionals and knowledge workers has seemingly been enhanced with the democratization of knowledge on the one hand, and devalued with the commodification and technologization of professional knowledge on the other. This is in the context of the deregulation of education labor markets. The 1990s was also a period described as one of a

1

crisis of trust in public institutions (Warren 1999). Students (and parents) have become volatile subjects, consuming individuals empowered by market discourses of choice while focusing on more instrumental vocational outcomes. Education has become less about what students learn and more about what students are worth. Success is measured in terms of what institutions are attended (high performing schools and elite universities) as much as by individual achievement. Bloland (1995) sums up the emerging tendencies of the performative culture of education and governance to state that "efficiency and effectiveness have become the exclusive criteria for judging knowledge and its worth" (522). Whether it is true, just, or morally important has been reduced to whether it is efficient, marketable, or "translatable into information quantities" (Bloland 1995, 523).

A tension thus emerged between modernist and postmodernist tendencies in educational organizations. It is a tension that this book attempts to unravel and one that produces contradiction, ambiguity, and paradox for all educational leaders, but with subtle gender inflections. Paradoxically, at a time when passion, creativity, and caring social relationships were necessary for individual and institutional survival, the tendency of education reforms has been toward technical expertise, standardization and uniformity, products of both markets that produce risk and the new managerialism that seeks to manage it. The colonization of education by markets and the new managerialism have produced new regimes of performativity that focus on appearance, on image, and on marketable performances. As such, performative technologies (e.g., performance indicators, standardized evaluations, audits) demand practices that are increasingly "decoupled" from the realities of the core work of education—teaching, research, and leadership (Elliott 2001). Academics, trainers, and teachers express a sense of loss of control over their intellectual property and autonomy in their professional lives due to the intensification of their labor and the simultaneous exploitation of their desire to perform, but with professional care and compassion. In turn, these new regimes produce new work identities and understandings of professionalism as educational organizations take on new responsibilities, functions, and priorities; and old knowledge hierarchies that once imparted prestige and power are supplanted by new hierarchies of performativity. Being seen to perform, we found, counts more than substantive social action such as addressing issues of inclusion/exclusion and social justice (Morley 2003).

We suggest that this decoupling is indicative of something more than the representations of leadership in the media, job descriptions, contracts, and management theory being at odds with leaders' practical knowledge and daily experience. It is symbolic of a shift in the sociopsychic and political economies of education professionals and a renorming of the field of education. In practice, these changes have heralded the emergence of "professional identity crises" concurrently with "the 'managerialized' structural realignment of lived practices, social relations, and intersubjective dispositions (especially ethical dispositions)" (Zipin and Brennan 2003, 352).

The data presented is thus a snapshot of the restructuring of all three Australian education sectors (universities, TAFE institutes, and schools) during a four-year period (1995–98). It represents a period of transition in educational governance and management and is illustrative of processes of corporatization (in terms of consumption and production) and privatization (in terms of costs and benefits) of education in many Anglophone nation states. We explore how the processes of marketization and managerialism shaped the position of women already engaged in or seeking leadership positions. We consider the implications of a shift from a welfare to a postwelfare state in Australian public policy in general and gender equity for women educators specifically. We question how the radical restructuring, reculturing and renorming of Australian education impacts on gendered work identities, understandings of leadership, and institutional politics. We draw from the new policy sociology to identify how similar policy frames and common historical legacies produced cross-institutional, cross-sectoral, cross-national convergences and divergences. During the 1990s metanarratives of neoliberal reform were rapidly transferred through the interchange of personnel and ideas among the international intelligentsia and the institutionalization of a narrow conceptualization of human capital theory and economics through supranational institutions such as the World Bank and OECD (Henry et al. 2001). Our study also indicates that this is not to downplay the significance of the local, or the interplay between the local and the global, or "glocalization" (Luke, A. 1997).

This book are framed around the following questions:

- How did women leaders, in formal and informal positions of leadership in schools, universities, and technical and further education institutes in four Australian states experience and negotiate the contradictions, paradoxes, and tensions arising from the process of educational restructuring?
- What professional and institutional contexts provided them with agency, and which ones disempowered them?
- How were understandings of both the global and local enacted in gendered ways through shifting structural, cultural, and material relations?

SITUATING THE STUDY

This study is distinctive in many ways. Through the comparison of women in leadership we bring together some commonalities and unravel some differences in the experiences and outcomes of educational restructuring across different organizational contexts (universities, TAFE institutes, and schools), in four Australian states (Queensland, New South Wales, Victoria, and South Australia). In so doing, we draw upon well-established feminist scholarship on leadership in schools (e.g., Acker and Feuerverger 1996; Chase 1995; Arnot, David, and Weiner 1999), a smaller but expanding body of research on gender and universities (e.g., Brooks and MacKinnon 2001; Morley 1999), and an emerging, predominantly English, research field in the further education sector (e.g., Shain 1999; Whitehead 1999; Avis 2002 in the United Kingdom; Seddon and Angus 2000; Brown et al. 1996 in Australia). From this literature and our research we argue, first, for the need to consider specific professional discourses arising from the historical relationships in and between each education sector and ask how these professional fields are both sector and culturally specific. Second, we acknowledge that within each sector different institutional cultures produce site-specific narratives and counternarratives about leadership, educational change, and gender politics that are informed by wider discourses about educational leadership in popular culture and the media (Blackmore 1997; Blackmore and Thorpe 2003; Thomson et al. 2003; Wilkinson 2005). Our analysis of highly localized interpretations of these different discourses revealed a common set of problems for women managers and leaders in the education field that resonated with women in other professional contexts.

We undertook intensive interviews with these women to explore the ways in which different professional and institutional cultures informed how they viewed leadership—and were viewed in leadership—at a time when education was shaped by both nationally driven policies seeking to internationalize Australian education and state policies that sought to restructure schools, universities, and TAFEs (Sachs and Blackmore 1998). While leadership was the primary conceptual lens, gender was also foregrounded. This made explicit an undercurrent of any remaining gender/sexual bias flowing through organizational practices (Alvesson and Due Billing 1996).

The book draws from data derived from a project funded by the Australian Research Council (1995–98) that focused upon three groups of women in education—the institutional achievers already in formal leadership positions, the aspirants to formal leadership positions, and the capable nonaspirants or informal leaders. Our focus in this project was largely on those women in management responsible for strategic and operational aspects of educational organization—from financial management, quality assurance, and curriculum through employment, professional development, and performance appraisal. We also interviewed women who were perceived to be leaders in some aspect of educational work—disciplinary, curriculum, and pedagogical leaders or directors of research centers, as well as those perceived to be change agents and reformers. All the women interviewed were from an educational background. Our sample was representative of different disciplinary specializations, the range of institutions in each sector, as well as age, ethnicity, and location. We undertook a total of one hundred and fifty interviews in twenty schools, five universities, and eight TAFE institutes. The identification of institutions and individuals was based on purposive sampling (typical case sampling, criterion sampling, and collegial-recommended sampling). On the basis of "typical case" sampling, schools were selected to include both those with women in leadership positions and those with no history of women in leadership across rural, urban, and provincial locations. Higher education institutions were selected to include "sandstone" universities (founded prior to World War 1); "redbrick" universities (established in the 1940s and 1950s); "gum tree" or regional universities (founded between the early 1960s and mid-1970s); "Utechs" (i.e., universities of technology) or reconfigured senior institutes of technology; and the "wanna-bes" or new universities, the colleges of advanced education not merging with universities (Marginson and Considine 2001). "Criterion sampling" of women in executive leadership meant that we included one of the three universities (out of thirty eight) that had a female vice chancellor, but interviewed two female vice-chancellors (or university presidents). The TAFE institutes were selected to gain a sample of different institutional cultures: on the basis of strong community or trades orientation; whether they were newly amalgamated; their size and the concentration of men and women in senior management and CEO positions.

Theoretically and methodologically we sought to problematize leadership as a concept and practice. To do this, we approached each organization from two perspectives (insider and outsider) to get a sense of the issues circulating around gender, leadership, and equity. Using "purposive sampling," we began by interviewing key "gatekeepers" in the organization—the CEOs, heads of departments, and school principals—gaining a "top down" mainstream perspective. At the same time, we interviewed the "outsiders inside," on the margins, the equal opportunity officers and teacher union representatives. We asked each of the initial interviewees to identify women they saw as leaders, both in and out of formal positions, that would broadly (without asking who, why, and how?) "fit" the categories: women in formal leadership positions, women aspiring for formal leadership, and women who indicated few aspirations for formal leadership but who were perceived to be leaders by their colleagues. This technique led to an additional sample of about ten to fifteen women who were perceived by others to be leaders in their institutions. These combined techniques allowed for the consideration of women who were perceived to be leaders outside a self-evident definition of "leader equals role position."

In the writing of this text, we identified cross-institutional and cross-sectoral themes and contrasted different institutional narratives to indicate how context shaped individual and collective possibilities. Our interview data has been used in a range of ways. We have used the biographical narratives to provide story lines in which individuals made sense of their lives and point to contradictions and dilemmas. These portrayals are selected on the basis that they typify a particular position or aspect of institutional life and personal experience that we wish to explore. Along with these individual accounts, we incorporate extracts from different narratives to build a more holistic picture that provides a sense of significant patterns of practice and belief (Stake 1995, 15) yet gesture toward the ambiguity, complexity, and paradoxes that characterize contemporary organizational life (Hearn 1998).

STRUCTURING THE TEXT

This text, therefore, focuses on how women negotiate the paradoxical relations of leadership in increasingly corporatized education systems. In chapter 1 we engage with recent feminist theorizing about the state, education markets, restructuring, and globalization (Taylor et al. 1997; Gewirtz 1997; Stromquist and Monkman 2001; Blackmore 1999a) and draw on profeminist elements of the new sociology of masculinity (Lingard and Douglas 1999; Connell 1995, 2000; Whitehead and Moodley 1999) and critical feminist organization theory (Aaltio and Mills 2002). We elaborate on how the concepts of performativity (Butler 1999; Lyotard 1984), habitus, and field (Bourdieu and Wacquant 1992) enhance our analysis of gender and leadership as agency. We have organized the book into three parts: in part 1 (chapters 2–5) we focus on the processes and gendered effects of changing relations between the individual and the state. In chapter 2 we map out the first-level effects of educational restructuring in terms of structural and cultural reform, then track how the strategies of corporatization, markets, and managerialism reconfigure the institutional and cultural arrangements of education. Chapter 3 considers the second-level (or substantive) equity effects and how restructuring was inflected by gender in both positive and negative ways, but in the context of increasingly toxic, volatile, and greedy workplaces. Then in chapter 4, we consider the differential effects of restructuring in specific organizational and professional cultures (e.g., the entrepreneurial cultures of TAFE, the academic cultures of universities, and the professional cultures of teaching in schools) and how this specificity produced possibilities and constraints for women in management or womanagers (Ozga and Deem 2000). Why are some institutional or organizational cultures more conducive to women in formal leadership than others? Chapter 5 considers how the emergence of new modes of educational accountability explicit in the rise of the audit culture in education leads to a focus on the performative rather than the substantive and produces a sense of cultural and functional dissonance within organizations and of psychological "splitting" for individuals about the purpose and nature of educational work (Walkerdine 1989).

In part 2, we focus more on the how corporate leadership and managerial practices reconstituted the professional identities of teachers, trainers, and academics, as well as institutional identities. Chapter 6 considers the formation of leadership habitus of our women participants arising from their life histories in education, activism in social movements, and individual experiences of and in leadership. Chapter 7 then focuses on how the discourses of management and markets constrained and shaped leadership agency, while chapter 8 maps out how the performative organization captures and exploits the emotional management capacities of women managers. We explore the renorming of education through the notion of "sociopsychic economy." Chapter 9 tracks how competing external agendas and institutional/sectoral differences position women in middle management within competing logics of practice where they act as both change agents and managers of corporate culture.

Part 3 considers different interventions by the state and other change agents, such as gender equity reformers. Chapter 10 focuses on how equity policies and practices have been reframed during this period. Specifically we examine the policy shift from more legalistic and explicitly focused discourses of equity and equal opportunity to looser and weaker notions of managing diversity and what this implies for future policy agendas. The concluding chapter picks up and elaborates on the ongoing paradoxical relations between performativity and passion in educational work during the first decade of the twenty-first century. We consider evidence relating to increased educational inequality and social division as a consequence of restructuring and the instransigence of masculinist forms of leadership. This, we argue, demands a rethinking on the role and function of education in democratic postindustrial societies from a view of social justice and the implications of this for new more inclusive modes of leadership.

POSITIONING OURSELVES

We work from a position that asserts that social relations are a central aspect of leadership work. Our focus on women and leadership in education is heightened by our own positioning within the discourses of globalization, restructuring, markets, management, equity, social inequality, and educational reform. During the writing of this book, we both moved into key policy and administrative positions in our respective universities and took up leadership roles on our respective academic boards and in senior management.[2] In negotiating what constitutes academic work and quality, we are located at the cusp of the shift from modernism to postmodernism in education. This shift is evident in the cultural clashes between two opposing views of what constitutes a university. On the one hand, there is the modernist university and its associated intellectual and disciplinary traditions that are rooted in a twentieth-century sense of democratic and academic freedom and public service backed by government investment. On the other hand, the corporate "lean and mean"

twenty-first-century university now has a clear strategic focus, line management structures, client service, and industry orientation. This is in part due to
government disinvestment in public education, training, and research and in
part due to the changing nature of knowledge, its production, and its dissemination. Working in one of the few remaining spaces within the university that
allows for professional discourses about academic freedom, academic boards,
we are both struggling over the changing role of the university and the role of
the critical intellectual in relation to the corporate state within our own specific cultural milieus and different institutional histories that have shaped our
own experiences of universities and leadership habitus (Blackmore 2003b). As
researchers in schools and TAFE, we are aware of similar processes reshaping
the field of education that impact on who we are and how we work in education as a field. As sociologists—one with initial training in history and the
other in anthropology—we have turned to "structural and materialist frameworks in order to offer more complex understandings of why patterns of social
inequalities remain intact despite the shifting, more fluid nature of modernity"
(Arnot 2002, 4). It is in this context that throughout the book we ask ourselves, are we "eyewitnesses, subjects and objects, of a break within modernity"? (Beck 1992, 9).

Hence, our analysis is undertaken from the position of two white, middle-class, feminist academics. As participants and observers in the restructuring of universities, schools, and TAFE institutes, we are in the advantaged
position to reflect upon the contours and fault lines of the educational and
organizational landscape of the 1990s with which we are familiar. In writing
this text, we situate ourselves as critical intellectuals (Blackmore 2003a),
activist professionals (Sachs 2003), and reflexive sociologists with a commitment to political action in and through research. Accordingly our project is
one of recapturing the capacity to define what constitutes "the problem" from
a theoretical position that is predicated on social justice and the possibilities
for action (Gunter 2000; Bacchi 1999). We hope that what we say in this text
leads to debates about educational values and raises questions about the role
of education and social progress.

ONE

Risky Times for Women Leaders

WOMEN MOVING INTO institutional leadership during the 1990s were not only managers of the processes of restructuring the education workforce but also the transformation of educational work and professional identities. During the last decades of the twentieth century, social, economic, and political relations were disrupted by the speeding up and intensification of flows of capital, people, goods, and images (Appadurai 1996). For these managers it meant "we are in fact multiple and contradictory subjects, inhabitants of a diversity of communities . . . constructed by a variety of discourses, and precariously and temporarily sutured at the intersection of these positions" (Massey 1994, 6–7). This increased interdependency also meant shared risk. The 1990s has been variously depicted as a period of high risk and low trust (Beck 1992; Warren 1999). The high risk is due to an increased susceptibility to more precarious and deregulated labor markets, as evidenced in the decline in a sense of the collective such as unionism, reduced protection for individuals by the postwelfarist state, more fraught social relations within new family formations, and changing gender relations. The low trust is due to a reduced faith in, and commitment to, public institutions, in particular the reduction of relations with the state to a limited economic model of contractualism rather than citizenship, increased social stratification, and "a lack of positive expressions of respect and recognition for others" (Sennett 2004, xiv). Working life is thus "saturated with uncertainty . . . which is a highly individualizing force. It divides instead of uniting, and since there is no telling who might wake up in what division, the idea of 'common interests' grows ever more nebulous . . . fears, anxieties and grievances . . . are to be suffered alone" (Bauman 2001, 24).

By the 1980s education policies informed by human capital theory in most Western democracies perceived and promoted education as central to knowledge economies (Brint 2001). Governments therefore sought to bind education more closely to work, industry, and the state. But in so doing, they refocused on the private rather than public benefits of education, with less regard for its unequal social and material outcomes. Privileging the economic was at the expense of the social, although public policy discourses of self-management, local participation, and choice captured a nostalgic return to notions of local community at a time when the notion of one unitary community with a single idea of a common good was disintegrating (chapter 2). Professional identity was being reconstituted around expertise, technology, and technique to service the new economy (chapter 4). We question whether the new work order is merely an extension of old industrial forms in a different guise, or whether it is capable of producing new work-based subjects and organizations in a knowledge society that is democratized in terms of its social, economic, and political practice?

This study was undertaken in the context of the resurgence during the 1990s of the cult of leadership (and indeed celebrity) in popular culture, politics, and economic and cultural life. Strong leadership was seen as a source of security, an easy solution to uncertainty in high-risk times. In education, the rhetoric of leadership supplanted that of administration and management as the dominant discourse in educational reform. Yet we found the management paradigm mobilized during the 1990s was more modernist than postmodernist. It was about reengineering education in "hard-line" ways, promoting images of being tough, entrepreneurial, and decisive, sidelining the human costs, and utilizing demoralizing and dehumanizing strategies of downloading responsibility, downsizing organizations, and outsourcing or casualizing core work.

These corporate and governmental processes not only reconfigured organizations but also reconstituted gender, class, and "race" inequalities. Paradoxically, the need for workplace flexibility in more culturally diverse societies also produced seemingly progressive postmodern discourses about women's styles of leadership as the way of the future in management. *The Karpin Report on Management Education in Australia* (Karpin 1995), for example, promised a paradigm shift in management. "Soft" management discourses were promoted, as was cultural and gender diversity in leadership, based on a prediction of "the feminization of management" and the shift to "relational rather than competitive values" (Barrett 1995, 1342). Thus, the "feminine" skills of people management were as critical to good leadership and management as the hard "masculine" skills of financial management. Increased interdependence was the key, so business opportunities had to be "nurtured through affiliation and cooperation rather than rationality, separation and manipulation" (Barrett 1995, 1342).

This view appropriated a now well-established feminist discourse of women being good change managers and drew on "new wave" management theory arguing that managers needed to continuously refashion themselves in a way that "involves a redrawing of the traditional masculine/feminine hierarchy of logic/emotion. Managers were now called to be 'passionate' in the workplace and in the performance of managerial practice" (Hatcher 2003, 392). Missing from the discourse were substantive feminist norms around mutual respect and equality. Individualism was not replaced, just redrawn. The characteristics of the feminine were "inserted in an old moral order as new forms of ethical practice, . . . made accessible to everyone, but conceived of as 'skills'" (Hatcher 2003, 399).

This decade also illuminated the paradoxes of "women's success" as women moved into middle and executive management in education, politics, and business.[3] The ongoing media interest in feminism highlighted the trials and tribulations of individual women's advancement as evidence of the achievements of equal opportunity policies (Blackmore 1997). Yet attitudes to women leaders wavered constantly between public adulation and harsh critique (Wilkinson 2005). For their part, successful women in high-stakes leadership, aware of the dangers of naming the barriers to women's progress, hesitated in doing so, despite significant evidence of the permanence and impermeability of organizational "glass ceilings" and the "boys' clubs." Mentioning any discriminatory structures, attitudes, or practices, covert or overt, was dangerous territory, casting them into the spotlight as troublemakers or encouraging labels of "token" women promoted on gender not merit.

Yet workplace restructuring during the 1990s also mobilized systemic and institutional dispositions inherent in organizational processes (e.g., promotion and transfer procedures, job descriptions, redeployment policies based on tenure and experience). Women were often the first redeployed, in acting positions, or retrenched—a form of "structural backlash" (Lingard and Douglas 1999, Blackmore 1999b). Educational organizations and education labor markets reflected the wider patterns of work, with the resilience of horizontal occupational segregation (women concentrated in traditional service occupations of teaching) and vertical segmentation (women concentrated in lower levels). The number of women entering tenured, full-time educational management plateaued by the late 1990s, replicating patterns in the wider workforce. In 1998, at the end of this study, women constituted 43.8 percent of workers and only 3.5 percent of them managers, compared to 9 percent of male workers being managers (Office of the Status of Women 1998). Family friendly cultural shifts in work practices remained arbitrary, usually mandated by executive fiat rather than the result of a bottom-up sea change in attitudes in the private sector. Even in the public sector, the major employer historically for women, policies often did not translate into action on the ground. Yet women's access to senior management is often paraded, "both as a symbol and a measure of organizational change" (Wacjman 1998, 1–2). This is because it is in the "top job" that women are perceived as the greatest threat to male power, a challenge to the gender regime that has naturalized and institutionalized the power relations in organizations. For gender is a "property of organizations as well as individuals," constituting how organizations work both in terms of the "symbolic order and in discursive and material organizational practices" (Wacjman 1998, 3).

SO WHAT IS THE PROBLEM HERE?

Studying women's experiences in middle and senior management in the context of the changing nature of educational work is important because the underrepresentation of women in authority, especially at high levels of management, is "not simply an instance of gender inequality but it is probably a significant cause of 'inequality' more generally" (Wacjman 1998, 32). We explore this connection between women's experiences of inequality and wider educational debates around education and social justice. To some extent, the discourses informing policies generated to support women's advancement in institutions has inadvertently contributed to making social change difficult to achieve. As Bacchi (2000b) comments, "this is due, in their view, not simply because opponents of change quash attempts at reform, but because issues get represented in ways that subvert progressive intent . . . and the ways in which 'social problems' or 'policy problems' get 'created' in discourse . . . problems are 'created' or 'given shape' in the very policy proposals that are offered as responses" (47–48). Bacchi's notion of policy-as-discourse allows us explore gender equity reform in the context of organizational and political change. Discourse is

> never disembodied or context free; it is always constitutive of the dynamic and ongoing process of making meaning. Gendered organizations thus do not "exist" as such; rather they are performed moment by moment through the communicative practices of their members. While such performances usually do not unfold capriciously, but rather, follow well-established scripts, it is still only in the doing—the performing—that such scripts are produced, reproduced, resisted, and transformed. . . . Discourse is not merely text or symbolism but it is something in which social actors engage with as real. (Aschraft and Mumby 2004, 116)

While we draw primarily on the voices of women in management or aspiring to be, we refute the view implicit in much equity policy that women are the problem. The "problem" of the underrepresentation of women in educational leadership is not about women's lack, whether of ambition or capacities, but rather, it is the consequence of the limited opportunities cre-

ated by the systemically gendered cultural, social, and structural arrangements that inform women educators' choices and possibilities *relative* to
their male colleagues.

Furthermore, while feminism has been seen by many men to be too successful, to the detriment of both men with their loss of privilege and women
due to overwork, the women leaders in our study often felt more weary and
worn out than successful. Sinclair (1994) also found a dissonance between
women's understandings of their success and their male colleagues' understandings of gender equality. This was because masculinity is "less about
power and more about a feeling of entitlement to it"; about perceptions of
who is powerful rather than how power works (Lingard 2003, 36). Australian
studies in universities (Currie and Thiele 2001), schools (Blackmore 199b)
and private industry (Sinclair 1994) confirm that many males believed women
were treated equally, most women did not agree and felt organizations ignored
or marginalized women's interests.

Spivak (1988) makes a useful distinction between how women are represented by others (representation that is subject to interpretation), and how
they see themselves or how they wish to be re-presented (self-presentation
according to their experience and perceptions of how others perceived them).
'Representations are more than mere symbols. They are the means by which
we come to know, embody and perform reality" (Moreton-Robinson 2000,
xxii). This is a critical point when it comes to understanding media, policy and
other representations of women that shape organizational discourses and gendered leadership identities(Blackmore 1997; Wilkinson 2005). Sinclair and
Wilson (2002) suggest that leadership is "constructed in the minds of audi-
ences" (176) as much as in the minds of the actors, producing a considerable
dissonance between how women see themselves, and how they are seen by
others.

Women leaders are positioned within popular discourses about "women's
styles of leadership" and women leaders being caring and sharing, powerful
discursive products of second wave feminism and feminist research (Blackmore 1999b, Wilkinson 2005). These limited gender scripts subtly continue
to draw upon the "symbolic power invested in the most powerful female role,"
motherhood, interestingly at a time when many women in leadership are
either without dependent children or are childless (Reay and Ball 2000). But
the dominance of this caring and sharing discourse during the 1990s meant
that regardless of whether men and women adopted authoritarian or democratic practices in management, how these practices were perceived and judged
was highly gendered. Furthermore, the actual capacity to undertake democratic practice was shaped by political, institutional and cultural contexts that
were more conducive to more authoritarian leadership practices. The problem
is both one of perception and structure as these strata work together in
unpromising ways for women.

GENDER, RESTRUCTURING,
AND EDUCATIONAL ORGANIZATIONS

Our project here is to consider how existing and emergent discourses circulating in and through educational organizations framed possibilities for women "leaders" as the principles of the market and new managerialism in the "post welfare," "managerial," or "market" state increasingly informed organizational practices in universities, schools and TAFE institutes. Specifically we are interested in identifying discourses around the changing nature of education professionalism and client based student/teacher relations; institutional discourses about entrepreneurship; management discourses about efficiency and effectiveness; and accountability discourses about quality and outcomes. Our analysis identifies trends towards the re-privatization of care and the privatization of the public, producing a blurring of public/private life, as well as changing priorities and practices in, and the intensification of, educational work. In this context women leaders, now moving into middle management in education as principals, department leaders and deans, are simultaneously positioned both as 'leaders' and agents of change and also as managers of organizational 'housework.'

In what follows, we identify seven areas where our analysis differs from other attempts to analyze women's experience of educational leadership. First, we link macrostructural shifts to micropolitical activities in organizations and to individual agency. The context described by these women in leadership is one in which government and management policies and practices signal tensions between the desire to gain control, on the one hand, and to encourage the creativity of "educated labor" as the source of productivity in knowledge-based economies, on the other. This is a tension echoed in the contradictory tendencies of centralization and decentralization, between innovation and maintenance work, and between care and compliance in organizations. As Rhoades (1996) observes: "Governance is not about centralization or decentralization—it is about regulating relationships in complex systems" (151). Whereas the 1980s saw academics and teachers as "co-participants in the exciting work of educational innovation and change" (Brown et al. 1996, 311), now they were repositioned as the recipients of decisions based on a decisional not dialogic process of reform. Limerick, Cunnington, and Crowther (1998, 21–22) argue that, in Australia, the public sector has been "plagued by problems of accountability and governments are reluctant to let go of the apparent certainty of hierarchical control. So they have developed an uneasy hybrid form of organization in which hierarchy is retained but which also attempts to implement some of the precepts of post corporate organizations [such as flexibility, localized autonomy etc]."

The product is the corporate neobureaucracy, a hybrid of entrepreneurial, masculinist corporate managerialism and paternalistic bureaucracy. While our study of leadership as a catalyst for personal and organizational change illuminated how women identify as leaders and change agents, our cohort inevitably contextualized any discussion of leadership within the changing context of educational reform. They saw the cumulative effect of hybrid managerialism and quasimarkets, together with new communication and information technologies, as fundamentally changing personal, pedagogical, and professional relations and, in turn, how they as women were represented.

Second, in attempting to better understand and theorize these transformations, we recognize that the processes of systemic, organizational, and personal change are gendered, as are their effects, a feature largely neglected in the literature on educational restructuring (Ashcraft and Mumby 2004). Educational restructuring, as organizational life generally, is gender inflected, in that the objectives, priorities, and processes of reform, despite the gender-neutral discourses, are highly gendered in their assumptions, values, practices, and therefore, effects (Alvesson and Due Billing 1996). In turn, the technologies of the market and management have produced new work identities that are gendered, "raced," and classed (Gee, Hull, and Lankshear 1996). Most of the women we interviewed saw women leaders as being dynamically repositioned between changing economic, political, and social contexts, the "reciprocal dialectical and mutually defining character of symbolic/discursive and material conditions of organizing" as both "macro political arrangements and the micro practices work on identity, body and sexuality" (Ashcraft and Mumby 2004, 123). They recognized that the shifts in values produced through policy texts, funding mechanisms, labor market relations, organizational cultures, and the lived experiences of people working within educational institutions all affected their orientation to work (see Brooking 2005). But we found women positioned themselves variably within this changing discursive space. Some saw this as being about increased control through self-management—becoming "designer employees"—as the corporate ethos discouraged voicing disagreement with corporate aims (e.g., Casey 1995). Other women were more comfortable with entrepreneurial discourses than others. Some women rejected feminism and did not see their role as one of advocacy for other women or disadvantaged students, thus problematizing popular discourses about women's styles of leadership that imply all women have similar value positions, and care for the disadvantaged. Regardless, our focus on restructuring as the context for leadership work moves beyond the current fixation of leadership research on personal attributes, skill development, and career paths, on the one hand, and generic "management guru" recipes for successful organizational reform, on the other hand.

Third, this study is informed by recent sociologies of gender that focus on the social construction of multiple masculinities and femininities and the different ways of acting out being male and female (Connell 1995). Femininities, like masculinities, "are defined collectively in culture and sustained in institutions" such as schools, universities, workplaces, unions, bureaucracies, and professional and voluntarist organizations (Connell 1995, 11). These different social spaces produce different communities of practice, ways of speaking, behaving, and doing that are not readily transferable to other locations and sites of practice (Wenger 1998). Hegemonic femininities and masculinities in workplaces and nation states also change over time, although the close association of masculinity with authority and power (masculinism) endures. But we do not suggest that educational restructuring benefited all men and disadvantaged all women. Feminist understandings see gender as not being "fixed," emphasizing change and fluidity (for example shifting and performative notions of gender) over gender continuities and stability (Dillabough and Arnot 2001, 32), as our study indicates. Changing organizational practices threatened the taken-for-grantedness of particular forms of masculine dominance in educational organizations, but it also reinforced others. While many individual women benefited from restructuring in some ways, gendered power/knowledge relations did not significantly alter. Indeed, the very processes of marketization and new managerialism arguably led to the emergence of refigured modes of masculinity. For example, masculinist images of leadership and success arising out of the new entrepreneurialism and internationalization in education revitalized in new forms old constructions of valued knowledge or desirable outcomes (Reay and Ball 2000; Reed 1995).

Fourth, we focus on the conditions of possibility for social change and leadership as well as conditions of constraint. Policy-as-discourse analysts have emphasized constraints, largely because they have emphasized the use and not the effects of discourse (Bacchi 2000b). We seek not to be "skeptical" postmodernists but "affirmative" postmodernists, critical of modernity but open to new ways of change. From our position as critical intellectuals and activist professionals, we support "affirming an ethic, making normative choices and striving to build issue specific policy coalitions" (Rosenau 1992, 15–16). This requires us to "identify sources of power and propose projects to challenge them" (Bacchi 2000b, 47) and to consider their symbolic and material effects. Restructuring altered the symbolic and material conditions of educational and therefore leadership work. We use the term *educational worker* intentionally, interchangeably with *teacher*, *educator*, *trainer*, and *manager/leader*, to highlight what we see is a radical transformation of the educational labor process underway in all education sectors. This transformation promised some possibilities with the shift toward knowledge-based economies, as educational institutions increasingly focused on managing the processes of knowledge production, dissemination, and legitimation. We consider whether educational workers (and managers) will belong to the new class of "symbolic analysts" or "knowledge workers," the designers and producers of knowledge, or merely become technicians or service workers in the transmission of knowledge (Aronowitz and de Fazio 1997; Brint 2001). A labor-process perspective links the numerical feminization of lower level management to a new managerialism incorporating women leaders and their skills, while seeking to drive down costs and intensify the return of labor in capital accumulation. "Knowledge practices capture particular subjectivities" and are "materially engaged in the production of reward differentials and segregation and subordination of work by women" (Prichard and Deem 1999, 324). Managerial work itself was in the process of being "deskilled in the sense that management is reconstructed as a set of highly codified technologies (budgeting, strategic planning and audit) and distributed to subordinate post-holders." So there is a tension between identities constructed through codified managerial practices and discourses that emphasize women's suitability for intensive people work that would appear to challenge "traditional paternalistic profession-ally-oriented knowledge practices" (Prichard and Deem 1999, 324).

Fifth, we see organizations as an array of fluid social practices and inter-actions, cultural representations, and meaning making that are gendered (see also Czarniaswka and Hopfl 2002; Ashcraft and Mumby 2004; Aailto and Mills 2002). "Gender is constitutive of organization; it is an omnipresent, defining feature of collective human activity, regardless of whether the activity appears to be about gender . . . the gendering of organization involves a struggle over meaning, identity and difference . . . [and] such struggles repro-duce social realities that privilege certain interests" (Ashcraft and Mumby 2004, xv). While multiple narratives of masculinity and femininity offering different versions of the self and others circulate, indicating their instability and lack of uniformity, "in practice they yield differential and consequential access to power and resistance" (xvi). Most often leadership is suffused with masculine images as the norm. In turn, it informs how women come to per-ceive themselves and be perceived by others as leaders and managers.

But if our lives as agents is recognized as a set of practices rather than structure or unreflective cognition that is determined elsewhere, then struc-tures can be understood as hierarchical relationships of power and processes that reinforce or subvert social relations. Organizations, for example, have a low tolerance for difference. There is a strong emphasis on similarity in under-standings and language and style, an expected commitment to corporate goals and to particular strategies and approaches. These practices of conformity are evident in the rituals of meetings (who sits where, how people dress, the lan-guage and level of formality and informality), in the symbolic use of space (who has the largest desk, location and size of office) and the cultural artefacts of dress. Resistance or signals of rebellion to organizational norms of mas-culinity and femininity are also symbolic—length of hair, color of clothing, size and design of shirts, skirts, and ties. The performative aspects of gender, therefore, are rendered evident in the repeated and subconscious gender per-formances in terms of codes for dress and behavior. They are

expressed in the design of the organization and of work, in the artefacts and
services that the organization produces, in the architecture of its premises, in
the technologies that it employs, in its ceremonials of encounter and meeting, in the temporal structuring of organizational courses of action, in the
quality and the conditions of its working life, in the ideologies of work, in
the corporate philosophy, in the jargon, lifestyle and physical appearance of
the organization's members. (Gherardi 1995, 13)

Organizations therefore "express a number of work cultures and comprise
of social constructs of workplace gender relations" because they are porous and
open to societal influence (Gherardi 1995, 3). Labor law and affirmative
action policies produce particular relations within and between social institutions, which assimilate and normalize demands for equality. Thus social
movements such as feminism in the professions or the media can impact on
institutional practices with regard to ethics and equal opportunity through
their extrainstitutional discursive power. In turn, wider political shifts in discursive fields toward neoconservative notions of gender can be mobilized to
delegitimate institutional equity discourses (Blackmore 1999b). Organizational cultures differ in terms of their gender regimes but are also shaped by
the wider "grammar of the social structures." "How gender is 'done' differently
is a crucial cultural phenomenon, and how it can be done differently is a challenge to all those who work in organizations and of the civilizing process
itself" (Gherardi 1995, 4).

Organizations and governments also practice symbolic violence (Bourdieu 1998). That is, they disguise inequality in the ways in which economic
and political power is represented and taken for granted through their logics of practice. Symbolic power is a subtle form of control and domination
that prevents this domination being recognized. It works through the structures and habitus inscribed in women's bodies (Webb, Schirato, and Danaher 2002). "Material and symbolic orders are internalized as a set of presence, categorizations and classifications that reflect existing gender
inequalities" and thus naturalized (Christie and Lingard 2001, 3). These
symbolic systems exercise power by making the self-complicit in the taken-
for-granted," the dispositions inculcated into the agent by insignificant
aspects of everyday life" (Bohman 1999, 132). Thus the academic world is
premised upon individualism and competitiveness and knowledge hierarchies where some disciplines claim objectivity and privilege makes women
complicit in devaluing their own experiences when they do not "fit." Likewise, when a woman's experiences of leadership do not fit that of the educational organization, they are positioned as not being ready or not appropriate, rather than considering that perhaps existing leadership
representations and practices are not inclusive. This constant reminder of
one's assigned social destiny works through the symbolic and the material,

the structural and the cultural, and is a key aspect of the symbolic violence in education systems. Through all this women receive contradictory messages: "[B]e equal but be different" (Gherardi 1995, 97).

Sixth, we identify and explore a hidden dimension of organizational life only recently addressed in organizational and educational theory—that of the emotions (Blackmore 1996; Fullan 1997; Sachs and Blackmore 1998; Hargreaves 1998; Boler 1999; Fineman 2000). Understanding the processes of organizational change means exploring individual emotional and intellectual investments in maintaining the existing circumstances or changing them. The focus therefore shifts to the relational aspects of leadership, as well as the matter of personal and professional identity. Emotions and motivation are connected. Many educators view education as a site of social action and change, as a political act. They feel a responsibility beyond their particular organization toward a wider public or profession. They gain rewards through productive collegial relations, recognition, and commitment (Nias 1999), yet career paths are premised upon reward systems based on authority. Emotional display can be the "surface tension" of educational politics. "[W]ithin Western patriarchal culture, emotions are a primary site of social control, emotions are also a site of political resistance and can mobilize social movements of liberation" (Boler 1999, xiii). Through the notion of a sociopsychic economy, we link emotional and political work to the collective organizational life and professional relations.

Our behavior is also governed by emotion rules. Boler (1999) also argues that "men and women across diverse cultural and ethnic backgrounds recognize similar patterns of gendered rules of emotion" (xiii). Women leaders, already seen to be the managers of "the personal" and "the private" in traditional gender relations, are now expected to also do the emotional management work of organizations—a "natural extension" of their domestic work of caring and sharing associated with popular notions of women being good at teaching young children and women's ways of leading and managing. Management is thus "capitalizing on emotions" . Yet success continues to be in the language of male-type behaviors and emotional expression, men and women abiding by the emotional rules of masculinist organizations.

Seventh, the reprivatization of care and work has produced new contradictions for women, given their usual responsibilities as primary caregivers of the old, young, and sick (Hancock 1999). The continual balancing act confronting women in leadership—between home, community, and work—highlights the contradictions between management discourses about flexibility (flexible workers, flexible learning, and flexible work arrangements), which are "family friendly" as opposed to the inflexibility of "greedy organizations" that demand more for less and actively undermine women's work as they intensify labor, casualize work, practice increased surveillance, and demand compliance (Summers 2003; Smulyan 2000; Franzway 2001). Even as an elite group of women, women educational leaders are positioned differently from their male colleagues in terms of the gender division of emotional management work.

In Western postindustrial societies, processes of detraditionalization, in which the traditional gender order is being transformed due to women's increased participation in work and leadership; and retraditionalization, as the neoliberal postwelfare state shifts responsibility back onto women for the maintenance of traditional family values and solidarity, are occurring simultaneously (Giddens 1994). Detraditionalizing forces, therefore, "may change the division of labor. But men and women have investments in particular traditional images of masculinity and femininity that cannot be totally transformed" (McNay 2000, 41). Indeed, the destabilization of gender at one level leads to greater intractability of the other. Thus while most women are more economically independent, many men's notions of masculinity and femininity fit neither new jobs nor the changing relations of gender. The effect of this is to lead to even more extreme versions of macho masculinities (Lingard and Douglas 1999; Whitehead 1999; Hearn 1998).

Finally, we take seriously McNay's (2000, 1–2) comment:

> One of the most pronounced effects of these macrostructural tendencies towards detraditionalization is the transformation of the social status of women in the last forty years and the restructuring of gender relations that it has arguably initiated. The effects of gender restructuring upon the lives of men and women are ambiguous in that they do not straightforwardly reinforce old forms of gender inequality; nor, however, can their detraditionalizing impact be regarded as wholly emancipatory. New forms of autonomy and constraint can be seen to be emerging which can no longer be understood through dichotomies of male domination and female subordination. Instead, inequalities are emerging in generational, class and racial lines where structural decisions amongst women are as significant as divisions between men and women.

We recognize that the white, middle-class women in this study (including ourselves) are advantaged relative to the majority of women. Indeed, we found a significant absence of ethnic and indigenous voices in the institutions we studied, a silence resulting from the Anglocentrism and heterosexism of mainstream management and leadership theory and the white, male hegemonic order in schools, universities, and colleges (Connell 1995; Sinclair 1998). Certainly the "embodied" presence of women disrupts senior management's culturally (masculine) homogenized environment (Sinclair 1998), foregrounding gender. Sadly, few male or female management practitioners undertake the painful analysis of their inherent whiteness and middle classness, despite a growing mass of critical and feminist organizational theory and research (e.g., Alvesson and Due Billing 1996; Hearn 2002. Moreton-Robinson 2000).

AMBIVALENCE, AMBIGUITY, AND CONTRADICTION

Central to this study was how most of the women leaders interviewed expressed a sense of contradiction and ambivalence toward educational change as it impacted on their own sense of professional self and agency. Women leaders often referred to a tension between the demands for corporate loyalty, particularly in management positions, and the capacity of educational leaders to exercise professional judgment and integrity at a time when there is no necessary consensus about the nature, method, or objectives of recent educational change. This, we have argued elsewhere (Sachs and Blackmore 1998), creates intellectual, emotional, and moral dilemmas for teachers and leaders as modernist notions of professionalism focusing on autonomy, judgment, activism, and advocacy are challenged (Sachs 2003). Professionalism was increasingly being viewed as a contractual arrangement, a technical capacity, part of emerging contractual relations arising from marketization and managerialism. It was premised upon competitive individualism rather than the collective aspirations of communities and groups, an individual rather than a shared sense of responsibility to a profession. This was even more intense for the espoused feminists whose professional identity and leadership habitus was tied to particular equity ideals. Such moral dilemmas led many women to exit educational leadership positions (Schmuck, Hollingsworth, and Lock 2002).

During this period of radical restructuring, we found that the women educators in this study expressed a sense of collective and individual alienation. This alienation arose from a dissonance between their commitment to particular educational values and the practices and values they were required to espouse in order for them to survive individually and as organizations. Policy shifts now focused on outcomes, on productivity through cost efficiencies, and indeed work for its own sake (productivism), rather than on relationships, quality, and effectiveness maintained through individual and collective work practices (Giddens 1994). Seemingly progressive discourses expected them to be consultative and collegial, yet new managerial and market regimes restricted them from being so (Sachs and Blackmore 1998; Blackmore 1999b).

Leadership in this context, we argue, is best understood as a set of social practices that arise out of particular relationships and conditions of work. In that sense it is undertaken by many at all levels of an organization and cannot be simplistically equated to formal position. Just as policy is the authoritative allocation of values, leadership has a normative dimension, as it is a moral and political as well as a social practice. The issue for educational leaders is not just how to "do leadership," but to elaborate upon the values that underpin the social practices of leadership. This notion of leadership raises matters of trust, expertise, and loyalty in the context of an erosion of trust in social institutions generally (Groundwater-Smith and Sachs 2002) and the rise of audit cultures in response to that erosion (Strathern 2000a). Interestingly, the desire for control and to reduce risk by executive management and government alike has led to increased surveillance of professionals in the name of accountability and a trend toward standardization at the same time we see a further trend toward numerical feminization of education.[4]

We explore women educators "crossing over" from the professional cultures of teaching and research into management, and how such experience can lead to a "cultural identification" as outsiders and reidentification as women (Wacjman 1998). As new immigrants they are inside, but as managers, remain on the outskirts of the culture, while bringing prior loyalties. As women, they are "strangers in a familiar world" dominated by men. Their gender leads to a range of cultural processes of assimilation, ghettoization, and positioning as the "other."

SOME THEORETICAL DISPOSITIONS

Dillabough and Arnot (2001, 32) claim that "[t]he current research traditions within 'feminist' sociology of education are even harder to 'capture,' drawing as they do upon divergent, yet sometimes overlapping, theoretical and empirical approaches to the study of gender and feminism in education." In general, feminists increasingly reject sociological binaries of structure/agency, objective/subjective, and individual/society and focus more on the dynamic and fluid relations in gender formation through structures and relationships. A central issue for feminist social theorists has been how to conceptualize gender identity in ways that understand how social (and therefore gender) change occurs in the context of wider structural and historical formations. How can feminists theorize the structure/agency dynamic in ways that address continuity and change in gender identities, institutional formations, and social movements?

McNay (2000, 5) suggests that "with regard to issues of gender, a more rounded conception of agency is crucial in explaining both how women have acted autonomously in the past despite constricting social sanctions and also how they may act now in the context of processes of gender restructuring." Negative connotations of agency in feminist theory position women, even in leadership positions, as powerless. Yet leadership as a central concept in administrative theory is discursively associated with a sense of agency, an assumed capacity to change oneself, "to become a leader," and to produce change in organizations. A theory of agency needs to explicate how leaders produce change within particular conditions of possibility and constraint that are not just treated as exogenous to gender identity formation ahistorically. Such a theory would recognize both the durability of gender identities and the potentialities for their reconstruction, as well as address issues of intentionality and reflexivity (McNay 2000). We draw from McNay's three foci on agency and change: the relation between the material and the symbolic dimensions of subjectification; the issue of identity and coherence of the self; and finally the relation between psyche and the social.

Symbolic and material practices are intertwined in the formation of the gendered subject. "While all social practices are linguistically mediated, they are not necessarily linguistic in nature; patterns of employment discrimination or economic exclusion are deeply sedimented, complex and reproduced in ways that a linguistic model does not adequately capture" (McNay 2000, 14). Women in formal authority are, in contrast to most women, seen to have both symbolic and material power—symbolic in terms of the embodiment of female sexuality as leaders in male dominated environments; and material power due to their capacity to allocate resources. Our data suggests that the women in our study struggle with, and negotiate, both the symbolic (representations) and material conditions (division of labor and resources) that shape possibilities for action (Walby 2000).

Yet gender identity, while "durable," is "not immutable" and is capable of reformation (McNay 2000, 2). Calling on Bourdieu, McNay (2000) argues: "Although subject formations receive their shape from prevailing social conditions, certain predispositions and tendencies may still continue to effect embodied practices long after the original conditions of emergence have been surpassed. This durability partly suggests that a coherent sense of self is not just an illusion but fundamental to the way in which the subject interprets itself over time (2)."[5]

Bourdieu's notion of habitus provides a way of explaining the "paradox" of the individual who can be directed or shaped toward particular ends but not totally driven or determined by them. Habitus recognizes the desires for both continuity and change critical to identity formation. It also distinguishes between a prereflexive "feel for the game" that cannot be reduced merely to socialization and the reflexive that indicates some intentionality and desire for action. Agents never know completely what they are doing because they often respond out of habit in "reasonable ways" (Bourdieu 1990, 109). For example, gender, as "practical belief," is more than the internalization of particular representations. Gender identity formation is not merely a "matter of consciousness but arises out of and creates naturalizing of agendas, strategies, goals and desires of habitus" (Webb, Schirato, and Danaher 2002, 16). "Habitus permits thinking about the synchronous nature of constraint and freedom expressed in the hybrid forms that women's social experience has assumed" (McNay 2000, 61). The durability and embeddedness of particular subject formations is evident in the different ways in which these women positioned themselves with regard to feminism, work, and family and the difficulty some people had in terms of their investment in particular self-images. Thus, not being labeled as a feminist was important to some as it meant that they had achieved success through individual merit, not because affirmative action policies advantaged them. Concepts of 'investment' and 'negotiation,' as much as 'resistance,' are perhaps more appropriate to understand the fragmented, discontinuous, unpredictable nature of gender identity and indeed change. We seek to explore how these investments and predispositions are negotiated in the context to specific educational environments of schools, TAFE, and universities.

PROFESSIONAL DISCOURSES, INSTITUTIONAL METANARRATIVES, AND WORK IDENTITY

Individuals' work identity is informed by the articulation between particular personal, political, and professional discourses circulating within and around educational organizations and professional communities of practice. These give rise to different understandings and readings of individual and collective corporate identities. Particular "professional" discourses are mobilized in each of the fields of practice of the three education sectors. The entrepreneurial field of TAFE, the disciplinary knowledge-based field of universities, and the pedagogical or caring field of school practice each produced different discourses of professionalism, but in the context of specific institutionalized "cultures" that shaped opportunities and inhibitors to women's advancement.

We suggest that organizations are "fragmented unities," although they can be discursively represented as a unified and uncontested "whole" by, for example, strategic plans seeking a "normative glue that can be applied and removed as the executive desires" (Parker 2000, 1). Organizations enact a set of changing relationships that at any one time appear to assume a dominant expression or narrative (often referred to as "culture"). Embedded in dominant institutional narratives are patterns of assumptions, not tangible or visible, that members of an organization develop to cope with its problems and daily lives, into which new members are partially inducted, adopting and adapting those discourses that make sense to them. These are usually not the expression of dominant philosophies or values made explicit in mission statements. What happens and how people relate and think in relation to each other is informed by hybrid arrangements and relationships arising from interactions of individual habitus, collective stories, and "management engineered programs of change" (Parker 2000, 2). Organizational narratives also assume the "more general features of the sector, state and society of which the organization is a part," such as the professional discourses of fields of practice, wider debates about leadership, and the wider gender order (Parker 2000, 1).

Following McNay (2000) we draw on Bourdieu's concept of 'field' to illuminate the relation between agency and structure. Bourdieu's notion of a field is useful in that it does suggest some reflexive dimension to agency. Thus, as a member of the field of education, or subfield of schooling, one is both produced by the field and is capable of producing effects on the field

(Bourdieu and Wacquant 1992, 80). Women have undertaken autonomous action despite structural inequalities from marginal and seemingly powerless positions in achieving equity reform. But the notion of 'self-conscious creativity' or 'reflexivity' as a generalizable characteristic of agency in postconventional societies is complex. Reflexivity (self-conscious consideration of action) and autonomy imply some level of intentionality. For example, some women leaders may be more "caring" because they see this as promoting particular democratic values and ethics, while for others these dispositions arise from performative practices that have become naturalized and unconscious ways of being (Bourdieu 1990, 116). Considering organizations from a perspective of the social relations of gender allows us to explore cultural meanings carried through corporate strategies, language, practices, and symbols that are specific to men and women. But most often, dominant values and beliefs in organizations and images of leadership are defined by forms of masculinity:

> Arguably it is the increasing movement of women into social fields which were previously confined to men that is crucial to an understanding of the decline of traditional gender norms. . . . [T]he concept of the field permits the conceptualization of differentiation within the construction of gender identity replacing dualism of public and private, workplace and domestic, the central and the marginal with a more complex logic that mirrors the expansion and uncertainty of women's social experience. This in turn offers a way of thinking about possible transformations within gender identity as uneven and non-synchronous phenomena. (McNay 2000, 36)

To continue with Bourdieu's argument, membership of a field of practice informs professional identity. The field is defined as "objective relations between positions, and the field's configuration receives its form from the relations between each position and the distribution of a certain type of capital, economic, cultural, social and symbolic, that denotes the different goods, resources, and values around which the power relations of the field crystallize" (Bourdieu 1993, 72–77). While fields are relatively autonomous, and there is no single all-encompassing logic, there is a hierarchy between fields. Thus TAFE or universities or schools collectively constitute the field of education. Each education sector or subfield has particular logics of practice that overlap in some respects and diverge in others, logics in which professionals differentially invest according to their location. Academic, teacher, and trainer habitus constitute, and are constituted by, their fields. However, all individuals bring to the field the "power at their disposal. It is this power that defines their positions, and as a result their strategies" (Bourdieu 1998, 40–41).

Each sector is part of a wider field of education that has a "central gravity" or "specific logic" that regulates the field in which there are "core" activi-

ties such as teaching, learning, and research. As a field, education is constituted by hierarchies of knowledge/power relations that permeate educational
organizations, in terms of what knowledge is valued and how power is
asserted, both materially in terms of the distribution of resources, and symbolically in terms of how particular knowledge is valued and represented. Significant groups with different interests compete for control of the field that is
underpinned by capitalist imperatives for accumulation. Power rests in the
complex set of relations within and between fields and does not rest in specific individuals or institutions, although these relations impart power to some
individuals more than others. Social control is therefore insidious. The efficacy
of symbolic domination is both strengthened and open for subversive misap-
propriation. Educators as teachers and researchers therefore have multiple
investments in different fields—in their profession, unions, social movements,
government authorities, and professional organizations. There are overlapping
values across these fields, such as notions of education as a public service. This
enhances how individual agency or acts of resistance "may transcend their
immediate sphere in order to transform collective behavior and norms"
(McNay 2000, 4). Thus the actions of educational players connect to larger
social structures.

Education policy as a bounded field of practice works through the educational dispositions and moral valuations of the various players in the field.
But increasingly it overlaps and is informed by other fields of economic and
social policy. The more autonomous a field the more powerful and capable
it is in imposing its logic on other fields (Bourdieu and Wacquant 1992,
105). Professions, as organizations, are "communities of practice" within
fields that have transcendence in terms of historical and cross-cultural
understandings that characterize professionalism as a specific body of
knowledge, levels of competence, public responsibilities, and ethics. These
alter over time and in specific cultural and organizational contexts. Leadership or professionalism are practices that arise out of specific fields of practice that are bounded by disciplinary knowledge but have both particular
and universal meanings, that is, how it is practiced within this school or university, but with wider cultural meanings. Identity and agency are not what
individuals do but are part of a set of practices arising out of networks of
relationships within particular communities of practice. Individual leaders
learn to play the game and negotiate the logics of practice within their subfield—universities, schools, and technical education. We map the intersections and convergences between the "education sub-fields" (schools, TAFE,
and universities) at a time when the field of economics (economic rationalism, human capital) gained precedence nationally and internationally, when
boundaries between the education subfields became more porous, thus
weakening the autonomy of the field of education.

PERFORMATIVITY AND PASSION

There was, we found, for the women participants in our study, a tension between performativity—that is, performing well through managing oneself better according to a new set of regulatory disciplinary mechanisms—and the passion for "doing good" in educational work based on a desire to achieve through education fairness and social justice (see Chapter 5). "Education is modernity's last stand" (Hartley 1997, 4). This tension emerged out of the competing discourses of new managerialism and old bureau professionalism that circulate within the field (see chapter 4). The promise of new management theory that postmodern organizations would invest in "feminine" leadership (good communication, consultative skills, negotiation and person management skills, recognition and understanding of diversity); develop teamwork and flexible work practices in an adaptive or learning organization; and utilize management practices of recruitment and reward that promoted performance and not position, contribution not status, we suggest were idealized and optimistic readings of post-Fordist organizational life. Instead, the hybridity of market and managerial practices interpellated in and through patriarchal bureaucracies produced neocorporate bureaucracies that were simultaneously modernist (hierarchical, individualistic, strong executive power) and postmodernist (teamwork, entrepreneurial, self-managing workers; see chapter 2).

The dilemma for educational managers that we explore in this text is that an intensified focus on the performative transforms the very practices, values, and processes from which educational workers derived their passion and pleasure, the motivating force for being in education. Being a compliant worker meant putting the organization's goals ahead of personal aspirations or the public good. Thus the performative practices of the neobureaucratic corporate organization have produced counterintuitive impulses that undermine what many educators described as "the real work," the "passionate work" of education, much of which was about promoting social progress and enhancing opportunity of all: that is, "doing good" (see chapter 8). We investigate how women leaders negotiated the tensions between passion and performativity in the context of shifting relations of power that created new possibilities and new constraints for individual and collective agency. The new work order provided both opportunities and costs for women in leadership (see chapter 3). We track the ways the discourses of management and the market mesh with older professional discourses within particular education sectors, based on the view that teachers, academics, and trainers identify themselves within a wider community of practice beyond their specific organizations and draw upon wider professional discourses to shape their practice (see chapter 5). Women leaders were expected to "manage the paradox" between promoting these accountability exercises or disciplinary technologies that have the tendency to control, monitor, and standardize along a narrow range of educational indicators (see chapter 9). This is at a time when improved outcomes for all students rely increasingly on the knowledge worker's curiosity, initiative, and creativity together with professional advocacy, activism, and autonomy based on the recognition of a complex range of educational outcomes (Sachs 2003). Our women educators spoke of a crisis in trust arising out of the loss of a sense of commitment to and alienation from their work as a result of the lack of reciprocity and mutual accountability within organizations and the sense of personal guilt arising from their to inability to meet their own desire for perfection and to provide a quality education for students and colleagues (Bishop 1999; see chapter 6). Our study suggests the need to reconceptualize education leadership in postmodern corporate times, our task in writing this book.

TWO

Restructuring Education

GLOBALIZATION AND THE PERFORMATIVE STATE

THE 1990s WAS a period of contestation between social democratic, neoliberal market and neoconservative political responses to globalization within many Anglophone governments (United Kingdom, United States, New Zealand, Canada, Australia). The restructuring of Australian education was indicative of the general convergence in these nation-states toward neoliberal market/neoconservative social policies that fundamentally shifted relations among the individual, the state, education, and work. Whitty, Halpin, and Power (1998, 12) refer to the "apparently paradoxical combination of state control and market forces, or, to put it more specifically, a combination of the 'evaluative state' and 'quasi-markets.'" For our purposes here, restructuring means "thinking in terms of relations" and "articulations" among identity, place, and space (Newmann, King, and Rigdon 1997, 42). It highlights "organizational features . . . that depart significantly from the conventional pattern of student experiences, teachers' professional work, governance and leadership, and connections to the broader . . . community" (Newmann, King, and Rigdon 1997, 42).

Restructuring, as change, is ongoing, through incremental adjustments and accommodations. However, we argue that something significantly different occurred in Australia during the 1990s with regard to the assumptions about how education "worked" in relation to the state, the economy, and society. This was a shift informed by, and in response to, "restructuring movements" elsewhere in the United States (Murphy 1997), the United Kingdom (Whitty, Halpin, and Power 1998) and New Zealand. Globalization was both the rationale and the context for this move. But globalization is as much a discourse generating a view of the world (Blackmore 1999). Globalization in the late twentieth century is also the recognition of growing economic, cultural, environmental, and social interdependencies; emergent transnational financial, economic, and political formations; and the intensification of flows of people, goods, ideas, money, and images across space and place (Burbules and Torres 2000; Appadurai 1996). Some have argued globalization spells the end of the nation-state. Others see globalization as changing the relations between individuals and the state in a time of "manufactured uncertainty," as the state now mediates global/local market relations rather than protects individuals against the excesses of the market. The state has readjusted to meet new economic, social, and political pressures. The state is "now less a unit of governance with respect to the self determining citizen community, and more a unit of political management with respect to how its internal subjects and their economic activities articulate with transnational markets and institutions" (Yeatman 1992, 449). It is with this understanding that we examine the local/global articulations specific to the Australian restructuring agenda of public-sector and education reform.

TRAVELING POLICIES

How discourses of globalization are mobilized in specific nation-states is contingent upon national policy responses to the discourse in the context of historically produced local political, social, cultural, and economic factors (Ball 1998b). Thus Australia's responses to globalization were informed by its English legacy, its marginal position relative to new regional economic blocs of the European Union and the North American Free Trade Alliance, and its proximity to Southeast Asia and Asia. Some nation-states have invested in education to promote economic growth and cultural identity (e.g., Singapore), while others have sought to protect their social structures and values (e.g., Nordic states). Responses were also mediated by local politics. Whereas conservatives were in government in the United Kingdom, the United States, and Canada during the late 1970s and the 1980s, conservatives were not in power federally in Australia until the Howard government of 1996. While federal Labor had initiated workplace restructuring after 1989 after the financial crash, the Howard government after 1996 was "much more minimalist and managerialist, emphasising policy outputs and a 'steering at a distance' modus operandi, and driven much more by market ideology, than the hybrid efficiency/equity, human capital/social justice collaborative national approach of Labor" (Lingard 2000, 86). Globally marginal nation-states, such as Australia and New Zealand, as well as economically developing nation states, voluntarily adopted or were pressured to adopt more extreme measures of reform relative to the United Kingdom and the United States, who being at the core of global economies were more protected from the exigencies of global market forces (Carnoy 1998).

There was also a "paradigm convergence" in education and social policies. Though articulated differently in modes of implementation and practice, convergence emerged in the "invocation of policies with common underlying principles, similar operational mechanisms and similar first and second order effects: first order effects in terms of their impact on practitioners, practice and institutional procedures and second order effects in terms of social justice— patterns of access, opportunity and outcome" (Ball 1999, 198). Common to the traveling policies of education reform nationally and internationally at this time was the language of structural adjustment. Developed by conservative economic think tanks, this strategy advocated internationalization, marketization, client service, efficiency, accountability, self-management, and devolution. Such policies "traveled" rapidly cross-nationally, advocated through international consultancies, research communities, and policy bodies, often prescribed by funding bodies such as the IMF and the World Bank. A new global policy community in education was emerging, in which such ideological perspectives took hold, with the OECD at the center. The OECD was connected both to governments through its reports and to the research community as authors of those reports (Henry et al. 2001). The ideological mindset of the OECD also shifted from a social emphasis in the 1960s, which construed education as a public good, to a "new instrumentalism" by the 1990s, informed by the new public administration and economic rationalism that saw education as a positional good (Henry et al. 2001). The OECD therefore implicitly and explicitly promoted human capital economic theory with all its assumption of a freely choosing autonomous gender and racially neutral autonomous individual and the principles of competition and choice.

Accompanying this were new modes of governmentality. In the Anglophone states there was a marked shift from *government*, where the state takes responsibility for the daily administration and universal provision of services; to that of *governance*, where the state steers indirectly from a distance through a range of disciplinary technologies (e.g., policy frameworks, financial contracts, and accountability) (Taylor et al. 1997). In the early stages of dismantling the welfare state in New Zealand, the United Kingdom, and Australia, governments sought to devolve responsibility for delivering service down to local public and private providers set up in competition while subsidizing services for the needy.

A central feature of corporatization in Australia during the late 1980s, as in the new public administration in the United Kingdom and New Zealand earlier, was the ministerialization of policy, where ministers take direct control over policy and appoint a senior executive service on contract from outside the permanent bureaucracy (Lingard et al. 1993). New policy relations were reformulated between the "policy generating 'center' of public bureaucracies and the policy implementing 'periphery'" of schools, universities, and TAFE institutes (Taylor et al. 1997, 59). The policy focus of the state shifted from a focus on inputs and reducing structural inequalities in the 1970s, to participation and inclusivity in the 1980s, and then to outputs and what could be readily quantified in the 1990s. At the same time, the state has become more inflexible. It addresses the demands for democratic participation by not abolishing these rights but by neutralizing their scope and power. One countermove was to mobilize neoliberal orthodoxies through the dual strategies of marketization and new managerialism. These linked rights-oriented discourses of individual choice and contractualism to participatory-oriented discourses of self-managing institutions in local communities and accountability. In so doing, parents were positioned as clients, employers, and citizens (Vincent 2003), and teachers and academics, as providers (e.g., Lauder 1994).

The postwelfare state in Australia, following trends in the United Kingdom and New Zealand, was characterized by a more deregulated, outsourced, and downsized public sector; strong policy and accountability frameworks; and government disinvestment in public education. On the one hand, there was a devolution of responsibility and risk down to individual institutions, institutional units and individuals to achieve new efficiencies as government expenditure declined. From 1975 through 1995 the percentage of Australian GDP expended on education decreased from 4.2 percent to 3.8 percent compared to that of the United Kingdom from 6 percent to 5.2 percent of GDP (Marginson 1997). This reduction of public funding was balanced by the privatization of education costs through the introduction of user pays. Work was privatized with increased unpaid overtime to achieve productivity gains negotiated through a newly developed and devolved industrial relations system of enterprise bargaining. On the other hand, reregulation and recentralization were achieved by developing strong policy and accountability mechanisms that fed back to executive government and executive management. This centralized decentralization constrained the possibilities promised by the greater autonomy arising from self-management. This mode of governance seemingly freed up the local unit or individual to be responsive to student needs and markets through greater self-management but also placed considerable restrictions on the nature of the responses to markets and clients by imposing institutional charters, strategic planning, financial contracts, administrative guidelines, and policy frameworks. In this way, the public sector was redesigned.

AUSTRALIAN EDUCATION RESTRUCTURED

Restructuring became the key means by which government could simultaneously reduce expenditure while linking education more tightly to the economy. During the 1980s, under the tripartite agreement among big business, big unions, and big government of federal Labor corporatism, business had an increasingly greater influence in education policy. Business and union leaders, chairing significant and important education reports (the Finn, Mayer, and Carmichael reports), directly impacted on the practices of universities, schools, and TAFE colleges. This was specifically in the areas of curriculum and pedagogy by importing the notion of competencies from workplace training (Blackmore 1991). Business and accountancy "best practices" were imported unproblematically into educational management through accountability practices such as total quality management, audits, and accrual accounting. Thus the structures, culture, values, systems of funding, and management roles were made subject to significant transformations (Lingard et al. 1993; Thomson 1998).

Stimulated by the 1987 global financial crisis and collapsed youth labor markets federal Labor reforms (emulated by the state governments) focused on macro- and microreform through workplace restructuring. In education, the emphasis was on the massification of higher education and increased retention in schools and postcompulsory education and training in order to address unemployment and skill deficiencies to meet the needs of a "clever country." Ironically, as skill requirements were rising, payment for skill was declining as individuals had to invest more in education and training only to receive lower rewards (Ferrier and Selby-Smith 1995). Education was set to be "rationalized" and vocationalized in ways that realigned the sectors in relation to each other and tightly coupled education to national economic interests. The early 1990s saw moves toward a unified national system of higher education, national school curriculum frameworks, standardized testing, and a national open training market in which private and public providers competed for competitive tenders for training programs (Lingard et al. 1993). The boundaries among the professional fields of practice of higher education, training, and schooling became more porous during the 1990s with the development of national qualification frameworks linked by credit transfer (e.g., Australian Recognition Framework, TAFE university amalgamations, and the commodification of curriculum in all sectors to make it more user friendly; Smith and Keating 2003).

Restructuring led to a redistribution of the "spatial division of labor" and "spatial differentiation" (Massey 1994, 51) in interdependent ways. Geographical specificity (rural/urban) and the symbolisms that people attached to them were contested. Nationally, shifting demographics, one consequence of deindustrialization, meant flows of populations from some states (South Australia, Tasmania) to others (Victoria, Queensland, and New South Wales), and from rural to urban centers. Regionally, there was a redistribution of opportunities for students and teachers in specific localities arising from new regional universities, on the one hand, and the closing down/amalgamation of rural and small urban public schools, on the other hand. Ideological shifts in the nature of educational funding and governance (increased funding to private schools and self-management, competitive tendering, and the emergence of private providers) interacted with "spatial restructuring" in terms of the redistribution of educational provision from public to private providers. This increasingly uneven market provision created new forms of differentiation of opportunity, producing new pockets of "locational disadvantage" as rurality, poverty, and race coincided to concentrate in poorer communities with downgraded educational, community, and service infrastructure. Highly capitalized (culturally and financially) educational organizations (elite universities and schools) and individuals could maximise their opportunities because of these spatial inequalities (e.g., Teese 1995).

Restructuring Australian Universities

Universities, already relatively autonomous institutions, were particularly susceptible to internationalization and external global pressures because of the modern university's role in a global intellectual community. The university was more open to a wider range of external political, economic, and social influences. The university was unable to appeal to tradition in seeking to defend a romanticized view of academic collegiality. To do so the university lay itself open to charges of being exclusive and elite, a dangerous position in a mass education sector seeking clients. Labor reforms after 1989 expected efficiency, effectiveness, *and* equity to be delivered. While increasing access (e.g., into regions), Labor also reintroduced fees in the form of a higher education contribution scheme (HECS) or deferred tax by 1992. While mature women had largely been the beneficiaries of the no fee regime initiated by Labor in 1972, there has been little increase in nontraditional users of bluecollar workers.

But the principle of restructuring was that "bigger is better" (and cheaper) to reduce costs by advantages of scale as with the massification of higher education in the United Kingdom. Institutional restructuring was achieved through the processes of closure, amalgamations, mergers between universities and the colleges of advanced education (teacher education similar to community colleges) or TAFEs (equivalent to the English polytechnics), and upgrading of status to a university, to become a unified system. The result was universities differentiated by size, status, location, and profile. As depicted by Marginson and Consindine (2001) they included the "sandstones," established midnineteenth century in each state, that could appeal to tradition, prestige, research-based cultures and size; the "redbricks" established in the 1960s to cater to postwar expansion; the upgraded technical instititutes or "Utechs," the "gumtrees" or regional universities; and the upgraded CAEs or "wannabes" (a university) (Marginson and Consindine 2001). The various amalgamation, conversion and 'stand alone' positions adopted after 1990 tended to be the result of expediency, executive personalities and status, rather than focusing on student access, mission, proximity or program.

Not surprisingly, long-held institutional dispositions persisted in each restructured institution that impacted on the division of labor and career opportunities. The newer universities in Australia, as in the United Kingdom, tended to be more "managerialist," a legacy of the patriarchal nonacademic culture of the CAEs and technical institutes (Marginson and Considine 2001). For many women in the old CAEs, the move into a university was welcomed and, as argued by Dianne, a dean (sandstone), for "those from the old CAE sector, it's clearly gotten better. There are more permanent positions available to academic staff in the old CAE sector than ever before." Another dean commented on the historical employment practices of TAFE: "There is no doubt that the women are still at the bottom of all the hierarchy in Australian universities. But the old TAFEs operated incredibly on those kinds of short-term contracts, and no contract up to summer . . . dreadful human relations policies, which almost only hire casual people whenever they could and never put anyone in tenure. . . . [T]he traditional university sector . . . tried to put people on tenure wherever possible."

For women in the former CAE sector, amalgamation provided them with new opportunities but also new demands in terms of becoming academics, such as getting a PhD. For those in the "old" university sector, the amalgamation with a CAE coinciding with new line management imparting "more power to the powerful" often meant a return to a hierarchy in universities at a stage when women had begun to be included, even if marginally, in academic governance (Blackmore 1992; Castleman et al. 1995).

Restructuring TAFE

The TAFE sector was funded predominantly by the states since its establishment in 1974, but with significant federal input for capital works and specific labor market and employment programs. This sector also underwent significant restructuring, with amalgamations into larger multicampus institutes, as in the further education sector in the United Kingdom (Avis 2002). TAFE institutes, relatively autonomous and large, were most vulnerable to discourses of entrepreneurialism, as their professional cultures were industry and community based. A female middle manager commented that "TAFE is very much the political football, and community responsibility is written in very small print as TAFE is being forced to become privatized and self-sufficient."

In 1992 the national Open Training Market (OTM) was created as a strategy of microeconomic reform by Labor in order to create a seamlessness of individual pathways for students among the schools, TAFE, and universities and to encourage life-long learning. "In essence this strategy aimed to address Australia's balance of payments problems by enhancing the productivity and international competitiveness of Australian industry" (Anderson 1994, 67). The OTM was based on the principle of competitive tendering for programs between public *and* private training providers (Ferrier and Selby-Smith 1995). Thus TAFE, schools, universities, and a growing private sector of educational providers, many of them church charity organizations (e.g., Brotherhood of St. Laurence) and training organizations run by exteachers, competed for federal tenders (e.g., English as a Second Language [ESL] and labor market programs). The TAFE sector sought increased income from customized and enterprise-specific training programs for industry, Commonwealth, and state government programs (Kell, Balatti, and Muspratt 1997). The sector moved away from its traditional community education orientation and "social service frame" that focused on participation and access for the individual student, contextual and generic curriculum, and personal development. Now TAFE shifted into an "economic utility frame" to promote national economic development, signaling a move away from "social equity" to gain success in the market, to "market equity" that ignored structural inequalities, unequal outcomes, but merely provided the freedom to enter the market (Powles and Anderson 1994).

Curriculum reform accompanied structural reforms with the introduction of competency-based training as a first step in an ongoing process of commodification of curriculum and pedagogy. Pedagogically based on a linear model of curriculum development (industry standards, development, delivery, and evaluation), teacher proof units were packaged in a lock step fashion to be delivered anywhere and anytime. CBT assumed a behavioral model of learning, assessment was based on mastery, and individuals progressed at their own pace based on demonstrated competency (Smith and Keating 2003, 120ff). The predominantly female teachers in adult and community education or working in access and equity units within TAFE were troubled by the vocationalization/commodification of curriculum and pedagogy (Butler, E. 1997; Angwin 1994). They argued that competencies reduced pedagogy to a technical set of procedures with predetermined outcomes, denied the professional judgment of teachers, and changed the strong pedagogical focus emphasizing self-growth and education as empowerment (Sanguinetti 1998). Many saw the shift toward the vocational and user pays as having detrimental equity effects, with the labor market focus replacing access and equity courses (Ferrier 1995).

At the same time, while TAFE institutes have been male-dominated bastions of the blue-collar trades, restructuring with its new focus on marketization, the service occupations, human resource management, quality assurance, and curriculum development opened up new spaces for many women in management and teaching. Raelene, a senior manager in a small, progressive, suburban TAFE, commented: "The restructure has meant more women in management. . . . [W]omen are all right with change—they have handled it better than the blokes have. Today's young women are more forceful." Margaret, a colleague, agreed that "since the restructure, TAFE has recognized women's ability and employed them in senior positions. We have more women than before." The reculturing of TAFE to be more entrepreneurial, service oriented, and student focused repositioned women favorably as they had expertise in the service industries, with students, in pedagogy and curriculum, and some had service industry backgrounds. It enabled many women to "jump into positions where they were back out dealing with commercial clients" (Raelene). Jane, in the same TAFE, agreed that "the changes in TAFE have given opportunities for women who wanted to work with them: women thrive on change; women who have been mothers adapt to change very easily." At the same time, as the federal government tendered programs out to private providers in the most profitable areas, TAFE was "left with low value, high cost programs in industries with poor employment potential," thus marginalizing the public providers as a residual service (Kell and Blakeley 1997, 54).

Restructuring Schools

The public school sectors in each of the six states and two territories underwent similar restructuring during the 1990s, with a spate of amalgamations and closures arising from demographic shifts and curriculum provision. The effects were larger schools and restructured relations among the central bureaucracies, regions, and schools. In all states, but most particularly in Victoria, competitive markets had always existed with a strong "private school" sector made up of the Catholic, low-fee sector (averaging 20+ percent of students) and an elite, high-fee, private sector (averaging 8–10 percent of students).[6] While each state government department of education adopted different levels of devolution, the general trend during the 1990s was toward dezoning school recruitment areas, funding based on enrollments of individual schools through global budgets to facilitate local flexibility, and the delegation of increased responsibilities for outcomes down to schools with stronger accountability mechanisms. This echoed similar moves in the United States and Canada to site-based management (Levin 1998), in New Zealand toward self-governing schools (Wylie 1997), and in the United Kingdom to self-governing and grant-maintained schools (Whitty, Halpin, and Power 1998; Gewirtz, Ball, and Bowe 1995). Some Australian state governments maintained a stronger regional support role, through clusters in Western Australia; some states such as New South Wales did not devolve structurally at all; and Queensland was initiating moves to devolve with the policy of *Leading Schools* in 1997. Victoria, with the election of the Kennett Liberal/National Coalition in 1993, moved most rapidly and radically toward a devolved model (though not as extreme as self-governing schools in New Zealand, grant maintained schools in the United Kingdom, or charter schools in the United States). Regional curriculum, welfare, and equity support roles were devolved to individual schools or outsourced, and 300 of 1,850 schools were closed as size was equated with efficiency. As per capita funding was radically decreased in Victoria, the private sector offered an attractive alternative, at a cost, to aspiring parents, a cost increasingly funded by federal government after 1996. As Angus (1994) then observed: "School based management seems to be employed as a euphemism for new right themes of privatization, corporate management and market control of schooling."

Nationally, the 1990s saw a move to centrally coordinate school curriculum, historically a state responsibility, through the auspices of the national Ministerial Council of Employment, Education, Training, and Youth Affairs representing state ministers and directors of education, and chaired by the Commonwealth minister of education. The 1989 Hobart declaration stating the role of Australian education was followed by three national reports (the Finn, Mayer, and Carmichael reports) resulting in a National Curriculum Standards Framework. This framework, adopted and adapted in various degrees in each state, shifted all systems toward a focus on outcomes. This trend was exacerbated as federal and state governments started to measure their success nationally and internationally in terms of standardized scores on foundational literacy and numeracy (e.g., PISA). Universal testing at grades 3 and 5 were introduced in most states during the 1990s, despite opposition from teachers, academics, and parent organizations. As elsewhere, there was a focus on increased retention of students to year 12 as a key indicator of system and school success. But the twentieth-century tension in secondary education between vocational and liberal education, and the systemic dispositions that privileged the academic over the vocational in both government and nongovernment systems remained unresolved. Instead, the social selection function of secondary schools was heightened as higher education became scarcer with increased demand as school retention rates increased. Socioeconomic background and location (surrogates for class) were more overtly the critical factors in individual and school success (Teese and Polesel 2003).

Government schools, due to their size, geographic dispersion, and public systemic responsibilities for all children, were more prone to centralized bureaucratic managerialism than even systemic parish or private schools. Structural reform during these years took on two interrelated forms as depicted by one south Australian secondary school principal. They "swept across the entire public service infrastructure: corporatization, privatization, outsourcing . . . and downsizing," moving toward corporate models of local school management based on small business principles (Starr 1997, 2).

> Power over policy, curriculum and resourcing has been consolidated centrally, whereas bureaucratic paperwork and minor capital works has been devolved to schools. The central bureaucracy is responsible for all policy matters, staffing, per capita financial allocations, major works and facilities budgets,

and the oversight and development of administrative systems and procedures. The central bureaucracy determine the form and content of quality controls for the performance of schools and their personnel, particularly the principal, through outcomes based criteria and verifiable performance indicators. Schools have lost much of their professional authority over curriculum, student assessment and evaluation, for example, but are expected to take more responsibility for staffing, facilities and financial matters. (Starr 1997, 3)

For teachers, this decade was a period of contraction and lack of mobility, partly due to declining student and aging teacher populations. Teachers were also paralyzed by fear of being labeled "in excess" to a school's requirements, to be made "voluntarily redundant," as occurred in Victoria for two thousand teachers (20 percent of the workforce) in 1993 and 1994.

THE STRATEGIES OF CORPORATIZATION

The corporatization of Australian education during this period of restructuring was achieved primarily through the interrelated but sometimes competing processes of marketization and managerialization. Educational organizations were encouraged to adopt a client/service rather than student/pedagogic orientation. The unrelenting logics of the market and new managerialism converged upon the view that educational institutions must market themselves in order to gain and maintain their competitive advantage and that improved management will deliver greater flexibility to do so. Individual self-managing institutions increasingly competed with each other in local, national, and global markets and between and within public and private sectors and were expected to be more relevant, client focused, flexible, productive, and market oriented (Yeatman 1994). There were rising expectations that educational institutions benchmark themselves against local, national, and international "best practice" exemplified in "like school" comparisons and consumer satisfaction surveys of students and parents (Thomson 2000).

LEVEL PLAYING FIELD?
"QUASIMARKETS" STRUCTURING OPPORTUNITIES

The 1990s saw education become an industry as a major employer and trainer of skilled labor. Education was now central to the processes of capital accumulation in globalized knowledge-based economies. Previously, markets, even in the business sector, were treated as an external factor to be nurtured. Now the consumption orientation of late capitalism saw "idealized principles" of "the market" permeate through the structure, culture, and value systems of educational organizations (Deetz 1992). Education markets were created through policies based on competition and contractualism (e.g., competitive tendering) that sought to create a "level playing field" for both public and private providers (Yeatman 1998a). Official policy tended to take up and adopt market principles relatively uncritically, but there was contestation at the grassroots. For example, Felicity, a senior manager in a large, suburban, community-oriented TAFE, perceived a significant shift in culture with increased expectations to be competitive and entrepreneurial: "It's just a dog-eat-dog approach at the moment. [It's] difficult to get the people who are paying. [It] creates ethical dilemmas for us, as teachers and managers, as we need more money and new markets. The market was not in mind when working with people in the past. Now we don't want to lose that market. But we need those markets where we get the dollar." Marginson (1997) considers competition-based policies assumed an "imagined line of causation from competition to consumer sovereignty to better efficiency and quality" (5).

But education markets are best depicted as "quasi" or "hybrid" markets (Whitty 1996). They have two dimensions: first as part of sociocultural frameworks, and second, as forms of regulation (Woods and Bagley 1996). With regard to regulation, "the government controls entry by new providers, investment, the quality of the service (as in national curriculum) and price, which is often zero to the user, as in schooling" (Levavic and Woods 2000, 167), and manages this through a range of regulatory procedures, policies, and contractual arrangements with providers. This produces contradictions and tensions between self-determination (self-management) and regulation (mandated policies). Markets as sociocultural phenomena mean that student or parental "choice" is not just exercised in simple demand-supply terms but is mediated by other factors such as the social selection functions of certification, government policies determining allocation of students and funding, perceptions of elite institutions, and the valuing of education for its instrumental and intrinsic benefits (Wylie 1997; Gewirtz, Ball, and Bowe 1995). "Individuals and providers engagement with markets is value led—not merely in terms of seeking to self maximise interest, but in terms of how that engagement occurs and is judged" (Woods and Bagley 1996, 653). Choice, as understood from Bordieu's notion of a field, is a "relational rather than an individual attribute" (Woods 1999, 2). Competition is a form of social agency in "public markets," where market elements are embedded in wider social political frameworks that differ from commercial markets because of the "significance afforded to the public interest" (Woods 1999, 2).

At the same time, those institutions at the center of the market are more protected from local market forces just as some nations are more protected from economic globalization. Because of their privileged status and intergenerational capital transfer in terms of resources, staff and reputation accrued over time, the sandstone universities, like the elite private schools, or well-established TAFEs, are able to command a strong market position relative to their poorer or regional counterparts (Meadmore and Meadmore 2004). The market ensures their privileged position "outside the economic exigencies and beyond the limits of accountability" (Meadmore and Symes 1997, 30). As one female VC of a Utech commented, the desire by VCs of the sandstones to augment that privilege by exclusive benchmarking and performance assessment programs was a "very effective counter attack by the old elites designed to turn back the spread of a mass system of higher education." In contrast, the regional universities in provincial cities and the outskirts of cities, as the public schools in these same locations, were precariously situated in terms of their capacity to perform against the norm of elite institutions in a market differentiated on status (Marginson 2004).

Thus, the market and state are not separate entities, as markets are both produced by and responded to by the state. Markets are neither free nor efficient but mobilized by self-interest and perception, infused with emotion and the aspirations of particular individuals and groups-students, academics and teachers, parents and managers (Blackmore 1995). Education markets are constructed through policy and in turn inform policy, as abstract economic models that do not reflect experience and that often ignore the material conditions that govern individual lives and choices. Finally, the articulation among education, certification, and the market works differently for men and women, different racial and ethnic groups, as gender, like race and language, brings negative rather than positive capital into the marketplace due to cultural biases, despite the rhetoric of gender/"race" neutral skills and qualifications (Bowman 2004).

Universities, TAFEs, and private providers competed for government labor market program tenders as the vocational education and training (VET) sector became an "identifiable" sector of postcompulsory education offered in schools and TAFEs (Ferrier and Anderson 1998) with the aim to enhance "flexibility, diversity responsiveness, adaptability and innovation" (Anderson 1994, 41). But competitive tendering increased risk for institutions, teachers, and students as the client base for TAFEs moved from the individual student to industry (Brown et al. 1996), and the capacity to reduce market risk was difficult, as cost not quality was the bottom line.

> TAFEs are very different to what they were . . . our department, the language studies department at this college, is probably one of the best English as Second Language (ESL) providers. . . . [It has] a very good reputation for innovation. Unfortunately we've just lost a major tender *because* we were the best quality and too expensive. On the ranking they gave us a ranking of 96 percent on our tender, but, apparently, the winning tender was around 70 percent. It was the price that made the difference. (Alice, manager, large, metropolitan TAFE; her emphasis)

The impact of this was severe, with the loss of staff, excellent programs, and students. But marketization required a new mindset as well. Felicity, a TAFE senior manager, commented that "now, a lot of our managers are not good at marketing because it doesn't sit comfortably with them . . . that aggressive role to go out and get the money. . . . [They find it] very difficult to call themselves sales people . . . and to demand dollars for a training course that is the right of every individual." Felicity, herself one of many multiskilled managers appointed in the public sector during the 1990s, did not see marketing as an issue because she had not "traditionally come from an educational background. I've always been in the public service areas—government aircraft factory, a defence factory." She had brought into education a strong business habitus.

In universities, the funding of teaching, since 1990 was based on an annually negotiated profile. The claw back of research funds to the federal government meant academics now competed for research funds through the Australian Research Council, the National Health and Medical Research Council, or other external government consultancies. Research and research training funding was measured by a formula or research quantum based on "inputs" (research income) and "outputs" (doctoral student completion rates and publications). As in the United Kingdom, after a similar unification of colleges with universities, this system favored the older universities with well-established research concentrations and capital (therefore income) intensive medical, engineering, and science faculties rather than newer, less research, and capital intensive universities that rapidly increased their output (in terms of postgraduates and publications) (Slaughter and Leslie 1998). Women tended to be concentrated in the newer universities and lower down the academic hierarchy, with a greater teaching load and intermittent career paths (Glazer-Raymo 2000; Morley and Walsh 1996; Currie and Thiele 2001). The university's increased focus on income production, large-scale research, continuous careers, science and technology, had cumulative and detrimental effects on women's capacity to develop a research profile and thus become more "marketable."

In school education, Victoria in particular, the funding model of devolved governance was based on enrollments in a dezoned environment through Schools of the Future (Blackmore 1999c). How local education markets worked was highly contingent upon the relative proximity of private or competitive public schools, demographics, and reputation, much of which was out of a principal's control (Angus and Brown 1997; Bishop and Mulford 1999; Meadmore and Symes 1997; Townsend 1997). Market discourses of choice facilitated the mobilization of middle-class agency, with the parent-client now exerting increased pressure on public schools by threatening to exercise their choice to exit the public system and move to the private, often in preference to seeking to have greater voice within the public sector. In these increasingly inequitable systems, "popular" schools more often "chose" students through a range of implicit and explicit marketing, enrollment, disciplinary and curriculum policies, and practices that were exclusionary (Teese and Polesel 2003; Power et al. 2003b; Thrupp 1999). Dempster (2000, 4) commented on how Queensland market-oriented reforms encouraged schools to adopt strategies such as student selection, streaming, exclusion, reduced access, teacher casualization, selective reporting, income generation, scholarships, commodification of curriculum, school specialization, competitive marketizing, advertising, and the "poaching" of good students from other schools.

"The market" led to increased tensions between schools within the public sector and between government and nongovernment. Colleen, a principal of a small, working-class, suburban secondary school with a declining population, considered that the introduction of markets meant that there is "no reason for loyalty anymore. Our lot are still committed to the state system, including me, and I'm reluctant to do what it would take to encourage my teachers and council to adopt a robber barren mentality about our kids and our school at the expense of any other school." Status, size, location, and reputation, together with a relatively homogenous middle class population, were the keys to market popularity (Lamb et al. 2004). Yet only government (public) schools had responsibility to take all students in their neighbourhood and follow government policies, thus being more externally regulated within a deregulated environment.

Small schools with a high cultural mix and in low socioeconomic areas, although addressing specific (market) needs of disadvantaged students in inner-city communities, tended to spiral downward due to middle-class flight to private schooling. Such a secondary college in suburban Melbourne had decreasing enrollments and numerous principals. Downsizing forced teachers to be flexible and inventive, although lacking in expertise, to protect the school and their jobs, as explained by Carol, an aspirant senior teacher: "We've got a lot of people teaching outside their subject areas . . . the result of being a small school. The administration is protecting our jobs by asking us to be more and do more. You are meant to be flexible, but it doesn't always work." Furthermore, the reduction in per capita funding (in Victorian schools particularly) based on enrollments meant an increased reliance on parental voluntary labor, funds, and expertise. Often the schools in greatest need due to cultural diversity and the wide spread of student ability had less capacity to raise funds locally (Townsend 1994). Julie, the assistant principal of a small Victorian P–12, inner-city school near a large public housing estate, with variable numbers of recent immigrants from Vietnam, Cambodia, and Ethiopia, commented:

> The current funding formula hurts small schools most as there is no base
> funding. We are only funded on enrollments plus additional [funding] for
> equity groups, based on an index for individual students that makes planning

difficult. Money is a real problem if you want to run good curriculum. Whilst it is harder here in a P–12, raising money in a small primary school is more difficult. You've got to do a lot of stuff with parents. I do community development because of our parent body. Many do not feel comfortable coming up to the school. . . . I don't try to get them to raise the dollar . . . just come here. I provide the afternoon tea, and they have an Easter egg raffle, and we raise fifteen dollars. They spend it on something they decide. We raise our school money through renting our facilities out of hours. I would be under considerable stress if that parent association had to organize a fete to raise seven thousand dollars for the reading program. . . . [T]hese parents lack the financial and professional clout.

While Victorian schools suffered declining government funding and a reduced teaching force, all Australian schools after 1996 experienced Howard's federal government budget cuts of specific general purpose programs such as ESL, the Disadvantaged Schools Program, Early Literacy, and the Country Areas Program, as well as the abolition of Students at Risk and the National Professional Development Program that had successfully linked schools and universities in teacher professional renewal projects (Kronemann 2001, 5).

Quasimarkets in education therefore shape leadership and management practices. Increasingly, money was invested in marketing programs, image, media, and glossy pamphlets to attract students. This often mean schools diverted funds away from educational activities to promote on their face value (image) and the most readily available evidence (achievement on standardized tests or examinations) rather than according to how they "added" value to their particular cohort of students (Blackmore et al. 1996; Meadmore and Symes 1997).

Institutional performances in the market were also embodied in the person of the principal, vice-chancellor, or director and therefore gendered (Thomson 2001; Blackmore 1995). Popular associations between leadership and images of hegemonic masculinity, for example, meant women managers carefully managed their presentation. One pro vice-chancellor commented: "When I perform publicly, for the media, I don't want to give them a chink of vulnerability about my gender identity, or my sexuality. It is totally guarded in every way. When I re-emerge into my personal life, I almost have to go into a decompression chamber to feel normal about being a whole woman. I almost desexualize myself" (Ellie, Utech). Her aim was to be both asexual and female, well-groomed, but not overly so. In turn, the particularities of local markets impacted on the possibilities for leadership advancement for women. This was particularly the case for schools in rural regions. School amalgamations in provincial centers resulted from closures in small towns, reconfiguring clusters of schools into senior/junior or multicampuses, reducing opportunities. Some schools benefited, as did a newly created and high-performing provincial senior college, Brentwood. A nearby rural secondary college, a 7–10 school of 650 students, was as a result predominantly boys. Gabriella, the principal, considered the move to self-managing schools favored Brentwood, but to the detriment of public education in the region. She stated that we did not "really want the Victorian Certificate of Education (years 11–12) component to be transferred to Brentwood Senior, or to be part of the Schools of the Future Program. The other neighborhood 7–10 colleges have become Schools of the Future, and we didn't. We see the trend as damaging of public education." A strong union branch and proactive male principal enthusiastic about Schools of the Future meant Brentwood could attract the best teachers, many from the local junior schools. But Frank, the principal, still found that "the figures are hopeless on the number of women who have been principals in the region: it's always been at a steady two out of thirty . . . I think the culture change is there, [but] the results aren't. We're not getting more women in leadership positions. . . . [W]omen have now got superior abilities and skills for a lot of the jobs that are involved in teaching."

Despite this, in this region women openly spoke of the close association between masculinity and leadership in the local community's minds, many who were on local selection panels of principals. A leading teacher was dismayed at her future possibilities with the appointment of "yet another young male to a secondary college as principal although a number of equally good females applied." Even when women were appointed in assistant principal positions, previously held by women, the comment was, "[O]h she was appointed because she was female." Yet if her male colleague left, and a female was appointed, "the community would be up in arms if a woman got his job. It's OK to have a male principal, a male AP and a female AP, but not two female APs. This is the unspoken rule" (Natalie, senior teacher, primary school). Education markets operated in highly gendered ways within each sociocultural milieu in that the rules are set by socioregulatory contexts and not the market itself (Blackmore 1996b; Waslander 1995). Markets are thus "sub-systems nestled into wider socio-economic contexts" that are also open to cultural and political influences (Woods and Bagley 1996). Education markets are for teachers and academics "lived" in terms of their career paths, where location, familial relations, and their personal ambition were negotiated on a daily basis (Gewirtz, Ball, and Bowe 1995, 5).

HYBRID MANAGERIALISM

The other strategy of corporatization was the new managerialism, referred to as the "New Public Administration" in New Zealand and the United Kingdom, and "economic rationalism" in Australia (Clarke 1998; Rees and Radley 1995). The "new managerialism" arose out of the material and cultural conditions of globalization, namely flexible specialization and a shift in orientation from production to consumption (du Gay 1996). Two discursive strands coexisted within this managerialist discourse: the soft-strand human relations discourse focused on people management in which diversity was the key to productivity, and thereby more open to the perceived attributes of women; the "hard" reengineering strand sought to streamline processes regardless of the human impact. The hard strand rewired organizations with only a veneer of empowerment and team work in a form of "functional humanism," reinventing hierarchy through a strong leadership that meant management control was extended into the domain of employee subjectivity without real democratic involvement and an imposed not negotiated common sense of purpose (Willmott 1995). The worker was now expected to be self-starting, self-disciplined, and self-motivating.

Managerialism takes on hybrid forms in particular contexts. Dianne, a dean, argued that "you can't talk about managerialism as though it's some *thing* without defining it. It doesn't actually exist in the business world as we know it in universities, so you have to figure out where this thing is coming from." Corporate management, as mobilized in the Australian public sector, was to devolve the daily management down to small subunits that competed for funds and that then provided regular feedback to the center through accountability processes focusing on outcomes. Thus, the state, and executive management, could steer indirectly and from a distance, while downloading the difficult decisions within policy and financial constraints to the local unit. But managerialism was in itself more than just a neoliberal "New Right tool." It also had an "imperialistic logic" of its own: "the ideological naturalization of organizational reconstruction, the articulation of modes of organizational power and calculation that have displaced bureau-professionalism as operating logics of public service organizations; and the creation of dispersed systems of organizational inter-relationships and control" (Clarke 1998, 173). Managerialism adds its own dynamic to conservative agendas with its logic of the "right to manage" in that it critiques the failings of other claims to power—the professional and political—that coincided with New Right agendas. Marginson and Considine (2001) comment how this impacted in universities, but its extent and nature varied in each university:

> University purpose and operations is now defined by strong forms of executive control, in which leader-managers take the role of strategic planners and re-engineers, guided by corporate style institutional missions. Institutional reform emphasises flexibility in resources deployment, personnel and mission. Increasingly decisions are controlled not by legislative style meetings but by plans, targets and formulae subject to executive control. (7)

The ideology underpinning this new organizational arrangement was that institutional competition and consumer preferences were more efficient resource allocation mechanisms than regulatory frameworks; explicit standards and measure of performance focused on outcomes are appropriate for all organizations; and senior management can resolve problems by assuming a strong executive management style and planning techniques of business.

In Australian public education sectors, corporate managerialism, together with policies framed by economic rationalism, produced a hybridized discourse incorporating both hard and soft management tendencies that then articulated with an instilled bureau professional logic that was rational, and rule bound, the twentieth-century professional logic of service and care (Clarke 1998). The product was a hybrid "corporate neo bureaucracy" (Limerick, Cunnington, and Crowther 1998). In universities, for example, where there are complex administrative structures with collegial governance through academic committees and boards, governance through faculties and schools (policy and implementation), parallel systems of executive line management (strategy and resources) were created, producing a more clearly defined vertical split between policy and execution (Peters et al. 2002). Increasingly, faculties (deans and heads of school, etc.) became embedded in the line management structure responsible to the executive, marginalizing, or incorporating academic governance (e.g., academic boards) (Miller 1995). Currie and Woock (1995) refer to the "clear shift from a collegial model of decision making within universities to a more confrontational model" (146). TAFE, without the same collegial discourse, saw the reassertion of its historical disposition toward hierarchy and executive power, while individual schools were partially protected by their distance from the now corporatized and streamlined center, but felt the direct effects of the increased power of the principal over their daily lives and reduced democratic decision making.

Performance was embedded into this new managerialism, both soft and hard versions, through the new technologies and regimes of performance management, "a free-floating technology" management tool that reconfigured professionalism (Mahoney and Hextall 2001, 175; Gleeson and Gunter 2001). What counted as performance was now to be determined by external rather than peer bodies by the disciplinary technologies of standards, benchmarks, performance indicators, and the audit. The predetermination of outcomes through standards, for example, while promising coherence, transparency, consistency, and purpose, has an implicit view of the nature of the world in which there is little room for disagreement. Standards have in mind a particular educational habitus of performing and conforming. Thus the new managerialism was the means by which the state and executive officers could manage resources in a recession in which staff were convinced through discourses of inevitability and self-interest to do more for less. Opposition was derailed by the individualization of performance reward systems. This was not the "high trust, high skill, participatory utopia" of the soft management discourses but a "low trust and low commitment" organization of reengineering where quantity comes before quality (Mahoney and Hextall 2001, 177–88).

Teachers and academics, used to professional autonomy and voice, were typically ambivalent to such managerial discourses as they were simultaneously experiencing new controls (to be more accountable) and new freedoms (to be more entrepreneurial). Discourses of both management and market were appealing to their professional sensibilities of being accountable and providing service (chapter 5), but such discourses were mobilized in particular ways and with heavy constraints. Any autonomy won by principals, directors, and VCs through devolution was qualified by the institutional charters, profiles, and policies. Self-management and devolution became more a means to deliver reform determined at the center, rather than encouraging local innovation and initiative, because of financial and policy constraints (Ball 1994; Gleeson and Husbands 2001). Fay, a head of school (Utech), saw devolution as counterproductive:

> Devolution as it is being constructed is not efficient. It will only be efficient if they close small campuses, retrench, and further casualize academic labor. This fear lies within us all. At the same time it is highly centralizing. We find people in HRM making work for us, expecting us to deliver activity logs, do CVs, and report to DEETYA to get research quantum points, listing PD work . . . run workshops and expect everyone to be about evaluating and managing their staff. We just get the sense at the bottom of the academic pile that we are not valued.

Gleeson and Gunter (2001) observe that "the preoccupation with performance obscures discourses of power, masking deeper issues of regulation, of control of teachers and academics . . . by steering market exchange relationships" (154) that characterize learner-teacher relations. This promoted a professionalism that is only about finer differentiation based on pay and status, but a professionalism more readily aligned with the entrepreneurial practices and performativities of the market. It was therefore ironic that despite claims that devolution under Schools of the Future in Victoria would lead to improved student outcomes, Caldwell and Hayward (1998, 93–94) the architects of educational restructuring of Victorian schools, admitted in 1998 that research on Schools of the Future "failed to explain what impact, if any, on learning outcomes for students. Although the *logic of reform* suggests they ought to have effects in this domain, especially in relation to planning and resource allocation, with a focus on building the capacity of staff to improve the quality of teaching and learning" (emphasis added).

CULTURAL RESTRUCTURING AND THE
"RENORMING" OF EDUCATION

These ideological shifts also produced a "cultural restructuring" in terms of attitudes toward education and training. First, with user pays (e.g., Higher Education Contribution Scheme) and the mobilization of discourses of choice, a new instrumentalism emerged among clients as choosers seeking competitive advantage. Second, globalization meant education changed as a cultural field. During the 1990s, universities recruited overseas students through twinning arrangements and "development" projects in third world countries; universities and TAFE sought to internationalize educational provision in the search for new income sources; state education departments and authorities (e.g., Victorian Curriculum and Assessment Authority) sought to sell their curriculum products and skills in assessment; and "popular" private and government schools began to recruit full fee-paying students from overseas (e.g., Malaysia), a practice already well established in New Zealand (Vidovich and Slee 2001; Matthews 2001). This required academics and teachers to be both flexible in terms of what and who they taught and more geographically mobile across campuses and countries. In 2000, of 181, 656 international students in Australia, 56 percent were in universities, 17 percent in vocational education, 7 percent in schools, and 20 percent with private providers (ESL) (Matthews 2001, 3). As with structural adjustment, the imperative was economic not cultural exchange. The new contractualism underpinning international fee-paying pedagogical relations based on "informed consent, negotiation by mutual adjustment and accountability" reworked professionalism by delegitimating any sense of protective paternalism that professionals had previously claimed and thus redefining teaching as client service (Yeatman 1994, 5).

As a field of practice, there was also a cultural shift in internal labor relations with a spatial/perceptual redistribution of labor and power in educational organizations between management and workers (Gewirtz 1997; Gewirtz and Ball 2000; Yeatman 1998a). Line management imparted the greatest control and rewards (performance bonuses) to those with personnel and financial responsibilities, that is, managers. The new emphasis on strong executive leadership at the level of the individual institution and performance appraisal based on a supervisory or peer review model produced a distinction between management and educational work. And, as in the United Kingdom,

> Managerialism comes to dominate collegial cooperation in the organization of both teaching and research. Explicit vocationalism displaces implicit vocational preparation. . . . [R]esearch endeavours are increasingly applied to meet the requirements of government or industrial demands. The don becomes increasingly a salaried or even a piece-work laborer in the service of the expanding middle class of administrators and technologists. (Halsey 1992, 13)

Anna, a senior lecturer in a sandstone university, saw "part of restructuring is about removing power from the faculties and with power either going up to the center or down to the schools . . . and partly about smashing the faculties which have been seen as too 'academic' . . . because they had that kind of autonomy and they are very diverse in their cultures."

There was also a shift in power/knowledge relations. The commodification of, and overtly instrumental attitude to, knowledge produced a significant crisis in educators' sense of authority and autonomy, particularly in universities, but less so in TAFE, which was already strongly vocational. When only utilitarian knowledge is valued, technical competence rather than professional judgement becomes the main game. The focus on measurable outcomes threatened notions of broader intellectual qualities, knowledge, and understanding, reducing them to skills or personal attributes rather than ethical behaviors, a matter of concern to academics. This vocationalization and technologization impacted on what knowledge and skills were valued most. Policies increasingly prioritized science and technology in higher education, with a heavy investment in on-line learning in universities, computers in schools, and new technologies in TAFE. In universities many women academics felt that the type of work that women generally did was less, not more, valued in the new corporate and entrepreneurial cultures, although they were contributing to "productivity" with high student-teacher loads (Deane 1996). "Material quantities—publication output numbers of student taught, or funds generated—rather than intellectual or educational qualities are very much on the foreground of how academics and their work are valued" (de Groot 1997, 134–35). Chee Wah, a senior lecturer in a science department in a red brick university, commented about the reification of particular versions of science: "It's not so much that it's arbitrary. I believe that the scientific dominance defining what counts is very narrow, very outdated in today's world. . . . [T]here is a fight back from this dominant view that was a bit lax in the last five years. . . . [S]cience is coming back strong. . . . But all that number crunching and often so little outcome at the end, what is the evidence that science does better?" This was particularly evident in the newer universities, many of which had amalgamated with teachers' colleges without the research cultures of traditional universities. As one "junior" academic and union activist commented:

> It was pretty clear that women where actually going to lose out in that process of amalgamation and restructuring because the dominant culture was going to be hard headed, research oriented . . . but research oriented from a very elite notion of research. What was going to be important was the blokes you knew who would referee, know all of your work, and it would be a self-perpetuated type of process. (Anna, senior lecturer, sandstone)

Like TAFE and universities, schools also underwent a cultural restructuring. Christine (principal at an inner-city progressive primary school) considered that earlier moves to devolve in Victoria in the early 1980s were "a real devolution of power under the Labor government, particularly in terms of curriculum and management of schools, when teachers had a sense that they had a genuine say in how a school was going to be run. . . . Now it has been taken over by a completely different culture." Natalie (assistant principal in a regional secondary college) identified the difference as a value shift away from equity to compliance and efficiency "in the early nineties, not just in teacher things, but in student things. People bent over backwards to be equitable; things were gained on merit. . . . [N]ow, it is, 'Here is the job, do it!' It's purely whether we can afford it, whether it is going to make us money, if this will fit into the global budget." Colleen, a principal in a working-class school, summed it up:

> The focus is switching away from a view of students based on an assumption that they can all learn, and that they are all entitled to access life's goodies, including tertiary institutions. There is a switch in the role of teachers from being here to assist students to achieve such access and recognition, recognizing that this required more resources for some, to a view of young people fitting into economical imperatives. If the teachers don't succeed in that, the fault lies in the teachers. . . . It is the switch from a system that gave space to an optimistic view of young people and their entitlement to learn and their entitlement for us to find ways to help them learn, to an instrumentalist view of students and therefore of the institutions that serve them and of teachers. Also, teachers have always been expected to be the repository of wisdom and solving all problems. That's not changed, but there is incredible anger as the government has given permission for the media to condemn teachers.

Gewirtz and Ball (2000) refer to a similar shift in discourses amongst English school principals or heads that matched the move from welfarism to new managerialism, from a "learner needs" perspective toward an "institutional needs" perspective, set within the paradoxical logic of market discipline. This assumed that the "self interest" of the institution would deliver "impersonal benefits" for the student (254).

In TAFE, in particular, the intensified market disposition arising from the growing reliance on commercial income required a new set of values and cultural orientations that jarred for many women teachers who had, as educators, by experience and training, valued education intrinsically and as a right. In particular, for many women and some men who had a humanities and social justice background in a suburban, community-oriented TAFE, their work had been to provide access and pathways into education for immigrants and older women returning to work.

So despite the similarity of the policy discourses, how they articulated in the Australian context in terms of the mechanisms of implementation and effects was contingent on a range of historical economic, political, geographical, and cultural factors. But during the 1990s, common to other Anglophone nations, there were the mobilization of neoliberal discourses informing policies that interacted to initiate fundamental cultural and structural shifts in the internal and external relations of Australian education; discourses based on concepts such as 'choice' and 'competition' (commodification and consumeration of education); 'efficiency' and 'entrepreneurship' (the managerialization and commercialization of education); and 'comparability' (imposition of centrally determined assessments, schemes of work and methods) (Ball 1999, 196–97). In the end, there was a shift in discourse in Australia, as in the United Kingdom, the United States, and New Zealand, between "two largely oppositional conceptions of the nature and purposes of schooling [education] . . . that relate to more general visions of the nature of society and citizenship" (Gewirtz and Ball 2000, 265).

THREE

Gender Restructuring: Toxic, Volatile, and Greedy Organizations

THE CULTURAL AND STRUCTURAL reforms in Australia, with the move to postwelfarism had, as in the United Kingdom, Canada, and New Zealand, fundamental implications for education and gender equity (Gewirtz 1997; Brooking 2005; Coulter 1997). This chapter considers the opportunities and challenges faced by women in the new education order. We consider how the processes of corporatization were also processes of gender restructuring, with particular effects in terms of the quality of life for women in restructured educational organizations, and how the structural and cultural reformation during the 1990s created a backlash undercutting women's progress in education (Lingard and Douglas 1999, 61–64).

The modernist welfare state was characterized by government investment in universal free public education for citizenship and vocational preparation. The growth of public education saw the emergence of highly centralized education bureaucracies "to tackle the anomalies, prevent departures from the norm, and defuse the consequences of norm breaking" (Bauman 2001, 22). It was built upon a division of labor in education as a feminized field of practice and a masculinized field of administration and theory (Gunter, Smith, and Tomlinson 1999, Blackmore 1999b). In Australia, the gendered character of the welfare state was premised upon the institutionalization of the "nuclear family" (male breadwinner, dependant wife, and two children) through a highly centralized industrial relations system and social welfare infrastructure in the public domain. The implicit sexual contract was that women cared for the private world of the family and voluntarist social relationships of private life. Weaker groups (women and children) were "protected" by the "nanny state" and strong, male-dominated unions in the centralized industrial relations systems of Scandinavia and Australia, where the gender wage gap was less than in decentralized industrial systems (e.g., the United Kingdom and the United States). By the late twentieth century, the Australian nation-state included immigrant and indigenous populations among its citizenry, but in a cultural not political sense (Hage 1994).

The shift from government to governance during the 1990s meant elements of welfarism coexisted with elements of postwelfarism. While the detraditionalization of the market gave women, young, and NESB workers access to casual and low-paid service work (underemployment), social policies of retraditionalization meant women, regardless of work status, were repositioned as the primary carers due to the withdawal of the state from care. Associated with this was a revitalized conservative discourse promoting a one-dimensional view of the nuclear family (Giddens 1994). This new policy paradigm significantly impacted how women as a group related to the postwelfare Australian state that had formerly been the most equitable employer of women, particularly in education (Yeatman 1992).

During the late twentieth century, paid work increasingly became central to women's identities as they entered employment. Most girls now assumed they would remain employed throughout marriage, as gender equity reform had provided them with multiple ways of being female (Arnot, David, and Weinu 1999, 166; Kenway et al. 1998). But women's economic independence also altered the social relations of gender. New knowledge economies provided new occupational niches for middle-class males in management and technology by reinvesting in revitalized notions of masculinity associated with fast capitalism, more entrepreneurial and management-style masculinities. But blue-collar masculinities remained fixed and narrow with a continuing emphasis on being primary wage earners. Thus the "tradies" in TAFE (Pocock 1998) had particularly strong investments in masculine identities fast going out of date (Connell 1995). Kaye, a middle manager of a small suburban TAFE, perceived shifting gender/power relations with TAFE's new entrepreneurial and service orientation:

> TAFE teachers have wonderful conditions and feel that they have an [in]alienable right to those conditions. We have courses and curriculum quite often out of date. This produces a culture of the status quo as it was ten years ago . . . very macho. Women are much better at changing because they come into TAFE later having taught community studies and the communication areas, new types of courses. The men are still teaching the same old things, apprenticeship. But our apprenticeship numbers are down and traineeships are going up. We've got to make people understand that we're not selling a

product, we're selling a service. The trainer is no longer the font of all wisdom. We've got to facilitate the training development needs of people. We've got to be consultants. Not five minutes ago I was told that if you go out and talk to industry you are a used car salesman type. I said you have to be an educator, explaining to people how education works, and the best way that we can help train their people and, oh, it's like being a used car salesman.

As in the United Kingdom, the creation of a distinctive postcompulsory sector during the 1990s was part of "a wider revolution . . . one influenced by New Right thinking which privileges the values of enterprise and market competition while seeking to substantiate managerial authority . . . and central to this transition is a 'new masculinization' of management, both as language and practice" (Whitehead 1999, 58). The cultural restructuring of education with the reprivileging of science and technology, the rise of entrepreneurship, business and management, and the rush into international education, on the one hand, provided arenas for new "entrepreneurial trans-national masculinities" (Connell 2000). On the other hand, localized middle management in areas of curriculum, evaluation and quality, became the new femininized organizational domain. Devolution led to a remasculinization of the center (executive management) and a feminization of middle management (Blackmore 1999b; Limerick and Anderson 1999b in Australia; Strachan 1999a,b in New Zealand; Young 1998 in Canada). In practice this meant that there has been less of a redistribution of power than expected with "restructured" gender identities.

Whitehead (2000) also points to the irony in the further education sector in the United Kingdom that restructuring provided a context for the "reordering of dominant masculinities" despite an increased number of women in senior FE management positions (from 5.5 percent in 1990 to 17 percent in 1997) as both numerical (gender) and cultural (entrepreneurial) shifts were underway (158–59). "The sector appears firmly embedded in a work and management culture that is difficult to describe as 'feminine,' no matter how flexible one is with the term" (Kerfoot, Pritchard, and Whitehead 2000, 159). Importantly, although hegemonic masculinities were outdated due to the lack of a service orientation (Lingard and Douglas 1999), and while women were being repositioned as managers against/within these old/new masculinities, the ideologies of management and market as articulated organizationally regendered educational work in a number of contradictory ways, some more favorable to women than others.

THE UPSIDES

Into this complex set of institutional arrangements and new relationships, the more progressive CEOs considered women to be the new source of senior management due to their "natural" management skills of negotiation, partnership, community, service. Jim, a CEO at a small, progressive, suburban TAFE, influenced by the Karpin report on diversity, explained that:

> there is a complete restructuring taking place which demands new skills and competencies which women are better suited to and prepared to do ... skills such as accepting accountability and achieving outcome through the performance of others, developing and supporting other managers, working collaboratively, developing human resources, setting out performance expectations via dialogue, underpinning all this with strategic planning.

Women were thus seen to be both more adept at personal change and changing others and also more compliant and amenable to "corporatization." The wider range and human focus of new managerial tasks created new opportunities for women. Jim believed: "Devolution gives individuals much greater opportunities to develop their skills and therefore be able to move into other jobs. There is a fundamental change in the view of management that recognizes that a lot of the skills that women have are the skills that are in vogue at the moment." Kylie, as did many other female managers in this TAFE, saw this discourse of women's change agency as a significant opportunity to enact major change agendas.

> There are so many opportunities in this organization to do whatever you want to do if you're keen and interested in doing things. Restructuring is a way of life, if you're positive about the thing, and if you're confident in your own skills and ability. It's the people who sort of dig down into the hole and want to hide from change who don't do well. It's good in promotion of women. I've done so many different courses that TAFE has paid for—fantastic support as far as training goes.

Indeed, restructuring was welcomed for having expelled many inefficient staff members through retirement, as noted by Ingrid, manager of a large, metropolitan TAFE: "The reshuffle has got rid of a few ineffectual directors and associate directors. Restructuring of TAFE is positive: it gets people out into industry, gives them opportunities they didn't have before. I think women are much more adaptable, much more flexible, much more creative, much more positive. . . . [T]he experience of working with capable women gets men to change their attitudes." Interestingly, while TAFE was more vulnerable and open to market forces, many women in TAFE were more positive than women in schools and universities toward the possibilities arising from restructuring. TAFE restructuring had shifted institutional priorities away from male-dominated blue-collar work and macho masculinities that discouraged promotion on merit toward women's traditional work areas (e.g., service areas, teaching, marketing) and developed more transparent policies and practices (job descriptions, selection, and promotion). Restructuring in universities had however privileged new modes of masculinist governance (line management) and old modes of masculinist knowledge (science and technology). New career paths emerged in TAFE required new management practices in HR, finance, and pedagogy. Jane, manager in a small, progressive TAFE felt, "We are going to be corporatized and outsource things that we do. We have to look at who we hire. I'm lucky in that I am employable anywhere in any training or education organization, not necessarily as manager . . . because of my curriculum instruction design ability."

Quality discourses also provided a leverage to transform the old male-dominated TAFE cultures so exclusive of women, as envisaged by Felicity, the quality manager in a large, community-oriented TAFE:

> It's about proving that we can be really good performers if we apply the best practice management principles that equate to quality management. I suppose my mission is to try to demonstrate to the whole of the system that quality assurance is OK . . . bringing out a reliable product consistently and to have really good programs. To be really good you need to adopt those sound higher principles of quality management.

Quality assurance and improvement comprised therefore another new arena in which the "feminine" skills of organization, perfection, and presentation were seen to be of value to TAFE. Women prepared to do this form of domestic labor, "tidying up" the policies and procedures, were well rewarded. Women, as managers of quality, were seen to be good corporate citizens (Acker and Feuerverger 1999).

THE DOWNSIDES

Restructuring also reinforced old gender regimes. The entrenched gender division of labor that located women in marginal, part-time, acting, or lower level positions, and with men tending to have tenure and located in upper level positions, meant institutions were predisposed toward particular ways of doing things. Summed up by a dean: "My gut feeling tells me that usually men are always advantaged in any restructure." Restructuring mobilized any systemic, group, and individual predispositions toward reproducing social relationships, practices and policies by those already in powerful positions, a form of self-protective reflex arising from their habitus. The cumulative effect of multiple institutional reflexes, though, was a structural backlash, as indicated in the following observations in each education sector:

In the restructure, if two faculties concerned with health came together, that would mean one dean position would have to go, and there are two female deans . . . two steps forward and one back. (Bronwyn, head of school, Utech)

We are amalgamating with a vocationally oriented TAFE. We were a community institute to look after the socially disadvantaged. The user-pays system creates an ethical dilemma because we are in a working-class area. We are currently awaiting the outcome of the TAFE review and, possibly, further amalgamations. Our female CEO has gone to a university-based TAFE. There is a large proportion of women in senior positions, but there is not a predominance in the trade area. The amalgamation could see the loss of many of these positions as our other TAFE has a high proportion of male senior managers. (Felicity, manager, Quality and Continuous Improvement)

We've lost some wonderful teachers out of the system. The ones we are losing are the best ones, who are employable outside the system. They are first to go, and they are mostly women. (Merilyn, school principal)

Studies in Canada of female superintendents (Young 1998) and New Zealand with regard to the principalship (Brooking 2005) report similar effects of restructuring—"last in/first out."

Backlash also emerged in the form of resistance to reform. Some men sought to subvert women when they did gain management positions. In a small, progressive, suburban TAFE there was "resistance from some men who think women have put good men out of jobs" (Anne, middle manager). Despite this, there was a widespread discourse among women that with time resistance to women in leadership would dissipate with the disappearance of a particular cohort of men: "We are still only one generation away from men believing, totally and completely, that a woman's role is in the house. . . . [S]ome of them just accept that because of their maleness they are going to be top honky around the place basically" (Trish, small, rural town primary school). Lingard and Douglas (1999, 64) argue that in these reforms the "hardest hit *psychologically* were the middle class straight white men from their twenties to their forties" who felt they were "entitled to power." They came from a period in which "a lot of these men like to lead in an autocratic type of way. Then they have difficulty with the different leadership styles that most, not all women, but many women, bring a more caring and sensitive manner" (Sara, provincial town secondary school). Or as another leading teacher reflected: "I see a number of men in this college are very stressed . . . and have lost their sense of being involved in decision making . . . and they found that they couldn't cope as they were not moving along as they thought they should traditionally advance up" (Marg, provincial town secondary school). Restructuring provided the chance for such men to reclaim their "proprietorial" entitlements (Blackmore 1997).

Put bluntly, those in power tended to protect themselves and their own. Any restructuring based on past practices, rules, and established patterns of organizational behavior, together with the mobilization of institutional narratives and mythologies by those in decision-making positions, tended to favor those in existing positions of power. Restructuring usually led to a redefinition of roles in limited ways. Ironically, the opportunity to develop new images of leadership, new expectations, and new ways of working was rarely taken up by executive management. Furthermore, the managerial discourse immediately privileged a particular managerial habitus, leaning toward proven management and financial skills, rather than potential interpersonal skills. Margaret, a manager in a small, progressive, suburban TAFE believed that "restructuring is driven by a male power base and economically driven. It's blocked women out; it's toppled them. Women are seen not to have the financial management skills. . . . In the eighties we saw disabled people in the workplace; now they are all gone. Men are better at putting themselves forward, use their physical size to advantage."

In amalgamations, women tended to lose out due to lack of seniority and status. In a P–12 inner-city school, Julie, whose primary school amalgamated with a secondary school reflected on her "downgrading" to assistant principal: "We've had a big structural change. A lot of people would say that I've been demoted because there were two principals, and I was one of them. We've made a decision that we will be a true P–12, and I'm the principal of the junior school. John, the principal of the senior school, is overseeing. But I've been here so long and developed an incredible power base . . . I do all the money." Symbolically, while she lost power, Julie was quick to argue that her power rested in her long history of strong personal relations at the primary school and her capacity to raise local funds. But her interpersonal and financial management skills were exploited not rewarded as the expectations for a P–12 school and the "automatic" rise of the male secondary principal into overall management. Likewise in the tertiary sector, Joan, the EO manager at a large sandstone university commented that "when two institutions merge, male competitiveness and the legacy of past advantage are the primary determinants of outcomes." Equal opportunity managers in universities commented that most amalgamations had set back equity progress for many years.

Furthermore, the time that restructuring took also tended to favor those in existing, tenured, and senior positions, largely male, and not in acting, contract positions in the lower echelons. Roya, from a large, outer suburban, community-oriented TAFE, reflected: "[W]e developed rules regarding redeployment processes designating only a small group of people who were eligible to reapply for their own jobs. But we didn't realize that it would take two years. Heaps of people have left, and as a consequence there is only a very small pool of people who can possibly apply for the jobs: you're not necessarily getting the best people for the job." In most institutions, equity issues were rarely raised during restructuring, despite the national Affirmative Action Agency requesting that EEO be central to the objectives, processes, and outcomes of restructuring. New managerial discourses about planning, processes, and priorities therefore coexisted/converged/propped up the old bureaucratic division of labor, subtly reinstating traditional gender orders. The backdrop was always the uncertainty around planning arising from rapidly changing political agendas. Sandy, a manager in a metropolitan TAFE claimed: "There is a great deal of uncertainty working at the level of government, huge policy shifts in terms of whether government is going to maintain its commitment to public infrastructure, huge changes occurring ideologically: the distribution of work is totally inequitable. Things would be better for my staff if I had enough people to distribute the load, yet we're going to have to cut down further because of cuts to funding." Reduced funding, volatile markets, and policy shifts had significant effects on the quality of life and real choices available to educators. Restructuring also led to an intensification and casualization of educational labor, often producing toxic and volatile work cultures while undermining the conditions of work, again with differential effects on women educators and managers.

WORKING HARDER: LABOR INTENSIFICATION

The intensification of labor in the education sector arose from multiple sources: reduced per capita funding; the negotiation away of set hours of work in return for pay rises in decentralized enterprise bargaining agreements; increased productivity gains achieved largely through downsizing of the workforce; outsourcing teaching, thus shifting the load of development and planning to a shrinking core of tenured educators; and the necessity for casual staff to work in multiple jobs. This intensification of labor not only changed the nature of the work teachers, trainers, and academics, in the form of whole of class rather than small-group teaching, large lectures rather than small tutorials; it also impacted on quality. In all sectors, teaching workloads and student-staff ratios increased, doubling in higher education from 1992 through 2002. The new accountabilities also escalated requirements for recording, reporting, and evaluations; and student and industry markets demanded more rapid client responsiveness. Evelyn commented that "everyone gets bogged down with all the repetitive information and going to meetings, and nothing gets done in the end." Henrietta felt that "school administration is being bogged down by faxes, in-services, constant paperwork. It is information overload."

Labor intensificaton became another mechanism of management control. Collective resistance through unions was less likely due to lack of time as well as due to the increase in marginal, part-time, and insecurely employed educational workers. Change was ever present even for the securely employed with the threat of restructuring arising with each new executive appointment as new executives often made their mark by structural reform. As explained by a dean in a redbrick university, Donna, her ambivalence to reform was because it was too rapid: "[I]t is a really important learning curve to get into new stuff, but it's the constancy of what I've had . . . the repeated changes have just been so enormous . . . I change who I am every semester."

How academics, teachers, and trainers positioned themselves in a context characterized by constant change and marked by labor intensification was dependent upon a number of conditions: the historical conditions in which they worked, the specific institutional culture, and the professional discourses they could call upon. Many, such as Anna, a senior lecturer in a sandstone university, expressed a growing dissatisfaction with the new work order of the university.

> I think the changes have been monumental; I can't think of any other work-place where people would have to totally revolutionize the sort of techno-logical basis of their work, its mode of delivery, its mode of communication. All of those things they would have to do at the same time to completely change the orientation towards their work. The only way academics can cope with the increased numbers of students is to develop a range of teaching practices that simply don't allow for the informal learning processes that used to take place and that were actually extremely valuable.

New funding regimes were established. Program budgeting in schools attached curriculum to dedicated budget lines, requiring fine-grained planning. In universities and TAFEs, local internal budget centers paid other centers for services and competed for funding provided centrally. Many academics saw the budgeting processes as being more aligned to the logic of management and accounting and less aligned to the logic of academic work of research and teaching, thus creating more administrative labor for academics to sort out the misalignment. Academics responded to multiple accountability demands rather than doing teaching and research, resulting in less, not more flexibility. A typical account was:

> In this university we have an extremely decentralized financial system where there is a one-line budget. Everything comes down to the department level and gets shared around a bit among staff members. There's an enormous amount of filling in of forms and going to meetings and working out this, that, and the other. Everything is devolved to the basic unit when there's no flexibility in budgeting. You're stuck with it right down there at the depart-ment level. There's no moving around of finances because it's already allo-cated. . . . [F]rom the time of Dawkins governments have required a lot more documentation from universities, and it all trickles right down the line to everybody. We're always filling in remarkable forms and codes about research and all this sort of stuff. (Helen, sandstone)

Central management, as did government, assumed such budgetary processes were more efficient and constantly reduced delegated budgets, with little regard for the costs in terms of organizing local relations on a competitive basis. Local units (faculties in universities, departments in TAFE, and schools) meanwhile increasingly spent time and energy raising funds for core purposes to cover the shortfall—through consultancies, research grants, commercialization of teaching, curriculum products, voluntary fund raising, business contributions, and ultimately fee-paying students. The paradox was that internal competition for limited funding led to reduced flexibility, increased entrenchment of positions, and incoherent program and research groupings resulting from attempts to gain market niches or additional funding. Chee Wah, a senior lecturer at a Queensland redbrick university explained:

> It's that one-line budget that divides people. Before, ecology and social sciences wanted to work together. Right now, we have to protect against ecology, so we actually don't really talk to each other any more. In fact we have become territorial, fighting over student numbers. When you have several different fields merged together into the one-line budget, you just fight . . . it's tremendously stressful and indicates the deterioration of our quality of life in academia.

The management discourse was to work "smarter and harder." In universities, "smarter" most often meant reducing contact hours for tutorials, larger tutorials and lectures, teleconferences and email, or using online student management systems with less pedagogical interaction. "Harder" usually meant increased staff-student ratios, a computer on each desk escalating expectations for instant communication through multiple modes from students and managers, without technical support. "One tech says I don't do that and sends somebody else, and the job doesn't get done . . . there is no loyalty or identity any more" (Meredith, redbrick).

In TAFE the daily administration was devolved down the line to middle managers and then teachers, altering the "rules of the game," summed up by Alice in a large, metropolitan TAFE:

> Maybe five years ago the paperwork used to be 5 to 10 percent of a teachers' work. Now it's closer to 40 or 45 percent The paperwork is astronomical because the students are receiving benefits from the Commonwealth Employment Service. We've got our own academic records. Then we've got audits all the time on the stats—how many students in your class are from this funding source. Every fortnight the rolls have to be faxed to the CES. Anytime a student withdraws from a class there's a fax. . . . Each time a student comes out of the class, it easily produces fifteen to twenty minutes' paperwork.

This labor intensification impacted on those lower down the ranks where individuals had less control over their workload and for those people made promotion more difficult. Samanatha, a middle manager in a rural TAFE, felt that "my job is paper chasing. It's not really a leadership role anymore . . . it's administrative now . . . it's a lot of organizational stuff that people, generally teachers, hate but what TAFE really want." Samantha went on to indicate how educational and management work was becoming more complex and more unmanageable with multicampuses, partnerships, consortiums, and distance learning. "I work on state-wide and national projects, often working in consortiums with other colleges. Egos, power, and inefficiencies come into it. Often there is a lot of effort into communicating with people at vast distances, getting people together, and things fall apart because people can't make it." The job then was too large and the pay too small given the escalating expectations from systems, managers, and markets. But labor intensification was accompanied by job insecurity.

WORKING FLEXIBLY:
CASUALIZING EDUCATIONAL LABOR

With funding based on enrollments, individual institutions were caught between the downward pressure to be efficient and the horizontal pressure of markets to be flexible. Flexibility for self-managing schools, universities, and TAFEs became increasingly dependent upon a casualized education workforce. Whereas flexibility and mobility produced additional rewards for tenured professionals and managers, mobility and flexibility were the preconditions of getting employment for marginal educational outworkers (Blackmore and Angwin 1998). In Victorian schools, casual teachers doubled from 7 percent to 14 percent from 1993 through 1999. This had multiple flow on effects. Principals, in manipulating global budgets, replaced expensive "retiring" senior teachers with junior, less experienced, cheaper, and often casual staff. Schools went for several years without employing new graduates on an ongoing basis. Parents, largely women, became a new source of voluntary labor, working as paraprofessionals, as policies linked good parenting to involvement, for example, literacy training programs (Blackmore and Hutchison 2001). For principals, local funds were the only source of discretionary expenditure that could support a more comprehensive curriculum beyond the basics, including sport, art, and music,. Principals were thus trapped between undermining teachers' employment conditions and promoting the best program for their school. Financial issues produced sleepless nights and anxious days (Thomson et al. 2003) for Julie, a primary principal in a poor, inner-city school:

> Over three years, we scrimped and saved and applied for grants. This year, for the first time, we had $168,000, which is the total cost of our curriculum

program, paid for in advance. We rent the facilities, and we are vigilant look-ing for money. The city council has community grants, and we have a break-fast program. We applied. If I hear of another local organization that is about "save the children" we apply. . . . Two toasters from the manufacturer free is two toasters we don't buy.

Universities similarly saw the doubling of casualization of staff to 16 per-cent. In 1995, women constituted 26.5 percent of continuing staff, 46.1 percent fixed-term contracts, and 46 percent sessional staff, yet they were only 38.9 percent of academic staff in all. Of female academics 36.1 percent had contin-uing positions, 23.7 percent had fixed-term, and 40.2 percent had sessional positions (Castleman et al. 1995). Increased research output was increasingly contingent on the invisibility of contract teachers and researchers, a marginal-ized pool of underpaid and undervalued research assistants and casual staff, largely women, without whom the intellectual and social wellbeing of the insti-tution, and indeed core workers, would not survive. "Academia's domestics" (Reay 2004) were the first to go when student target numbers were not met, institutional directions changed, or budgets cut. Dianne, a dean in a sandstone, agreed that "universities already have a high casualization. Now it could get much worse. . . . [M]ost university employers would like to move people into more and more contract positions. . . . [C]asualization is an issue for the future." Likewise a vice-chancellor observed that the consequences of "the casualization of academic work means there is a big pack of women who have come in at the bottom at a time when the whole environment has changed—it's horrible for them." Yet "women, in particular, with other responsibilities at home, were less flexible at a time when workplaces required increased flexibil-ity of the part of workers to 'fit' organizational needs" (Joan, EO manager, sandstone). Sandra in a rural TAFE saw her career limited as "women are not given opportunities to do certain things, often because they are sessional or part time. When I was point eight the director said to me, 'We'll have to think about your commitment.' It made me realize how hard it is for women. You have a child, and someone is saying that is showing lack of commitment."

The trend to outsource teaching to casual workers has historically been greatest in the TAFE sector, a trend that was exacerbated and spread into other sectors with the open training market as increased competition developed between public and private providers, but usually not recorded or monitored (Anderson 1994). Many TAFE institutes had a majority of their staff working as casuals (to gain industry experience). The requirement of competitive ten-dering for labor market programs increased sessional casualization as govern-ment contracts often only lasted for six months, increased the time expended by middle managers on writing tenders and managing sessional staff, often only employed for three months at a time. Year-long contracts in this context were highly valued but not rewarded in competitive tendering as too expensive:

[I]n spite of the tough reputation of our management, the director of the college, especially, over industrial issues, this department has got an excellent record of contract employment in terms of the ratio of contract and sessional. We've got 80 percent contract teachers, which is exceptionally high. But now our conditions will just go because we lost the tender. We'll lose a lot of our students, the superior programs, and contract staff. (Alice, manager, large, metropolitan TAFE)

Casual TAFE staff (many expublic school teachers) in the private- and public-sector labor market thus became mobile educational outworkers, virtually teaching out of the back of their cars in up to five casual positions, and without collegial support, professional development, holiday leave, or superannuation (Blackmore and Angwin 1998). Institutional flexibility effectively was achieved through the labor of a "lost generation" of teachers and academics:

Our teachers have been living with this for years now. The casualization of the teaching profession in VET, which is predominantly women, means when the teachers' contracts come due the teachers are pitted against each other in competition for their own and others' jobs. They're all on six-month contracts, the coordinators on three years. Seven of our coordinators' positions are all up in December, competing against each other for our jobs. I don't know whether to go for my coordination position again or go back into teaching. Doing something else, being forty-six, the realities are bleak. But here we've got no pathways, no career prospects except marking time and grabbing whatever we can get. The name of the game is surviving. People will work for below award conditions, with less job security and fewer ongoing positions. Each year we're told there's cut backs again. (Alice, large, metropolitan TAFE)

Many graduate teachers and postgraduate students with PhDs left the education sector as the contract staff were more readily "detached" by nonrenewal of contracts. An associate professor commented on the impact of retrenchment: "The prospect for some of the young women coming into the [university] system, I think, is profoundly disturbing. We could, in fact, lose an intellectual generation . . . [and] in casual work they're not going to get the opportunity to develop as a mature intellectual and grasp the disciplinary area. . . . [I]t's a sort of vandalism" (Anna, sandstone). The casualization of labor, together with its intensification, had significant effects on practice. A casual academic commented about the tension between being involved and being exploited by organizations, and the lack of access to professional development and advancement possibilities. Meg, a sessional staff member at a wannabe university:

It's totally difficult if your only time on campus is when you are paid to actually teach. A lot of people I've worked for did not see me as a human being, just someone . . . they could leave work to. But I was shut out of the planning, as they were careful not to exploit me by calling me to meetings. But no professional learning, no direction. The structures were inflexible. People like me couldn't crack into networks and systems simply because I was not in a position . . . where I could access them.

Another effect of casualization and contractualism is compliance. "People remain silent about a lot of things—they become secretive and because everything is to do with information they start to get protective about their own bit of information" (Maureen, school education system bureaucrat). Information was power. So communication became more instrumental through choice and lack of time. Frequent restructurings led to constant redeployment of staff, ongoing job applications, and a deepening sense of powerlessness. "The workplaces are becoming less flexible, the school works longer hours, and there is not much part-time work. The flexibility comes from the cheap labor of the employees" (Margaret, small, progressive, suburban TAFE).

Finally, there was an evident lack of investment in staff and professional development, as Jane (manager, small, progressive TAFE) commented: "[One of the] big problems we've had with our staff is that I don't think they've had the opportunity, and the rules change very quickly. They're supposed to be able to teach ongoing students, but at the same time we're supposed to be able to hop out to the workplace and train everyone from managers through to operators. This college is investing an incredible amount of energy into training managers and half that amount in training staff to work in this environment." Educational restructuring, in one sense, produced the appearance of coherence and direction as policy integrated education into government planning, cascading down into organizational strategic planning. At another level, organizational and social fragmentation arose out of these same processes, so that "members work together on temporary alliances, consolidating power and isolating potential threats to the illusion of stability" (Calbrese and Roberts 2001, 270).

WORKING "SMARTER"?
VOLATILE AND TOXIC CULTURES

Cost cutting and downsizing was evident across all sectors. Little care was taken about how to manage these radical shifts, and indeed the culture of restructuring produced more volatile, toxic, and greedy organizations. Structural reform was the symbolic means by which CEOs and managers made their mark, often with little concern or awareness as to the organizational costs in terms of equity, worker morale, loss of institutional skills and memory, or alienation. Janis, manager in a metropolitan TAFE, commented on the poor change management that "funding was dropped, and there was a lack of negotiation. Working closer with state budgets and funds seems to have meant that there was less interest in the good things happening at 'the tech' and only an interest in the facts and figures. Change wasn't too rapid, but the system fell down where it didn't explain the changes to people." Another TAFE manager commented about how she came to view her institution after restructuring: "All I was seeing was the hardness . . . the really masculine use of power, the financial management, not getting recognition for doing a good job, uncertainty, staff afraid of losing their jobs, feeling frustrated with decision making processes and compromised. The loneliness for me was a rude shock" (Janis, large, metropolitan TAFE). Others saw the level of toxicity and volatility resulting from "a politicization of education in the last eleven years" together with restructuring that meant "lots of complaints and issues to deal with, tight schedules, long hours, and high demands in terms of time and commitment" (Sally, small, rural TAFE). Both anxiety and compliance were exacerbated by "people's uncertainty about job security. Even tenured people wonder, will they have a job tomorrow? I don't trust them. The world is changing so quickly; I'm no longer in control" (Nicole, redbrick). This feeling of lack of control, insecurity, and distrust heightened lower down the organization. It had significant effects, as "junior academic staff have very low self-confidence. It is really important for senior women to mentor them or at least point out that they are doing a good job" (Dianne, dean, sandstone).

Institutions were also toxic for feminists. Institutional discourses articulated with media discourses denigrating feminism, multiculturalism, and reconciliation (Blackmore 1997). Feminists were open targets for male anger arising from fear and dislocation in workplaces, and around (un)reconstructed gender identities. The marginalizing of discourses of gender equity in Victorian schools during the Kennett era "permitted" the vocalization of male discontent locally. In a regional primary school, Terry, the principal, had sought to equalize women's employment opportunities in a region with the lowest level of women in leadership in the state. A male teacher "verbalized" in a staff meeting that women were "getting jobs unfairly" in their district because they were "favored."

Likewise in TAFE institutions under restructure, antagonistic and degrading antifeminist/female discourses infused traditional "trady" discourses as a last stand in shoring up blue-collar masculinities (Connell 2000). Raelene, a manager from a small, progressive TAFE, recalls how "women were categorized as dumb and fat. The men would talk to the good looking ones and not bother with the married ones. Even when sexual harassment charges are made the men always get off and don't get dismissed." One TAFE manager commented that "there is an element of resistance if you are working within a male-dominated area of a trade department. TAFE is a very male culture due to traditional apprenticeship training. Before the restructure one out of the thirteen managers of teaching centers were women. After the restructure the culture is still about 'life wasn't meant to be easy'" (Cora, small, progressive, urban TAFE). Many senior, male administrators did not see EO as their responsibility. Some actively generated sexist discourses at the executive level, as described by Tricia (large, metropolitan TAFE):

> In this environment women probably start behind the starting block. The college has a male director. It is a male-dominated field. There expectation is that males take on the leadership. All of the upper levels are occupied by men, except one female deputy director, who is not in a position of power. This sends a message about women's opportunities and the way women in leadership roles are facilitated and encouraged. There is no expectation that women will be in those jobs.

In the university context, Elle, a DVC at a Utech, considered that "women are a minority in leadership, not surrounded by female colleagues. This produces stress and loneliness, whereas men are so good at protecting their own interests and promoting their interests. Women are still being 'good girls,' yet power is defined in male terms, and men collude against women all the time in formal and informal ways." Peta, at a redbrick university suggested that "misogyny in this school is part of the invisible implicit culture. There is a group of half a dozen males between fifty-two and fifty-five who are neither up to date, nor are they committed to the very real issues of social justice and equity." A dean, likewise, commented on one sandstone university being "right down at the bottom in terms of leadership when she went there. The department was filled with male, senior lecturers champing at the bit to become professor. There was a lot of hostility between people" (Dianne, sandstone). This antagonism spread to her as the newly appointed dean and as a female. One senior lecturer commented that "within this institution there are misogynists and sexists and racists, who do what they do out of absolute ignorance. I hope they are a decreasing majority" (Francesca, Utech). Some cultural milieus were not only misogynist, but also racist, as experienced by Chee Wah (redbrick), a senior lecturer working in a faculty of science in the area of public health: "Well I really feel being Asian and a woman is tough—a minority, and this particular faculty is known to be sexist . . . not sexist in a conscious way." Some workplaces were perceived to be more women friendly, as in the case of one Utech, because it has "both symbolic support backed by infrastructure. . . . There are a range of systemic things, sexual harassment contact officers . . . [and] there's a sense that those sorts of things will be taken seriously" (Deana, Utech).

Even the institutions where women were in executive leadership were not necessarily women friendly as external imperatives (policies, overseas student markets, funding) dominated agendas. Georgina, a professor, commented: "I think this university is one of the most volatile ones I've ever worked in." Even in more "women friendly" cultures, behaviors of individuals changed. One dean, Jodie, commented on how she was "treated badly by men in meetings outside her university. My usually supportive male peers were siding with the nonsupportive blokes: the boys sticking together yet again." The TAFE culture in many instances was described variously by managers as being fraught and toxic because of "having to tell staff members that they aren't performing, being dependant on grants and DEET for funding which affect staff hours (contract and casual staff)" (Janis, large, metropolitan TAFE).

Restructuring, therefore, brought particular toxic effects and provided an environment for encouraging latent prejudices. A deputy principal in an inner-city primary school refers to the reassertion "symbolically" of masculine leadership with the election of the neoliberal government in Victoria after 1993: "The boys who had put their suits away during the 1980s now dusted them off and put them on again as they now saw new opportunities for promotion with EO gone." Amanda, an assistant principal, recalled how "I used to go to the monthly principals' meetings because I was called a principal, and there were four women . . . suddenly now the regional manager sits at the top table with an inner group sitting at that big table and the rest of us in rows without tables." This behavior of intimidation and fear permeated throughout organizations and systems. In Victoria, it was embedded in particular policy discourses that positioned teachers as resistors. Media discourses about public school failure silenced teachers, while government gagged public debate by threatening to invoke long-forgotten legislation that disallowed public servants to criticize government (Blackmore and Thorpe 2003). A culture of bullying emerged in Victorian schools, as described by Helen, principal of an inner-city primary school: "Principals are in the firing line. If they try to deny their staff or go against the government line they end up being threatened themselves. . . . [There have been] letters with an underlying threat to block promotion . . . [and] teachers feel if they don't toe the government line and the principal's line they are in danger of being made in excess." This in turn influenced how teachers related to students. Evelyn, principal of a lower socioeconomic school in a provincial city argued that "the current climate of bullying by the system is becoming entrenched in teachers' values and attitudes because they have no control over anything anymore except their classrooms. . . . [W]e are regressing to 1950s behaviors—they stamp on us, so we stamp on kids."

While women were used to chilly cultures during the 1980s, constant restructuring in the 1990s produced a volatility in organizational life that shaped social relations in debilitating ways. Under the rules of the new public administration, senior bureaucrats and ministerial advisors were under contract and increasingly vulnerable to changes in government, which in turn produced rapid and significant policy shifts in bureaucracies and schools. Estelle, a bureaucrat working in the area of "students at risk" reflected on the rising toxicity of one school education bureaucracy:

> I am on the social justice floor, with the aboriginal and Torres Strait Islander group next door. We are the gender equity, cultural equity (i.e., for people from a non-English-speaking background), and disability services area. All of these groups (largely women) intersect and make connections with each other. Now government policies have shifted dramatically to the Right. Instead of being called the "Supportive School Environment," our team is called the "Discipline Team" . . . to stop disruption in schools. . . . My job is to write policy statements and "ministerials" that go up through three layers of editing. Any woosy words like *social justice*, *equity* or concepts like 'barriers' get red penned out. Really strong words like *cost effect* get straight through.

Her inclination was to leave, but she was persuaded to stay to keep the new minister well informed. But "he hasn't shifted his position, hasn't read anything. . . . [T]wo minutes after he became minister he gave principals the power to suspend students for thirty days for disruptive behavior." Apart from her concern about how policy had shifted from schools working with students at risk to excluding "students who are disruptive," she spoke of a wider policy shift away from social justice that manifested itself in her everyday work relations. "[W]e are not allowed to talk to each other. Different groups have been told 'don't talk to gender equity'—gender and cultural equity, both gone. The Torres Strait islander group have not yet been named but feel it coming. We are in an open plan office. . . . [T]he aboriginal and Torres Strait islanders' group area next to ours was always noisy, busy and lots of talking going on. Now it is silent, and that is distressing." Compliance led to social tension, closure of debate, and lack of collegiality.

Such bullying was becoming typical of universities. Leesa, an associate dean at a Utech, commented that "leadership in most organizations is quite abusive, and I'm not comfortable with that." Meetings were often confrontational, and there were expectations for rapid responses, strategic thinking, and sure-fire solutions. Reflection was not part of the game. "I think it's a female thing, not being good at forming an opinion quickly, having the right words. Until I can do that I'm behind the eight ball. I can't articulate what the problem really is, what they should do. I'm not totally comfortable functioning in an all-male environment" (Pauline, senior lecturer, Utech).

For one's presence not to be recognized, least of all heard, was a form of symbolic violence experienced by many women. Women's vulnerability in institutional life was exacerbated by these policy shifts in terms of what and who was valued, the intensification and uncertainty of work, the volatility, and a new equity politics. This vulnerability meant they were unenviably positioned as being too compliant or too resistant. As Estelle decided, philosophically: "I can't write 'stop disruption in schools' . . . I don't want to stop it; I value it; I think it is a useful thing. If we don't have disruption, we are dead." Disruption in her terms was about recognizing difference, about addressing the needs of students who are not succeeding or who had difficult home lives, about provoking the system to respond to certain types of students by problematizing categories such as "at risk." When this was no longer possible, she left the bureaucracy and returned to teaching.

Those who stayed in management adopted a range of survival strategies. One dean indicated she "won't tolerate being bullied, and men are not used to that. When I'm pushed I present more like men—I don't retreat or look the victim. I argue more, and I argue from principle. But like most women I work most times to preserve a relationship even if I disagree with someone. I've got great personal confidence to do that" (Jill, Utech). Another strategy was to "sit back and listen." Loretta, a Dean, did not see her job as directing or providing quick solutions: "One thing I hate is walking into a room and somebody says, 'What do you reckon we should do?' I do probably control the agenda, but I try to identify the problem with them . . . I avoid open conflict. People heap abuse on me, say the most horrible things to me in public at meetings. I just blank it out, never respond, but I think about it a lot . . . I just gloss over the rudeness and conflict, work around it, but never publicly."

Managers came to see the main aspect of their job as "managing conflict because a team approach is not encouraged in the department. It's divide and rule" (Alice, head of department, large, metropolitan TAFE).

Loretta considered the rising level of abuse as being part of a wider shift in how people related to each other in organizations more generally with recent managerialist and market oriented reforms. It was more than anxiety or distress. Rather, she argued: "I think there's less time for tolerance of individuality: now we don't have space for these people. If you are not performing (with a capital P) according to the sorts of expectations established both outside the larger system but also inside the system, because of resource constraints, you feel under threat and marginalized. There isn't that sort of tolerance, it's just that managerialist thing."

So while individuals took on new responsibilities and risks, there could not be an expression of individuality outside organizational parameters. *Anxiety*, *turmoil*, and *tension* were terms that our participants used to characterise their workplaces. This could be expected with wide-scale reform. The difference was now belief systems were being transformed through consent but increasingly overt coercion. This produced significant dilemmas for womanagers who managed casual and contract staff (hiring and firing) but who were often their advocates and now felt complicit in their exploitation. Institutional survival ultimately won over individual or collective rights, sidelining any ethical implications, through a paralyzing incrementalism. Indeed, there were fewer outlets for appeal as most casual staff were nonunionized. Tricia, a middle manager in a large, metropolitan TAFE, commented:

> It's just another thing that will be imposed on us. We've got no control over it. There is no forum to fight it. At one stage we were not allowed to have a union meeting before 5 o'clock . . . directive from our Associate Director. We're used to it now; people are just busy in their classrooms; just busy surviving. When you work long hours, the agenda is survival. One of the problems in TAFE is that there is no career path. There is no promotional structure to work through.

GREEDY ORGANIZATIONS: REPRIVATIZING WORK

Halford, Savage, and Witz (1997) argue that the training sector in particular depends on "a particular configuration of relationships between home and work which valorises the independent, lone individual with no other commitments" (75). But this was becoming the norm across all sectors. Most women participants jokingly commented that "we all need a wife," someone to organize the everyday life of family and relationships (Jane, small, progressive, suburban TAFE). While many women were without children or partners, supposedly an advantage in the promotions game, other responsibilities shaped their capacity to be flexible, mobile, and work long hours in order to assume higher responsibilities. Typical of most women's careers in this project was, on the one hand, their subjugation of their own career, desires, and needs for others that was indicative of how women's choices are highly constricted, particularly since many of them were sole parents or primary carers. A study of 3,872 academic and general staff in Australia found that 50 percent of women academics were the main carers of their children compared to 4.3 percent of male academics. Despite this, women academics were no less committed to academic work and careers, and their research productivity was not significantly different over a comparable time span (Currie and Thiele 2001, 92). Career was very important to their identity *because* of their responsibilities but also their professional commitment to education.

Responsibilities weighed heavily, together with professional priorities and quality of life issues, to inform individual career "choices." Andra, a senior lecturer, gave up being deputy dean with another impending restructuring on the grounds of restructuring exhaustion: "I have decided that I am now fifty-five and have poured enough energy into this university, and I am rethinking my priorities. I haven't been too bad as deputy dean, but I don't want to do it any more. I could have gone further, finished my book, been promoted again, done the career thing, but this last restructuring has lost me altogether" (Utech). But embedded in organizations were also subtle and overt discriminatory processes and practices positioning women as outside the mainstream if they were primary carers of the aged, sick, or young. This included "scheduling a meeting from 3:00 to 6:00 PM—an acceptance of these extracurricular hours is part of the job and the unspoken assumption by men that this is OK. . . . The requirement to be available for teaching from 8:00 AM to 10:00 PM and having to work in school holidays has affected women with children. Many of these women chose the profession so that could fit in their childcare responsibilities" (Sheila, large, metropolitan TAFE). Raelene, manager in a small progressive TAFE, commented that "restructuring and the new teaching responsibilities meant that the job I do is time consuming. I believe that a manager's position will be even more time consuming. The new timetabling from eight in the morning is particularly tough on families, both teachers and students, with family priorities."

Consequently, "family life suffers: staying back, taking work home. There are some conflicts where there are high standards applied. Trying to have a career and be a mother—one will suffer. As far a nontraditional areas, we haven't shifted too far with EEO" (Felicity, large, outer suburban, community-oriented TAFE).

The privatization of educational work, its penetration into family time and private life, was significant for most of these women. For some, taking up leadership positions was not possible due to the logistics of parenting. Jenny (leading teacher, rural senior secondary school) could not undertake leadership because "in the five years that I have been part time, I've got one off to kindergarten; so, after that year, life will be easier . . . I have been involved with the 'collegial situation' here at school, where I have teamed up with a male member of staff, and we've learned from each other how we will operate in the classroom, how we will operate within the programs." Speaking out against this new corporate work ethic and against such practices was not acceptable. "It's not just hard for women to compete with men when the men haven't had an interruption to their careers with childminding stuff, but when I mentioned it my dean said: 'Oh that gender thing; you're not going to go on about that are you?'" (Bernadette, Utech). In another university where the issue was also raised, the male dean let slip a comment about "all that motherhoody stuff" while reporting strategies have been implemented to support family friendly workplaces. But "policies without changing practices do not change results" (Alida, redbrick). As one dean, herself a single parent, commented: "Family issues have not really been resolved for staff or students at the university. There could be significant improvement in the culture allowing people to look after their child-rearing roles. The possibility of flexibility is there, but not taken up. The changing nature of academic work could be worse for women due to casualization. Future jobs could become so unstable that it puts women off" (Dianne, sandstone). Again, this had significant implications for the next generation of leaders.

Young women have got families and are trying to juggle all of that. Two women have got young children, one doing a PhD, one finishing off her masters. They're marvelous, but they're going to be burnt out if I don't protect them. We've got to have recognition in this university that there are structural and cultural barriers against women making it in academia, despite EEO policies. (Jeanette, head of school, Gumtree University).

Many women felt torn between competing demands and emotions of work and home. "I lead the life of a mother who stays at home as well as a mother who works full time and it's very difficult: I don't want my children to miss out on the opportunities because I work full time, so I make sure I put the effort into enabling them to do all their things and their activities. It's just exhausting" (Jo, metropolitan TAFE). Or, Roya, a manager in a large, outer suburban community TAFE, without children, but who finds work consumed her waking moments. "I keep having resolutions that I'm just going to not worry about working too much and try and concentrate on seeing friends a bit, but it's really hard to do. I'm too tired to talk to them, and you sort of lose interest in trying to keep up contact."

Women were balancing work/home with little support from either employers or government. They did not indicate a preference for work over family, or family over work, but rather sought to balance the two. They were not happy to be in low-paid, casual jobs without any benefits and few opportunities for advancement, but pragmatically accommodated to it because of their familial responsibilities and because choices were between limited options. Work was important to their sense of identity, as with men, but women's relationship with work was informed by their familial responsibilities, whereas male attitudes to work rarely addressed family. This dominant "job model" for men and a "gender model" for women considers women only experience conflict between work and family roles. (Probert 2001b). Those women who do advance into formal leadership generally had institutional support in family-friendly workplaces. In a study of women academics post-1987 restructuring, Deane (1996) summated that "the struggle for balance, what we have termed the 'holistic academic,' where quality of teaching and the pursuit of research can coexist with family and personal commitments, was, however, often a frustrating quest" (3).

WEARY, WORRIED, AND WORN OUT

The cultural fields of higher education, schools, and TAFE institutes are merging as sites of new cultural practices. Leading and managing in one sector increasingly required knowledge of the other sectors. There was also increased fluidity between education labor markets, with the integration of

TAFE with universities, and many TAFE and university staff previously from schools. But the restructure of education labor markets and of educational labor, we suggest, reasserted old masculinist dispositions in new forms without changing household domestic labor. Furthermore, educational organizations exploited the new gender dynamics of the 1990s, providing work for many women, but without full rights and benefits. This was done through exploiting women's educational capacities in curriculum and pedagogy, while corraling off such core work as marginal to line management; by inviting women into middle management, but only to manage the crisis of restructuring. The modernization of management also appropriated particular essentialist feminist discourses of women's capacities to its benefit: "Women are much more interactive with . . . strong interpersonal communication skills. They're much more able to talk about their feelings, and that is sometimes very important in this working environment. If you've got the shits, you should be able to say, 'I have got the shits' and not indirectly manifest that through behaviors which then are destructive of others" (Renate, CEO, metropolitan TAFE). Women have therefore been "greenfields labor" to management. The "greedy" organization invited women into what were fast becoming volatile and toxic cultures on its own terms. Teaching and the academy, previously seen to be equitable workplaces with some flexibility were no longer family or woman friendly. Instead, management, with its generic skills and competence as the basis for promotion, rather than well-established profiles in research or long-term teaching experience, was emerging as the better career option for women as late entrants into the game. But in general, greedy organizations practiced symbolic violence in the sense that women were simultaneously called upon to be good organizational citizens by moving into leadership, but subtly continued to be excluded as full corporate citizens. This raises "the paradox of being an organizational citizen by right and an outsider by fact may suggest ways to make an organizational culture more woman friendly, or, alternatively, why this may not be possible" (Gherardi 1995, 5).

FOUR

"Lived Contradictions": Gender, Professionalism, and the Crisis of Trust

---

PROFESSIONALISM MADE OVER

IN THIS CHAPTER we consider the changing nature of professionalism with the restructuring of schools, TAFEs and universities, and what this means for educational leadership and women leaders. Education is itself a contested cultural field with its interconnected institutions, rules, conventions and categories that "produce and authorise certain discourses and activities" around notions of professionalism (Webb, Schirato, and Dahaher, x–xi). Education itself has a particular discursive logic around research, pedagogy, curriculum, assessment, and within some sectors, social justice and democratic practice. Professionalism is an "occupational strategy" that shapes patterns of power, place, and relationships in organizations. Professional fields are also highly gendered, with quasi "caring" professions, such as teaching, being numerically feminized. Gender in each education subfield assumes a particular symbolic capital. Thus, femininity has negative capital in a field of educational management that is masculinist, but positive capital in the field of early childhood, where discourses overtly link young children to the naturalness of "mothering." We argue that women moving into management assume material and symbolic capital in terms of control and power but retain the negative capital associated with their gender.

Professionalism came under scrutiny in the context of both the rise of the performative state and the fast capitalist work order that sought to "manage professionals" in the late twentieth century (Rhoades 1996). The status of the service professions—education, health and welfare—had risen with the emergence of the welfare state after 1900, the state having "underwritten the institutional knowledge production and codification (universities, research organizations, professions, unions) and institutions of dissemination (universities, schools, and TAFE) (Seddon 1997). Women had made their greatest gains in the feminized professions by working for/with/against the state. Twentieth-century professionalism was premised upon discrete expertise, the monopoly of a professional/practical knowledge base, often imbued with discourses of service to citizens and public advocacy. In Australian education, the blurring between unionism and professionalism was most evident in the strongly unionized school and TAFE sectors (Blackmore 1991). This close professional relationship with both unions and state bureaucracies was more in alignment with Europe than the United Kingdom, where the weaker state was "less an organizer of division of labor and more an object of attention of the organized occupations" (Brint 1994, 175).

Educational restructuring in Australia, as elsewhere, together with the move to postwelfarism during the 1990s, changed the relationships among government, public bureaucracies, unions, and the professions, ending "licensed autonomy and public service professionalism" (Seddon 1998, 230). Demands for accountability focused increasingly on quality assurance and external standards set outside the profession rather than self-monitoring based on trust. Industry influence increased while union influence decreased. Neoconservative governments (e.g., Kennett in Victoria and Howard) sought to undermine the legitimacy, and indeed the public advocacy role, of the "old professions," strategically excluding them, local councils, public-sector unions, and other nongovernmental organizations (women's and parent organizations) from policy formation because they were the major opponents to restructuring the public sector (Blackmore and Thorpe 2003; Pascoe and Pascoe 1998; Hancock 1999). Professional expertise was substituted by market surveys as "sources" of government policy.

As in the United Kingdom and New Zealand, neoconservative Australian governments framed debates about professionalism through a number of discursive moves and media spin: by positioning the professions as self-interested powerful groups who had "captured" the public sector, and by promoting seemingly democratic discourses about market-driven services making providers more responsive and accountable (Peters, Marshall, and Fitzsimons 2002). The latter discourse was seductive to professionals and lay alike. Neoliberal theories of the market promised choice and as such were "a means towards destabilizing professional bureaucratic expertise and demonising professional autonomy. If the consumer was to prevail, then the producers' influence would 'diminish' (Menter et al. 1997, 7; Pascoe and Pascoe 1998). These discourses undercut idealized discourses about professionals as public servants, being altruistic, and needing autonomy to exercise professional judgement, thus effectively generating a crisis in trust in the professions.

The "new public administration" introduced during the 1980s led to increased hands-on professional management in public-sector bureaucracies, explicit standards and measures of performance, greater emphasis on output controls, and the breakdown of monolithic units into smaller, manageable units for flexibility, underpinned by principles of efficiency and competition (Hood 1995). Senior bureaucratic heads, often without public-service experience, but trained as economists, were employed on limited contracts, accountable to their political masters. These multiskilled managers were moved often across fields (e.g., transport to education) to "multiskill," but also avoid them being "captured" by the field. The newfound status of this generic manager in government bureaucracies elevated them into a "new professional class" regardless of their lack of expertise in a substantive field other than human resource management, financial management, and planning. These new professional managers were given the executive powers to shift public-sector cultures toward entrepreneurialism and a consumer orientation—"the right to manage" (Clarke and Newman 1993). Performance management with bonus payments meant such individuals' interests (and loyalty) were linked more upward to the government or immediate superior, and less to their citizen clients, their professional colleagues, or indeed the public, reconstituting these relationships as a contractual rather than a moral obligation (Yeatman 1998a).

The contractual regimes of corporate managerialism in public bureaucracies were replicated in universities, schools, and TAFE institutes in Australia during the 1990s, although earlier in the United Kingdom and New Zealand. Whitty and colleagues (1998), Gewirtz and colleagues (1995), Peters and colleagues (2002) and Wylie (1995) identified similar tensions arising in school self-management policies in the United Kingdom and New Zealand as in Australia between markets and equity; between individual institutional (and professional) autonomy, and mandated policy; between collegial relations of school-based decision making for school improvement and imposed external accountabilities for quality assurance; and based on an artificial separation between policy and operations. In Australia, executive power in schools was reasserted through the establishment of leadership teams comprised of teachers in designated leadership positions, replacing in many instances elected teacher advisory or decision-making bodies, as in Victoria. School council composition was altered—in Victoria, for example—to reduce teacher representation but also to remove representatives of organized parent organizations whose policies opposed devolution (Blackmore 1999c). Staff and community representation on university councils and TAFE councils was reduced, but business representation increased (Blackmore 1992).

These professional generic managers within education system bureaucracies and increasingly universities and TAFE institutes were the new class of "symbolic analysts" organizing work. The discourses informing this emergent field were those of human resource management, accounting, and business focusing on client service (Townley 1997). These fields of practice lacked traditions in redressing social inequality and social justice similar to those embedded in the disciplines of health, welfare, and education (Gewirtz 1998). The "old" professionals (academics and teachers) were now being repositioned as servicing and not running this new regime. The new managerialism shifted the networks and locus of power in favor of managers in terms of decisions made about what courses met market demands, what counts as relevant knowledge, and what was good pedagogy and research. Universities in particular exhibited the "full panoply of symbolic trappings from the new cultural paradigm—mission statements, strategic plans, total quality management, multi-skilling and staff development" (Currie et al. 2002, 270).

Meanwhile, executive management increasingly "managed professionalism" through the incorporation of professionals themselves into management (Rhoades 1996). New "line" middle managers were recruited from *within* the professional ranks of teachers and academics, as line management overlaid/sidelined/incorporated collegial forms of governance. Previously academic and often elected positions, such as heads of school and deans, became line managers. Gleeson and Shain refer to the new managerialism in the United Kingdom in further education driving "a wedge between lecturers and senior management interests . . . that finds expression in the conflict between lecturers in defence of professional and pedagogic values and senior managers promoting the managerial bottom line" (461). The new managerial habitus required significant accommodation by all staff as it was misaligned with the old professional habitus with all its progressivist aspirations.

At the same time, performance management, competitive tenders, and short-term contracts meant professional relationships were based less on trust and obligation and more on legal, contractual arrangements and obligations. Professional expertise was also being outsourced with increased use of consultants from an emerging industry servicing the public sector. This repositioned professionals as "individual experts for hire" based on "the conception of experts working in markets for services organized in a mixed economy dominated by the larger corporations. Convergence around a model of marketable expertise has been encouraged by the waning of social trustee professionalism in the Anglo-American world and by the decline of the distinction of state service in Europe" (Brint 1994, 176).

The new managerialism also assumed multiple hybridities in specific "occupational fields of practice" (schools, universities, and TAFEs) as each education sector was characterized by different power/knowledge relations and gendered divisions of labor. We identified embryonic debates, for example, about the practical relevance of research and teacher education. This perceived theory/practice divide (e.g., between universities and schools, universities and TAFE) was sustained as "a problem" (largely of theorists by practitioners) but exploited by government. The discourse of "practical relevance" was central to the reconstitution of professionalism as expertise rather than as an ethical or theoretical practice, and also to change relations between these subfields of educational practice, another discourse of state control based on use value. In the university-based field of educational administration, there was, for example, as in the United Kingdom, a more overt disposition to be relevant to teacher and principal practitioners (Gunter 2000, 628). In Australia, the split between policy studies (too theoretical and ideological) and educational administration (relevant to practitioners) was not as evident historically. The discourse of practical relevance was generated to justify the creation of leadership centers in universities and the "generative habitus" of recruitment by education faculties from school and TAFE practitioners to sustain immediate practice experience (Gunter 2000). Practical relevance was also the driver underpinning contractual research, tenders that also improved education faculties' income-producing capacity and shifted attention away from "fundamental" knowledge generation. This discourse drew instrumentally upon more emancipatory discourses of action research, while claiming to dissolve the theory/practice divide. But overall, the discourse was mobilized to refocus educational research to "enable reform" (in other educational sectors) rather than "study the impact of change on practitioners," leading to an incremental redefinition of "practical activity" as "leadership" .

Discourses of practical relevance in the context of self-management in competitive environments also encouraged short-term school-based teacher professional development supporting government and school priorities over "theoretical" postgraduate study that was seen to be self-indulgent and self promoting (Blackmore 2002a). Thus the 1990s saw education research focus on "policy service" rather than "policy critique" in Australia, just as contractualism increasingly drove research in the United Kingdom and New Zealand (Atkinson 2000). More broadly, the field of educational administration research was internationally premised upon assumptions of rationality and gender/race/class neutrality, happily absorbing discourses of "learning organizations" and "reflective practice" in a thoroughly "modernist makeover" (Hartley 1998, 154). This reinforced the dominant mindset of government to train technically proficient practitioners rather than consider "the practitioner having interests that go beyond the institutional requirement of the right to manage and be managed" . Professionalism framed by public choice and neoliberal political theory promoted a new type of professional self whose interests lay in being practical, relevant, and providing a service.

THE DISCURSIVE UNDOING OF EDUCATION PROFESSIONALISM

Discourses about professionalism are the contexts, texts, and subtexts in this study. Women entering middle management were caught in the bind of managing professionalism and, in turn, being positioned as management professionals. Our interviewees talked about professionalism, but in quite different ways; some foregrounded relevance and competence of "being professional" by meeting external standards often set outside the profession. This was in line with the corporate discourse of professionalism's focus on being technically competent and able to achieve organizational goals set by others, discourse that promoted a tendency to be self-serving and inward looking and more susceptible to serving its own and others' political ends (Sachs 2003). Most of our cohort took a more oppositional, critical, and democratic stance, seeing pedagogy as empowerment and education as promoting social change, a form of "activist professionalism" (Sachs 2003) based on articulated standards agreed upon by the profession, a sense of commitment to the wider profession of teachers, and a sense of obligation to the wider public that promotes a form of civic responsibility not just to the individual student, school, or local community but to the wider public, that is, "being a professional" (Brennan 1996).

These coexisting discourses of managerial (technical) and educational (activist) professionalism were suffused with gender. For many of our middle managers, to be a "good woman" (and a good feminist) was to be an advocate for less powerful colleagues and clients, a form of loyalty and obligation beyond the organization (Acker and Feuerverger 1996). While managerial competence was perceived to be a precondition to good leadership, there was a growing tension between managerial professionalism in conforming to the regimes of strategic and quality management and outcomes-based performance and educational professionalism based on process and relationships of trust and mutual responsibility. While posed as solutions to the crisis of poor status of teaching as a profession, many viewed the managerial "moves" such as TQM and professional standards with irony (Bensimon 1995). Given the intensification of labor, increased surveillance over teachers and academics, and emphasis on technique rather than on substantive ethical issues, this position has a certain level of credibility. The imposition of external measures was experienced as reduced autonomy and control over professional knowledge rather than improving standards, and leadership competencies were seen to technologise social practice, indicative of a form of deprofessionalization (Seddon 1997; Shacklock 1998). Such sentiments were shared by teachers in England who experienced a "dumbing down" by the Teacher Training Agency (Mahoney and Hextall 2001). For the marginalized "educational outworkers" without any organizational base, professionalism provided meaning to their work, a sense of work identity, and collective engagement in a community of practice (Blackmore and Angwin 1998). Part-time and casual educators and researchers were particularly reliant upon professional networks for renewal and support as they lacked institutionally based collegial support and professional development.

The breakdown of the postwar political, economic, and social settlement that had been negotiated between professionals and the welfare state (Clarke and Newman 1993), produced a number of tensions for "womanagers" during the 1990s (Ozga and Deem 2000; Yeatman 1998b). Feminists found the notion of professionalism problematic because of its paternalistic roots (Bascia and Young 2001: Clegg 1999; Hey and Bradford 2004), a concern heightened with the discourse of crisis in teaching linking a lack of male teachers as models to declining professionalism (Mills et al. 2004). Feminists recognized that liberal feminist strategies seeking gender equity for professional women relied incorrectly on the "neutrality" of bureaucratic state *and* professions that had "masculinist" dispositions. They also realized that feminist networks among education/government sectors, professional organizations, and unions were unraveling as the femocrats fled the chilly climate of education bureaucracies (Hancock 1999). Education feminists were trapped by New Right backlash against "political correctness," and "democratic" discourses of local autonomy and market responsiveness in education. Both discourses exploited any disenchantment client groups had with the professions, unions, and advocates of equal opportunity and antidiscrimination policies.

The discourse of "managed professionalism" readily exploited such contestations over status in and between the different subfields (Rhoades 1996; Randle and Brady 1997). While academics historically had greater cultural capital than teachers as the educational "pace setters" and "tune callers" (Bauman 2001, 128) and teachers more than teacher/trainers in TAFE or community education due to their training, now academics were being positioned as providing courses that were not as "relevant" as TAFE nor as accountable for standards as schools, while academics lacked teaching qualifications. Expertise and status were further challenged across all sectors as entrepreneurialism became a criterion for promotion and in job descriptions (Mahoney, Menter, and Hextall 2004). Educational entrepreneurialism, with its focus on practicality and applicability, was more readily adopted in the service areas of TAFE and the disciplinary areas of business and science in universities but viewed as contrary to the "feminized" cultures of pedagogy in schools and adult or community education or the disciplinary fields of humanities and social sciences. But entrepreneurialism was increasingly linked to reward systems and encouraged a form of competitive individualism that undermined the status of educational work:

> Professional staff expended their human capital stocks increasingly in competitive situations. . . . Participation in the market began to undercut the tacit contract between professionals and society because the market put as much emphasis on the bottom line as on client welfare. The raison d'être for special treatment of universities, the training ground of professionals as well as

for professional privilege, was undermined, increasing the likelihood that universities, in the future, will be treated more like other organizations and professionals more like other workers. (Slaughter and Leslie 1998, 9)

Discourses promoting choice, client service, accountability, and practical relevance were difficult to counter, given the professional desire to "service" student needs. It readily subsumed discourses premised upon rights (academic freedom or good pedagogical relations), thus subtly reconfiguring relations between client and provider. Yet it was industry and parents who were now the primary clients, rather than individual students, an "ethical retooling" as professional judgements became subordinate to markets (Ball 2000).

Cumulatively, these processes shifted power relations between those who managed and those who taught and researched. Thus in a progressive, urban TAFE, recently restructured, Jane moved sideways into a key leadership area with strategic significance to promote online course development. This sideways step exploited her substantive curriculum and technical skills but did not earn her status or promotion. As Jane put it: "I realize now, because people review your performance on whether you're head of department or associate director, that it's got nothing to do with what you might have achieved in terms of new innovations, new products, new ways of doing things—total lack of recognition." Management and the consumption of knowledge work, rather than its production, was becoming the core work of organizations. Institutional rewards went to those controlling money and managing people, rather than teaching and research.

TEACHING: DEMOCRATIC OR MANAGEMENT PROFESSIONALISM?

At a time where educational reform was premised upon a sustained attack on teacher professionalism "based on a low trust model of accountability" (Ozga and Walker 1999, 109), teachers were negotiating conflicting discourses of democratic and managerial professionalism. Yet teachers, pressed for greater innovation, creativity, flexibility, teamwork, higher order thinking, and problem solving appropriate to postmodern times, were confronted with work intensification, rising expectations, exhortations to raise professional standards, and media-generated and political criticisms regarding teachers' lack of professionalism. An Australian Teaching Council report (ATC 1994) concluded,

Australia's teachers are ambivalent about their profession, they believe their central role—teaching and learning—to be worthwhile and personally rewarding. But there is also considerable frustration, anger and even despair among teachers, mainly arising from aspects of their working lives which are outside this function. . . . [S]ome of these include structural reforms in education which do not appear to have a necessary relationship with the "core business" of teachers. . . . [T]eachers are not contributing to the debates and policy changes reshaping how they live and work. (2)

The democratized workplace reforms of the 1980s in many Australian school systems had provided some degree of autonomy and space for professional judgment and collegiality. Research during the 1990s, as did ours, found that managerial professionalism "degutted the professionalism out" (Grundy and Bonser 1997, 158). Teachers felt deprofessionalized and reprofessionalized simultaneously. But overall, new controls outweighed new freedoms. As one teacher said, "teachers have been disempowered." Empowerment, Bishop and Mulford (1996) argued, was about "recognition, support, respect and reliability." Studies of primary teachers concluded that economically driven reform challenged conventional versions of public sector service professionalism (Blackmore et al. 1996; Menter et al. 1997; Gewirtz, Ball, and Bowe 1995; Bishop and Mulford 1996).

Increasingly in marketized systems, professionalism had to be displayed, outwardly, to parents and managers. Teachers and principals alike referred to how the performative aspects of their work changed relations with parents and influenced their sense of a capacity to make professional judgments. Noelene (principal, secondary college) explained: "I don't see any change in community relations except for the fact that if parents are unhappy with your school they think they can threaten you that they will remove their child from the school." Angela, in the same school, stated that "parents have a lot more power, and the students have a lot more power. The students are starting to realize it and are becoming more vocal. They've found out that they are entitled to more out of education. They are demanding more, and they are not shy at all." Many saw this as a positive, a new energy among the students, but based on principles of consumption rather than education, "in that we need to be offering more so that the community will send their kids here—it is like a private industry— we need to be showing better grades" (Lois, leading teacher, large, suburban secondary college).

Teachers' professional successes also had to be made visible, outside the classroom, before they were recognized as "leadership material." Karen (leading teacher, large, urban secondary school) commented on how the reforms meant that "as staff they had to pull their finger out and do a lot more. We also need to show that we are having input into almost everything, otherwise we are seen to be not doing anything. It is not enough just to teach anymore— indeed that is less relevant by the day in terms of how you are judged." An aspirant female teacher, Harriet, commented on how you "have to spend money on clothes now. Some teachers don't look professional. Kids expect you to look the part." Debra (returned teacher on contract) reflected on how "I've changed totally. I've had to. Before I was constantly concerned about my curriculum. Now that's second. I have to sit an interview at the end of the year as I'm on contract. I've got to compete against the rest of my department and show what I have done this year. So I'm constantly getting involved with things outside the classroom. I have no job security."

Another commented, "I have tended to be less innovative, to stick more to the status quo, particularly with curriculum development and stuff like that." Teachers were becoming more risk aversive, working within the policy and organizational frames. Karen reflected on the impact of the demand for strategic planning: "Charters, priorities are rearranging the deckchairs. These issues would have emerged, and people would have done it anyway. It's more the case of being seen to be doing something. People/schools have always identified issues and attempted to deal with them. Schools of the Future are an accountability device instead of treating schools as professional organizations."

The desire to be seen not only distracted and diverted energy but fundamentally changed the nature of professional practice itself. Angela, a primary teacher in a popular, inner-city school, changed her pedagogy with rising demands for recording and reporting in larger classes. "Things will have to go, such as, for example, working individually or with small groups. The temptation is to teach them as a whole group as the curriculum is getting fuller and fuller." Another primary school preparatory teacher, Liz, identified how, "I get parents to come in and work with little groups of children. Whereas previously I might have had them listening to reading. Now they do letter recognition and word recognition games. They are actually teaching." Parents (usually mothers), then largely in middle-class schools, were being incorporated as quasiteachers in literacy; literacy and teaching young children are both associated as an extension of mothering (Blackmore and Hutchison 2001). Gender, professionalism, and parenting then are discursively intertwined through policies institutionalizing parental involvement as quasiliteracy teachers and also as employers of teachers, fund raisers, and clients.

This new transparency is both paradoxical and disciplinary because it "bites deeply and immediately into the practice of state professionals—reforming and re-forming meaning and identity-producing or making up new professional subjectivities" (Ball 2000, 7). This desire for visibility permeated through professional appraisal and school review in what Ball (2000, 7) calls the "flow of performativities" in which teachers and principals were being judged constantly by others, and indeed themselves, and in different ways at different times, with different combinations of rituals (special events) and routines (record keeping). Lines were being drawn between those who performed according to the new rules of the game and those who did not in the sense that "the more you put in the more you are expected to do, whereas those who don't put in appear to be rewarded by fewer classes or being named in excess" (Debra, returned teacher on contract). Thus "the space for the operation of autonomous ethical codes based on a shared moral language is colonized or closed down" (Ball 2000, 9). Corporate professionalism encouraged new forms of individual calculation for enterprising subjects—when to be seen, with whom, and in what space.

Principals Renegotiating the Corporate Professional Space

The reregulation of teachers accompanied the deregulation of principals' work to allow them to operate competitively in market-oriented school systems. Competitive market relationships between individual schools even within the public sector reshaped the "cultures of autonomy of the primary school work" and the "amateurism of its management" (Menter et al. 1997). Principals were expected to become more entrepreneurial and professional managers. Visibility was critical for principals. Harriet commented about her principal "who likes to jump onto every bandwagon that's around and be involved in everything." Debra commented about the same principal that "the school is looking for a new direction. It has lots of pies but it has branched out too far." At the same time, teachers recognized that "the principal's job was a reactive one—reactive to the system to the kids, the parents. It is very difficult for them to be proactive" (Karen, leading teacher). But in effect, "the principal has less time to be about the school, to interact with the students" (Debra, returned teacher on contract). Yet our cohort of principals liked how they were more autonomous in some areas in ways that facilitated quicker resource decisions about personnel, materials, and buildings, although this was a devolution of responsibility of management tasks. But they considered that the new accountabilities of performance management, together with outcomes-based curriculum and assessment, reduced their capacity to focus on the "situatedness" of student, teacher, and local community educational needs, with less space for curriculum and program innovation outside system priorities. Rewards (performance pay) for being professional (technically efficient and competent) did not necessarily reward being a good professional (working for disadvantaged kids).

Women leaders negotiated meaning by adopting particular discourses of professionalism to suit their purpose within specific fields of activity. Thus, in Victorian schools, "the difference between Schools of the Future and other programs is the lack of democratic process. It is all driven top down" (Helen). This reconfiguration of governance shaped principals' relations with their staff and peer collegial relationships (Bishop and Mulford 1999). For some, it meant networking with other principals rather than teachers, moving out of the teachers' union and into principals' associations, and learning to judge those below them in the new management hierarchies. Others adopted an overt oppositional stance, therefore endangering themselves (and their school) of being marginalized in resource redistribution (Bishop and Mulford 1996).

In turn, principals were judged centrally through performance management contracts as to the extent of their rule compliance. They were also judged from below, on a different set of criteria, by teachers. In a Victorian multicampus, urban secondary college, while teachers recognized the pressures on the female principal and her three campus principals to perform, they felt that "the staff have no input, it's being totally forced onto them. They've been told they have to have professional development and appraisal, but there is no support or assistance to help staff cope." Another commented that "they're bringing in all those new things, the middle-school restructure, without finishing anything." Karen, a leading teacher, goes on to say that "they've changed the structure of education and curriculum so the normal, everyday teacher doesn't get a say. There's very little decision making available to the grass roots anymore: it's all done through committees. So unless you're one of the privileged enough by being on a committee, as a head of department or an advanced skills teacher, you don't get much say."

Not surprisingly, teachers felt alienated from both central bureaucracies and the principal, a loss of agency summed up by one teacher on a junior campus of a large secondary school, "[T]he administration is not seen as being for guidance and leadership but more as the prison guard—the enemy—because they're implementing government policy, and they tell us we have to do as they instruct us. We get some input, but basically it's down to 'you do as you are told.'" In response, Noelene, the principal, commented: "I only see them at meetings and PD. There is less opportunity for informal discussion." Teachers were withdrawing into more individualized relationships as "the staff is fragmenting into their own areas; there's not much cross curriculum communication" (Debra). Restructuring was about increasing the size of schools for efficiency only.

Other principals worked harder to maintain collegiality, forming alliances with other principals and teacher unions to keep social justice on the agenda, and tempering the new hierarchies with democratic processes where possible to retain a "professional culture, while bureaucratized and gendered, [that] provided considerable solidarity and constructed identity" (Menter et al. 1997, 9). In a small community-based, urban primary school, Amanda, the principal commented that "there is a lot of peer support, a group of people . . . Helen [the principal] tries to do that, making sure people are aware of opportunities, encouraging them to take them, and providing professional development where possible." One working-class secondary school with a highly supportive female principal focused on transparent processes to counter increasingly competitive promotion policies. Carol, an aspirant leader, "applied for a teaching and learning position. . . . [W]e'd talked about applying for it . . . all very open and supportive. This year we were showing each other our CVs and talked about interviews . . . as a way of improving our chances, helping each other rather than feeling in competition."

Any professional mythologies of autonomous judgment were being replaced by a sense of contradictoriness of purpose and blurred motivations. Teachers were cynical when principals introduced a new idea: "[I]t must be down as part of their performance management plan to earn their next bonus." Principals felt trapped, expected to implement imposed top-down imperatives while being innovative locally. Teachers' fear of being made "in excess" (redundant to school requirements) produced a cynical compliance, working to their own competitive advantage. Adele, a young teacher in a multicampus, secondary college in a middle-class suburb felt that "When teachers are up against each other for a job in a school where there is excess, they become more protective of their curriculum and less sharing and supportive as they have to show they are different, a 'better teacher' than their colleagues." These reforms were increasingly about managing oneself and each other better (Blackmore, Bigum, Hodgens, and Laskey 1996).

ACADEMICS: PROFESSIONAL EXPERTS AND/OR PUBLIC INTELLECTUALS?

Universities were reengineered after 1987 to better align higher education and training with national goals. New modes of governance and control premised upon efficiency (measurement of knowledge production) and relevance (what is taught and researched) were installed. Market and managerial principles, while adopted in most nations, have penetrated Australian university systems more than in the United States and the United Kingdom, managerial cultures competing with and remaking traditional collegial cultures (Slaughter and Leslie 1998). Traditionally, academic habitus was informed by professional discourses idealizing academic freedom, disciplinary expertise, and being public intellectuals. This favored men as universities were "highly gendered workplaces for all staff, and male culture based on male experience continues to affect the way women's work is valued in higher education" (Currie et al. 2002, 273; Castleman et al. 1995). Indeed, women in universities generally tend to spend more time on teaching, being good corporate citizens in terms of institutional work (e.g., committees), and student pastoral care (Acker and Feuerverger 1996; Morley and Walsh 1996).

Marginson and Considine (2001) argue that Australian universities in the 1990s indicated only three characteristics of the "entrepreneurial university" that policy makers espoused—a strengthened steering core, an expanded development periphery, and a diversified funding base. But they did not, as in the United States elite research universities, have a "stimulated academic heartland" and an "integrated entrepreneurial culture." Indeed, academic culture was weak in amalgamated and newer universities after multiple restructurings, many inheriting the legacy of the more hierarchical CAEs and technical colleges that lacked entrenched research cultures (Blackmore and Sachs 2003). Everde-creased funding and the tightening and rapidity of policy changes meant more executive management. Jill, dean in a Utech, argued:

> You need to talk about styles of management whereby more power is basi-cally wielded by vice-chancellors. So they may use devolved structures, but there is less time spent in traditional academic committees making decisions over a long period of time, getting everyone's view. There is a transition . . . getting to make decisions quickly, primarily in response to federal govern-ment directives, that began with Labor in 1987. . . . There is more time on committees that monitor and report. . . . You get to a point where one more thing where you have to gather information for some response to something outside will drive you insane. It's not any worse for women than men . . . I don't think the managerial or efficiency direction of university administra-tion necessarily disenfranchises women more than men. I think it's a pain in the ass for all academics. It makes universities less pleasant places to work.

Newer universities without prior histories as universities tended to be more innovative and open to more equitable practices, whereas academics and female managers felt restructuring had impacted detrimentally on women's opportunities as academics. Jill felt that in her university managers had proac-tively sought to mobilize EO discourses and recruit women into management:

> Restructuring has not affected women as much here. . . . [T]he EEO requirements have actually put more women in senior administration, acad-emic and administrative. Perhaps there are a lot of women who are very good administrators and like detailed work. Most women are good organizers. They have to be, in terms of their multiple lives [and] . . . the fact that uni-versities aren't as worker friendly as they used to be is a put off for both men and women.

As teachers in schools and TAFE, academics experienced an intensifica-tion of work, new modes of accountability (performance appraisal), and an everwidening breadth of activities—teaching, research, consultancy, course development, online teaching, and internal administrative and community service. The new contractualism of client service and user pays changed rela-tions with students, the community, the professions, and industry, reposition-ing academics as paid professional experts rather than public intellectuals, as "piece workers" serving the professional managerial class, the new "heros" of the university (Blackmore 2002c, 5). Formal commercial contracts were encouraged rather than voluntarist community service. Paradoxically, at the same time that academic work was systemically being encouraged to expand into consultancy, commercial activities, online learning, and industry/professional partnerships, system-wide measures of academic performance (research quantum) were narrowing. What constituted valued research was defined by research measures that privileged input (income dollars), throughput (graduations), and output (publications in refereed international journals). Yet academics were also expected to be more practically relevant, work in partnerships with industry and the professions, do research that had immediate and measurable outputs, and inform professional practice. Thus policy discourses of excellence and practical relevance came into conflict when operationalized in practice. Working with professional practitioners, as expected in professional courses such as education, went unrecognized and undervalued in research quantums.

These performative regimes encouraged self-advocacy as academics reconstructed themselves continuously for the needs of the institution, their students, their markets and their professional fields. Chee Wah, senior lecturer in a redbrick university realized this tension: "This university culture is composed of a lot of very ambitious people . . . with a pretty high publication record and a reasonably good grants record. . . . [T]here is a kind of pragmatism nowadays and recognition or resignation that academic life is not what it used to be." Some academics felt that women lost out in this new competitive game as "many women are more reticent about their abilities than men. Some of my male colleagues, not crash hot, seem to have absolutely no inhibitions about applying for things and promotion. Women have got to be absolutely sure they can get promoted before they apply" (Helen, sandstone).

Academics were also expected to work more flexibly, with new demands on their time arising with the push to excel in new pedagogical approaches using learning technologies, to "deliver" courses on- and offline. While becoming more technically "upskilled," these same learning technologies demanded new models and templates of instructional design that commodified the process, disaggregating curriculum development from pedagogy and assessment, more of a "down skilling" (Brabazon 2002). Finally, standardized student evaluations as the new mechanisms of strategic planning articulated with top-down teaching and learning management plans that focused on generic skills, graduate outcomes, and academic codes of ethics focusing on speed in response times (Blackmore 2003b). Meanwhile the status of academics as the producers, disseminators, and legitimators (i.e., as knowledge workers) in defining what counts as valued knowledge was being undermined by the commercialization and proliferation of multiple sources of knowledge production arising from new information and communication technologies and the rise of alternative private producers of research (Brint 2001).

The multiple demands of the performative university and its environment meant adjustments of the academic habitus as academics were in a constant state of "remaking the self." Academics began to let go to old notions of academic freedom and to compromise professional rigor, identity, and the rules of "togetherness" in the face of the "short term mentality" (Bauman 2001, 23). The desire to achieve was fraught with both new risks and opportunities. The system only rewarded the risk takers who worked within organizational objectives. It was this postmodern tension between planning for perfection and a readiness to "risk it all" that caught women out, encapsulated in Helen's (sandstone) comment:

> Women want to be sure that they've written the absolutely best possible research application before they put proposals up: less a fear of failure, more about seeking perfection . . . with a few shining examples of women who used the system to their own ends, do very well and kept their togetherness. . . . If you're a perfectionist you are frightened of taking risks. And women have good reasons for not taking risks. They've fought very hard to get where they are.

"The world of impression management, judgements and penalties is creating new professional subjectivities, new modes of description and new organizational identities" (Morley 2001, 3).

Power/Knowledge Hierarchies

Higher education reform also shifted, through the mechanisms of accountability, what counted as valued knowledge and how "counting" was done. Surveillance accompanied management technologies. Amanda, a senior lecturer (sandstone), commented on the damaging impact of transparency and visibility regarding performance: "We now get lists that come round saying you've only published two things in the last two years, but so and so published sixteen, so this isn't good enough. Or you didn't get a research grant last year, why not? Its not necessarily a bad thing but. . . ." But there was also a rejigging of power knowledge relations. Dianne, a dean, commented on the implications of a reinvigoration of science in universities that produced a type of epistemological backlash against the social sciences that

> the biggest issue is really an intellectual issue. . . . [A] feminist perspective has pervaded the social sciences and humanities to a substantial amount. Women's history is acceptable; it's okay to talk about gender from an analytic point of view in the social sciences. It's not really pervaded the sciences. And technology areas are still heavily dominated by males, even though their student bodies have changed. They don't understand feminist interpretations, are hostile to them, and feel very threatened by them. So how do you raise the consciousness of science-based academics, men especially, about the analytic ways they might understand the position of men and women in the disciplines in which they operate? (dean, sandstone)

Government policies such as the research quantum at the institutional level reinforced particular disciplinary subcultures of universities (e.g., science being based on teams publishing multiple papers in refereed conferences and journals), and failed to recognize different disciplinary practices and cultures such as the more individualized mode of research in education and the humanities in which book publications were also high status. Chee Wah, a senior lecturer in a redbrick university's science faculty, recalls her university promotion committee asking, "Where are your refereed journal papers? Books don't count. Then how many papers? Social scientists' papers tend to be long—twenty pages rather than one and a half pages. So we don't have the right number, we don't have fifty-six joint papers with six people's names listed on it, cycling through the names each paper." Women were continually confronted with hegemonic views and hostile cultures within specific discipline-based fields of practice. Even within social science, male academics have "studied themselves" and others "in reflection and contrast to themselves" (Blackmore 2000c, 4). Jill (dean, Utech) considered that the "law faculty is very male orientated; people have worked here together for twenty years, and there is a sense of this is the way things are done. These are largely men who have wives at home and so have more time to do things." A study of research productivity by Deane (1996, 3) concluded how there was a strengthening of old hierarchies: "There was widespread ignorance of what might constitute both high achievement and normative activity in various disciplines. The role of institutions in offering career guidance and collaborative goal setting for individual academics was nonexistent. . . . [T]he academy is not blessed with an acceptance of a diversity of ways of operating nor a diversity of research paradigms within disciplines."

This new instrumentalism has put the dual historical role of universities as producers of knowledge as science and knowledge as culture in opposition. Academic work has become a "top class," high-achievement sport.

TRAINING: ENTREPRENEURIAL OR JUST PRAGMATIC?

For TAFE, the "culture transformation" is to become "entrepreneurial," a discourse that quickly permeated parts of TAFE because of its historically strong industry orientation (service industries) more than others (trades-based teaching). Entrepeneurialism also fed off the dominant discourse of practical rationality that imparted "primacy to practice" over theory and to "practical knowledge" over "knowledgable practice" (Edwards 1997), the "get things done" mentality was to the "performative management culture" evident in further education generally (Kerfoot and Knights 1996). At the management level, it was evident in the strong cultural proclivity to perceive that "management is doing." Esoteric notions of visionary or educational leadership were absent in this sector. TAFE's well-institutionalized management culture premised upon hierarchy and hard "trade" masculinities (Pocock 1998), readily accommodated new managerial discourses of efficiency, rationality, and responsiveness.

Angus and Seddon (1998) refer to two other overlapping marginal discourses in the TAFE sector. A discourse of professionality largely emerged out of a sense of collectivity and of solidarity based on staff union activities now actively discouraged by management; and a discourse of educational progressivism mobilized in the lower echelons at the level of classroom practice where issues of pedagogy and social justice did not disappear, particularly in the access and equity, and community education areas inhabited largely by women teachers. Both came under severe challenge from managerial and entrepreneurial discourses of responsiveness, flexibility, industry service, and client choice driven by the need for self-funding. Janis, middle manager in a large, metropolitan TAFE, commented: "There used to be a distinctive TAFE educational culture. I am not too sure any more. The focus has changed over the last three to four years to be corporate: the dollars come before education with the drive to be commercial."

TAFE's distinctive historical culture and traditions also produced two distinctive teacher habitus—that of the "tradie" and that of the community educator. The introduction of competency-based approaches had been strongly opposed by women teachers and managers in access and equity areas and community education, most with teacher training, on pedagogical grounds. "I don't like competency-based training [because] . . . it breaks up things too much into little bitsy things. We get round it by grouping things together here. . . . [T]raining should be a bit more integrated . . . I can only think of it like being office administration—packaging mail and handling customers as separate units. [It] just becomes reception duty, breaking it up into little things" (Raelene, small, progressive, suburban TAFE).

Competency approaches were seen to perpetuate old theory/practice divides embedded in TAFE culture and curriculum with its lock step approach to pedagogy deskilling teachers and providing certainty, not reflection. By contrast, "staff in areas of technical or practical focus welcomed competency-based approaches, claimed they were industry focused. The language of standards made sense to them" (Raelene).

Despite these general trends and tensions, Lesley, a new manager in a progressive, suburban TAFE considered, and what became evident in our study, was that

> each TAFE has its own flavor. There is a subculture in most TAFEs that looks almost indistinguishable from a technical school culture (automotive and engineering). Some TAFEs have moved on. Some still use the notes of the technical school. There are pockets in not all, but most, where nothing

looks the same. The differentiation between TAFE, and what you see in private enterprise, private providers or consultancy, is significantly less. The notion of "a TAFE culture" makes little sense now.

Raelene talked about how differences between rural and urban, large and small TAFEs, and the breadth of their activities, impacted on "localized cultures and practices. . . . There are differences between TAFEs that have a strong international focus and others largely working with the domestic industries. This would not be evident five or ten years ago." In a community-based TAFE, Felicity commented on how a more feminized work culture operated.

> Well it's different here because it's got a large proportion of women in senior positions. The trade areas are now the minority. We never felt overshadowed by trades as in other TAFEs . . . where men in senior positions tend to be more outspoken and dominating and the business and social service areas of other institutes have a lesser voice. We've had the reverse. . . . We've got trade areas and aero space, but also business management areas, social and applied science areas, and women in all. But we've also got men in community and business areas emulating behaviors when it comes to best practice. Behavior breeds behavior. You see those female characteristics now common in men managers. Some have female managerial styles that are caring, sharing, structured approaches, which makes people quite happy.

But against this internal trend toward soft managerialism in some institutions were policies encouraging the reengineering TAFE to be contractually bound to the workplace, rejecting past practices of a handshake or trade networks. TAFE's legitimacy relied on its unique relationship with industry and its relevance compared to universities, a discourse that "softened internal professional resistance to policy demand for private sector emulation" (Brown et al 1996, 316). Raelene considered that "one of the good things about TAFE culture is that it comes into contact with a lot of people from industry. We employ enormous numbers of sessional people. . . . [I]t keeps a good balance . . . not just that high school sort of people" (small, progressive, suburban TAFE).

Although framed by seemingly soft discourses of flexibility, entrepreneurship and client choice, restructuring exacerbated particular hardline management practices by devolving the stress, administration, and difficult personnel and financial decisions down the line into a fractured environment. In all of this, teachers were rarely mentioned in policy, and indeed competency-based training was lauded because it was "teacher proof." Roya believed "TAFE is very much about bureaucratic processes, and it's getting worse. The area where money is always being reduced is staff training, and the money goes to less important areas" (large, outer suburban, community-oriented TAFE).

New Spaces and Places

Women middle managers in TAFE worked through a number of different "managerial identities or positions," drawing from often contradictory discourses as unionists, feminists, professionals, and community workers (Whitehead 1999). As Sachs (2003) comments, there are

> incongruities between the defined identity of teachers as proposed by systems, unions, and individual teachers themselves, and . . . these will change at various times according to contextual and individual factors and exigencies. Identity must be forever reestablished and negotiated. It defines our capacity to speak and act autonomously and allows for the differentiation of ourselves from those of others while continuing to be the same person. (126)

But there was limited space available for alternative approaches to leadership due to the enduring, strong masculinism of executive management in most large, urban, rural TAFE institutes, as in the United Kingdom (Shain 1999; Gleeson and Shain 1999). In one rural TAFE Sally recalled: "I was only one of six women actually on the permanent staff. . . . [W]e had women's network meetings, just so we could speak to each other. This helped when I was staff representative on the Institute Council . . . meetings with twenty five men, maybe you and one woman; most of council were community reps, men forging career paths in the council. It has not changed."

Despite this, some TAFE institutions were seen to have management cultures favoring women. One TAFE middle manager, Cora, in a small, suburban TAFE, commented, "I don't honestly believe there is any cultural and organizational limitation here now, but we still haven't got the numbers to prove it, but they are improving." The male director, Jim, was perceived to be progressive in his attitudes to management and in his promotion of women into senior positions. Jim stated, "I'm trying to implement a modern management structure with a team approach—collaboration and devolution without an autocratic style." Yet his promotion of women into senior executive roles was received with some cynicism: "There are people in TAFE who think that a woman manager is in her position because of EEO and because she is a woman, not because she is good at her job" (Jim). In this institution, the dual roles of worker and mother were recognized and accommodated. Lesley, recently appointed general manager, found that her family role did not work against her professional advancement into a strategic development program because her ability was recognized. To do so, she traded off some income for six weeks' leave to be home with her children on holidays. This was not EO policy, but it had resulted, she felt, from enlightened management practices. Her business experience had given her the edge in seeking promotion in the new orientation of this TAFE; her presence encouraged other women to apply for leadership as "the internal restructure has been positive for women. There was the recognition of women by promoting several to be general managers. That has been very affirming to women overall in the organization" (Lesley). Margaret, a manager who had shifted from an older trades-oriented TAFE to this new entrepreneurial culture identified how "this TAFE really does value people. It doesn't get it all right, but it really does try, whereas my other TAFE made no attempt. You were either in or out. It was the senior male managers, basically. And . . . there were two female senior managers, but they were on the outer, clearly."

Likewise, in a large, community-oriented TAFE in a lower socioeconomic, outer suburb, with a female director

> The director gives a high profile to women in senior positions—she grooms and nurtures women. She has given women the confidence in interview panels to get the job on their own merits. Most of the women here can prove competency and are as good as any male. She has encouraged women through her role modeling, positive approach and her constant reassurance. She creates the impression that she has achieved director level, so there is no reason why other women can't also. She has identified competent women (and men) and tells the women, "You don't have to be one of the boys, just be competent." She has forced a culture of equality toward women. She will not appoint people that are not competent. (Felicity, manager, large, community-oriented, suburban TAFE)

Ironically, this TAFE was to amalgamate with a large, older, traditional TAFE with a large, male leadership team. As one of female managers ironically commented, "it probably means toppling more towards men in the amalgamation."

Other TAFE institutes did not undertake the same cultural shift. There was significant consensus among women within another larger metropolitan TAFE, not seen to be women friendly, that women working in management were "probably self selecting. They can cope with the pressures and cope with change" (Leanne, large, metropolitan TAFE). These women were seen to "act like men" once in formal positions to better "fit" the corporate culture, and often did not experience the corporate culture as exclusionary (Wacjman 1998). Such was the case of Joy, an executive manager, in this particularly harsh management regime, prone to poor industrial relations. Joy believed the system worked on merit and that "human resources have worked very hard to ensure that equity issues are not issues. I don't believe that men have an advantage at TAFE. If you show merit you get the job." Many women felt an ambiguous professional empowerment due to the coexistence of power and subjection (Chase 1995). There was for them "the tension between the discourse about professional work (with its emphasis on gender and race neutral individuals), and a discourse about inequality (with its emphasis on gendered and racialized groups)" (Chase 1995, 6). Discourses of inequality are more "self conscious" as they are more contested, arising from reflection, as people are aware of others assumptions and ideological frameworks of every day practices. Women such as Joy found comfort in appealing to gender-neutral discourses of professionalism, in assuming the new managerial habitus and denying experiencing discrimination or inequality, because their identity was closely tied to a sense of professional competence. Being professional meant adhering and performing better than anyone else within the frame set by the organization. For others, there was no easy "fit" with the corporate educational organization. To "become a manager" meant disinvesting in certain aspects of their professional habitus, sublimating, accommodating, if not relinquishing those aspects of the professional self seen to be critical to how they were viewed by others and wished to be viewed. This abandonment of elements of habitus produced a new habitus, a colluded self (Casey 1995).

Some TAFE institutes would appear to have undergone a positive culture shift in gender politics. The context was that the traditional trade habitus and working-class masculinity of TAFE teachers was under threat with deindustrialization and the expansion of feminized areas of service and business communication industries. Any anti-intellectual dispositions of "tradies" were confronted by a new of instrumentalism of "practical rationality" that arguably claimed to integrate theory and practice through practical knowledge gained through service as well as application, but that was now underpinned by principles of efficiency and effectiveness with strong evaluative aspects (Edwards 1997). This mode of practical reason, as understood by Bourdieu, was a new form of managerial habitus that is a consequence of dispositions and orientations that "do not simply 'regulate' their action, but define just who and what they are" (Bohman 1999, 129–30). The move from a public service bureaucratic culture toward privatized contractualism was accompanied by the managerial shift to emulate "best practice" from business. Education managers could now become "real men" operating in the "real" marketplace. So while blue-collar masculinities were under threat, professional managerial masculinities were under reconstruction in TAFE.

Women managers, many from the community education sector, by contrast, were able to draw upon pedagogical discourses of professionalism and service, thus repositioned favorably within both managerial and market frames to take up the expanding activities required by entrepreneurialism, the internationalization of curriculum development, evaluation, quality, communication, and marketing. Softer modes of masculinity and more aggressive femininities were now in use, at least at the middle management level, as described by Janis:

> The industry focus has given women opportunities at the college. It has broken down the old boys' network. Before the restructure it was the old boys'

club. The men in the new management team are gentle sorts of men, very good, strategically excellent, not at all powerful, macho types. We have more women choosing careers rather than family, some women are making conscious decisions not to have children or to have them later in life.

But as with universities and schools, the micro-politics of gender relied upon an institution's location, history, strategic directions, and executive leadership, with another restructure, another executive director, another policy shift, casting the everpresent shadow of uncertainty.

CROSS-SECTORAL PATTERNS, TRENDS, AND LOCAL GENDER POLITICS

Despite the variance between the different educational sectors in terms of the professional discourses mobilized within their fields, the above discussion indicates conjunctures and disjunctures across the three professional fields. There was a discursive move in policy texts and managerial practices to emphasize professionalism as competence, expertise, training, and competitive individualism rather than being about service to community based on sincerity, trust, and collegiality (Chase 1995). The 1990s saw a search less for a professional knowledge base in educational administration and leadership and more for a set of "generic leadership competencies." Leadership was subsumed by the discourse of practical rationality.

While women's competence was confirmed by gaining leadership, the discourses they mobilized in all sectors was most often about loyalty and commitment. One female director was seen as "passionate, she's got a commitment to the institute, and she exudes that loyalty. . . . She loves the place. If you're not committed to the institute, then you're probably not going to enjoy coming in every day . . . a passion she reflects onto people. . . . There's the strength of her conviction" (Sandra, small, rural TAFE).

Her multidimensionality was evident in how she articulated a sense of purpose, imparted trust and mutual respect, developed social relationships, and gave material support, providing an alternative model that was not about denying the feminine. Felicity (quality manager, large suburban, community-oriented TAFE) said:

She demonstrated that she can still be feminine and powerful, an awesome type. She's very political, and I admire watching her. She proves that to be up there you don't have to know everything: you just have to be quite dedicated. . . . She's had that respect for people and had time for every single staff member that wants to chew her ear. So she's patient and tolerant . . . [and] people respect her. If she makes a decision she'll see it through to the end.

The values that we have in the institute are really her values. She's got those values through to people and who say they're the sort of things I like. . . . She's got vision, and she makes sure that people move towards that same vision.

This director created new management structures with clear role definitions and transparency of process as well as strategic direction to remove what some saw were the vestiges of male networks that were subtle, underhand, and not always based on merit. "So there was no sleazy way of getting to the top or how women have to either be men, or you know lie down, you know, on coffee tables" (Sandra). But what energized and made a difference at this TAFE was the way we "prided ourselves on the fact that we were going to be very much looking after the disadvantaged groups represented in those socioeconomic areas" (Felicity). This commitment to the local community and social justice was now endangered by the entrepreneurial thrust.

In contrast, there was gender politic of the TAFE rural college in which the male director's approach had mixed messages for women but that overall constrained women managers and teachers in particular regressive ways within a masculinist frame.

And he will stand up and argue. Its a certain sort of woman he likes. He likes you to be intelligent, to look good, to act professionally. He has this image of the women who are going to be part of his organization. So if you are a nice person, but a bit drab or a bit plump . . . he doesn't see those women as effective. . . . And he has chosen women for positions, in the past, probably based on how they have looked rather than really whether they should have the job. He has difficulty with someone good at her job, but who doesn't look the part, like me. So it's a dilemma for him. I don't think it's conscious. It's a mindset. . . . When I represent the college, I always look professional, always prepared, got what he needs, and I know what I am doing. I don't let any flak come back . . . so there are no nasty surprises. (Sandra, TAFE)

Sandra's positioning as a manager was shaped by both her own sense of professionalism and femininity, while conscious of her institutional positioning as a woman by the director. Professionalism, therefore, was not just enacted but also embodied in a particular form of femininity based on appearance as well as competence or expertise. Ironically, the male director in this case was large, heavy-set, and not well dressed, tending to confirm unnervingly persistent images of masculinist "successful" leadership that are resilient despite going out of date in the more corporatized metropolitan context.

The new professional self was trapped between the competing technical discourses of professional competence and standards, new work order discourses about being self-reliant and self-motivating, and old professional discourses of service and advocacy. But increasingly the inner moral self was being called out to service the external world of work, as the new professional habitus was forced to ignore other aspects of the self with which there had been strong personal and professional attachments. There was now little security in old connections, with the transformation of the nature and role of institutions, unions, professional organizations, and voluntary organizations (Casey 1995).

> If there is stability, it is that of the individual as a unitary self in managing him- or herself through a never-ending series of work identities and working relationships. But in such a world there may be no inner identity either. The working person in the modern corporate self has no self. The self becomes an assembly of components, some of which may be useful in one environment and others in different environments. In this milieu, identities, practices and assumptions are easily discarded. (Barnett 1997, 120–21)

What these cross-sectoral studies indicate is how particular discourses of professionalism worked with/against the new corporate discourses of entrepreneurship and managerial efficiency and effectiveness. As Gleeson and Shain (1999) argue, professionalism and managerialism were not necessarily in opposition, but rather the contestation over meaning and overlap between these fields of activity were "mediated by changing identities in the workplace" (466). Professional discourses offer "particular kinds of subject position and identity through which people come to view their relationships with institutions, colleagues and students" (Clarke and Newman 1997, 92). Understandings of professional autonomy, for example, are now framed more tightly by the strategic direction of the organization, decided collectively by senior management. To break out of that frame is to put both the organization and the individual at risk.

Education has therefore tended to move from an autonomous to a heteronomous field as a result of the pressures arising from business, government, and individual demands. This transformation of the field has significant implications for professional identities, practices, dispositions, and values within the field. Educators' "subjective relation to the profession" has altered as "gender, generation and cultural relations are interwoven with educational system and labor market structures" (Olesen 2001, 291). Professional subjectivities are now informed, at least discursively, and not just by notions of service, advocacy, and commitment to the public, but also by self-preservation, promotion, and profit. This reshaping articulates with the new sense of professional destabilization. This arises from the cumulative effects of professional legitimacy and expertise being challenged by competing sources of knowledge production with the democratization of knowledge, on the one hand, and the proliferation of private educational and research providers, on the other. Professional insecurity also arises out of governments' exclusion of "the professions" in the production of policies of education reform, while they seek greater control of the professions, from reconstructed notions of occupation, work, and social regulation, and the increased emphasis on individualization of professional self-renewal to reinforce this. These have been substantive changes in the "occupational order" in which the professions are losing status and as flexible production systems have led to organizational "delayering" and the decline of the long-term, single, organizational career (Gee, Hull, and Lankshear 1996). The processes of professional destabilization were stimulated and shaped by the penetration of the orthodoxies of management and market and the commodification of professional knowledge and labor.

Now the managed and self-managing professional manager is herself undertaking the administrative work of performance management, accountability, quality assurance, prescriptive curriculum, standardization, and control in the manufacture of consent (Casey 1995). But educational workers' cooption and incorporation is always incomplete, provided education professionals promote a clear sense of a wider commitment to their profession, their discipline, their colleagues, to social movements, and to their students as citizens. Academics and teachers will have to increasingly look outside organizations for discussions about professional purpose and ethics, and to develop a strong civic professionalism informed by professional ethics and a knowledge base that will allow public organizations to survive. Despite New Right protestations in "denial of collective public vehicles of transcendence and the abandonment of the individual," individuals still experience "white hot passions which accompany the desperate search for communities" (Bauman 2001, 6). The long-term issue is whether the professions can take up the moral and liberal humanist imperative of social trusteeship, if at all. Professionalism, as a "constituency of conscience," is under threat as organizations require increased loyalty but offer less security for more democratic professionalism.

FIVE

Giving an Account: Performing Educational Work and Working to Perform

THE BALANCING ACT for the nation-state in more risky times is to gain legitimation from its perceived capability to perform as a player in global/local markets and its capacity to meet the democratic claims of different social groups. This is in the context in which institutions for overcoming social and economic problems (e.g., schools, universities, and TAFE institutes) have been transformed into institutions for causing problems (Giddens 1992). Education in particular has increasingly been perceived as both a cost and a source of income in the pursuit of skilled labor and knowledge commodification and therefore has to be channeled more instrumentally towards the national good. In balancing between its desire to manage more efficiently and yet to be seen to be accountable, the "performative state" of the late twentieth century developed loose structures (deregulated and devolved) and tight policies (targeted funding and accountability). In the context of increased uncertainty and a desire for greater control, accountability has therefore become the key to the management of risk and a perceived "breakdown of the trust" in institutions (Warren 1999). A theme throughout the interviews was not only how the exercises of performance management and accountability that focused on quantifiable outcomes failed not only to adequately represent the complexity of teaching and research but also that they were increasingly shaping the nature of that work due to labor intensification, standardization, and the narrowing of acceptable processes and outcomes. In this chapter we explore the central managerial dilemma in schools, universities, and TAFE institutes as they mediate the market and policy and manage risk locally, as it is for the managerial state. That is, how to, on the one hand, sustain, but also appropriate, the creativity, passion, and good will of educational workers; and, on the other hand, to direct this passion and commitment toward predetermined organizational goals and more immediate, measurable, and income-producing outcomes under conditions of constraint.

THE PERFORMATIVE STATE AND ORGANIZATIONAL PERFORMATIVITY

The 1980s saw policy become increasingly important as it provided a capacity for the state to steer indirectly from a distance in increasingly devolved and globalized systems of governance (Taylor et al. 1997). With more intense global competition in education, national educational performances were being more finely calibrated through international rankings based on standardized assessments on the basics of literacy and numeracy (e.g., OECD Program for International Student Assessment, PISA) (Luke and van Kraayenoord 1998) and institutional benchmarking (quality assurance and research assessment; e.g., Shanghai Jia Tong World Ranking for universities). Educational productivity increasingly has come to be measured by performance indicators, proxies for outcomes, such as standardized test and university entrance scores in schools, graduate outcomes, publications (as measured by citations and esteem) and research income in universities, and industry earnings and throughput in TAFE (Taylor et al. 1997). These measures do not necessarily indicate what was actually learned or achieved. In this way, "performance indicators translate macro-policy into micro-practices" (Morley 2003, 57). By targeting policies, and connecting funding to outcomes, in a cycle of accountability, the state and organizations have been enabled, through policy, to provide "symbolic" solutions, often without necessarily expending the effort and resources required to actually solve "the problem" (Bacchi 2000b). A key feature of this "new educational accountability" is an emphasis on measured student performance equated to institutional performance, complex systems of standards which allow for comparison between institutions, teachers/academics, and students, and rewards and penalties for improvement (Newmann, King, and Rigdon 1997).

There are three aspects to the performative state in Australia. First, in the context of reduced public expenditure and structural adjustment, the policy field of economics (Treasury) has been able to impose its "specific logic" of efficiency onto the policy fields of education, health, and welfare, signifying the "relatively lesser and declining autonomy of 'academic' fields in relation to the powers of political and economic sectors" (Zipin and Brennan 2003, 359). It also has encouraged efficiency to outrank equity in systems already predisposed to do so. Second, the disciplinary technologies associated with accountability have produced "audit cultures" within educational institutions that manage risk and uncertainty by equating and ensuring "quality" with process within this form of governmentality which is about the conduct of conduct (Strathern 2000a; Power 1999). The state thus "indirectly regulates the performance of schools and teachers through a technology of audit" (Elliott 2001, 193; Newmann, King, and Rigdon 1998; Gleeson and Husbands 2001). Finally, the media has increasingly media/ted both the politics of education policy production and education markets, circulating blame/shame and win/lose discourses, creating another mode of public accountability and judgment together with management and markets (Blackmore and Thorpe 2003). The media also produces "repetitive trauma" for educators because of its repeated representations of underachieving public schools, stressed teachers, overworked academics, and underresourced TAFEs that impacted on the professional psyche (Thomson et al. 2003).

The process of educational restructuring that commenced in Australia after 1987 saw the state become less a provider (other than a residual system for the needy), and more a regulator, as provision was increasingly left to the market. The "evaluative" state now encouraged public and private organizations to exercise "self-discipline" through the internalization of financial and performance targets set by the state through charters and institutional profiles negotiated with individual universities, schools, and TAFE institutes. In return for institutional discretion to determine how they achieved these goals in "self-managing institutions" with fewer government funds, strong accountability mechanisms were built into these contractual arrangements. Self-management was justified, at least rhetorically, on the view that central reform had failed, that institutions exercising professional judgment were more capable of reforming themselves, while financial flexibility would "release entrepreneurial initiative and spirit" (Troman 1997, 346).

Devolution at the system and organizational level also linked curriculum for the first time in schools to financial management through one-line global budgets, feeding systemic models of accountability that emphasized student performance as the touchstone of state governance—"a steering by results" (Taylor et al. 1997). Similarly, increased institutional autonomy of universities and TAFE institutes was matched by tighter contractual arrangements with government based on audits (e.g., quality assurance reviews of universities and in TAFE 1993–94) as institutional profiles determined allocation of government-funded student places. These "accounting systems represent an encodement of values and priorities. They also structure and construct desires, aspirations, and ambition" (Morley 2003, 57). The discourses of accountability were imbued with the "technical property of a role or contract, structure or system. Territories are clear and demarcated and accountabilities uncontested. The language used . . . is abstracted, detached and rational," "delivered and controllable" (Sinclair 1995b, 224).

Within this new mode of educational governance, organizational and individual "agency" was repositioned within vertical and horizontal fields of forces of managerial and market accountability:

> The vertical axis aligns agencies as delegated authorities between the central-ized power of the nation state and the "consumer" power of the periphery, whilst also subjecting them to rigorous forms of financial and performance evaluation. The horizontal axis characteristically repositions them in a nexus of marketized or quasi-competitive relationships. Within this field of forces agencies are typically given the "freedom to manage." (Clarke 1998, 176)

While markets were to become the mechanism of distribution of educa-tional services, managerialism provided the mode of coordination for the per-formative state, the discipline necessary for efficiency, particularly in relation to the claims of welfare professionalism for discretionary authority. Manage-rialism articulated a new basis for "discretion," as attached to a managerial rather than a professional calculus, and expressed in the claim to be given the freedom to "do the right thing" (Clarke 1998, 176). Self-management, framed in this manner, would provide a capacity for flexibility, responsiveness, and local control. But the cost of that freedom was to be accountable; "autonomy being exchanged for accountability" (Morley 2003, 56). Accountability as a "linguistic construction" was therefore about meaning making through images and texts, about who we are, not just "representation and control" (Sinclair 1995b, 224).

The push for accountability has also led to renewed interest in assessment and evaluation of students and staff. The function and nature of assessment has undergone significant shifts—with increased emphasis on institutional quality and system-wide standards—as governments are under pressure by international credit-ranking agencies and their constituencies to be financially responsible, while developing more responsive and productive education sys-tems in globalized economies (Broadfoot 1998). Institutional assessment regimes have taken the form of quality assurance in universities and TAFE, performance appraisal of teachers and academics, self-reviews, publication of formal standardized test scores or postgraduate destinations as performance indicators, and the national monitoring of standards (Chadbourne and Invargson 1998; Mahoney and Hextall 2001).

These new accountabilities, shaped by management, markets, and the media, provide the state with a capacity to tighten control over the profes-sions. The discourse of transparency and accountability is common sense where public funds are involved and to facilitate choice. The proliferation of information-gathering exercises provided by universal testing required close reporting and monitoring, and new modes, managers, and technologies of information production such as Kidmaps (a software program tracking individual students' progress) and consumer satisfaction surveys in Victorian schools, and student evaluations of teaching in universities and by the federal department (graduate exit questionnaire) emerged. These were increasingly linked to individual teachers and institutions. "While purporting to provide consumers with a basis of selection, and funders with evidence of output, performance indicators also provide powerful managerial imperatives" (Morley 2003, 57). The desire for data to feed the rapacious but limited diet of performance indicators allowed for "deluded visions of control and transparency which satisfy the self image of managers, regulators and politicians but which are neither as effective or as neutral as commonly believed" (Power 1997, 143).

In practice this meant that teachers and academics were caught between being both "steered" and "rowed," between the "imperatives of prescription and the disciplines of performance" (Ball 1999, 202). Opposition was difficult. To resist was to risk being identified as "outmoded" or defending elite/sectional interests, a dangerous position when structural redundancies were the norm. Overall, individuals, when exorted to be accountable, felt caught between the demands of performativity and their professional dispositions to improve student learning, producing an ambivalence toward the reforms that was expressed in our interviews a "dispositional dissonance" between different ways of being accountable, or what Sergiovanni (1999) refers to as "conflicting mindscapes" between competing managerial/market/professional value systems.

PERFORMATIVITY RULES

We have argued that the state and institutions increasingly have sought to maintain legitimacy in complex conditions of uncertainty through an emphasis on the symbolic and the performative. There has been a shift "from a focus on issues of value and ideology to issues of institutional systemic and economic performativity" that has produced a "shift in governmentality, and a shift in systems, discourses and practices for the legitimation of governments, public sector work and educational institutions" (Luke, A. 1997, 3). We argue that performativity, as rendered in contemporary society, has three interrelated dimensions—as a disciplinary technology, as a representation of being seen to be good, and as a production of a regulated self—that have significant effects on educational practice. First, performativity is about "getting more for less" or, as Lyotard (1984) so aptly puts it, "be efficient or dead." As Jameson comments in the introduction to Lyotard's *Post Modern Condition*: "[The decision makers] allocate our lives for the growth of power. In matters of social justice and scientific truth alike, the legitimation of that power is based on optimising the systems' performance-efficiency. The application of this criterion to all our games necessarily entails a certain level of terror, whether soft or hard; be operational . . . or disappear" (Lyotard 1984, xxiv). In that sense, "performativity works as a disciplinary system of judgments, classifications and targets" toward which teachers and academics, schools, universities, and TAFE must "strive against, and through which, they are evaluated" (Ball 1998a, 190). The prevalence of global achievement standards, professional standards, and industry standards supports this view.

Second, the shift to consumption rather than production inherent in fast capitalism has meant that image has become more significant than substance. Performativity is as much about "being seen to perform"—producing a simulacrum in that the actual substance or original is lost. This mode of performativity is about representation. So images of ivy on aging walls represent elite universities and old schools in which "the images themselves, not the products, become the objects of consumption. Individuals receive their identity from the signs and meanings they consume" (Wells, Carnochan, and Allen 1998, 339). Performativity therefore "provides sign systems which 'represent' education in a self referential and reified form for consumption" through processes such as TQM and performance management borrowed from commerce. Performativity also resides in the "pragmatics of language" (Ball 1998a, 190) and what counts as performance, as for example, the instrumental orientation of the school effectiveness and improvement movements. Language itself is the means of performance as language games are associated with the "performative"—the "taking of tricks," the "tripping of the communicational adversary" (Lyotard 1984).

Both these aspects of performativity are "linked to and valorized in the educational labor market. . . . Teachers [and we would add academics and trainers] are inscribed in these exercises through the diligence with which they attempt to fulfil the competing imperatives and inhabit the irreconcilable subjectivities" (Ball 1998a, 190). Much time is therefore spent producing the image of "being good" (as indicating quality) through TQM and audits, but also efficient and effective against predetermined performative exercises. At the same time, the audit is most often presented under the guise of a search for quality. The audit allows institutions to be seen to be doing the right thing, claiming both transparency and accountability, while promising quality *and* efficiency under conditions of scarcity and unpredictable consumer demand.

Finally, there is a third perspective on performativity and subjectivity. Butler (1997) sees performativity as the effect of individuals internalizing particular behaviors, actions, and practices through repeated performances, such as being embodied as female or male, changing the practices of the embodied self while recognizing the contradictions within that self. Performativity is not a singular act, but a repetition and a ritual, which achieves its effects through its naturalization in the context of a body. Gender is performative in that "an internal essence of gender is manufactured through a sustained set of acts, posited through the gendered stylization of the body" (Butler, J. 1997, xiv–v). Femininity itself becomes for many women a form of performance, a set of practices repeated, that then become part of the embodied self (Butler 1997). The notion of performativity, therefore, "highlights how constraint is constituted but not fully determining of gender subjectivity" (Butler 1993, ix). It captures both the cultural arbitrariness of the performed nature of gender identity and the deep inculcation of gender inscribed through repeated performances.

Performativity is not a voluntarist process of performance but rather a "forced reiteration of norms" that is often unconscious. Change arises from the instability of symbolic and discursive structures but also works within the limits of the logic of practice. Performativity also assumes its own logic of practice in the search of more refined calibrations of measurement in tests and rankings to measure quality, rather than questioning whether what is being measured makes sense or represents substantive difference other than a category constructed for a particular purpose. The notion of performativity thus captures both the state's managerialist (efficient and effective) and evaluative (symbolic) aspects, to produce new "managerial or managerialized identities."

REHEARSING THE PERFORMANCE

Restructuring based on market and managerial principles brought new performative regimes that implicitly and explicitly reordered who and what were valued in organizations. This is aptly illustrated by the "game" of promotion. Increasingly in the performative university, the message was that presentation (image) was the key to success. Many women learned the rules of the promotion game through failure rather than mentoring or professional development. This was obvious in one Utech that was simultaneously developing new processes with regard to both promotion and equal opportunity and where the rules of the game were rapidly changing. Pauline, a senior lecturer in this Utech, reflected:

> I applied for senior lectureship three times before being successful after five years. The first time I went up, I didn't have anyone to model as no one was in a higher level in our school. I got fine referees, but at the interview they said I probably went for the wrong area and should have gone for the professional area, as I had been on every committee and stuff at the federal level. So the next year I specialized in that area. After the interview they said, oh really, you should have gone for. . . . It wasn't so much that I hadn't done what was required; it was just that they didn't like the way I had written it as I had not provided evidence. Luckily, I didn't take it personally. Well, the third year I thought I'd beat the system. I did the Women in Leadership program. I took the application down to the EO . . . the same application. They said you've

got all the stuff, but organize it better: local, Australia wide, and international. Then it was obvious what I'd done, and they had to give it me. It was about presentation—the EO people were good at picking up the language.

While many academics felt positive about the range of skills and the relative autonomy they enjoyed compared to other occupations, although increasingly less able to remain focused on their core work, they were disenchanted with the lack of positive feedback or recognition because "the bean counters did not value staff." At a redbrick university, Chee Wah, a public health lecturer in a science faculty, unsuccessfully applied for promotion four times. Her history, as that of many women academics, was of being appointed to levels lower than the two men she replaced, of being downgraded through one restructuring and then blocked because she had failed to "serve her time" at each level as had her male equivalents (Castleman et al. 1995). Merit was not the issue here. Chee Wah had written three books, established an international center attracting significant funds, and supervised eight full fee-paying PhD students. Her research was used strategically as examples of "best practice" in the international area by her university and by the faculty as "a case study in excellence in the public review." She ultimately applied for associate professor, the level at which she was operating, and was given a senior lectureship. She continued to work longer and harder:

> I am angry about it, but I don't get upset anymore because I get the external rewards—I have been invited to work in London, Jakarta, Mongolia, Vietnam, and China. I have no regret or anguish. I will just keep applying for promotion. But you can only apply every second year, and there is so much time spent on it. I also have to understand the politics, to protect my own skin. If you appeal, people have to admit they were wrong. Threatening to appeal further marginalizes me. (Chee Wah, senior lecturer, redbrick)

Common across all three education sectors was the lack of formal institutional support and recognition of staff. For those who had moved outside the promotion pathway into marginal (e.g., equity) areas, such as Monica, an EO manager at a sandstone university, advancement was even harder: "We're not in the academic administration stream. At the end of five years there has never been, either from the faculty or from the university, any acknowledgement of my achievement. I'm discriminated against by my success; it's going to be difficult to move; it's in the university's interest that I stay here, so they ignore my international contributions."

These stories were not unusual. The game was "that they like you to try a bit harder, so they knock you back the first time you apply for promotion" (Donna, dean, redbrick). A senior lecturer in a sandstone reflected how "the culture of the institution certainly gave women very, very few opportunities" and was "definitely chilly, if not frigid."

Feeling marginalized and isolated by the disciplinary and organizational networks that were required in corporatist academies, women also sensed that performativity reinvented old gender dichotomies between reason/emotion and mind/body, not explicitly, but implicitly in the ways of working and viewing what counted as success. Chee Wah reflected on how both her gender and her race disadvantaged her advancement in a restructured institution as new practices and modes of managerialism shored up old modes of white masculinity and reasserted old knowledge/gender hierarchies and binaries under new guises of how science and technology promised efficiency, enterprise, and commercialization. She was located within a particular disciplinary area that modeled itself on an unrealistic and indeed anachronistic view of what constituted science. So while there had been wider recognition of different forms of research in universities (e.g., feminist, qualitative, etc.) during the late 1980s, the dual fears of litigation (most evident in reinvigorated ethics procedures based on the medical research model) and the national research quantum (measuring publication output) during the 1990s led to a narrowing of what constituted research and acceptable research methods. Ethics committees tended to presume that a simplistic health science model based on large populations and statistical analysis was the norm, all other approaches therefore being questionable. This signaled a return to "modernist" ways of working rather than postmodernist recognition of diverse ways of doing research, making it more difficult to undertake industry partnerships and practitioner-based action research advocated by policy makers. Chee Wah said, "But see, even within public health, it is dominant. They don't know about theory; they don't know about people or context. You just twist the research question to fit the tool. But that's what they regard as scientific. Social science is not a science to them. Yet we have four hundred students. But teaching about women and development, that's not important."

Chee Wah envied those women in faculties where there were strong collegial groups and networks. Indeed, she was performing well, on all external accounts, but the research audit measures meant she missed out. "I feel rewarded in the professional sense, outside the university, getting consultancies, finishing books. . . . But I can't say the same about being rewarded by the university." Despite this, Chee Wah continued to perform because she loved doing her research and gained significant pleasure from it. In that sense, her emotional and intellectual labor, her investment in her professional and personal identity as an academic, was exploited by the institution, yet she remained an "outsider" in terms of her gender and race as well as her mode and focus of research. "Race," as gender, operated as an organizational signifier of marginality.

How people are seen to get promotion is central to institutional narratives that inform individual desires, ambitions, and expectations, and institutional narratives of fairness and worker friendliness, as well as how leadership is understood. Such narratives are constructed through texts (position descriptions, promotion applications, mission statements) that mediate institutional processes and inform individual perceptions (Blackmore 2002c). The narrative of an aspirant leader, Carol, a teacher in a working-class, secondary school with a high cultural mix, is a case in point, in indicating how understandings of leadership had changed:

> And I got an interview. But in deciding how to write the CV, you think, what skills do I have? I read the description of what a leading teacher is and thought, that is not me. The first thing is "outstanding educational leadership in the school community and beyond," and I thought, well that's not something that I do. So I decided not to write my resume in that way. I did not satisfy the "outstanding" part of the selection criteria. I suppose with the word "outstanding," people use it in different ways; but what I would call "outstanding," I don't think I do that, yet I feel what I do I do well, and that is always recognized by others. The other point was the very narrow focus of what I've done: . . . basically involved with the ESL program and literacy—classroom-based stuff. [I'm] not a jack of all trades, as is now required.

Classroom success, working in student care and for less advantaged students, while central to her students' progress, was not enough against what is now expected of any performing leader and the need to make exaggerated claims of outstanding and best practice across a widening range of organizational activities. So while educational work was encompassing a wider range of "competencies," there was little time for consolidation or reflection on how they might engage more with students.

REFORMING TO PERFORM
THROUGH ACCOUNTABILITY

Much of the focus of reform in the 1990s was structural, with the devolution of responsibility for daily administration and outcomes to the local unit in the form of the self-managing, "learning" organization. Similar public administrative reforms in New Zealand, the United Kingdom, and the United States sought to "delegate authority to act in specific ways to subaltern organizations" such as universities, TAFEs, and schools and to the market (Clarke 1998, 176). "Dispersal was a strategy of reconstruction bypassing old sediments of power of the bureau-professional organizations and moving beyond them to the citizen, as well as increased central control through fiscal discipline and evaluation" (Clarke 1998, 176). Structural devolution had produced new forms of possibility but also new forms of constraint. In management terms, while there was discretionary activity possible at the level of the local decision-making unit "at the interface," this was informed and shaped by the policies and contractual obligations imposed, on the one hand, and the increased data collection, reporting, and auditing mechanisms back up that in turn delivered institutional and individual rewards and punishments, on the other. In this cycle of management, while executives of self-managing institutions had increased control over their workforce and the internal priorities, they experienced reduced control over external factors of markets, student enrollments, and government policies that established and enforced the rules of the game.

Schools had increased discretion to allocate increasingly reduced resources to meet externally set guidelines. Government also decentered the blame for reduced capacity, positioning individual schools and not systems as failures, a discourse mobilized quite strategically through the media (MacMillan 2002; Blackmore and Thorpe 2003; Myers and Goldstein 1997). Karen, a senior teacher in Victoria commented: "People fear they are going to cop the blame for not delivering in a situation where the government is reducing resources. All Schools of the Future has done is enable the government to point their finger at schools when people have come to them with complaints—a shift of accountability" (principal, multicampus secondary college, middle-class suburb).

This was what Hargreaves (2004) referred to as the "emotional politics of school failure," and how in "inter generationally unequal societies, distributions of dignity create emotional economies of distinction and disgust . . . the basic emotions of social exclusion" that "demarcate success from failure" (34–35). Structural reform (devolution) as a structure is itself neither implicitly good nor bad. But devolution did increase the power of policy, justifying new modes of accountability that changed cultures as well as a value shift focusing on efficiency and performance outcomes. A university EEO manager commented, "Our VC is pushing a very strong public-sector reform mode, with implications for equity in terms of accountability and performance appraisal, which we all see as good. But you can't just change structure without changing culture. I mean you have to look are the underlying values and culture. The idea that one is just going to make people do things through restructuring is simplistic." Policy discourses and accountability technologies changed the rules of the game through privileging efficiency and competition over equity and cooperation, shifting priorities, reallocating resources, contractualizing relations, producing systemic value shifts readily identified below.

Market-driven reforms, where funding was reliant upon student numbers, encouraged CEOs to put their institutions first, altering loyalties toward the immediate and the local and away from the idea of "a public." In order to be seen to perform well in the market-driven system of self-governing schools in the United Kingdom and New Zealand, competitive relations encouraged a move away from access to selectiveness, from participation to ranking, from cooperation to competition, from collegiality to hierarchy, from process to outcomes, from comprehensiveness to specialization (Gewirtz, Ball, and Bowe 1995; Gleeson and Husbands 2001; Campbell and Sherington 2003). This value shift in turn exacerbated any systemic and organizational predispositions and practices to elitism or exclusion.

The nation and "local" state increasingly sought through the development of national curriculum statements and profiles and the introduction of new vocational standards framework of employment-related competencies to extend the scope for school and school system accountability. "This was seen as . . . useful in terms of ensuring that schools delivered on requirements set for them by governments as a means of providing information to the consumers of their services as they moved more into a market mode of operation" (McCollow and Graham 1997, 63). They also enhanced steering capacity of the state to improve performance. By the mid-1990s, school teachers felt that despite the differences between each state along a structural reform continuum from centralization (NSW) to self-management (Victoria), the key commonalities changing systems overall across states and structures were the technologies of performance in the form of increased workloads, standardized assessment, performance management and appraisal, centralized curriculum, increased competitiveness between schools, and focus on outcomes driven from both Commonwealth and state agendas (Dempster 2000).

Performativity not only increased regulation locally but also intensified labor. School principals, despite the various modes of devolution cross-nationally, had to respond to a new range of accountabilities tightly articulated by integrated information management systems that facilitated and expanded exponentially demands for reporting and data collection at the school level. Devolution and its reporting requirements led to anger over the waste due to duplication. Barbara, a secondary school principal of a small, inner metropolitan school, said,

> I go from being angry about some of the management issues because I am getting sheets of figures that I am ploughing through with the calculator. Every school is reinventing the wheel under a guise of self-government. But to do that routine stuff in every school . . . is an abrogation of responsibility by government and not a devolvement of responsibility. The [principal's] role has changed, and that sort of work, it is not satisfying.

These new regimes of performativity reconstituted core work as these management tasks were redistributed. Compliance to mandated reporting meant, according to Celia, a leading teacher in Queensland, that "all teachers are expected to take far more responsibility outside the classrooms as well as inside, extra time on professional development, extra responsibilities on committees, extra paperwork, administration, and departmental work. Increased class sizes make work particularly heavy when it comes to assessment, reporting, and data collection for each child."

Added to this market compliance, as identified by Elwyn (advanced skills teacher) in Victoria, "New accountability demands have led to a huge amount of administrative tasks that we have to do now. Parents ask teachers to be more accountable and are more comfortable coming to the school and ringing you up at the same time that the students expect that you are going to have time for them whenever they want you."

Market and managerial accountabilities became new mechanisms of control and compliance, reducing time and energy for opposition. In a suburban TAFE institute, Alice, a section head, commented that "people are just busy in their classrooms, and they're just busy, busy, surviving: when you work longer hours, the agenda is survival. You really haven't got time to worry too much. We have no control over it, so we just go with what we are told." Tricia, a new department head in a large, metropolitan TAFE, commented on the additional layer of work required by accountability and now quality assurance: "There is a lot of pressure. I work every night. All the handout material has to be reworked for the competency-based format, creating a huge workload. There are lots of administrative tasks need to be done under quality accreditation on top of the teaching load and changed working conditions for teachers. There are only twenty nonattendance days instead of twenty-seven, with no salary increase."

TAFE, with its bureaucratic proclivities, took up quality assurance, a key mechanism of performativity, more enthusiastically than universities, still struggling with structural reform. Whitehead (1999, 67) similarly reports that in further education in the United Kingdom, "TQM emerged in the form of devolved accountability, quality circles, cost center management, and budgeting." The new discourse of performativity materialized everywhere through staff appraisal, new job descriptions, and contracts and set targets for staff and the focus on income generation. Quality took over in terms of value and effectiveness, with increased documentation to provide evidence of "quality structures," at the same time that class contact was reduced by half (Whitehead 1999, 67).

In Australia, curriculum and assessment was also a new managerial focus with nationally developed competency-based training packaged into readily consumable "teacher proof" modules to maintain consistency in TAFE and new learning technologies online in universities (Sanguinetti 1998). The uncoupling of curriculum development from pedagogy and from assessment (Brabazon 2002) not only deprofessionalized teachers and academics but also produced a tension between "pedagogies for performance" and "pedagogies for learning": the former saw pedagogy and performance as separable; the latter saw pedagogy as process, inextricably related to knowledge (Stoer and

Magalhaes 2004). Pedagogies for performance tended to be "thin," with a narrow focus on norms, limited repertoires, and standardized outcomes. Pedagogies for learning tended to be "thick," complex, interactive, focusing on difference and multiple outcomes.

Academic pedagogies were modified due to rising student staff ratios, and the ability range and aspirations of students broadened, at the same time that the administrative load was dispersed down (McInnes 2000). Brenda, an associate professor in a redbrick university, commented about how "recent changes include larger classes, progressive shortening of tutorial small group times, increased marking loads, and more administration." Academics, previously perceived as having greater control over their work, and therefore "choosing" to work hard, were frustrated as "increasingly demands required them to be involved in administrative and quality assurance work, a form of managerial accountancy with endless form-filling, data collection, and benchmarking that involves, seriously disrupts and over-regulates teaching and research," and in one sense "proletarianized" academic work (Currie, Thiele, and Hams 2000, 271). A 1996 survey of academics' responses to a first round of quality assurance in 1995 concluded: "The intrusion of excessive accountability processes, the regulation and codification of work practices associated with teaching and research and the pressure for compliance to routine management requirements undermine the primary work motives of academics, and paradoxically, put both quality and productivity at risk" (McInnes cited in Currie, Thiele, and Harris 2000, 272).

Additionally, planning in all sectors was being developed on two to three and five-year plans that inducted managers *and* staff through corporate culture programs "to constitute the subject in correct behavioral norms" (Whitehead 1999, 66), another time-consuming activity linked to performance.

Thus the coupling of strong upward managerial accountability with market accountability skewed and indeed transformed organizational life. The stories of these women leaders in schools, universities, and TAFEs indicated how these "performativity exercises" intervened in, and undermined, what they referred to as their "real" work. Furthermore, institutional resources were increasingly diverted toward performativity exercises in the form of image and income production. Jane, a manager in a small, progressive, suburban TAFE reflected:

> I seem to spend too much time on money making rather than getting anything done. We've spent an inordinate amount of time on economic rationalism. So I have tendered for money to assist our literacy tutors in community education. I can no longer, as I used to in the eighties, call on teacher goodwill. Then we could be innovative and start new things to assist the community. Now everything that we do has to have some funding source, and I regret that.

Managers, predominantly men, were at the "fulcrum of the inculcation and dissemination of this managerial discourse," in which "new discourses of masculinism/managerialism purport to offer 'solutions' through 'objective' measurement and assessment, applied in a highly competitive, yet still bureaucratic, environments" (Whitehead 1999, 68). And as in the United Kingdom, we found in our study that, ironically, "as a result of performance, women may well come to be more prominent in the sector, displacing men/managers who under-perform and fail to achieve targets," indicating a "feminization of management" (Whitehead 1999, 68; Prichard and Deem 1999); yet "the new masculine work culture required women to relate to it in a masculine fashion" (Whitehead 1999, 68). In internalizing through repeated performances the performative aspects of the new managerial habitus, women assumed the position of "the masculine subject" (Kerfoot 1999).

"REAL" WORK

Ball (2000) suggests performativity leads institutions and their leaders in particular to construct institutional fabrications that are about escaping from the gaze rather than being more transparent. This reduces the organizational capacity for meaningful evaluation and the ability to identify and resolve problems openly. To signal that an institution has a problem is dangerous in a market-driven environment. Institutions thus invest in these fabrications, and individuals are expected to live up to them. In that sense, performativity is also, but not only, about representation and control. Apart from a generalized first-level effect of institutional energies being dissipated away from teaching and research toward collecting data, producing reports, and developing measures, there was a second, more fundamental, effect. Performativity does not just get in the way by acting as a distraction; it also produces a sense of organizational splitting between the imperatives of core and performative work. Performativity was actually changing the nature of educational work with a "fundamental change in the relation between the learner, learning and knowledge" where these relations are desocialized (Ball 2000, 16). Our respondents spoke of how performativity was affecting both staff and collegial relationships, as well as defining content.

A dominant performative effect on management and market practices was standardization and uniformity. Institutions and individuals were increasingly compared with each other through benchmarking and normative models of "best practice" with the drive to constantly improve performance to maintain comparability between subunits and institutions (Brabazon 2002). The macromeasures of benchmarks, improvement plans, student evaluations, accreditation processes, and performance appraisal enabled the matching and benchmarking of "like" institutions locally within systems, nationally between systems, and internationally between nations, a network of quality control. At the chalkface, these global networks produced micromanagement of individuals as they were operationalized into checklists, proformas, data bases, graphs, and online templates that shaped daily work (Thomson 2000; Smyth 1995; Gewirtz, Ball, and Bowe 1995; Vidovich and Currie 1998; Williams et al. 1997).

Standardization (of curriculum and evaluation) "presents substantial role conflict for teachers, pitting the reform's values of performance, efficiency, and academic achievement against teachers' values of care and investment in broader cognitive, social, and emotional development of students" (Vanderberghe and Huberman 1999, 73). Universal standardized testing was experienced by teachers, for example, as undermining their sense of professional autonomy in that "first, they felt the need to move away from the teaching that they thought was important for their students towards what the tests measured; and second, they saw the standardized test results supplanting their professional judgements in administrative determinations of student progress" (Wylie 1999, 73).

In universities, the drive for "customer satisfaction" and the focus on graduate skills outcomes meant that teachers' and academics' professional judgment was weighed against what students wanted and what students liked as measured in surveys, as if students knew what they needed and wanted in the professional field of their choosing prior to training (Blackmore 2003b; Scott 1999). With the need to raise more external funds as government funds were reduced, the recruitment of international students was seen to be the "solution," requiring further rejigging of institutional priorities and policies: "So it's about the overseas market. It is about re-packaging and packaging, you know . . . lots of money is going to the marketing people" (Chee Wah, senior lecturer, redbrick). This focus on student demand as a planning priority meant institutions geared up to produce programs that sought to attract particular types of students that matched their image (demand oriented) and that challenged professional judgment over what was a desirable curriculum in a field of research or practice (supply oriented). The increasingly instrumentalist focus on industry needs and graduate outcomes as defined by professional bodies also redefined the benefits of education as prespecified skills rather than a more holistic notion of education as a process with multiple outcomes. Performativity was encouraging pedagogies not for difference, despite the increased cultural diversity of students, but for sameness. This constrained imagination within limited parameters of management by objectives was as if there is some certainty based on "customer satisfaction" (Scott 1999).

In TAFE, the discourse of student centeredness competed with discourses about responsiveness to industry, requiring teachers and trainers also to do more outside the classroom into the workplace, as elaborated on by Sandra, manager in a small, regional TAFE. "The big rhetoric in the whole TAFE system is that we really should be delivering in the workplace. . . . [T]hat's the only *real* delivery: and delivering with students in class, doing workplace delivery programs, is given a lot more validation, because it's industry driven, you know. The TAFE emphasis means industry tells us what we want to do, and then we do it." Academics, trainers, and teachers alike considered that too much time, effort, and money were being expended on marketing the institution, quite often, some felt, falsely, given that they had less time to develop and perfect their "quality" programs.

> Marketization and quality stuff is . . . making us do lot more things administratively. So there is less emphasis now on teaching. If you can get away with teaching . . . if you can get the same product, but spend less time in class, so then you can go out there and liaise and spruik and develop other networks, terrific. Essentially, the view is that it is a bit of a waste of time being in class. (Heather, large, metropolitan TAFE)

Thus quite contrary technologies of surveillance embedded in the hyperrationality of corporate managerialism (e.g., performance management, TQM, research quantums, student retention and graduation, annual reviews, program evaluations, outcomes) subverted institutional and individual capacities to improve quality (Rowley 1995). Yet the assumption of quality assurance is that if teaching objectives are clearly communicated, "then it is understandable and reproducible by students" (Elliott 2001, 197). That is, learning is judged according to its "immediate assimilatibility" (Strathern 2000b), thus ignoring the complexities of the pedagogical process. Unit descriptions in handbooks about curriculum, pedagogy, and assessment have to be both "sexy," to incite student interest, and also clear and immutable so that there is nothing unexpected as the outcomes are predetermined. Pedagogies of discomfort that focused on addressing issues of inequality or privilege, challenged personal identities, and invited engagement and critical reflection through exploring the unexpected are within these parameters less acceptable (Boler 1999). Discomfort does not make for customer satisfaction.

Finally, the accountability mechanisms themselves added to the intensification of labor and created unrealistic expectations about "quality" teaching in expanding but downsized and underresourced systems, with some ironic effects. One senior academic commented:

> Over the past two years . . . I was in charge of quality of Teaching and Learning. We now have twice the size of tutorials, and the assessment requirements have been reduced at the same time that quality control was instituted. It is rather a joke. My administrative job, monitoring quality, is going to disappear in the restructure: it will be moved to central office—to people who don't know the units and the students. We decided to start a email protest, [but] nothing came of it as people didn't want to raise their heads.

The emphasis on the performative, with its focus being seen to be accountable, in effect realigned how an organization's time and energy were invested. In this case it was away from staff development, networking, mentoring, sharing ideas and innovations and became the "invisible to audit" processes so necessary in educational work, while quieting opposition to its dulling effects (Strathern 2000a).

CONTESTED ACCOUNTABILITY

Accountability is both a cherished concept and a chameleon and has contested meaning for individuals and in particular occupations and organizations (Sinclair 1995b). Theories of accountability are "infused with unexamined commitments to particular moral and social orders," but

> the factual context of that story is never separable from the duplicities of language and the rhetorical strategies which support it. Like power, accountability can be understood as something a person is or feels (a personal attribute or affect), something a person has been granted (an obligation bestowed or part of a job contract), something a person exchanges for authority (a property of a relationship) . . . a more abstract and impersonal property of an authority structure, or an artefact of scrutiny. (Sinclair 1995b, 221–24)

Accountability can be a financial matter, a matter of legal obligation, or a matter of professional ethics, based on a shared agreement and shaped by social norms. The women in our study, in all sectors, were not averse to "process" accountability, as it focused on adherence to procedures, nor "program" accountability, as it was about effectiveness. As one head of school in a Utech commented, "more and more I think academics are taking responsibility for the sorts of things such as quality of teaching and learning" (Carla). Few would deny that they, as professionals, should be accountable to their students in terms of giving an account of what they have done and why or to adhere to standards or ethics of professional associations. Public accountability was more about transparency, fairness, and the right to know (Sinclair 1995b, 221). Rather it was the form, focus, and effect of these new accountabilities that were contested. Many educational workers saw market accountability (supplying information about a service to facilitate choice), fiscal accountability (efficiency), and managerial accountability (delegated authority to be accountable for measurable outcomes, that often incorporated program, fiscal, process, market and outcomes accountability) as taking precedence over professional and public accountability (Sinclair 1995b, 221).

For our cohort of women, accountability was contested. Personal conflicts arose when professional accountabilities clashed with managerial accountabilities. The irony was not lost on them that the government rationale for these new disciplinary technologies was premised upon democratic discourses of the public's right to know, professional responsibility, greater transparency, efficiency in the use of public monies, and measures of effectiveness of policies. Such discourses were difficult to counter. Most were ambivalent but felt that the balance between autonomy and accountability was weighted increasingly toward the latter. Colleen, principal of a working-class, high cultural mix, primary school, elaborates on this theme: "The fantasy of the desire for data was that if we get everything pinned down, if we have the curriculum standards framework, if we get results recorded, then if we match one school with another, and see one school has better results than the other then we may be able to identify those missing ingredients in the teachers that will fix it all up. . . . People, schools, and communities are not like that."

Underpinning their opposition was also the view that both managerial and market accountabilities signaled a lack of trust in the professions at the same time that they also provided a way for organizations and the state to manage professionals (Bishop 1999). Indeed, "the more intense the gaze of the audit, the less the trust invested in the moral competence of the practitioners to respond to the needs of those they serve" (Groundwater-Smith and Sachs 2002, 341). Managerial accountability has the tendency, in its operationalization, to "elide into policing, reductive templates, and disciplinary mechanisms" (Shore and Wright 2000, 557). Furthermore, managerial and market accountabilities were seen to work against improvement. Indeed, improvement in standardized tests was often closely associated with a reduced curriculum and a focus on basics that sidelined liberal arts and critical pedagogies, with less emphasis on the interests of children and social relationships. This was particularly the case in working-class schools where teacher opposition to standardized tests was greatest in Victoria with many parents withdrawing students in protest because of cultural bias and the long-term impact of "teaching to test." These testing regimes had little to do with authentic learning and assessment. The tests were neither of value diagnostically or for remediation, as funding did not follow when problems were identified. As Newmann and colleagues (1996), suggest: "The heart of the matter is whether performance information can serve both educative needs of individual pupils and national standard setting simultaneously, and how these can be combined in a reporting process that is meaningful to parents as well as a wider public audience" (195).

Indeed, managing performance against externally set targets can produce unfair approaches to school improvement, such as focusing on examination results that can enhance successful students or, by focusing on borderline students in order to indicate some "measurable" improvement, to the neglect of the perceived failures it becomes a type of educational "triage" (Gillborn and Youdell 2002). That is, "the logic of performance management is most likely to encourage a search for tactical improvements which bring about short term improvements" (and bonuses to managers for meeting PIs) and not systemic structural improvement (Husbands 2001, 13). Any improvement in current terms does not necessarily represent a "better education," as this depends on who you are and where you are located, while real improvements in performance tend not to be on the register, such as students' increased enthusiasm and attendance (Gillborn and Youdell 2000).

Woods, Levacic, and Hardman (1998) argued in the United Kingdom that the strongest "*general*" effect of the market's focus on visible and measurable performances was "in conjunction with, or as an arm of, public regulatory measures (such as the introduction of league tables of performance) and a revamped and more public national inspection system" (5). This meant "*local* instances of high competitive engagement, over and above the general system-wide digestion and subordination of competitive pressures, and involves not strategies to enhance student learning but strategies that are aimed at other forms of market responsiveness, such as promotional activity and social targeting" (31)—that is, attracting high performers and excluding low performers. In Australia, while there are no league tables per se, the marketization of public schools during the 1990s exacerbated existing tendencies toward positioning public schools as "the other" to the more desirable (or so perceived) norm of the elite private schools, a ranking propagated through consumer choice publications about schools and universities in the media. The local practice, though not new, of elite private schools "creaming off" high achievers from public and Catholic sector schools intensified as schools undertake the selection function for scarce university places (Teese and Polesel 2003). This becomes less about "genuine" educational performance (in terms of schools adding value for individual students) and more about "public indicators of apparent performance," such as university entrance scores. So there is sufficient local pressure (particularly in high socioeconomic areas) to reinforce this trend to improve, to exacerbate "performativity," across the system, but in so doing it reinforces the academic bias of schooling to disadvantage the majority of students. The public market "encouraged a constructed conception of good performance and effective 'production methods' which is promoted by the government for social efficiency reasons" (Woods, Levacic, and Hardman 1998, 32).

Being seen not to succeed publicly is therefore dangerous in the context of markets and "name, blame and shame" environments. Both market and managerial accountabilities converge in a focus on failure as depicted by limited quantifiable outcomes. For professional educators, the effect is that "accountability has been exchanged for autonomy" (Barnetson and Cutright 2000, 289). This led to particular struggles between professional desires to both be accountable but also to be able to make professional judgements based on multiple forms of professional knowledge in order to address specific needs appropriately. But autonomous judgment requires some level of trust. Currently, the transparency of the processes substitutes for integrity in practice (Strathern 2000b). As Morley (2003) comments, "we are asked to trust the measures, rather than the professionals delivering the service" (56). Documenting practice in quantifiable ways becomes a ritualistic practice that in turn fails to account for what is not quantifiable, but that is equally important in professional knowledge production and judgment.

LOGICS OF PRACTICE:
ANOREXIC ORGANIZATIONS LIVING ON AUDITS

The wo-managers in this study were ambivalent about implementing such measures. On the one hand, teacher and academic performance appraisal in many instances improved relations and conditions for teachers and academics as their supervisors met and planned with them their professional development individually, often for the first time (Chadbourne and Ingvarson 1998). However, when performance appraisal systems were tightly linked to productivity agreements between unions and employers in workplace bargaining rather than reward or support systems for staff, they became another form of control by closely aligning professional autonomy, aspirations, and development to that of organizational outcomes (Townley 1997). This sidelined notions of professional renewal as a reflective practice, often individually tailored, as central to a individual identity and collective professional knowledge. Learning technologies provided another layer of skill, yet the management of these same technologies could "dumb down" curriculum development and pedagogy (Brabazon 2002). In schools, professionalism appeared to be enhanced with the adoption of systems of discourses of action research, teacher practitioner research, and evidence-based practice, only for these empowering practices to be operationalized in an instrumental way in order to fit the systemic preference for limited modes of accountability that is data driven rather than research driven (Blackmore 2002a).

Professional development in teaching, learning, and leadership encouraged innovation and risk taking to improve student learning, but professional development was tightly channeled through planning toward systemic and institutional priorities. Professional development in leadership focused on psychological models (e.g., Myer-Briggs personality types) rather than encouraging critical reflexivity. The state and the performative institution publicize awards for excellence in innovation, teaching, and learning and leadership, but this was against the backdrop of "innovation fatigue" and "submission angst." Such developments provided a positive cultural experience for many womanagers who gained an increased sense of professional expertise and self, but most also felt a pervasive pressure to self-manage and self-promote. Being a performing leader was both self-fulfilling and "feeling good," but also meant "feeling bad," as they were under excessive scrutiny (Acker and Feuerverger 1996). Jane, a manager in a small, progressive, suburban TAFE, considered that "sometimes in focusing on getting the management right the products have suffered: being bossed into assisting with management and being told to attend meetings, having to justify why at the moment I don't feel the need to be involved in professional development. It's not painful, just frustrating. About 50 percent of our time is spent contemplating our navel."

Morley (2003, 72–73) captures the complexity for womanagers, particularly feminists, describing how they "are being forced to promote the practices many of them criticise" as management is dispersed down. New managerialism has demanded that all academics (and teachers) display characteristics of the "hegemonic" rather than "counter hegemonic intellectuals." For some, relief lay in being rejected: "[M]aybe I would no longer feel so vulnerable if the university would just say to me we no longer need you. I know I could make a successful life somewhere else" (Donna, dean, redbrick). It was also evident that as women progressed further up the hierarchy, they were driven by a desire to succeed. They entered the field of educational management expecting familiar rules of the game to work but found the rules had radically changed. A feminist unionist commented how systemic predilictions, in terms of how power was wielded coercively, were often internalized:

> If a woman recently got a job, she is going to do the job in the job description, despite the fact that all the evidence says her job will sometimes be to bully and to ring up and yell and abuse. She knows that the people have been doing that to her; it is part of the job. There is real putting aside of values. But she is also fired up and knows where she wants to go, and while she won't say it out aloud, she will do anything she has to do to achieve it. That is the core of the very destructive force we have initiated.

Women's capacity to reconcile their leadership habitus and "doing good" with their expected managerial habitus meant "one's habitus tends to shun the practices that inculcate such secondary dispositions, perceiving them as alien and 'other' to produce a comfortable coherence of 'onself'" (Zipin and Brennan 2003, 358). This often meant that they had to outlaw emotions as they faced the contradictions between being "caring women" and "productive administrators." Performativity at work and the self-governing mechanisms of performance management and strategic planning exacerbated what Walkerdine (1990, 144) calls the "unbearable splitting of identity" . Yet we also found that teachers, academics, and trainers adopted strategies whenever possible that are more in line with their own professional habitus that focused on collegiality and trust rather than competitiveness (Bishop and Mulford 1999, Sachs 2003; Butler 1996; Currie and Thiele 2001). This "resilient public professional regulatory principle—enacted by [school] leaders and others—acts as a pervasive dampener on competitive pressures" (Woods, Levacic, and Hardman 1998, 33).

But in general, the technologies of performativity did have paralysing and even numbing effects in discouraging the type of public dissension and debate necessary to strengthen the capacity of individuals to change the organization in often principled ways. The contrast of our account with the literature on the learning organizations is stark in terms of the lack of horizontal collaboration, communication, and consensus building (Choo 2001). In the performative organization, "One wants to work collaboratively but when you are in a system you are forced to work with the system: it is all about competition" (Janis, large, metropolitan TAFE). The dox (core values and discourses that the field articulates as self evident and true) produces a "doxic attitude": that is, a "bodily and unconscious submission to conditions that are in fact quite arbitrary and contingent" (Webb, Schirato, and Danaher 2002, xi).

Thus the new accountabilities based as they are on a limited range of performance indicators produced "selected visibility" and diminished rather than enhanced transparency (Sinclair 1995b). There was little reciprocity between organizations and employees. Employees were to achieve predetermined outcomes without any guarantee that organizations provided the conditions of work that make such outcomes possible. The assumption was that strong external accountability will impel organizations and workers to improve. Such theories fail to recognize the human, technical, and social resources of educational organizations. Indeed, "what makes an effective collective enterprise" is an organizational capacity that highlights the importance of internal accountability to each other in ways that reinforce that capacity (Newmann et al. 1997, 41). As our participants argued, good leadership was premised on democratic accountability to community, educational accountability to parents and students, and professional accountability to colleagues. Sinclair (2000b, 143) argues:

> While people say that managerialism has led to a clearer focus and outcomes, whether the organization is more effective, whether practices are more equitable and people feel better, whether the quality of life is good . . . this they cannot answer. [In that sense,] excellent customer service is not enough. The sign of an organization with emotional and moral anorexia is one living on a diet of thin measurable outcomes (and thin pedagogies which arise from that). This is slender spiritual nourishment.

SIX

Accidental Leaders
Acting Out and Acting Up

LEADERSHIP AND THE DISCOURSE OF REFORM

LEADERSHIP HAS BECOME the lexicon of reform, a term supplanting administration or management during the past decade. This shift is apparent in the proliferation of leadership texts by management gurus, the focus of systemic professional development on school principals and managers in TAFE and universities, the establishment of national leadership centers, the multitude of leadership courses in universities, and the on-going debates about different styles of leadership. The dominant image is of the single-headed and single-minded individual who somehow has a capacity to change systems, cultures, and outcomes. "There is a pervasive belief that different forms of leadership have different effects and that these forms arise due to the interplay of the individual attributes and dispositions of leaders (habitus), the knowledges and networks they use (capitals) and the contexts in which they operate (fields)" (Lingard et al. 2003, 128). During the 1990s women were moving into the middle management of education organizations as heads of departments, deans, and school principals. This "moving up" was a consequence of a range of changing demographic, institutional, and professional career patterns, with a cohort of highly qualified women creating a new leadership pool at a time of radical restructuring of education systems. The intermittency typical of this generation of women's careers meant many women educators had reached the management level later than their male counterparts as past practices had privileged seniority and experience over merit. Equal opportunity legislation and policies embedded institutionally during the 1980s, particularly in Australia, had prepared their way. Now, in new line management hierarchies that recognized merit and the capacity to get things done, many women found themselves "in the right place at the right time." Leadership during the 1990s became an enterprise of the self in relation to others.

Much has been written about leadership, yet conceptually there is an ongoing lack of clarification about what leadership means. Epistemologically and theoretically, approaches range from interpretive, to culturalist, cognitive, poststructural and feminist. Each of these approaches brings into account and emphasizes different dimensions of the nature, scope, and practice of leadership. For example, "interpretive styles of leadership see leaders seeking to understand how people see and understood their lives and then channeling those values and emotions towards organizational goals" (Middlehurst 1993, 38). Culturalist approaches depict leaders inventing organizations and meaning and recognize the power of the symbolic (Parker 2000). Earlier cognitive approaches were about how organizations selected leaders with particular personal attributes, producing longstanding leadership myths about the capacity of particular charismatic individuals (usually male), for decision making, decisiveness, and direction. Recent cognitive approaches (distributed leadership and organizational learning) emphasize the capacity of leaders to develop conceptual maps and schema, delegate, self-manage, and deal with complexity (e.g., Gronn 2000, 2003).

Distributive leadership means that individuals are able to "differentiate and undertake a large number of projects simultaneously, for example, to differentiate between competing views of an organization's purposes and integrate them into a range of potential activities and strategies" (Middlehurst 1993, 40). Missing from both the cognitive theory and the activity theory that informs some notions of distributed leadership is recognition of the unequal social relations of power in hierarchical organizations (cf., Gunter 2004 to Spillane 2003) and the emotional aspects of change in organizational life (Fineman 2000; Boler 1999). The recent escalation of interest in distributive leadership, which is more about the "balance between control and autonomy" within a hierarchical organization, is, it could be argued, eclipsing and colonizing long-standing notions of democratic leadership (Woods 2004, 254). Where notions of democratic leadership have been invoked, they are rarely informed by substantive political theorizations about democratic life in organizations.

> Democratic leadership differs ontologically, epistemologically and ethically from distributed leadership based either on cognitive activity theory or a school effectiveness position framed by neo liberal and utilitarian views. The latter emphasises technical professionalism within a straitjacket of professional standards, competencies and quality assurance, where managerial tasks and responsibilities are redistributed but not power and agency. Both ignore

power inequalities and the unequal conditions of teaching and learning. The democratic approach views schools as sites of learning about democratic processes through shared decision-making amongst stakeholders (teachers, parents *and* students). (Crozier and Reay 2005)

Likewise, those mobilizing the recently popularized notion of transformational leadership within the same managerialist frame forget its critical origins in the civil rights movements that emphasized inequalities in politics, culture, and power (Sergiovanni 2001). Indeed, embedded in discourses of transformation and empowerment is the assumption that leaders somehow "empower" others, failing to attribute agency to, or leaders' reliance on, "followers." Inherent in many notions of moral leadership are assumptions of hierarchies in which both initiative and moral authority rests with the leader or particular group. Poststructuralist accounts, while eschewing such hierarchies and normative universals, have focused on leadership as performance constituting multiple subjectivities, emphasizing a capacity to deal with uncertainty, ambiguity, contradiction, and paradox, Leadership is about being "multilingual," managing multiple layers of relationships, activities, and responsibilities and mediating managerial and local discourses simultaneously (Gewirtz, Ball, and Bowe 1995, 96). Meanwhile, feminist accounts of leadership have been "negotiating a relationship between emancipatory ideals of the modernist Enlightenment grand narrative and postmodern appeals to local knowledge, multiple voices and truths," while remaining suspicious of both as mere reinventions of masculine domination (Ashcraft and Mumby 2004, 82). Christie and Limerick (2004, 2) capture the limitations of contemporary studies and writing on leadership.

> In mainstream management and educational-studies, leadership is a valorized concept associated with success, not failure or even mediocrity. Seldom is it probed in ways that reveal the conditions of its own construction. The ethics of its power dynamics are often glossed over. The interplay of unconscious as well as conscious, of irrational as well as rational dynamics in human relationships, is often overlooked. Its embodiment in gendered and raced forms and its emotional evocations are often not confronted. The macro-structural contexts within which it operates are often not considered, as is the fact that leadership is more often concerned with working within those structural contexts rather than changing them.

Organizations and systems (policies and bureaucratic cultures, structures, and processes) are productive of leadership identities. Leaders work within networks of constraints and possibilities (e.g., markets, line management, professional networks, promotional hierarchies, performance management) (Brown et al. 1996). These are the "macro-level social structures and cultural processes that affect the character of the generalized self at any historical moment" (Casey 1995, 74). While men and women may seek to practice the same styles of leadership, whether authoritarian, managerial, or democratic, women more consciously experience organizational life as gendered because societal and organizational expectations and responsibilities are different for men, and because of women's location in a gendered division of labor (e.g., women do the pastoral care and teaching) and its associated processes (e.g., women are the most casualized; see chapter 3). Moreover, as we argued earlier, organizations are gendered in terms of the assumptions embedded in their daily practices. Women's subjective and objective experience of organizations is shaped by these factors, constraining and influencing their choices, understandings, and perceptions of themselves and others.

Women's performances—behavior, emotions, appearance, language—are also interpreted differently by others because of their gender. The gaze is particularly intense on individual woman leaders, who are highly vulnerable to failure because of popular but contradictory discourses about women leaders being caring and sharing, superwomen balancing work and at home equally successfully. This becomes especially the case when women are seen to be acting like men and being too hard or acting like a woman and being too soft (Blackmore 1999b). These are reductionist and dualistic readings that rest on a "tired and problematic logic of difference" (Ashcraft and Mumby 2004, 7). This logic ignores differences among women based on intersections of "race," class, and sexuality, as well as how particular organizations construct, or are receptive to, particular leadership discourses. And it is the absence of these "other" differences in leadership that foregrounds femininity (not masculinity) in what has traditionally been a white, male, heterosexual domain.

Even the liberal feminist tradition that informed gender equity reform discourses during the 1990s (see chapter 8), while seeking to confound gender difference, ultimately asserted that women's access to leadership was justified due to their difference. Women were brought into management because their "feminine selves" "fitted" the new corporate order, complementing not challenging the male norm, "adding value" through an "essential" connectedness now necessary in organizations relying upon people for sustained productivity (Blackmore 1999b). This appeal of the discourse of "feminine styles of leadership" was also promoted by the shift in organizational theory away from an earlier rationalist "partitioning of emotional effort from reward" (Coates 1996, 3). Whereas individuals sought emotional and instrumental rewards outside the organization, the desire now is to encourage employees to develop new emotional ties and bonds with organizations in an attempt to recapture their emotional lives by a commitment to more collaborative workplaces. People are the last untapped resource left to add value to productivity, and women, this universalizing discourse goes, are good people managers able to do that work.

For all women educators during the 1990s, assuming formal management positions therefore meant mediating radical reforms and negotiating competing discourses that positioned them in quite contradictory ways as leaders, managers, and also women. Hearn (1998) describes the "lived contradictions" of organizational life with its ambiguity of expectations and interpretations and ambivalence in that individuals felt both persuaded by, and resistant to, the organizational logic. Gender in particular is an "ambiguous discourse" (Hearn 1998, 31) as is evident in Shirley's (dean of engineering) comment that "I certainly want to be womanly, but I don't want to be in your face with it . . . I want to be one of the pack. I don't want to be singled out as female. I'm actually quite tough but . . ." (Utech). Shirley did not deny her femininity, but she also sought to belong as a professional and a peer, to render gender less relevant to her work, but without relinquishing her gender identity.

LEADERSHIP HABITUS

Identity formation is part of a wider set of interpersonal, social, cultural, and structural relations in which there is an ongoing process of simultaneously being a leader (both in formal positions and informally as a change agent) and becoming a leader (learning through experience and observation) with specific objectives in mind. Individuals bring particular dispositions to the job and are also subject to a range of contingencies that require "learned" responses that derive from well-articulated notions of how things work. This leadership habitus is constituted from past experience in different communities of practice within the field of education. It is constituted also from intuitive responses arising from tacit and implicit personal and professional knowledge that is experientially based, often not articulated, and rarely learned through professional development. Habitus also arises from theorizing about leadership practice, often articulated through partial knowledge gained from formal professional learning. In that sense, the self (and the self as leader) is both a "convenient fiction" and a "narrative construct" (Casey 1995, 3). The self is not fixed, but at the same time there is a sense of inwardness and individuality associated with agency, as well as a "fluid locus of one's subjective experience. It is where effect and reason are experienced and the capacity to act beheld" (Casey 1995, 3).

Our women participants had a strong leadership habitus developed through their activities in numerous communities of practice as volunteers, carers, workers, and educators. Leadership "habitus" in the discursive field of education also has its own tradition and learning trajectory that derives from the relationships and practices in which individuals engage. Identity is in that sense the "pivot between the social and the individual," accessing broader constellations, styles, and discourses as there is a "profound connection between identity and practice" . Trish (principal) comments: "I've thought of myself as a leader for a long time; it is not something that just came to me . . . I come from a family of leaders" (Her father was mayor). This leadership habitus provided cultural capital in her occupational advancement. For many women moving into management, their leadership habitus had been formed by unionist activism during the seventies and eighties that also imparted a strong sense of collective action (Kaplan 1996). Margaret provides a typical account of the diversity of leadership experiences women brought into education. Now a relatively young middle manager in a small, metropolitan, progressive TAFE, she

> fell into jobs . . . I was manager of the Australian Competency Research Center, a commercial, autonomous unit . . . a huge experience of change and reform in that sector. I have a teaching background. This combination . . . is the ticket to this job. The critical thing is to do with change. My TAFE institute made the decision to restructure and spill positions: they wanted people in there that knew what change was about. Change is how I have operated most of my working life . . . I've always been in relatively tenuous employment situations. . . . The cultural pattern is very strong: my father was a teacher and a principal. The educational influence was always pretty strong at home.

Leadership habitus for Margaret was both alterable and distinctive. It was how she understood herself, and it was routinely created and sustained through her reflexivity. Her individual biography indicated a predisposition to educational leadership, but institutional restructuring enabled her to make the moves as a self-identified "change agent." For Amanda, an older primary school principal, class, location, ethnicity, and gender shaped her leadership habitus as an educator: "I wanted to be a teacher from the day I went to school. My father was a policeman moving all around country Victoria until I was thirteen." Colleen, now a secondary school principal in a working-class suburb, joked about teaching as a family tradition. The product of teaching parents, her father was a principal, bringing "salvation success stories" from a "progressive to left wing to socially just and ethical stance," and she was "a high achiever . . . with good timing in that I had access to teacher's scholarships, commonwealth scholarships, studentships, and a multiplicity of reinforcing factors encouraging us as women to enter teaching." Her experience, as that of many of our participants, was also that of the power of collective action as she "learnt union strength in dealing with a very conservative principal, reinforcing my capacity to see a whole school as distinct from just me."

Colleen's predeliction for working in education for social justice, as with many of these women, often arose from her own experience as outsider and from her parents' belief in education. Julie, as a second-generation migrant, now principal of an inner-city, multicultural P–12 school, was one of the few Italian principals in Victoria, although Italians were the largest migrant community in Australia. For her migrant parents, "the aim was to make money and go back home," but they settled down. "My father," she recalls, "had this view that education was incredibly important . . . and refused to let me leave school. I applied for teaching, liked teaching, and was good at it . . . but can't forget how when dealing with my kids at this multicultural school how I was treated as different at school because of my name, what I ate, and that I could speak Italian." Barbara's leadership habitus and attitudes to education were also shaped by her experience of discrimination by senior male staff when a young mathematics teacher. "I realized I was going to earn my money the hard way being put down as female in a male area. . . . I applied for jobs and signed my initials on job applications so I could not be identified as a woman. Being in science and maths they assumed you were male." Sandra in a rural TAFE worked first in industry where "I experienced sexual harassment; women tolerated [it] in most cases. I've never forgotten it. I think that really stands you in good stead as a teacher and a leader in a school because you become so much more attuned, so much more conscious, of what people are saying. [You develop] a sense of purpose."

Experiences of gender discrimination imbued them with a desire for social justice. Being the object/subject of "othering" was therefore embedded in these women's leadership habitus.

OFTEN "ACCIDENTAL," SOMETIMES "RELUCTANT," BUT FOREVER "ACTING" LEADERS

The formation of a leadership habitus was contingent, forever emergent, and situated. Many of the women principals had, early in their careers, leadership responsibilities in rural schools at a time of rapid expansion in secondary schooling. For a few, opportunities arose from teaching overseas, working in curriculum units in the bureaucracy, undertaking postgraduate training, or working in unions. A large proportion of our participants began as teachers and moved into TAFE and universities. Many had serial jobs as a result of following partners, divorce, being widowed, or redundancy due to structural reform. Their career trajectories were rarely planned, often determined "by default," and then most often in "acting" positions. Few had aspired to leadership: "After twenty three years of nontraditional academic work, with fourteen of those years as part-time lecturer, with children growing up, if you'd asked me fifteen years ago what I wanted to be, it wouldn't have been dean in the faculty of engineering" (Anne-Marie, dean, Utech). "My career has been all by default. I was one of these reluctant managers. I always loved teaching . . . I didn't apply for it, I was asked. . . . [T]hey actually formed a coordinator's role for me. A year ago, when the head of center left, she asked me to go for the position. I really didn't want it" (Raelene, progressive, suburban TAFE).

Any reluctance to lead was overcome through persuasion by a boss or colleagues, often out of a sense of loyalty to the institution or an individual. Margaret, a senior TAFE manager, for example, commented, "I've never actually planned a career move in my life." Elle, a university EO manager reflected on her circuitous route from sessional teaching in politics and women's studies. "When a restructure eliminated the external studies department where I was primarily based . . . I didn't have a contract, so I found myself out of job . . . I ended up, four years later, back at the university but in the equity area. It was the result of a series of accidents really" (sandstone).

Significantly, their choices were shaped by their relationships to others, "getting jobs because I was either following my husband around or because someone else said you'd be good for that" (Cynthia, head of school, sandstone). For Denise, "I may have had more flexibility in chasing positions around the state, rather than staying where my family was established." Jill's "choices" were framed by institutional restructuring as well as familial responsibilities:

> I've been at the university since 1991 as a level B [lecturer]. Even with a PhD I came on a contract position. I left my practice in law because, while I enjoyed it, I didn't want to be continually on a merry go round all day and all night like the young boys. I progressed to senior lecturer in law and then head of school. We then merged with another institution, so I was head of [the] Department of Law. Then we merged and created this university. Someone else became head of the school. I didn't apply because I had three and a four-year-old kids and an unhappy marital situation. I did research. (Jill, Utech)

But a typical account of women educators' career paths was that of Kaye, a single mother, now manager in a small, progressive, suburban TAFE, who was adaptable and assertive:

> I was teaching and a divorced woman with four children under the age of eight. I was hired by the Utech—because of my status as a mother—to take part in a tertiary orientation program for women . . . but the travel was too much. I applied to the Education Department and was offered three possible TAFE colleges. I chose the closest. My teaching load was to start up a women's access program. I was lacking confidence, returning to work without qualifications, but fought to have a childcare center . . . I couldn't afford life on a teacher's salary, so my first move to be a coordinator was to get a pay rise. As a single woman, my job has meant an awful lot to me. I enjoy managing and making working environments as good as they possibly can be for people.

"This nexus between work and home in the formation of particular gender regimes is central" as women in formal positions still tend to be single, divorced, or sole parents more than male managers (Wacjman 1998, 87). Work, as well as family, constructed their leadership habitus under particular material, social, and ideological conditions shared by most but not all women.

OPENING AND CLOSING WINDOWS OF OPPORTUNITY

Restructuring meant that the nature of leadership and managerial work was changing, creating new demands, and requiring new skills. On the one hand, continuous reform produced confusion and a sense of lack of control, with educational labor intensified due to multiple contradictory reforms. Nicola, assistant principal at a small, rural, primary school, commented on Schools of the Future:

> In leadership positions, so much of what is required is administrative and technical: things like annual reports—it's never-ending. Then a departmental memorandum arrives, and a week later it's altered. Hours wasted. If things were more clearly defined it would be good. If you have the capabilities named then I would pursue it. Whereas I just sort of feel it's just such an enormous and ever-growing and ever-changing sort of thing. I like to feel that you are not doing things well.

The managerial habitus required being able to deal with ambiguity, constant change, uncertainty, and lack of closure (Blackmore and Thomson 2004). On the other hand, restructuring also provided new opportunities for women, some proactively building a career portfolio, developing their skills base in line with future organizational needs across a number of areas, positioning themselves within the managerial frame. Felicity, manager of quality in a suburban, community-based TAFE said that

> my career ambition on my resume states that I want to be a senior person in an organization as a director of an institute or as a senior center executive officer. I don't necessarily see myself staying in the TAFE sector, although I do love being in education. I don't think I've learnt enough yet. . . . So I'd like to take the traditional steps and try to get into an executive position. I'm trying to get a well rounded profile that can prove to them that am I good at things other than quality. . . . [I'm] looking at jobs in administration that embrace educational aspects, program profile, and funding.

Few women were as clear and articulate as to their ambitions and future. For Jane, in a small, progressive, suburban TAFE, restructuring had an unexpected twist despite her plans. While she felt that she was "more useful to TAFE now. I went to a professional training board to acquire the skills that would assist me. Ironically, the skills I got to be useful (in my current job) conflicted with the skills necessary to give me a promotion." Being useful did not necessarily lead to institutional rewards.

Typically, women were appointed not just because of their ability but also because they were perceived to be outsiders in existing power arrangements and most likely to initiate change. Jill felt that her dean asked her to be acting dean because she was efficient and trustworthy but also because "he knew he could trust me to give him information and to record things, whereas some of the other blokes will pull the wool over his eyes" (Utech). Also she believed her colleagues liked that "I get the point, I am clear, and I certainly get things done." Many were encouraged to stand for management positions by colleagues who had experienced their leadership informally. Paula, head of school (Utech) recalls:

> My career wasn't planned at all . . . from the time I graduated I had a combined role of parenting and teaching. I taught in the United Kingdom, working with the top people. I came back half time as a tutor and worked my way up through the ranks . . . I am now one of five specialists in Australia. I decided that I wanted to do my PhD. The head of school became dean, and her deputy went to Melbourne. I was approached by eight or nine staff who asked me to apply for head of school. I said, no, I was doing my PhD and teaching. I got here by default.

This "accidental" nature of the career trajectories of women into leadership was indicative of the failure of personal, professional, institutional support; lack of formal mentoring; and little access to informal networking. Women were learning the game from the sidelines, through observation, experience, and reflection: that is, leadership as a form of "praxis," based on pedagogy and dialogue, and through extraorganizational networks and relationships.

MOVING UP THE LADDER: A MATTER OF COMMITMENT?

Motivations for seeking or accepting promotion into formal management positions were varied. Many made career choices for financial reasons, and others were based upon a professional commitment to a particular program or issue. Some did so with regret, as did Jane, manager in a small, progressive, suburban TAFE:

> I built up a department at a TAFE college from a women's access department. When it came time to select a head of department for that area, I

stepped aside because I still wanted to be in the operational area as it was embryonic. . . . The management position would have taken me away. Now I find it difficult to live with that decision because it affected, obviously, how I was seen. Management is about becoming a head of department and not managing another project, to manage staff and look towards an associate director's position. The director's position doesn't come through being innovative or building up projects or outside work; it comes from the accepted tradition; I have cut off my alternatives.

Jane's commitment and misreading of the institutional politics benefited her program and the students. But program work was marginal to organizational priorities and did not count as there were no line management responsibilities for staff or budgets. Any reluctance to take up managerial positions, particularly in larger organizations, was seen to signal a lack of commitment or a lack of ambition (Sinclair 1998; Wacjman 1999).

Commitment was also about the length of tenure in a position and providing evidence of one's ability and influence. It meant "you have to stay there and be prepared to bide your time there and then build up the role to make it as important and make it a key role so that you can have some degree of clout in the institute too" (Joy, large, suburban TAFE). Being committed to one's career (and the organization) also meant taking on jobs one did not enjoy so much to expand one's experience. Miriam, a school principal in a popular inner-city primary school mapped her pathway under a strong female mentor: "The first year my principal let me be the curriculum coordinator. So I was in classrooms every day, teaching and modeling. But the next year resource cuts came with Schools of the Future. She gave me two jobs I hated, integration and facilities, bloody grounds and buildings. . . . [She] said I had to move on to new things, to move out of my comfort zone."

But the primary measure of commitment was the willingness to work longer hours, even less so than the capacity to produce outcomes. For these reasons, many women saw management positions as life consuming. Liz, a TAFE teacher, did not apply to be head of department because it had made her home life very difficult when she was in the acting position:

I totally wore out any welcome in the neighborhood. There were difficulties with my kids' music and sports commitments. The family was clearly against, especially the kids. Professionally, I would have liked the job, and I knew I could do it. I sometimes feel like, there went my career. I have already been overlooked for a program coordinator's position (which is the next level down), in an area in which I have experience. It went to someone from a totally different area. I resent that because I think the organization has not been able to recognize what I thought was a very honest decision. I feel that I have now been labeled as a person who is not going to put in for the organization.

Lesley, a TAFE manager, was not seen to be committed by her organization because, "I have been attempting to work .8 for three years while working very long days, ten-hour days, physically. Really doing five days, but trying to keep that fifth day free. . . . [M]y mother is dying, I have a daughter who is in her last year of school, and a second marriage that is very important to me . . . yet knowing I was losing points on one level, not to make that commitment of going full time."

Time for these women was the most valued resource, and lack of time was central to their incapacity to move up. For those who did, such as Felicity (TAFE), "my family had to get used to the fact that I was going to stay back until I finished the job as I was not prepared to take work home . . . while high standards are implied, children need child care. You've got to pick the kid up by 6:00." Commitment was, therefore, understood differently. Commitment in organizational terms was about putting in the hours and focusing on organizational goals. Commitment, according to many of these women educational professionals, was a desire to improve student learning and opportunities, to work with colleagues productively, to work in other organizations such as unions in ways that that will produce beneficial effects for students and staff, and producing outcomes. "I was doing it not because I wanted to be promoted but because there are important things to do, and other people weren't doing them" (Kim, nursing professor, Utech).

Women's career trajectories into management were thus informed by professional *and* personal circumstances, the need to be flexible to support a family, to fit in with their partner's careers, or to fulfill some organizational need. Organizational and workplace restructuring did not impart these women with less agency, but did require a level of openness to change (and disappointment). Women's careers were also "protean," in that the person—not the organization—was the driver, with the individual developing, exploring, and refining a "sense of 'career identity' in relation to one's multiple roles while maintaining an awareness of the whole system. This was matched by ever-increasing personal/professional adaptability that breaks down the traditional work-life distinction" (Bascia and Young 2001, 278). But these changing workplaces also reinstitutionalized organizational gender regimes (between casual/contract/tenured staff) that also position most women as marginal, reinforcing the wider societal gender order of unequal opportunities and risk. Women educators' professional identity was shaped by their "peripheral participation" in the organization's community of practice (Wenger 1998). These narratives indicate that women have always had "boundaryless," "portfolio" careers—portable, flexible, contingent and transitional—more typical of the twenty-first-century "new" work order than the twentieth-century masculine and modernist model of career as a fixed, linear, and continuous process of developmental progress (Gee, Hull, and Lankshear 1996).

LEARNING LEADERSHIP THROUGH DOING

The image of professionalism and educational leadership that most women leaders entering formal positions in the 1990s had encountered in the 1950s and 1960s was the product of the "masculine project of repressing and denying those values culturally assigned to femininity" and more about being "objective, competitive, individualistic and predictable" as well as "scornful of the nurturant, expressive and familial styles of personal interaction" (Davies and Hollway 1995, 5). Nicola, principal of a small, rural primary school, recalled her impression of male principals: "I found them distant, I found them quite separate from staff. It wasn't the era where you had discussions. . . . [Y]ou were informed what to do. I didn't particularly like their style—distant, well suited, immaculately manicured—but they wouldn't know the kids." Others also learned how to lead from watching others' mistakes or "bad leadership." Kaye, now a TAFE manager and a former teacher, saw "a lot of managers who were very authoritarian and very domineering and I loathed and detested them." For some women the desire to provide positive "female alternatives" was a personal project. Jenny, an advanced skills teacher in a secondary college in rural Victoria sought to develop more democratic and collegial practices because of one critical incident: "One principal tried to make quite reasonable changes to yard duty without consultation. It was a mess. People have to be consulted. . . . Even those who did not necessarily like the policy can accept that fact that they had been heard, argued their heads off, jumped up and down, and that some of their ideas were integrated. I can understand the need for that. It's useless to say 'Here is the policy, follow it.'"

Many learned about leadership by working with colleagues lower down the organization, and not from mentors or role models among senior staff, as Bev, principal of a rural primary, noted:

> There are some people I've hugely admired for their style. One woman was very much an administrator and manager; had her finger on the pulse of many things and constant paper work flow across her desk, cleared by the end of the day. But there are other workers in the field, not senior administrators, but coordinators, [who have the] ability to be politically right on and to operate in a diplomatic way and forge ahead in those negative days when equal opportunity and feminism were dirty words. These are the ones to learn from.

Others recalled critical incidents that informed their understandings about themselves with regard to leadership. Colleen, principal of a small, multicultural secondary college, recalled:

> I only won an appeal because I knew so little. I developed a theoretical position that stood up very strongly, so I never cluttered my mind with detail. I'm

learning this again in hindsight. Leadership also gave me a chance to see if I could communicate with strangers. I did have a strong sense that I was only powerful and effective when I was secure in those relationships. In one of the many restructures that led to a regional organization, I was transferred to a region and got to polish up my capacity to deal with strangers. I learnt to manage upwards quite well then, cause I didn't like being told what to do. Then a principal position became available. I applied, on the strength of other people's recommendations. You have that theoretical commitment that women should apply.

Despite this, many women aspiring to leadership tended to view the woman at the top as exceptional and not necessarily to be imitated. Such positions were increasingly out of reach and daunting to aspirant leaders due to ethical dilemmas, work intensification, and challenging gender identities. Janice, a senior teacher in a secondary school said:

I don't think of myself as a leader in a formal position. I don't have great ambitions as I've got a six year old and a four year old. I work full time. I've a husband just starting a business. I love doing what I do and have a great fear of becoming desk bound. I have no wish to apply for head of department as the size, administrative, and leadership positions by nature tend to isolate you from the student body; your contact is often disciplinary, administrative rather than pastoral. I've got leadership qualities, and I have been encouraged . . . but a leadership role within this school is very time consuming.

Many younger women were deterred by the position descriptions privileging the functional and the financial over the interpersonal and the educational (Blackmore 2002c). Leadership discourses were increasingly colonized by market and managerial language and practices and leadership equated to formal positions. Doing management was seen to have negative connotations in terms of relationships. For Raelene, a manager in TAFE, middle management was perceived to be no longer about people, more about policy and finance, so she applied with trepidation. She retained those aspects she enjoyed only by moving horizontally: "I'm a people person. I felt being in management I would be divorced a lot from people. I went for it and enjoyed lots of it . . . not the administrative nit picking, like checking student contact hours, and the accountant's work. . . . But once in a position like that, it would be very hard to let it go, and you can't balance teaching and administration. I gave teaching away. I moved to be director of studies, so I am again involved with students."

Institutional leadership positions were seen to require changing values, being and doing something different. Likewise, Carol, a young teacher in a small, working-class secondary school with high cultural mix, commented on why she was deterred from applying:

Leadership is about personal values, about how you treat people or about what people deserve. You might have to make a decision that contradicts those values. . . . [T]hat's what would put me off. I'm not very good at confrontation or conflict. I don't see myself as a leader. But then I haven't really thought about what a leader is. . . . [Y]ou just tend to think of it as principal, full stop. So then I think of all the negative things that a leader (as principal) has to do. Not negative so much as difficult things that affect people's lives. You've got to be so sensitive in the way you deal with everybody's feelings, and in the end you hurt some people's feelings in management decisions. That's the key because it could be in conflict with your personal values; . . . that's why I'm a failure.

Moving into leadership in the context of denigratory discourses and representations of women in leadership more generally also challenged gender identity (Wilkinson 2005). One organizational message readily articulated by Sarah, a young coordinator in a working-class secondary school was that you have to be "more like a man to be successful . . . to have balls on you." Doing leadership like a man was like yet another form of performance: "I can act like a man when I want to, but it depends on when I choose to. I am, generally, with the students, aggressive and tough. But it is hard to separate sometimes when you come out from school—acting like a boy and being yourself again." These women were incensed by dominant reform discourses that linked leadership to hard-nosed aggressive and authoritarian behavior, stereotypically masculine. Most learned how to be leaders by subverting what many perceived were masculinist norms. Bev, a principal in a rural secondary school was "determined when [she] started trying to get into principal class, not to be better than the boys. I was determined to be an effective female, so I wasn't trying to outdo the boys at the boys' game." But some like Carol also felt positioned in contradictory ways by feminist discourses about leadership: "I don't see myself as a leader. I don't see that as relating to being a woman either. I'm not particularly interested, but historically, women fought for the right to have a career. Now you feel like you have to have a career if you don't have a family. You are not allowed that middle ground. Colleen [principal] is keen for women to become leaders."

This dissonance between how the job was perceived and what leader/managers actually did once in the job produced ambivalence among aspirant leaders. It was also about self-presentation and a sense of mismatch between position and identity. Colleen, principal of a working-class secondary school in a provincial city, attests to her own inability to see herself as a principal for a long time, because "I still didn't see myself as doing anything except becoming a better and better teacher." As with most women in this study it took someone else, a colleague, often a male in a position of authority, to "name" them as leaders and to point out that what they did was leadership.

Doing leadership was something women did not associate with their everyday professional practice and personal lives, because the discourse was so strongly associated with formal positions. Even as a teaching principal in a small, rural, primary school, Merilyn reflected that "if all else fails in management, you always have great interaction with kids every day."

Some interviewees articulated discourses about "women being their own worst enemies." Pat, an EO manager in a sandstone university, suggested that women are insecure in spite of themselves: "But also there is fear of the unknown. Leadership and power is not part of the way women are socialized. And there are quality of life issues. Many women perceive leadership positions as too stressful and time consuming." But across the three sectors there was a sense that shifting leadership habitus (from informal to formal positions, from teaching to management) meant difficult identity work. The leadership habitus they brought to management was regulated and regular but without being obedient to the rules of the game. They possessed the habitus to enter the game, and for those who chose to play the game, it required a conscious and unconscious set of practices that provided a "sense of the game," an investment, even if reluctant, in the game (Bourdieu, 1990, p. 43). For many it was a game they did not wish to play.

Whereas men tend to see promotion as leading to more opportunities to delegate and hence more freedom and autonomy, our cohort more often saw promotion as leading to an intensification of labor, ever-increasing demands of deadlines against home life and balancing domestic labor, and demanding practices with which they were not comfortable (Coates 1996). Formal positions required women to put work first, family second, and self last. What these women valued most was to be independent enough to work things out efficiently on their own terms and make both their private and work lives manageable, as stated by Lois (small, progressive, suburban TAFE).

> I suppose I think of myself as a leader because I've been in adult education for twenty years. I feel comfortable with my skill level. I have plenty to learn. I know I can deliver and generate enthusiasm. Generally, in any organization, I've moved into that role. And it's the sense of self, and a desire—not just blind ambition—that I need to balance with interest. I've enjoyed positions of leadership because generally they have given me more freedom to work in projects that are interesting.

Others did not see this as possible once in middle-management positions. In the end, for many watching women leaders and managers from the wings, their perception was one of serial ethical dilemmas, struggle, and an overwhelming workload. So, while formal positions of management were highly problematic, leadership as a social practice, as a way of knowing how to initiate, implement, and evaluate change through action and political commitment was not (Gunter 2004a). They had all led in different contexts, leading in multiple ways, although some leadership identities were more secure than others due to the recognition by their colleagues.

"FEELING DIFFERENT": ISSUES OF REPRESENTATION AND RE-PRESENTATION

Underlying the polished presentation of the identities that produced the stories of leadership in our interviews there was considerable rough ground. For women in formal positions, there was a sudden sense that they were now under constant surveillance—as women, not just as leaders—requiring a "bracketing on the level of practice, of possible events that could threaten" their sense of identity and purpose (Giddens 1991, 54). Taking on management in universities, schools, and TAFE institutes was likened to assuming another identity, offering if not demanding a disjuncture in their autobiographies. Management felt like a misfitting, uncomfortable cloak. Some felt that they were in the wrong place and "unsuited" for the job. It was, for one TAFE manager, "feeling like a fraud. I felt I didn't have the skills that were needed" (Sinclair and Wilson 2002). Another TAFE manager stated she "would choose her life differently, I don't feel successful yet, because I've had to battle. I cannot envisage the future" (Gabriella, large, metropolitan TAFE). The thought that she may have to take on another senior role in the next five years was "awful." Yet, once in positions of responsibility, most women managers, while assuming a managerial habitus, drew upon an array of discourses to redefine their work, seeking security in their previous leadership practices and experiences, while exploring other possibilities. But contextual factors forced/produced particular subtle but significant accommodations, producing a constant state of being and becoming something different.

Initially, there was the realization that they were both seen and expected to be different in some way, although such representations contradicted what many women felt or how they re-presented themselves in interview. Lesley, an executive manager in a small, progressive TAFE commented: "I'm perceived, by others, as being somehow different. I'm much more of a peasant than I look like on the organizational chart. I'm more inflated than I feel. But that's people's projections to cut through. And the essence of staying joyful, and ensuring that your work has meaning and value, is to recognize that it doesn't in fact shape the essence of who you are. The thing is to not to cling onto the projection that comes with the job." A university dean said that "the experience of being the newcomer is quite fascinating in attempting to get up to speed in terms of identities, commitments, taking on board new stuff. It's just quite overwhelming. People who never knew who I was now talk to me as though we've always had this long set of relationships" (redbrick). Particular incidents produced new understandings about expectations of them as leaders and as managers but also as women. Megan, a newly appointed executive-level manager in a small, progressive, suburban TAFE, found how gender and leadership were so inextricably mixed:

> I mean, the moment that crystalized with me that I was different was when the old Business Management Team invited me to speak to the staff. I was not officially in the job, but having to address a hundred people I didn't know and give them a vision and a direction. So I thought long and hard . . . and invited people to introduce themselves. A lot did, all women . . . pleased to have a female manager and leader, quite excited, and very positive. Then I realized I was a senior manager *and* a role model. They had expectations of me because of me being female.

As Wacjman (1999, 2) comments, "management incorporates a male standard that positions women as out of place. Indeed, the construction of women as different from men is one of the mechanisms whereby male power in the workplace is maintained." Age and appearance also come into play. Margaret reflected:

> In my last job I was obviously younger but dealt with senior people nationally . . . not a problem in the long term, but certainly in the short. They look for someone more senior, then realize it is me . . . I have to work harder to establish myself. In the dynamic of meetings and decision making, I think men and women do it differently. I'm not good at loud voice yelling, power, assertiveness. I do think I have to change, but I don't want to be like Margaret Thatcher. . . . [T]here's clearly a line. I think it's changing the culture of how we work. I'm not prepared to exploit or sacrifice my femininity. (progressive, suburban TAFE)

But there was also a dissonance between others' perceptions and one's sense of self. Alice, a TAFE departmental manager, represented herself as "a better person when I'm a team player. I don't have the big picture visions expected of leaders. I certainly can identify who would be a great head of department, but not me. I'm a better organizer than a leader. I cultivate leaders and make sure they're in positions where they can lead." Yet to her colleagues she offered an alternative approach to the managerial leadership of this male-dominated college because she did not assume to be out in front but actually practiced democratic leadership. Ultimately, Alice's refusal to shift her loyalties upward was recognized. She was dissuaded from thinking about higher administrative positions by her male supervisor, who told her she was "just a teacher without management skills."

Women are particularly caught between accepting dominant masculinist images and constructs of leadership as being what is expected and how one has to do the job. For these women, "identity functions as points of identification and attachment only because of their capacity to exclude, leave out, to render outside" that with which they could not deal (Hall 1997, 5). Moving into formal leadership positions often meant some past leadership practices had to be discarded, requiring a significant redefinition of self and a reimagining of what was understood as leadership and also being female. Dianne, a dean in a sandstone university "confessed" how she was concerned, prior to taking on her first position as a dean, about her "femininity, not her feminism." The latter provided her with a sense of purpose, but she felt her femininity was more under threat:

> I thought you had to . . . as a dean or an administrator, . . . adopt a male style. In other words it was my image of being a leader was connected clearly in my subconscious with male qualities. The first year and a half was pretty difficult. But in the end I found that if you just did what you thought was best, that was fine. And you didn't have to be different: you didn't have to be somebody other than yourself. But I didn't have the confidence to recognize that before I got in the job. I, too, had a stereotype about what the job involved, and in fact I've got it again right now, as I apply for promotion.

Women struggled, therefore, between how they were perceived by others and represented in discourses about women and leadership and how they sought to re-present themselves. A dean in a Utech thought that the image she was projecting was of a "mind like a steel trap, decisive, reasonably confident but humble, with a sense of humor, with a bit of vulnerability thrown in." They struggled with how they were represented in popular and dominant discourses. Dianne, the dean, was outraged at how media representations at the time of her appointment focused on her appearance and youth coupled with references to her past history as a part-time "barmaid" to fund her studies. Such representations, she felt, positioned her as "unsuitable" and, by implication, "an outside female being drafted by the female vice-chancellor." When male vice-chancellors appoint male deans, masculinity is not an issue. Thus the media, scholarship, and literature are like narrative threads or fragments, partial and drifting representations of women with which our women leaders struggled. The women in our study both "recite[d] and elude[d] these representations, drawing upon and/or resisting them in the performances of everyday organizational life" (Ashcraft and Mumby 2004, 18). Such discourses had "constitutive power of the micro (interactional), intermediate (institutional) and macro (societal) levels of discourse" (Ashcraft and Mumby 2004, 28). How women leaders acted and reacted was not only framed by policies, accountabilities, and relations of power, but also limiting gender scripts that informed others' perceptions of their actions.

There was a constant struggle about gender and leadership identity, being caught between discursive binaries positioning them as being both in and out of control. Being in formal positions of power provided some opportunities for women to re-present themselves differently, to problematize dominant discourses about women and leadership, to trouble the oppositional binaries between rationality/emotionality, mind/body, objectivity/subjectivity, hard/soft. These binaries were central to women's subordination and continued to position women unfavorably as they were recycled. Moving into formal leadership positions at a time when managerialism was becoming the dominant paradigm rather than traditional "educational" cultures of academia, schools, and the trades was for many women about accommodating new practices and priorities expected by the institution and the position, while seeking to maintain particular valued relationships, ways of working, and principles. They did this by mobilizing discourses of leadership as counterhegemonic discourses to management and by utilizing formal authority only when necessary to focus on what they saw as important for staff and students.

REFLEXIVITY: MAKING MISTAKES AND PRACTICAL ACTION

At the same time, as females in what was still felt to be a masculinist culture, these women were outsiders, peripheral participants, in many ways "othered" by dominant societal and organizational perceptions and expectations. Being located in positions of authority as women (and in the interview) led them to reflect on their own practices and others' perceptions of them of what they did. "So I do find myself being seen as different. But it's allowed me to stop, look back, and take stock of myself" (Colleen, principal, working-class secondary school). In order to be able to do the work required, they had to track, and learn to work strategically, through the webs of power and discourses of possibility that many, but not all, men take for granted. Being positioned also as change agents required deliberative reflection in and on practice as ongoing learning about self and others. Teresa, secondary school principal in a working-class school in a provincial city mused about how she learned from her mistakes: "I can't lead from behind . . . I've got a very big picture of a school. I'm not a little picture person, and as a consequence I run in front of everybody else. It's not a healthy leadership style because I tend to get a long way in front, seeing where things should go. People don't like that. All the time I've got to stop and step back and just drop an idea in." A secondary school assistant principal in a provincial town commented about leadership as a collective practice and her role as merely one actor in a process:

The fact [is] that a lot of the work I do isn't work that *I* do; it's work with other people. I am good at getting teams together to look at a problem; we work out a solution. I just help along the way. I throw in ideas at various points and make models. I made the process happen. A leader is only as good as the team of people they work with. I am good at defining what the problem is, and sometimes I have to learn to slow down because people don't want you to give them answer. Rather, I offer different possibilities.

Many reflected upon how their understandings of leadership influenced their priorities and practices and how they differed from managerial definitions of leadership. One young teacher in a small school decided she had to broaden her repertoire of skills, as leadership was increasingly less about what one did in the classroom and more about performing well outside (Bishop and Mulford 1999). She indicated a heightened awareness about the game of "becoming" a leader without neglecting important practices in terms of what benefited her students and colleagues. This was a struggle between performing and re-forming (herself and others): "I need to probably take on leadership positions and start doing a range of other things within the school. But maybe I even need to identify what leadership is . . . I suppose it's a lot of self-discovery. I enjoy working with teachers and helping them to plan, and the rorganizational things, in getting everything together."

Many expressed the feeing of being both powerful (as an academic or administrator) and powerless (as a woman). Trish, an assistant principal in a rural, primary school summed it up: "I have a suspicion that I'm seen to be a very strong person, and perhaps too strong. But I don't perceive myself that way. I struggle with that. You look as if you are in control, and I don't feel that way at all." Moving from professor to a manager as head of school also led to new levels of awareness about the institution, its practices, strategies, and one's own position in larger institutions such as universities. One professor reflected on one articulation of the emerging academic/managerial divide "I think in large universities professors are treated like teenagers. You are too senior not to get any respect, and yet you don't get any respect. And you suddenly realize that there is a whole hierarchy above you, which you can now see, which you couldn't see getting up there" (Cynthia, sandstone). Advancement here meant changing one's perspectives on the institution, as well as facing desires and fears and questioning one's beliefs. Most of these women were reflexive, constantly reassessing their sense of self as leaders, of meaning in organizational life, and seeking to understand how to work strategically and ethically in that context.

Such reflexivity is often seen to be a characteristic of modernity, "not as an individual but a societal quality, organized in the division of labor and differentiation of individuals' conditions for learning and knowing" (Olesen 2001, p. 291). Reflexivity may be part of the condition of modernity, but

"reflective self-awareness does not necessarily produce a corresponding capacity for the enactment of change. It may instead produce a form of self-sur-
veillance in which reflective practice becomes managerial orthodoxy" (Clegg
1999, 169). This was most evident in how reflective practice in leadership
training tends to be more about reflection along a narrow range of parameters
(professional journaling and predetermined leadership competencies) and cir-
cumscribed by particular sociopolitical circumstances in practice. Reflective
practice can be pleasurable because it appeals to the need for a sense of competence, autonomy, and relatedness, and empowering because of a greater
sense of personal confidence, but it does not necessarily lead to change in
practice and can encourage "apolitical introversion" (Clegg 1999, 169).

Bohman (1999) refers to second-order socialization that provides a normative dimension beyond the notion of how cultural practices socialize
according to Bourdieu's practical reason. This normative dimension is about
"being a certain sort of person who has particular desires and goals" (147),
and this requires public learning. It is in the space of the organization that
"public learning can subject beliefs to public testing from diverse points of
view; similarly, public deliberation can be institutionalized in complex practices of belief, revision and deliberation" (Bohman 1999, 147–48), such as
through deliberative policy making (Forester 1999). Gunter (2004b, 7) suggests that "the activity of challenging is more intellectual than operational,
but it still requires the doing and the evidencing of the doing through writing and talking. Conversely, the action of delivering change could be more
operational than intellectual, but it does require cognitive and affective
processes as well as public expressions through writing plans and chairing
meetings." As knowledgeable agents, most of these women were enacting
practical rationality in "getting things done," but many also had a heightened
sense of intentionality informed by their desire for social justice, second-
order reflexivity, and a way of theorizing organizational change, a praxis
based on practical ethics.

This heightened level or double loop of reflexivity was also a condition of
their organizational survival as women. Gender figured large. "If reflection is
considered as a single epistemological loop, reflexivity might be conceptualized as a double loop, an ontological loop whereby the knower's social being
in terms of gender, race, sexuality and class form part of the basis of knowing"
(Olesen 2001, 175). It is this second loop of reflexivity that is so often missing in professional development. Reflection without a critical and theoretical
stance that locates personal experience within wider relations of power, and
how those relations of power produce particular leadership practices, does not
"transform." A more critical professionalism would provide "a set of literacies
that enable us to 'read' various scenarios within the educational field and to
promote them effectively offer us something good to think with" (Webb,
Schirato, and Danaher 2002, 141–42).

SEVEN

Managing the Self: The Consuming Passions of Performing and Re-forming Leadership

RESTRUCTURING LEADERSHIP

DURING THE 1990s, strong executive leadership was crucial in the broader education reform agenda cross-nationally. In particular it was critical in mobilizing and directing the shift to self-managing institutions based on new public administration reforms and marketization (e.g., Wylie 1998). In chapters 2 and 3 we argued that centralized-decentralized corporate management, as a mode of educational governance, produced a hybrid of corporate line management and neobureaucratic practices rather than postmodernist idealizations about flatter and more democratic organizational structures (Limerick, Cunnington, and Crowther 1998). Accordingly, university vice-chancellors and TAFE directors were renamed as CEOs, and there were frequent suggestions that school principals be recruited from the ranks of generic managers from business rather than from the teaching workforce. Leadership was equated to executive positions of authority, and considerable professional development was invested in training and maintaining CEOs and their leadership teams. In such a context, leadership had a purpose, and that was to restructure and reform education, and it was highly political. The executive officer was the linchpin of reform and gained considerable power during this period. In this chapter we examine how education restructuring appropriated discourses of educational leadership as it transformed systems of educational governance. We consider how the conflation of management into leadership discursively positioned the women leaders and managers in our study who were passionate about education promoting more equitable social change.

Lingard and colleagues (2003, 128) argue that leadership is not something that is an actuality, but more a discourse that is active in its own construction and rearticulation, that "constitutes its own forms, functions and interests" in ways that are "temporal, spatial and contingent." The success of the structural reforms of the 1990s was dependent on redefining management in ways that both subsumed educational leadership and created a discursive space distinct from teaching and/or research. Management was redefined as something requiring different skills, attributes, and knowledge, a distinctive managerial habitus with a "right to manage" (Clarke and Newman 1997). With self-management, the nature and substance of educational management changed with its increased emphasis on financial management, marketing, strategic planning, leadership teams, accountability, and vision building. The buzz-word was *change*, and the most repeated phrase *change is the only constant*.

The new public management reforms introduced corporate management discourses and practices into universities and TAFEs by promoting a seductive discourse to executives of institutional autonomy and self-management. The move to self-governing/managing schools in Victoria, New Zealand, and the United Kingdom, for example, was reliant upon principals' cooperation and enabled by their desire to have greater control over their schools. In Victoria, after 1993, support from principals' associations was gained by moving principals into a different industrial award from teachers on the basis of promises of increased staffing and financial flexibility, salary increases, and performance bonuses (Pascoe and Pascoe 1998). Likewise, the involvement of the vice-chancellors and TAFE directors, individually as CEOs with particular institutional investments, and collectively as national policy lobbies (e.g., Australian Vice Chancellor's Committee or AVCC), was central to tertiary education reform.

Paradoxically, while power was distributed upward, it was also a period in which much of the responsibility for doing financial, personnel, and industrial relations management work was devolved and dispersed down and throughout educational organizations. This set up a contradictory tension between a "seductive discourse" of team building and its implied participatory activities and line management's hierarchical relationships based on functionality and strategic planning (Sinclair 1995a). This was particularly evident in schools that were now likened to "small businesses" (Caldwell and Hayward 1998). An assistant principal in a large, senior secondary college commented about the tension between past practices of democratic decision making and the new managerialism: "It is unreasonable to expect principals to make all these decisions about how money is spent in global budgets. But the principal who works in a consultative manner and the people they consult have a heavier work load in terms of deciding how maintenance budgets are spent, how cleaning contracts are negotiated, or staffing decisions, as we hire our own short-term replace teachers and contract staff."

This was devolution of responsibility rather than devolution of power, given that key resource and policy decisions were retained at the central level. This mode of governmentality was echoed at the institutional level. Policy frameworks, strategic plans, and internal and external contractual arrangements constrained decision making in local "autonomous" subunits as tasks cascaded down producing a proliferation of information feedback systems and regimes of accountability back to the center. Principals, directors, and VCs as did government, had more control over their staff and ways of utilizing depleting resources but less control over core issues of curriculum or profiles, now tightly linked through financial agreements and accountabilities.

MANAGING LEADERS OR LEADING MANAGERS?

With the corporatization of education, management increasingly became conflated into leadership, part of learning about making strategic moves in the corporate game, with a focus on process, generic skills, and measurement rather than substance or content (Saul 1995). A TAFE's best management strategy (1995–99), for example, referred to management capability as an

> all round human quality that represents and all round integration of knowledge, skills and personal qualities that are used effectively and appropriately in response to varied, familiar and unfamiliar circumstances. Capability is about mastering the direction of change through integrating values, self esteem, awareness of needs, problem formulation and solving, evaluation skills, creativity, intuition and imagination with critical capability aimed at continuous improvement. (Institute 1995)

Corporate strategic skills were defined as "strategic management, participative planning, and knowledge and understanding of best practice," and leadership skills were defined as "the ability to be a learning opportunist, to take effective and appropriate action, to be innovative and entrepreneurial, confident to use and develop skills in complex circumstances, undertake change management, learn from experience and pursue continuous personal improvement" (9). "People element capabilities" included "communication skills, team working and developing skills, networking and peer skills, cooperative behavior, performance management skills and coaching skills." There was little mentioned here about corporate ethics or social justice, and leadership was compartmentalized as an entrepreneurial rather than relational activity. As Bauman

(1993) argues, such texts replace "agentic ethics" with a "heteronomy of instrumental and procedural rationalities" (124) in which the organization claims both agency and distributed ethics as "responsibility" is distributed elsewhere—that is, everywhere and nowhere (Thomson 2001, 14).

Similarly, principal and head of school/dean position descriptions and professional development focused on financial and human resource management, entrepreneurialism, and outcomes (Blackmore 2002c). Thomson (2001) maps how causal relations and agency were slipped over within such texts with benign statements such as "valid and reliable school level information on student's performance is collected regularly and reported to community," which was read by principals as "principals will ensure that teachers collect regular information on students' performance which they will then report to the community" (Thomson 2001, 12–13). Yet in the same text principals were exhorted to be democratic and nurture collegiality. There were significant internal tensions in these "heteroglossic" policy texts between performance management and teacher teaming, market curriculum and inclusive curriculum, student testing and student engagement (Thomson 2001). Likewise, heads of department and deans' position descriptions, now appointed not elected positions, were linked to strategic plans and performance management against a range of criteria in which academic leadership was one of many key performance indicators. Management positions were retained if they met the measurable PIs (i.e., within budget, achieving targets in fund raising, maintaining standards in student evaluations, etc.) without regard to the types of behaviors (interpersonal and ethical) that were utilized with/against staff.

Such policy and organizational development and planning texts blurred any distinction between management as immediate maintenance work and the CEO as operations and problem solver, and leadership as long-term vision work with the CEO as the catalytic change agent. Leader/managers were "expected to actively shape themselves in the likeness of prevailing cultural and social models" (Hatcher 2003, 392); be life-long learners who developed a personal management style but who could also refashion themselves to meet organizational needs, disregarding personal ethics; and being constantly appraised by others in discussions over strategic plans, priorities, and performance indicators. Managers were now the key to the corporate heart, and they must be open to corporate values to be successful. In so doing, the multiplicities of logics, rationalities, and techniques induced them to self-regulate about what is permissible to do and say. Managers were simultaneously disciplined, but also encouraged, to shape themselves as individuals, as "works of art" (Hatcher 2003, 393).

The decade was also marked by a shift from a dialogical to a decisional process of reform, with TAFE moving more rapidly than universities and schools into new modes of contractualism in their relations with staff, students, and industry (Brown et al. 1996). Internally, decisional modes positioned leaders differently in relation to their colleagues. During the 1980s, there had been a sense that academics and teachers were "co-participants in the shaping and implementation of educational reforms in that they asserted their professional status as a way of contesting managerial prerogatives which took the form of bureaucratic regulations" (Brown et al. 1996, 314). By contrast, the reforms of the 1990s were imposed decisional processes seeking to ensure accountability, with little consultation with constituent groups, and decisions based on economic criteria. Previously, teacher unionists, academics, and feminists who had previously opposed the paternalistic bureaucracy in the name of education professionalism, had been included, even if marginally, in policy production within an increasingly responsive bureaucracy (e.g., femocrats—see chapter 10) during the 1980s. Such constituencies were now excluded from policy forums that were often dominated by business. Educational policy was fast becoming a field distinct from that of educational practice. At the same time, a perceived theory-practice divide meant academics were exhorted to become more relevant (i.e., practical, vocational, and less theoretical), as in the United Kingdom (Gunter 2000); and schools were expected to be more relevant to students and the workplace. Relationships among universities, schools, and TAFE sectors were also being contractualized and profit driven, with schools paying TAFE for new vocational education programs and some TAFE institutes integrated administratively into universities or linked through credit transfers and course articulation initiatives.

So there was a politicization of education policy at the same time there was a depoliticization of education as a field of practice. "For principals [and heads of school/departments and deans] to act as moral subjects, then, as is it urged by many of those who are engaged in the textual practices of compartmentalization (implicated in the removal of face and ethical agency), they must find and use resources that are outside the dominant amoral disciplinary managerial discursive formation" (Thomson 2001, 15). In what follows we present some vignettes to illustrate how aspects of restructuring were experienced and acted upon not as a discrete activity, but from a perspective that recognizes that organizations work in relation to other agencies, interlacing gender and labor and that despite the desire to "neutralize the organizational subject's moral impulses" that the women as managerial actors, in mediating the new arrangements, drew from other sources to assume ethical positions (Thomson 2001; Dempster and Mahoney 1998; Gold et al. 2003).

CONTEXT AND THE CONSTRUCTION
OF THE SELF-AS-LEADER

Restructuring through multiple reforms mobilized simultaneously across organizations produced curriculum change, industrial relations reform, and organizational restructuring, marked by a sharpening divide between the policy actors that produced education policy reforms (politicians, consultants, bureaucrats) and the practitioner actors expected to implement them (teachers, academics, managers). While different fields of educational practice were also productive of particular leadership identities, our study indicated that these shared processes of restructuring produced new contexts that "change because people are actively making and remaking their worlds, their contexts" (Seddon 1994, 5). Wider sociological understandings of restructuring, or for that matter gender, class, and race are never understood as such. Rather we "experience contextual change in an integrated way as an array of contradictory problems, issues, pressures and demands to deal with. We understand context from a position of immersion because 'we are part of the context' and experience it from a particular standpoint" (Seddon 1994, 5). The women leader/managers in our study were managing downsizing, amalgamations, casualization, and staff redeployment at the same time that they were expected to fit with stereotypical notions of women's ways of leading as being caring and democratic.

In schools, the performing principal of the self-managing school was meant to be both entrepreneurial and responsive to cultural diversity. Julie was an assistant principal of a P–12 inner-city school with high cultural mix and low SES. Her leadership was shaped by the constantly changing conditions within her school and also wider education, social policies, and political ideologies. Her leadership habitus, as a first-generation Italian immigrant, was well suited to this local community as she understood what it felt like to be "different" from others at school. Her imagined community for the school was "invented" through developing a shared vision with her staff, students, and parents and acted upon accordingly. Julie encouraged her students and teachers to be advocates for the school, to realize that their actions represented the school and created a public image, and that students as teachers were under scrutiny. In so doing, she was well aware of the games of a highly competitive local public and private education market and the media focus on failure and crisis.

Julie's school was located near public housing apartments where many refugees with no English language or schooling would be located on arrival. School numbers would rise and fall regularly depending on federal immigration policies and state government housing and welfare policies, as well as the flux and flow of the local education market in which her school was seen to be closely allied with public housing, poverty, and a nearby street renowned for drug dealers. The school and its teachers became highly adaptive and responsive to a breadth of student and parental needs, providing, for example, a language center that offered literacy programs that many parents attended. When the flow of refugees stopped, she created a Rudolf Steiner program with local parents within the school. A work education annex was part of the school that met the needs of students at risk who had disengaged from the academic curriculum. She gained such institutional flexibility to constantly renew the school profile by renting buildings on her school site emptied by declining enrollments. Even so, reduced government funding restricted her capacity to provide the full range of support programs needed. The community parents were in the main poor, many not speaking English, most not comfortable with schools. Her leadership "capacity" was thus shaped by multiple policy frames, location, demographics, and "self-management," but she was judged primarily on academic outcomes and numbers.

TAFE leaders were also expected to be highly attuned to industrial needs, entrepreneurial opportunities, and marketing promotion. Historically bureaucratic, old hierarchies in the larger metropolitan and small, rural TAFEs were reinvented in the guise of new corporate management practices, while smaller or newer TAFEs were more open to new structures. Declining funding intensified the push for new sources of funds, and the competency-based curriculum reforms of the 1990s required innovative program development. In some institutions, this provided new opportunities for women's transition from teaching into management. It also marked a shifting in leadership habitus from the margins where the focus had been on "social rescue, holistic education and social justice" (Seddon 1994, 2). For Alice, in a large, metropolitan TAFE, the irony was that it was a particularly macho leadership that provided opportunities for her as an individual woman to become a manager. But the same hierarchical environment framed the way in which she was able to work in ways that denied other women similar opportunities:

> The commitment from the executive team has always been demonstrated through the male model that I hate. So I suppose we have been able to empower, to create policy and initiatives that are going to better the institute and sort of do it in a hard, masculine fashion. . . . [I]n a way the executive looked to us to show that leadership because they want us to get quality awards. But there is also a dependency relationship due to the hierarchical environment: "You show us how we have to manage our department. You know the right way in order for this alignment to occur." [You have to] display good leadership qualities, be respected across the institute . . . I've got enough leadership ability to at least get people to follow. Whether they agree or don't agree is another thing.

Here, the executive relied upon the relationships of trust Alice had built up with her colleagues and her knowledge of the institute to undertake change management that tightly limited her discourse and actions within the managerialist and market frame.

There was a significant shift around leadership habitus in universities directly affected by federal education policies. Universities have traditionally been globalized in terms of their students, professional networks, and knowledge production. The academy conjures up the image of a community of scholars and public intellectuals, self-governing collectives appealing to notions of collegiality, consensus decision making, academic autonomy, and common ideals. Women academics have long been cynical about such idealizations, seeing the academic culture historically more as a closed shop or club run by male professors. Discourses of collegiality were often more a democratic veneer to obfuscate quite hierarchical relationships in which women continue to be in a position of structural and discursive subordination (Harley 2003; Morley 1999). Indeed, although feminism and feminists had challenged dominant intellectual hierarchies, the female presence rarely intruded into male managerial bastions during the 1990s. Women had gained limited advancement up the organizational hierarchy during the 1980s through the committee systems of academic boards. But restructuring after 1987 captured mythical notions of institutional autonomy, collegiality, peer review, and professional critique, at the same time that executive power was reasserted through line management rather than traditional academic structures. Vertical managerial hierarchies and a horizontal management/academic split were emerging, exacerbating any academic predispositions toward competitive individualism and now mediated by a new layer of executive policy advisors (Marginson and Consindine 2001, 10–11; Currie, Thiele, and Harris 2002).

The traditional conceptualizations of intellectual leadership founded on teaching, research, and scholarship; of professional leadership; and, in particular, of professorial authority (even if masculinist) were under challenge, an ironic realignment of power given women's late entrée into authority. The role of dean and head of school/department rapidly moved to a budgetary and planning role, marketing more so than academic leadership. Paula, Utech dean, said, "The leadership that you're looking for in heads of school these days has changed enormously because of the change in the role in the last five years. When I came in it was very much academic leadership. Now more of the administrative work is devolved down, but I have less time to do either. I try to maintain my academic leadership within my area."

But for some individual women the rise of the managerial "class" was fortuitous. Given the difficulties in acquiring an unbroken good academic record, particularly in the colleges of advanced education, a move into management after amalgamations out of academic work was advantageous as administrative experience, competence, and a profile as institutional change agent were the main criteria. For one vice-chancellor, such a move was an easy choice given her circumstances at the time of restructuring in 1987:

> Even prior to 1987 when it didn't matter whether you had a PhD, I was far too old and far too busy. All the jobs I had early on in the 1980s were major academic administrative ones. It wasn't feasible to be doing a PhD. I barely

managed a masters degree because I lacked time with four kids. I was doing lots of external stuff that I thought was really important. I think I have a good policy mind, and that's why I moved onto the national committees and stuff.

Deans and heads of school dealt with the conflicts arising from the differing organizational cultures within and across campuses in amalgamated institutions, while trying to promote a more entrepreneurial culture and international redirection for survival.

[Y]es a number of things are having to change . . . with some quite major rationalizations. But the hardest thing was that nearly all the staff trained here in the old CAE. So we've all come through the same teaching mould. Whilst a number of us have worked in other universities they still come back to the fact that what we do works very well, so why do you want to dismantle it? But we need an international reputation. (Paula, dean of health, Utech)

Overall, there was a marked "shift away from notions of service leadership in which senior administrative officers service academic work, to where the senior administrative officers take on considerable autonomy and decision making which directly shapes academic work" (Middlehurst 1993, 92–93). Academics in particular noticed the marginalization of the academic voice in the "lean and mean university" as membership on committees was increasingly based on functionality rather than on representativeness, while line-management committees sprang up creating parallel but powerful budgetary decision-making processes as if academic matters (policy) and financial management could be separated. Meanwhile the operational was left to middle management, where "concentration on the operational leaves discussion, debates and the framing of educational social and cultural matters to others" (Thomson 2001, 13).

This shift to executive prerogative, which altered institutional power relations within schools, TAFE, and universities, was exacerbated by the new accountability mechanisms such as performance management based on supervisor-subordinate roles. The corporate ethos had severe effects for the academic habitus, grounded as it is in notions of academic and individual freedom as well as the "right of voice" within the academic community. While there has always been a tension between individual autonomy and operational decision-making, it was now made transparent. Janette commented how being head of school in the climate of a Utech with all its imperatives and demands had changed her practices:

I feel very uncomfortable doing some of the things I'm asked to do. They are neither good feminist practice nor good democratic practice. On the other hand, I think democracy is an over-rated thing. It is so hard to wait to go through those processes. The more I'm in the job, the more I short circuit process. I put the information out and say, "Come and volunteer." When they don't, I pick my committee. I would have been contemptuous in the extreme of that as a management practice, but it's the only way to get things done.

Like the VCs and directors, the school principalship had been traditionally positioned as embodying both the academic/educational and administrative aspects of leadership. But the privileging of efficiency and effectiveness over academic/educational values brought the normative and operational domains in conflict. Our leader/managers brought their own cultural capital, a professional and leadership habitus, to work within a rapidly changing organizational milieu. Drawing from their own experience, discourses of leadership were called upon to counter some of the more detrimental effects of managerialism. Leadership was enacted as attending to content, process and outcome, democratic process, and participatory decision making where possible, about listening to stakeholders, being seen to be fair, and in particular, effectively communicating ideas and decisions. But principals, as heads of school and departmental heads, found dialogic communication often did not count for much and could often potentially count against them as being "ineffective" as democracy works against demonstrations of "corporate loyalty."

EDUCATION AS PASSIONATE WORK

Educational management during this time became a new field in which different games were played with their own inherent logic and "truths." Players who wished to stay in the game to some degree acceded to these logics of practice, partially or fully. This often required individual leaders to forget how the field was constituted in which educational ideas were privileged. Leaders "learnt the rules of the game, the strategic moves necessary, the particular dispositions ranging from anticipating policy directions, manoeuvring to gain advantage, consistently reassuring other players, while recognizing the need to be persistent, coolheaded, multilingual, to work long hours and make judgments about what can wait and what is urgent" (Thomson 1999, 78).

A central theme throughout the interviews was the strong commitment to education, not only for its vocational but also for its intrinsic value, as a democratic practice and a vehicle for social change. This passion for educational work permeated through any discussions about educational reform and change and informed individual stances taken toward leadership. Most women interviewed articulated a clear sense of purpose that went beyond their individual advancement, as Hilary (EO manager, Utech) commented that "the greatest pleasure is gained from setting something up and seeing it happen, taking up an issue, fighting it through the various systems, getting it into policy. I really enjoy the work. I have a passion for it and a commitment to it." This passion for teaching, leading, and research emerged in most discussions about preferences, choices, and opportunities and was closely linked to professional identity. Institutional promotion was structured so that many of these women were torn between their pleasure in teaching, leading, and research and their desire to move into management positions that provided a capacity for wider change. Those who did tended to be equally passionate about initiating, promoting, and managing change in ways that supported teaching, learning, and research.

Pleasure was gained not just from reforming but vicariously from the institution and colleagues performing well. "The faculty has done extremely well in the quality rounds. Employers' surveys of new graduates have been very positive. We have increased numbers of research students. The academic staff are working together to achieve goals" (Alida, dean, redbrick). Another dean agreed that her reward was "seeing the staff do well, seeing the school perform well, and getting good feedback from employers" (Paula, Utech). Our womanagers referred to the "endless pleasure of seeing my staff achieving. I love to see change and the staff doing it themselves" (Justine, TAFE); from "getting positive feedback" (Sally, rural TAFE); from "traveling with the job, new projects, learning about them, selling them" (Leanne, large, metropolitan TAFE), while enjoying "the autonomy, the ability to make decisions, to take action, to see things through, and watching people grow and develop creative ideas" (Uta, community-oriented, suburban TAFE). For Joan (manager, large, suburban TAFE) it was about "establishing and maintaining a good reputation for the institute as well as achieving things and having them recognized." For these women, the pleasure came from the capacity to change things for the better; from communicating what was happening and why; from nurturing good relationships with students and colleagues; or from producing a new program that met community, student, or industry needs, that is, making a difference.

The discourse was often one of care, but increasingly about quality and service to industry and student needs, both markers of distinction in competitive markets. Quality was understood as process and product, but also quality in relationships within a nurturing culture. Good management, therefore, was integral to being able to lead. It was the base upon which they could articulate and justify their actions as "it's not just about administration; it's about educational leadership and making sure that everything is good for teaching" (Alida, TAFE). Some work to reform how management was done and understood, as articulated by Shirley (head of school, Utech)

What I enjoy most is the team stuff and working with people . . . building a new culture, breaking down this nonsensical, frustrating notion that management is different. "Management are us"; we are management. We need to promote the understanding that management is trying to help. We are there because we believe. We are there to set a context and an environment for people to achieve, recognize things come into fruition, actually playing a role in developing an institution that is really exciting. There was such a mystery about how decisions were made. It is a great pleasure to make certain they can get on with being academics, do their research, creative work, work with the big picture.

Leadership was about providing support, imparting a sense of agency to others through encouragement and resourcing initiatives, promoting good personal relations and productive spaces for research and teaching. This meant teaching others about leading and sharing the responsibility to act. According to Jane, manager in a small, progressive, suburban TAFE, "The experienced staff have to be able to assist their staff to do the job. I've seen too many managers take on projects and tell their staff to go off and do it and then when it comes down to delegate work they can't. I expect my staff to write a research paper or to manage a project that involves developing learning materials to teach." Working with others in teams was significant for many but not all. Ingrid stated that "I love my work; I am very locked into a community. I'm one of a team of three, sharing my experiences and expertise and all the social pleasures of coming to work" (large, metropolitan TAFE). And central to this pleasure was sharing ideas and experiences that focused on learning. Cathy, a leading teacher in a small, working-class secondary school, said that "what I love about teaching is watching some of the women here talk about learning. They really care about how is it the child learns and how the child gets better at learning."

Formal leadership higher up the institution, particularly in universities and TAFE, imparted an authority to "manage" and to change, an overview that was exciting and broadened their sense of what the institution was about within the local and global context. A dean (Utech) reflected on the sense of "extreme pleasure when you carry the group along with you where everybody feels as if they've got something out of it. The power is nice. . . . [I]t's wonderful, and I mean seductive, and you know you can make things happen. I really like being up with the executive management group and making long-term strategies." Anne Marie, dean (redbrick) stated, "I do like to influence policy. Being in management you can effect something far longer than your own lifetime." Leesa, also a dean, described how she was "setting a national and international policy, so I'm making a difference at every level. Also [you have] great control over where your contribution is, [which is] not possible in a conventional academic role—being able to set up your own small unit and hand pick staff, with the autonomy to do different types of work from what has previously been known by the university" (Utech). Infused throughout these commentaries, particularly among deans and above in universities, was a sense of a capacity to direct, influence, organize, mobilize resources, and set their own agendas. Power was gained through information, on "seeing how others and the institution worked' (Jill, acting dean, Utech). Enjoying problem solving, moving into different fields, and facing challenges motivated many, a common statement being "I love a challenge and get bored easily." Professors or project managers in TAFE promoting research or development in their specific area of expertise gained pleasure from learning to play the game: "My job is satisfying, rewarding, and challenging. It is always interesting to see if you can outwit the opposition and out maneuver them" (Elle, EO manager, sandstone). Some womanagers were seeking to be more transgressive in leadership. Leesa, an associate dean of engineering (Utech) enjoyed "trying out different management models, to challenge the status quo"; others gained satisfaction from the mundane "committee work . . . where you can go in and do it and get out a sense of completion. I still get that excited feeling about finding out about new things just at a personal level. I enjoy staff development, working on committees, making sure that they are going to make a difference to people, support people" (Utech). The dominant discourse in each sector was about energy and significant investment in getting things done, that at first glance was highly instrumentalist and pragmatic in the focus on the "how" rather than the "why" and "with what effect." Gabriella (manager, large, metropolitan TAFE) laughed about how "I'm a doer, I make things happen. Staff say I'm exhausting to watch and work for." Likewise, Shona, director of a regional TAFE stated: "I've got a taste for management, I like opening new ground and starting things up. The experience of opening a new college has just been wonderful. I've started a lot of things in my working life, and that's a privilege, a sense of pride in how they have developed. I really enjoy solving the problems. Also when you're working with good people, and they're going forward, you can clear the path and help them go even better." In that sense, women were good corporate citizens.

PURPOSIVE LEADERSHIP

While some women managers were more open to meeting organizational objectives and enthusiastic as indicated above, sometimes uncritically, others were more resistant to imposed reforms, usually because they felt the changes would not benefit their students or colleagues, improve learning, or produce more equitable outcomes—the litmus tests against which they judged new policies. While these women had a sense of purpose that often differed from the organization, they also sought to support and persuade others to work collectively to achieve that purpose. When asked further about why they sought to change things, many teachers and academics argued that they sought to "promote equity," "to make a difference," to give the "best opportunities for all," or to "improve society." For Elle, an EO manager in a sandstone university, motivation arose from a strong sense of politics and desire for social justice: "But my interest had been for many years in the theoretical aspect of gender equity. Because I'm a political animal it was logical for me to find my way into affirmative action type work. When I was teaching I was doing a lot of political stuff. . . . [B]eing an academic was not purely just being a teacher and researcher; it was political."

Leadership for many women was accompanied by a sense of responsibility to act, summed up by Julie, principal of a working-class, multicultural school. "I feel a great sense of responsibility. I've got two hundred little kids. If anything that we do as teachers makes it a slight difference to their lives I feel OK. I think my teachers understand that if they give me 100 percent of their working life, only their working life, I don't want to know about what happens after work. I'm a hard taskmaster when it comes to slacking off."

A critical mass of newly promoted women in senior management in a small, progressive TAFE now contemplated, according to Lesley, "whether or not collective support mechanisms are established because of the oppressions of this male-dominated organization. We are in this interesting position where that's been rolled, . . . and the potential to make a difference is now on us. There is a real shift in terms of recognition that there is no 'they' any more." For some, promotion into management provided space for resistance as well as reform. "I always classify myself as an accidental academic. I did research because it was important, but my great love and life is teaching. But then I recognized that we definitely needed people up at the higher level where the decisions were made, who would argue for those who did love teaching, and felt that it's an important [part] of university work" (Anne Marie, dean, Utech).

But, as one dean jokingly commented, to resist or overtly promote equity was dangerous, for example, by raising issues of equity in management spaces: "Yes, I raise the principle of fairness and equity all the time, and they're now used to it in executive . . . but it is tough on you all the time to do so" (Paula, Utech). The capacity for her to argue from a principled position was strategic because she carefully aligned it with institutional profiles and objectives, exploiting the discourse of performativity to shift the focus, practices, and policies toward equity (Gold et al. 2003). But it also meant that "in this profession, a lonely, isolated struggle against inequality is the requirement and cost of professional success" for her (Chase 1995, 33). The issue was whether and where to invest energy and activity, when to resist, and when to accommodate, what feminists would call "revolutionary pragmatism" (Ashcraft and Mumby 2004, 57). This position indicated a level of reflexivity and intentionality, asking why this should occur and with what effect. But not all who argued for social justice did so from a feminist position. Barbara indicated her ambivalence toward feminism, rejecting any dependence on feminism as a movement, but agreeing with its principles.

> I guess I am very strong in support of . . . perhaps *feminist* is too strong a word . . . equality and the rights of people. Where I don't see myself as a feminist is that I always reckon I could stand up for myself in the system. I believe that women should have equal rights, and sometimes we need to be enabled to gain those, which is really a feminist point of view. . . . [Y]ou have to actually believe there is some systemic disadvantage, which a lot of people don't. (Principal, working-class secondary school with high cultural mix)

Leadership was like a "web of associations, inclusive, emergent, and flexible . . . transformational and interactive . . . in which they invoke personal bases of authority to stimulate participation, share power and inform and enhance others' sense of self worth and energy" (Ashcraft and Mumby 2004, 5). But this passionate identification with leadership work often became all consuming, creating a vulnerability and energy readily appropriated for organizational purposes. Once in formal management positions, many experienced feelings of discomfort and ambivalence and sought to modify and negotiate their official responsibilities in line with their own sense of professional purpose and identity or drew upon their leadership habitus to counter systemic dispositions toward control rather than collegiality, by resorting to dialogical communication, and converting surveillance into support. This process of situated negotiation was made evident in a number of ways: how they treated colleagues, worked in teams, and delegated authority. But at the core was the leader's own personal ethical position and integrity characterized by "consistency and dependability, moral and intellectual honesty, with beliefs and values in evidence in day to day operation" (Bone 1997, 24). This integrity generated trust and was expressed in "fairness, magnanimity, belief in others, and commitment" (Bone 1997, 24). As summed up by a deputy principal talking about her principal:

> What is seen as being a good principal is probably not the things the Department would like to see. She cares about people and has a social conscience. She tries to involve people in decision making. She is not about power, and she cares about curriculum and providing school leadership. She is not on about "You do as I say," although there are occasions where that is necessary, and she will do that too. And that is what I like; she does it when a decision has to be made, and other times she will consult. What is being pushed at the moment is "We are going to make these principals separate people.". But we are educators first and foremost, and that is the reason we are here; we are here for the kids not to keep pushing their stuff from above. I like the fact that Christine has strong principles, and she is a feminist, she stands up for women.

While cultural practices in corporate organizations socialize people to acquire certain dispositions, how they are formed relies upon desire as well as practical reason, as social practices are based on recognition, respect, and deliberation. "Private and public deliberation can lead to changes in individuals' dispositions . . . but any revision of beliefs and desires is made explicit through public conceptions of legitimacy and authority. Reflective agency is not only about changing beliefs and desires but also the social conditions under which agents reflect and deliberate" (Bohman 1999, 148).

POWER/AUTHORITY

Leadership is undeniably about exercising multiple modes of power and influence through networks, rules, regulations, and systemic authority, as well as individual capacity to develop, synthesize, communicate, and enact ideas, and to motivate, persuade, and nurture others to adopt particular practices. Power is exercised variously: through systems and by individuals through influence and persuasion, consent and coercion, consciously and unconsciously, through the exertion of authority and relationships of trust, without a source. Yet in corporate educational organizations, while the discourse was about the visionary leader/manager as the catalyst and creator of cultures, the reality was that managers' formal authority imparted the right to manage. How power and authority were understood and exercised was therefore central to both leadership and managerial habitus. Women moving into management positions were often bemused by how they were perceived as suddenly "possessing power" and how corporate structures changed their relationships with others in particular ways. Colleen elaborates on this:

> Sometimes I am shocked by it, when parents refer to you as powerful. With the latest developments and higher duties performance review processes, I think I'm a bit scared because I believe relationships that used to be able to exist in open democratic schools as one of the gang [have] ended. I'm seen by parents and staff as the boss, the ticker off, the person that will hire or fire. I think that with power comes aloofness that separates. (Colleen, principal, small, working-class, culturally mixed secondary college)

Because of their reluctance to assume power indicated by Colleen's apprehension, many womanagers resorted to their own well-rehearsed leadership practices, depicted here by Nicol, assistant principal, small, rural primary school).

> A good leader has to set a good example, number one. They have to be able to do and carry out all the things they are expected in the school; they have to be good teachers; they have to get on well with children; be a good com-

municator, honest and direct; they need to give praise where it's due; they need to make hard decisions and be able to stand by their decisions. But the decisions need to be based on principles. Empathy as well as consistency, so that you know where you stand, not how that person will be today, what sort of mood they're in. Be personable. Put the job into perspective and [be] realistic in their expectations of their staff.

Much of their credibility as managers was gained from their prior understandings about how to work through the emotional issues of change, their professionalism, and the trust they had earned from colleagues. They understood what motivated educators to change their practices, and they mobilized those discourses that tapped into their own and others' personal and professional desires. Leadership was the exercise of influence through ideas, sometimes but not always through force of personality and not necessarily arising from status or position. Margaret expressed the view that she could make a difference because they were not just managers with particular authorities, "but the real issue is leadership: it is a more difficult issue; it's a bit more nebulous; it wanders around; it's not as easy to pin down. People will react to you differently for a whole lot of personality factors. But at the end of the day, I don't think I could do my proper job, without dealing with leadership things" (small, progressive, suburban TAFE). Influence came more through trust and not positional authority.

The institutional authority that they derived from their new role, therefore, was a surprise to many. Their skeptical attitude to the formal authority was evident in their preference not to use its coercive possibilities, emphasizing referent and expert power, not authoritative power. But there was a form of splitting, between how they were represented as powerful and how they wished to represent themselves. Clara, an assistant principal who had been acting principal in regional secondary schools observed:

> Power, I think, is in the minds of other people. I see myself more as having a set of aims, visions, whatever you want to call them, that are connected with charter goals for the college. And we sort those out as a college. It's really an empowering and enabling process to bring the staff and the community on side so that we're achieving our goals that we've set. So if that's power, then I suppose it is, but I don't really perceive it as power.

An assistant principal in a primary school felt that "in some circumstances I do feel powerful. I prefer to see myself as someone that works with other people. I think in this position there is a responsibility to give leadership, but there are occasions when it is just authority." For Margaret in a small, progressive, suburban TAFE, power was gained collectively, by working together. It was "a job to be done rather than power." Natalie, a regional secondary school principal, considered that "power is getting things done for the benefit of the school. If it hadn't been me, it would have been someone else. I just happened to be there."

But management also facilitated an overview of the organization that many women would not have as academics or teachers. Power was derived from this knowledge of knowing how to work within the wider institution and a sense of its complexity. It also brought significant personal learning for some, like Lesley, who was "now privy to what's happening at the corporate level and working very closely with the CEO. I am conscious now of things in the broader perspective that I wasn't when I was working only within the Human Resource Development unit" (small, progressive, suburban TAFE). Some saw this knowledge as an additional responsibility. Jane, manager in a small, progressive TAFE felt she was "extremely powerful. It means passing on new information I've gained, especially if I can save a bit of pain, assist people to carry out their job using my experience. But it's important to me to know what is important to other people."

Positional authority also increased the scope of their leadership relative to others. Dianne, a dean (sandstone) observed: "In this position, I've got four thousand students, and several hundred staff, five hundred academic and general staff. I've got all the resources and power. Obviously you consult and do all the rest of it. And I also have a lot of influence at the center in terms of what stuff comes down. So, I do definitely feel powerful within my area. I think I am listened to." Such power was to be acted upon, but carefully. Power used positively meant being able to listen, recognize, and rectify mistakes and to provide a rationale for decisions when possible. Paula, a head of school, commented about her VC "that she'll listen to you and you can choose when you disagree. But I'm also most impressed with her academic pull. A student can stand up and disagree with something she's put up, and she'll listen. She'll say, "Yes I agree with you. I'll take that back and redo it." I am very impressed with a senior person who would do that" (Utech).

Authority came with the position, but there was no automatic redistribution of power to the incumbent, as power was also embodied. With restructuring, redistribution of jobs meant loss for many men in power. "Men have to lose authority, and women have to gain it. Women have to work hard for people to take them seriously, whilst men are automatically credited with authority" (vice-chancellor). And some, such as Jeanette, enjoyed managerial power and did not feel constrained by that: "I've become comfortable with using the position of power. I expect people to do as I say. I feel powerful and I am comfortable with that" (head of school, redbrick). But while women were learning to enjoy power, they could not make that known publicly, both because as institutional leaders they could not acknowledge the unequal distribution of power, and as women they could not admit to enjoying power. Jean, an EO manager in a Utech said:

At a presentation I talked about difficulties arising from the gendered context of being a woman in a relatively powerful position in a university. Afterwards I was criticized for it because it wasn't a good role model. I should have just shown myself to be happy and powerful and happy in my power: you're meant to make it; you're meant to look after women when you've made it, and then you're meant to tell lies about it and say it's not hard.

While recognizing this right to manage, and sometimes being prepared to wield this acquired authority, the preference of most women was to work through persuasion, networks, sharing decisions, and imparting ownership where possible. And in turn, institutional and personal power was wielded by others in relation to them, which they accommodated in some instances and resisted in others. The relations of power are therefore simultaneous processes of resistance, reproduction, and transformation. Many of our educational managers, while disagreeing with dominant managerial discourses, were framed by them. They therefore used discursive strategies to reappropriate meaning, by, for example, tapping into managerial and market discourses about responsiveness to promote equity, or quality discourses to push for improved teaching, and in so doing to "work against demoralizing institutional technologies by tactically taking up submerged and lesser discourses, mobilizing other aspects of the 'non-unitary' self" (Thomson 2001, 15).

PERFORMANCE AND MANAGING
THE "EMBODIED" PUBLIC SELF

The dispositions of the high-achieving woman, therefore, suited the new push for management, organizational change, and accountability. But the service ethic of women, together with the critical element of self-centeredness, and their identification of their success or failure with that of the organization, made these women highly vulnerable. This was "the irony, ambiguity and contradiction in gender-work relations" arising from "the connections between micro-level communicative processes and macro-level discursive, political and economic forces" (Ashcraft and Mumby 2004, 120). As Bone (1997) comments, the strengths of women in such circumstances also have deficits. First, in the type of psychological and physical stamina required, the constant debate, ambiguity, and uncertainty. If one adds to that, as was the case for many women leaders in our study, the desire for perfectionism and over-heightened sense of individualism, where self-esteem was "linked to the seductive sense of being needed. The capacity for selectivity and prioritising required to maintain effective performance may be jeopardized" (24). Second, the desire for some women to make a stand on ethical issues led to high levels of anxiety. Third, while organizations promised that merit was the tool for the distribution of work, for many women it soon became evident that there was no meritocracy as "competence was not an absolute defence against organizational or gender politics" (Skrla 2003, 116). Some women spoke of cases of discrimination, being ignored and left out of decision making.

So these leadership identities were fragile when identified with the "new managerial practices and performance expectations." This led to two psychosocial responses, often felt simultaneously—a sense of being outside the track and lacking in confidence to meet performance requirements and therefore vulnerable; and inside the track "exemplifying the new corporatist values, but in a defensive rigidity that renders their identities as vulnerable and problematic" (Saunderson 2002, 398). Casey refers to a range of defences among workers in corporate organizations: the abandonment of self, the adoption of the colluded self, or the mismatched self who continues to adopt oppositional positions to the dominant culture and for whom there is little future. No such clear-cut distinction was experienced by these women, who felt they were colluders one moment and oppositional the next, sometimes compliant in the short run but subversive in the long run. All agreed self-management was the key to the job. Being seen to be able to perform, promote, and persuade others above and below were valuable attributes to the organization. Promotion of self was also central to the managerial habitus of the performative culture. Jane considered that

> in our educational institution 50 percent of your time must be spent attending the necessary committees, writing the necessary papers, and promoting yourself to your managers to enhance promotional chances. Women are not good at that: they have to be more aggressive, more assertive. People who spend a lot of time and who achieve a certain amount of recognition on process-related things get promoted. (Small, progressive, suburban TAFE)

Managerial habitus was a not just enacted, but also embodied, as a constant presence at work for long hours, in the use of space, and with regard to appearance and bodily display. The body is a "conceptualization of corporeality," which links both the "surface" features of physical performance and the "depth" features of emotion, desire, and anxiety (Brooks and MacKinnon 2001, 16). Dress was critical to credibility and image for women in leadership. The women interviewees, in middle and particularly those in executive management, had, in the main, a carefully nurtured elegance and subtle femininity. Each made conscious decisions about what she wore and why. A newly appointed senior executive of a university commented about "how I have markedly changed the way I dress. I consciously make sure that I'm well dressed, have makeup on, and look as though I'm on top of things, because I know people are watching, and I know, in general, that women's clothing signals more than men's." She dressed in light, bright clothes to stand out from the crowd of business men and politicians (and indeed academics). She also quickly realized that "height is an advantage: I never go and speak at a conference without wearing high heels. I quite deliberately make myself tall, to get noticed, to stand out." An executive manager spoke of how her sense of body permeated what she did and how she did it: "We get noticed for what we wear and judged on it, and whatever I wear will be interpreted one way or the other. I did wear red for my interview so I look like I'm out being powerful. I don't have a big voice, I'm not a tall person, so I just sort of try to bolster my confidence by dressing up" (Margaret, small, progressive, suburban TAFE).

"Dressing up," a sometimes pleasurable aspect of these leading women's lives, had less predictable effects on others. As exemplars to aspirant leaders, they were extraordinary in every way—their performance, their appearance, and their tenacity. Neat and subdued dress, style, and manner clearly were indicative of a "managerial habitus" that was an expression of control and competence. One senior lecturer aspiring for promotion spoke of attending a course to improve her dress and posture in order to be seen to be promotable and able to perform publicly. But for those at the top, particularly those seen to be feminist, there was a fine line between feeling presentable and feeling comfortable and desirable. One DVC commented: "I was irritated the other day when I was asked to do a press conference suddenly. I would have felt better dressed in a suit with lapels than in casual pants. It's not that I want to look fantastic all the time. . . . [D]ressing frees me. It's not that I want to be attractive to men. I just don't want to give them a chink of vulnerability about my gender identity or sexuality."

Other measures of self-control were expected of managers. Many of these women had been promoted because they were good communicators, able to build trust, influence, and persuade. But now

> I know that there is a level of discernment that is necessary for me to practice. That wasn't the case when I was lower in the pecking order. I know what I need to do in a change management role is to be a conduit for information, to check out what are the hot spots in the organization between departmental levels. And in order to maintain the relationships, it's important to give information as well as to get information, just so that you are not being seen as a spy, a CEO, going around amassing stuff, without sharing, without trust. . . . [But] I find that there are certain things I can't say to certain people. It is a tension for me, because I would like just to be able to tell everybody everything. (Lesley, small, progressive, suburban TAFE)

This required changing leadership habitus as her desire to inform was the product of "lifelong learning relationship formation and maintenance" (Ashcraft and Mumby 2004, 4). Amanda, principal of a regional secondary college, commented: "I believe good leaders have to be good communicators because perceptions are these days as important as realities. If you cannot communicate to people in such a way that they see you as honest, open, consultative, and inspirational, then they won't listen." Alice, a TAFE middle manager, felt that she had to manage herself better in terms of what and how she said things because of her seniority, but she saw it less an issue about the appropriateness of information disseminated and more a matter of not being seen as a dissenter within management circles. "I try not to compromise. I've had to compromise a lot. I've had to bite my tongue. I've always been very outspoken, but I'm less so now." Recognized as a leader because of her capacity to speak up to power, she was now silenced once in power. The corporatization of the self was "a process of colonization characterized by repression and absorption" (Casey 1995, 150).

LEADERSHIP AS RELATIONAL AND ETHICAL WORK

Good management was the groundwork that facilitated the types of leadership practices the managers in our study favored. But managerialism as a logic of practice did not nurture the leadership habitus of these educators. Many struggled to reduce the distinction between managerial leadership (as denoted through their position and its associated responsibilities) and teacher leadership or academic leadership, as leadership should be about creating "a [school] community where there are many leaders" (Lingard et al. 2003, 20), where there are exchanges of ideas, space, and time for reflection and evaluation. Many of our participants continued to resist the managerial discourses informed by the rational purposive model of corporate management and its understandings of "best practice" focusing on efficiency and outcomes. Leadership was to them about process, substance, and relationships, about identity and relational work in many sites, across multiple fields of practice.

The dominance of managerial discourses was indicative of how the changing nature of the field of education arising from new public administration and neoliberal market philosophies was clearly shaping agency and leadership practices. The managerial discourse drew primarily from human capital theory and school effectiveness research, not that of the research literature on leadership, which does address, even if marginally, relational and ethical issues (Thrupp and Willmott 2003). Furthermore, the distinctive leadership habitus of each of the specific educational fields (academic habitus interlocked with hierarchies of knowledge and specialist expertise, teacher habitus linked to the duty of care, and vocational habitus associated with practical knowledge) were now converging into a common language and logic of practice of managerialism based on "generic attributes" of competence and compliance, entrepreneurialism and efficiency, which assume an appearance of neutrality. Thomson (2001, 15) argues that neither the impartiality of old professional bureaucracies nor the seeming neutrality of managerialism is appropriate with the politicization of education in current times, as "impartiality, particularly for principals [and other educational leaders] is as much an ethical liability as it is a strength." These women drew upon their own experience and ethical dispositions, their professional leadership habitus, and external sources as the discourses of management were lacking. The irony for women leaders was that in seeking to "belong" in educational management by adopting too uncritically the corporate logics of practice, they could lose the very subversive aspect of leadership that made it ethical and capable of deep-seated change.

EIGHT

Caught between Acts: Middle Managers Mediating Change Up and Down

---

Educators as knowledge workers, particularly in the public sector, are trapped in the paradoxes arising from competing logics of practice. They are expected to be "catalysts of knowledge production, counterpoints to threats of inclusiveness, security and public life in a residualized public sector," and as a consequence are casualties due to escalating expectations "being met with standardized solutions at minimum cost" (Hargreaves 2003, 3). Colleen (principal, working-class secondary school with high cultural mix in a low socioeconomic suburb) captures the challenge for middle managers in education mediating local/global relations: "We are expected to be change agents. Yet we are also managers of multiple crises being passed down the line on a daily basis." Middle managers continuously mediate competing institutional logics (market rationality, bureaucratic rationality, community obligations, professional commitment) about educational work and purpose. These competing discursive logics are "constructed through institutionalized practices and historical experiences which construct normative models of organizational legitimacy" (Townley 1997, 262). Despite the carefully manufactured strategic plans and policies of performative institutions, there is "no one institutional logic or monolithic environment; rather differentiated societal spheres, each with differing belief systems sustaining different types of social relations" (Townley 1997, 262). This chapter focuses on the changing practices of organizational change from the perspective of the female middle manager now mediating macro-/microrelations. The telling of such organizational tales has an "illustrative and heuristic value" (Zipin and Brennan 2003, 352).

PEOPLE MANAGEMENT: SOLUTION OR PROBLEM?

Whereas under industrial capitalism staffing was marginal to productivity and therefore of peripheral executive interest, in globalized postindustrial service and knowledge-based economies, productivity gains are to be achieved through managing people better by getting more for less. Despite optimistic "new wave" management discourses of a "deregulated" autonomy and team-work in flatter learning organizations, the educational reforms of the 1990s, we argue, were characterized by increased regulation, both internal and external, of educational labor in organizations, regulation that was process and out-come driven, not learning centerd. Women as the new "recruits" (David 2003) into middle management were confronted with tensions between professional and managerial habitus (chapter 7). The recruitment of educational professionals into management simultaneously encouraged an "internalization of control and the surveillance of professionals in education" through strategic planning, benchmarking, and performance management, while "turning senior professionals, who might be resistant to a loss of professional autonomy, into managers" (Gleeson and Shain 1999, 463).

Furthermore, our cohort was typical of an aspiring, well-educated, and enthused cohort of women being discursively and institutionally positioned as "change agents" (see chapters 6 and 7). Middle management was the first step to accessing power in preparation for more senior appointments, as "middle management actually is where the action is to a very large extent. And I really think that women have a huge amount to contribute in their interpersonal and organizational skills" (Dianne, dean, sandstone). Womanagers were therefore positioned as both good change agents *and* managers.[7] But their advancement accompanied a transfer of authority up to the persistently male-dominated executive level down to an increasingly feminized education workforce. This was a no win situation, for if women failed to succeed within predefined institutional terms it was their fault, and if they did succeed there are no obstacles anymore for women in general. Failure is individualized, and success is a product of a fairer society.

Middle managers managed up the line. This meant imagining and working within the global "big picture" in a "free market/strong state" scenario (Gleeson and Shain 1999, 464) according to parameters set by executive management and central bureaucracies. Their aim was the survival and success of the unit they managed and with which they and their success were identified. They also managed the everyday work practices and minutae of organizational detail required when distributing limited resources down the line. This ranged from counting the paper, faxes, negotiating leave, employing casual staff, and stretching people resources to meet a range of often contradictory but everincreasing demands for teaching, community work, research, and of course, administration. This was the "classic boundary position-between top management and departmental staff, moving in and between two different gendered cultures" (Hearn 2002, 171). They were also increasingly visible and vulnerable externally, expected to manage clients (students, parents, industry, and professional and community groups), as well as image (media, marketing) locally, nationally, and internationally. Renata, CEO of a large, metropolitan TAFE, associated the cultural restructuring of TAFE as requiring the process of responsibilization of all workers by distributing management downward through "the internalization of structural requirements and dominant rationalities" (Woods 2004, 11) to create a self-starting, self-managing, and self-evaluating worker.

> Well in this institution we're blessed with a huge number of senior women. . . . [A] greater number of the women probably had much better management skills than a lot of the men who have been accustomed to . . . traditional styles of management which are basically . . . "I'm the boss and you do as I tell you." . . . We're trying to break down this culture through team processes, working collaboratively, accepting responsibility for a greater range of issues, instead of waiting for somebody to tell you what to do . . . understanding your job clearly so that you can actually discharge your responsibilities. . . . We've tried to build a strong, collaborative culture. Responsibility has to be accepted at the level each person is at. If you're a teacher, you have certain responsibilities, and you have to ensure that you discharge them professionally, with sensitivity to your students and their needs, making sure you're properly prepared and that the quality is of a standard you're prepared to defend. We have very good men, but many are unable to take on the modern manager's role. (director, suburban TAFE)

"RESPONSIBILIZATION" AND THE DISPERSAL OF MANAGEMENT WORK

The seduction of management made it attractive to men and women alike when the opportunity arose to make a difference, to position their institution favorably, and to do new things (Avis 2002, 65). Ostensibly in control of others, exercising power, feeling powerful if not omnipotent meant management can provide quick if not instant satisfaction, a sense of a job well done, being proactive, and making changes; the more hectic the work environment, the more likely opportunities for instant gratification (Avis 2002). For most of the women in this study the seduction of the job was to try to do it differently (e.g., Court 1998, 2004), because they saw leadership and management as being about problem solving. Once there, they described the job as about managing serial crises. Identifying the problem was difficult due to the increased complexity and rapidity of change. "The solution" was often imposed from above regardless. In practice this thwarted attempts to "develop alternative perspectives, adjust interpretations, make sense of what is happening and use experience to reflect on cherished beliefs" (Cooper and Heck 1995, 198). There was also significant "role straining" given their professional habitus, as the job was less about leading teaching and research and more about "line management" (finance, industrial relations, markets). For many, it produced dichotomous thinking about whether they were administrators or teachers, producing the "presence of two deeply structured and mutually exclusive role definitions" (Bascia and Young 2001, 278).

Any opportunities for alternative conceptualizations were framed by institutional and government practices and policies. One effect of the recentring of executive power in government, education systems, and organizations was delayering. Professional knowledge workers found themselves carrying out all the activities of hierarchical control above and below them. This drive for responsibilization was increasingly imposed on teachers and academics, who bore the brunt of managing often irreconcilable demands. Helen, a senior lecturer (sandstone), expresses the extent of this:

> Overall, I think that research has been disrupted because of the amount of time you spend with administrivia. We have an extremely decentralized financial system where there is a one-line budget everything comes down to the department level. So that gets shared among staff members; there's an enormous amount of filling in forms and going to meetings. I think it's particularly bad where everything is devolved to the basic unit—there's no flexibility in budgeting because everything is allocated. . . . There's no moving of finances around because it's already allocated, and you live with it.

This downward dispersion of management tasks to be done more effectively with less money was a pervasive feature. Janice, an assistant principal in a rural secondary college commented on how increased administration led her to manage her work differently, invading private space and time:

"I like administration and teaching, and I'm struggling coping with both of them. . . . So I tend not to prepare and correct at school—it goes home and gets done at ten o'clock at night, after the ironing." Middle managers such as Alice, manager of a TESOL program in a large, suburban TAFE, had to manage the flow on effects of loss of tenders. Policy makers, bureaucrats, and executive managers did not see the "face" of "the other" (teacher and student) that might remind them of the consequences of such policies (e.g., loss of work for casual staff, poorer quality teaching) as devolution "rendered central decision-makers as morally neutral or indifferent" (Thrupp and Willmott 2003, 82).

Another feature of responsibilization was pseudodevolution as strategic control was retained at the center by establishing systems and procedures to control all aspects of reporting, thus reducing autonomy and discretion.

Despite discourses about being autonomous, the reality was that educational workers felt increasingly disempowered and dissatisfied, and this had to be managed. From the executive position, Renata, as a director of a large, metropolitan TAFE institute, also commented about her lack of control, with the shifts toward privatization and also the contradictory expectations placed on institutions with little capacity to improve.

> I have enormous frustration with national policy directions, the push to privatize the entire education system, and too big a focus on the bottom line. We can't meet the demand that our community has for courses, nor do we have the power to sack people for incompetence or obstruction. We are caught within the industrial relations framework that is centrally controlled and government directed. Nor do we have much authority to reward staff.

A third feature was to use competitive relations to manage reward systems within and between organizations. Government competitive tendering was replicated within institutions that forced departments to compete with, and charge, each other for services. The new contractualism facilitated staff reduction or downsizing, now a middle-management responsibility. Funds crises were resolved by not rehiring contract staff or employing sessional staff because there was no "contractual" obligation. In a "gum tree" university, one faculty that went into debt due to a change in central university policy about funding retirements did not renew contracts with twenty staff members in one year, eighteen of them women. While their expertise was required, they were the easiest to offload . This decision struck at the heart of the sociopsychic economy of the faculty as tenured academics felt guilt at retaining their jobs and sensed their own vulnerability. In a Victorian school, a leading teacher found it difficult to relate to and support the numerous contract staff because they had little future in a system that had not employed new permanent staff for years. In TAFE, sessional staff came and went, their absence not noticed.

Responsibilization was not mutual or reciprocal. Policy makers never had to come face to face with students or staff impacted by their decisions. Managers mediating these relations are forced to discuss these issues in technical rather than moral terms as contractual arrangements. Bauman (1993,127) suggests, "The totality of the moral subject has been reduced to the collection of parts or attributes. . . . [Actions can therefore be] targeted on specific traits of persons rather than persons themselves." In this context, managers became risk averse rather than risk taking, into decision avoidance (giving tenure) in terms of budgets, selection, and promotion so not to be "slapped" for financial mismanagement. "Middle level managers required significant savvy to stand up to such performative pressures. . . . It is thus understandable that at the habitus level, [they] would seek strategies for avoiding sanctions from above . . . as well as avoiding painful ethical self-questioning in fulfilling the dictates from above" (Zipin and Brennan 2003, 364). Systems reduced ethical considerations to contractual obligations, and procedural dispositions overwhelmed ethical ones, providing a way out. This dispersion of managerial responsibility, we have argued, was integral to the manufacture of consent and struggle over professionalism in each sector (see chapter 4).

POSITIONS, PERSPECTIVES, AND POSSIBILITIES

The storylines in our studies indicated variability according to seniority, sector, and institution. Our interviewees were located at the executive level (deans, directors, and principals), in middle management (principals, leading teachers, departmental heads, heads of school), and at the chalk face (teachers, academics, trainers). Three discourses about educational reform and organization emerged from the interviews that largely reflected this divide.

Looking Out

At the executive level, the women managers' discourse invoked notions of a strong corporate culture, collegiality and purpose, a clear sense of mission, working with teams, initiating significant cultural change, sharing one's sense of the future, providing a sense of a unified corporate self. They were well aware that they had to keep an eye on the "patterns of change" rather than one off issues or "snapshots." Being strategic was crucial. The emphasis was on the external, organizational relationships with the wider community and seeking ways to advantage their institution. They recognized the fluidity of their position as women and as advocates for the university, of being flexible and adaptable. This discourse was most obvious in the tertiary sector, where community included industry and international community. Even so, despite any extensive administrative experience, the capacity of individual women to enact change was still reliant upon a progressive executive culture. Dianne, dean in a sandstone, recited, "I am involved in a professorial appointment based on equity. I couldn't get more support from the people I need—the vice-chancellor, key academics in and outside the university. I can do that now. The people who could block it are no longer in positions of power. That's the change."

Her capacity also derived from her wider knowledge of the system, its priorities, and its personnel. Agency also came through reading the corporate climate and working with supportive allies. Positional status derived from managerial authority meant she could bypass any opposition lower down. Her experience of a reformed gender politics at the executive level was evident in other universities. Jeanette, a head of school in another sandstone university stated:

I've taken on the boys, and I've said this is not the culture that's going to be in the school: I wanted to support research; I wanted to support people that have ideas; I want different things to happen. I have had to show courage about issues of gender, in what I won't allow to be aired in the staff room. If I hear stupid names, jokes that are sexist, racist, homophobic, then I'll stand there and say this is totally unacceptable behavior.

But Margaret, an executive manager in a small, progressive TAFE, commented that the gender politics did not go away altogether, despite her supportive director. "It doesn't happen in senior management here, we've got a good culture going. It doesn't happen within our business unit. I certainly wouldn't tolerate the meetings being that way, but I know it happens elsewhere."

Getting Messy

Lower down the institution or school system, corporate discourses mingled with discourses of survival and crisis management on a daily basis. Paula, head of school in a Utech, commented about how it was difficult to explain why some decisions, budget cuts in particular, were imposed. "Management is devolving down the responsibilities with no budget. It's emotionally draining when people come in with their problems and assume it is the boss' (my) job to sort them out when I have little power to do so." The balance was between system-wide demands for efficiency and the need for rapid response time, which worked against building collegial social relationships, the apparent logic of strategic plans, and the seeming eccentricity of professional judgment.

School principals, ambiguously located as both middle managers within large school systems and executive managers of their school, became multilingual as they mobilized corporate, community, and professional discourses simultaneously. But the dominance of systemic discourses became apparent to Colleen, a principal of a small, working-class, suburban secondary college in Victoria, because as system compliance was exerted, it changed her relations with staff: "The current model forces dependency. The principal is seen to have the authority. This encourages people to revert back to a dependency model. To me that is a source of dismay. . . . The system is infantacizing not only the kids and the staff . . . but also principals. Principals have supposedly got all this authority but are told what to do."

Principals felt isolated, lacking support from staff and from government, particularly if they did not "toe the line." Noelene, junior campus principal in a large, suburban, multicampus secondary school believed principals "copped all the blame." Yet "there are number of issues that have been in the media that I think schools should have had more support on from the system, and we haven't had that. We have given more than our pound of flesh." Indeed, in Victoria, the government regularly and publicly denied responsibility for increasing class sizes and the conditions of schools, attributing them to poor school self-management (Blackmore and Thorpe 2003). The dilemma, shared by all managers in performative systems, was whether to be honest or cover up issues (MacBeath and MacDonald 2000). Covering up was the least line of resistance to avoid negative media publicity in the context of heightened media interest in conflict, transgression, and failure in education. Falling enrollments, financial mismanagement, union activism, parental discontent, poor student outcomes, sex, and drugs all made good headlines.

Furthermore, with devolution, the downplaying of equity policies and downsizing of infrastructure, there had been a reemergence of misogynist discourses with self-management, although this varied according to local school cultures and principals (Court 1998; Brooking 2005; Blackmore 1999b; see chapter 10). Yet governments developed Women and Leadership programs to capture women's leadership talent, frequently positioning women principals as "saviors" of schools in crisis, only to be readily cast aside. Barbara, a secondary school principal recalled:

> When I first arrived at this school as principal it was a failed reorganization. I was asked to restart negotiations between the local primaries and secondaries. That took a lot of energy to work through the process. Otherwise all those secondary schools would have been shut down. It took two years to negotiate staff followed by the total depression of closing down your own school. So I took a year off. This worked against me. I applied for a new principal position and was down to the last two. But I had only two years' principal experience, and he had eighteen years but done nothing like I had.

Principals under such circumstances learned to transgress and manipulate system-wide rules not only to achieve mandated system-wide objectives but most often to obtain fairness for staff and students.

With marketization and devolution, driven by an economic rationalist agenda, systems exerted "considerable pressure on institutional managers to deliver" (Deem and Ozga 2000,141). In TAFE, the context was increasingly about organizational survival, with diminishing budgets as the National Training Reform Agenda relied increasingly on commercialization. Markets reshaped the internal organization of TAFE, with, for example, humanities departments being split up to teach communication skills in all the vocationally oriented departments (Brown et al. 1996, 317). Middle managers had to manage inflexible line management while dealing with a high level of bottom-up cynicism about TAFE management's religious fervor for strategic planning and quality assurance that they were expected to advocate. But for many, despite the equation of planning to efficiency, line management was a tedious and difficult process middle managers such as Sheila felt unable to affect. She commented, "I get frustrated in decision-making processes and a feeling of isolation. I want clear guidelines. The slowness of the system of the decision making doesn't support business opportunities. My frustration is encapsulated in a bigger team where consensus never occurs, while you also feel a loss of identity" (large, metropolitan TAFE).

Some institutions provided greater autonomy than others due to their size, location, and institutional histories. Yet managers at all levels were seen to be "authors of situations" by those above and below. Middle management was "not a very rewarding role" (Alice, middle manager, large, metropolitan TAFE) because "the dynamics and the problems about dealing with people all the time are really taxing." The search for connectedness through teamwork was reduced to a form of "simulated relatedness" due to lack of time (Casey 1995). Any desire for emotional intimacy was denied many middle managers (Kerfoot 1999). Supervision confused professional collegiality/development with professional appraisal. For many female middle managers in TAFE, managing alone meant they experienced a lack of horizontal collegiality and support, being forever vulnerable to ongoing restructurings themselves. Jo, manager in a large, metropolitan TAFE, said, "During restructuring work almost stopped. Why are we doing this project if nothing is going to exist, no time frame in place? You felt totally devalued. Will your position exist? I'm trying to change a very old culture. It's like banging your head against a brick wall and very frustrating when you work alone, no support structures to talk things over with people."

In some universities there were a range of institutional mechanisms that reduced isolation for middle managers. But competitive tendering between budget lines meant deans and heads of school, like principals and departmental heads in TAFE, were forced to compete with colleagues for the center's funds and students. However, they were also reliant upon their colleagues in terms of battling for greater autonomy and discretionary capacity, while seeking to limit additional responsibilities being dispersed down from the center without any funds. Horizontal collegiality often emerged as the units (departments, faculties) constructed a "them" (the center) against "us" (the providers), so that many large institutions or even departments and faculties, as well as schools, did not think of themselves as entities or part of a system. Self-interest (survival) prevailed, fracturing relations between core/margins and within the margins.

Those workplaces that had a strongly consultative climate sought to create an environment of debate through transparent planning processes. Although this could eventuate in compulsory redundancies or "excess," the effect was "a very collegial environment in terms of the heads of school and myself. We meet every two weeks for half a day, and I'm hoping that sense of trust and working together that I believe exists will see us through the tough time" (Jill, Utech). In this space, deans and heads of school aired issues and garnered support. In a progressive TAFE, Margaret referred to "a group of women, some senior managers and some middle managers. We go out occasionally, talk about work, more a friendship network. That's my support base. I can be quite honest to them and talk about issues or problems." Likewise in schools, strong horizontal networks developed between principals of like politics, forged to proactively work on local agendas for more socially just practices and mutual support (Blackmore 1996). Less frequent was support from the center, particularly in schools. The exception was a university: "I find Marion [the VC] is an excellent role model for me because she's a real worrier, and I'm a real worrier too. But she's strategic in her thinking. I have learnt a great deal. It's nice to be able to reflect and discuss matters that I would probably not feel right to discuss with a male vice-chancellor . . . just issues about how you might improve, areas that are not one's strengths" (Bronwyn, head of school, Utech).

This homosociability, or preference to work with people of the same gender, the basis of male networking, was emerging as a critical mass of women in management (Blackmore et al. 2004). But peer relations for a woman in a male-dominated environment were more unpredictable. Leesa, dean of engineering (Utech), seeking to develop an equity initiative in engineering, felt that "the deans, all men, who have been very supportive of a business issue, have been disappointing. They did not have the decency to agree, and there was no support from the top. I think it was too hot to handle. I was very disappointed. I have certainly been a woman in a sea of strange names. I felt quite intimidated by the wall-to-wall masculinity of engineering." This confirmed a common sentiment echoed in all sectors by female middle managers that certain things had not changed. Womanagers still had to work twice as hard when promoting equity or in male-dominated environments.

Managing Chaos

At the interface between institution and "client," the corporate discourses of corporate solidarity and collegiality, of forward thinking and strategic planning, were treated with some cynicism as were the discourses of necessity ("We have no money and therefore no choice," "We will not survive") and inevitability ("They will do it to us if we do not do it to ourselves"). Indeed, the dominant discourse circulating in staff rooms indicated a sense of lack of purpose, disorder, chaos, fragmentation, discord, loss, and fear. One senior lecturer commented on the shift in purpose, culture, and practice of her university, in part due to its corporatization and in part due to lack of funds. "The students, the quality of life, the freedom, the social makeup of the university was worthwhile. Now it is getting to be an insignificant big institution without a clear identity anymore" (Brenda, redbrick). The most common grassroots sentiment was that "those at the top had lost the plot," and that "machismo" displayed through performance in particular intellectual arenas was being displaced by "machismo in business culture" (Spurling 1997, 44).

Women at the top were attributed with the best and worst characteristics of leadership and management. A senior lecturer in a redbrick university reflected on her perceptions of a pro vice-chancellor: "She's very good, and I really like her. But they have in a sense sold out. You get up there, and you have to give up loyalties to the faculty, to the academic faculties, and to teaching and learning. If that is the case, I'd rather be down here." Discourses of "best management practice" articulated by senior executives jarred up against discourses of "good educational practice" articulated by teachers and academics. Many considered there was little executive understanding as to the detrimental consequences of imposed decisions because of lack of consultation and the distancing of management in universities and TAFE from the interface, a distancing not as possible for school principals. Anna, senior lecturer in a sandstone university said: "Our present VC has absolutely no understanding at all what it is like working at the chalk face: he's invisible; people don't know him. That's not entirely his fault. It's a huge institution. But most of the senior management are also invisible. That increases disaffection."

These perceptions had a significant impact on how academics and teachers viewed their future opportunities. One associate professor (Utech), Jessie, felt "slightly jaundiced about jumping through hoops—just criteria and outcomes, what you need to do and how many things you have to count. We need to specify what academia actually is. The problem is that people have worked very hard and aren't valued." Teachers and academics questioned both the logic and the substance of the changes being invoked. Fay, a senior lecturer, suggested that in her redbrick university "we have an unimaginative VC who thinks merely in terms of growth without being aware of the implications for people who work here and students. Bigger is better. We have had to amalgamate, restructure, and bring in all small satellites and be one happy family . . . and campuses hate it. They feel very threatened. We just get the sense at the bottom of the academic pile that we are not valued." At the same time, Anna reflected on how the "them" and "us" cultures stimulated counteractivities that were sometimes productive but often destructive. For example, "the level of collegiality amongst the women was sufficiently strong. Indeed, having a hostile vice-chancellor helped to galvanize them. They've nothing left to lose." Staff in lower ranks felt devalued with the decimation of particular courses due to student demand or management fiat; the incapacity to undertake good teaching and research practices because of reduced resources; and the lack of time and the intensification of labor with little recognition of the impact this had on quality or stress.

NEW MODES OF GOVERNANCE

Dialogic to Instrumental Communication

With the permeation of market and managerial language throughout the structures and processes of institutional work, line management supplanted more representative modes of decision making in universities and schools, but less so in TAFE, which had typically been more managerial and hierarchical. In Victorian schools, democratic modes of decision making and staff-elected administrative committees were replaced by leadership teams comprising of leading teachers, a more hierarchical-, age-, and experience-based model. Colleen, a principal, considered "what is different now is that this current model is about getting the lines of authority so clear that the principal has all the authority. But teachers are reluctant to be involved in decision making now because they feel that instead of just fighting for their school they are softening the burden for the system with no benefit to them as teachers, either in career or other terms."

In a multicampus secondary college, a relatively young teacher commented, "I certainly feel that things are being imposed upon us. You are just a resource." Many teachers in this school expressed a sense of the fracturing of collegiality in staff relations that arose from performance pay to those in leadership positions and the increase in contract staff. "The curriculum is both constantly changing and being mandated: VCE, drug education, sport, languages other than English, vocational education." There was significant decline in staff morale and in union strength, accompanied by a "lack of opportunity to speak against the reforms" and a "sense of disunity" increased by lack of time to nurture collegial relations. "We used to feel united as a group. That has changed with the new role of the principal. There is a perception of a bit of self-interest there with principals getting performance bonuses whenever they initiate anything" (Down, Hogan, and Chadbourne 1999).

This was accompanied by a shift from dialogic or hermeneutic to more instrumental modes of communication. Meetings became information sessions from managers down the line rather than an opportunity to provide feedback to executives. "It's common at management meetings to have more information passing down and no feedback" (Janis, large, metropolitan TAFE). Principals in Schools of the Future referred to how regional and central professional development sessions were more about how to implement what was prescribed and policy briefings than discussions about issues or feedback on how reforms were impacting individual schools. This mode of instrumental communication was about "non-reciprocal relationships, less about understanding and more about strategic action" (Barnett 1997, 55–56).

In response, many sought to short circuit the paralyzing and demoralizing effect by maintaining or developing "dialogic relations premised upon a genuine attempt to understand the other party and mutual respect that is structural" (Barnett 1997, 55–56). Bronwyn, head of school, made the following observation: "Women try to communicate a lot before the final decision, to make it a shared decision. Some people see that as a weakness (you can't make decisions on your own). But decisions are agreed by the faculty and executive. Once a decision is made it is owned and shared" (Utech).

Margaret (manager at a progressive TAFE) commented: "I find the language deliberately mystifies finance . . . and they are all men. And you know, financial stuff has been one of their traditional power bases. So, I don't feel intimidated in the long term in a sense, but I feel a bit underskilled at the moment. . . . [Y]ou can actually present it quite simply if you want to." The focus on performing as the substance of communication rather than on improvement also led to a level of obfuscation and poor decision making. A TAFE manager commented about how the focus of meetings was only on the strategic and not on understanding or problem solving. This reluctance among peers to talk about common difficulties meant managers dealt with issues alone, often replicating solutions, not learning from mistakes. Janis, in a large, metropolitan TAFE commented on how "every manager has their problems with staff, especially the industrial stuff. Each coordinator struggles with their own agendas. At management meetings I say, 'let's talk without naming people. This happened to me. How would you deal with it?' But that was discouraged." Adopting alternative modes of communication to the dominant decisional mode was critical to those womanagers seeking to develop shared meaning across levels. It meant, for example, modifying how privileged certain types of quantitative data (that which can be measured) informed decisions with qualitative judgment and taking seriously the capacity of those lower down the organization to inform change and indeed initiate change, as this is where creativity can most often be found.

Pseudorationality and Strategic Planning

Our womanagers' narratives continuously slipped between encouraging people to work together well and expecting everyone to conform to organizational objectives, between control and support. What was most difficult was to move outside the parameters of the organizational goals and structures but still play the game, because the processes of consultation and strategic planning were tightly structured and monitored through centralized strategic planning. While school principals had more direct influence, this was modified by system-wide policy and governance imperatives that determined how plans were informed (triennial school reviews), produced (pseudoinclusion of school councils) and operationalized (school priorities tended to be system-wide priorities because usually linked to funding). Yet the language of policy texts was about evidence-based policy and practice and action research (Blackmore 2002c). Many saw strategic planning as both useful and coercive, as Felicity, quality manager in a community TAFE reflected: "It's very helpful having a lot of the things that we want to happen being built into our strategic plan. Our planning process forces deployment down to the operation level so every single department develops strategies to maintain key performance indicators. A lot of those strategies can't help but be beneficial. Whether or not they are, ultimately you have no choice."

Into this mix of strategic planning were constant invocations to "do better with less." Bev, a principal of a small, rural secondary college, commented on how this impacted on her sense of agency and being out of control as 95 percent of her budget was on staff. "I feel quite powerless . . . I have no control over staffing to any extent, and I don't have huge control over budgeting. And then all the changes brought down from Schools of the Future have too frequently to do with reporting." Despite the apparent rationality of management, it was also arbitrary. Many managers were cynical as to how such plans elaborated any sense of "shared mission," as usually strategic plans were written at the executive level and sent down for consultation. Consequently, middle managers spent considerable time trying to second guess what such plans meant for their unit and how to position themselves favorably in terms of group or individual recognition (necessary for funding and promotion) within the wider milieu of their respective client groups, "industry," and institutional politics. But all planning was cast aside when external events, new policies, loss of students or income, produced new crises. An acting dean commented on how announcements of higher education cuts by government meant her Utech strategic management group went away and worked out a plan. The heads of school went to a meeting, and she was given an executive statement that her faculty had to lose eighteen staff members out of a hundred and seven. "And now that's all been decided, and the letters are going out on Monday. . . . If that hadn't happened, I would have been able to have a bit more balance, but I didn't get the chance" (Jill Utech). Systemic planning often overrode local planning. Middle managers' focus vacillated by the minute negotiating competing demands of good money management and good person management.

Yet the "the managerial logic was difficult to penetrate without attacking its very assumptions . . . the reasonableness of the approach depicted any display of anger, anxiety or frustration as being difficult or aberrant" (Deem and Ozga 2000, 141). Once you were a member of a planning group, your loyalty to the product and process was expected and thus appropriated at all ongoing public discussions as you had your chance "to speak." That detrimental consequences may only become apparent later in a planning cycle was downplayed. Alternative approaches, thinking outside the box, were often silenced if managers could not provide evidence or immediately mobilize institutionally strategic discourses to argue a counterposition. Individuals who pointed out problems were often seen to be negative and oppositional. The expectation was that if you did not have a solution to the problem you named, you were silent. Staff at all levels become complicit through a silence that is not about agreement with their immediate superior or about a particular resolution of a dilemma but out of an awareness "for the person put in a position that might seem to force her to extract extra work from them" (Zipin and Brennan 2003, 355). In return, managers come to rely upon staff by appealing to the troubling positional dilemmas in which they find themselves. Both self and soul are thus "co-opted and self-divided, by institutionally coded governmental suppression of other virtuous dispositions" (Zipin and Brennan 2003, 356).

Finally, distrust and division increase as the individual middle manager, despite the shared grieving over loss of staff, gets credit (performance bonuses) for any efficiencies achieved through aggregated staff productivity. Executive managers could distance themselves from the ethical dilemmas confronting the middle managers, who in turn cascade decisions down to those who teach and research, where there is no place to disperse, dispense, or delegate, only to resolve the messiness of daily work. These circumstances enabled and encouraged particular institutional dispositions, of executive managers "making a virtue of necessity" and looking for magical solutions of "working smarter" at the expense of those with nowhere else to go (Zipin and Brennan 2003).

BUFFERING CHANGE

Managerialism was at the same time not "complete or uncontested" as these womanagers were "mediators of change" in reconstructing the new organization, acting as "an ideological buffer between senior managers and lecturers through which market reform is filtered in the [further education] workplace" (Gleeson and Shain 1999, 461–62). They dealt with ambiguity and contradiction in working with a "complex duality of control and support," a duality that gave expression in the "double identities of middle managers as they broker materiality and meaning in their work" (Gleeson and Shain 1999, 462). Insightful managers acted as syphons of the multitude of reforms where possible, filtering out what could be ignored or deflected (Blackmore et al. 1996). Barbara, secondary school principal, commented that "there are some things that the teaching staff still haven't come to terms with. They have been protected from it by me." Middle managers as leaders could influence, mediate and articulate cultural norms—reinforce some aspects or seek to influence others—through a redistribution of resources, but primarily symbolic activities of recognition, establishing legitimacy in decisions through collegial relationships, listening, and providing others with a sense of agency. One dean commented that "management is very important, but leadership has a legitimacy about it, that is to do with professional legitimacy." In uncertain times gaining legitimacy professionally often meant transgressing managerial norms and rules.

While expressing concern about the overall directions of reform, change management was also exceptionally seductive for many women, and they took on the job seriously, negotiating identity and self as leader/manager, as well as the multiplicity of desires, dilemmas, and difficulties arising from rapid and radical change. Societal and policy context provided the framework of interpretation and orientation of their action as to how they assessed their professional situations and formulated action-strategies. As womanagers have in other studies, they described the "contradictory experience of support and discrimination in their everyday working life . . . the ambiguity of an environment that is simultaneously supportive and demanding" (Wacjman 1999, 35; Smulyan 2000). Paula (Utech), saw the role of head of school "as a political hole, playing political games all the time." Cast into ambiguous positioning as teachers/academics *and* managers, they were highly reflective about the nature of organizational change, about their expectations, responsibilities, strategies, and processes. Czarniawaska (1998) argues that "organizational theorists often refer to changing behavior, but the difference between action and behavior is critical" (4). Action is part of a life narrative, of habitus, and not just a discrete event. Nicola, a primary school teacher leader, believed that "I do it in the way that I know what I want, and I know how to go about getting it. I know I can influence people. I can get a team rallying and moving."

Strategizing

Each womanager had strategies for change shaped by her specific institutional politics. Sandra, a relatively junior middle manager in a rural TAFE, ruefully reflected on the linguistic strategies she employed to get her point across when she could not change the cultural context:

> It was really difficult, but I worked out after a while how to make it work for me. The tradies are perfectly fine with you as long as you defer. In one meeting with very strong council president . . . you could virtually say anything you liked as long as you reframed what he had just said like you were validating it. Of course, you said something completely different. . . . So he would feel very good. Now I just hook on to the most powerful person in the room to get a voice. Otherwise, you would try to speak, and he wouldn't acknowledge me, because I was a female, even though I was representing all the staff.

Barbara's story line as a "savior principal" indicates how she identified and encapsulated short- and long-term needs to symbolize a "new order" and thus mobilize her community.

> When I first came to this school it was as a result of three principals being in acting positions because the substantial principal had had a nervous breakdown, the result of massive staff friction between her and the staff. . . . [T]he structural reforms had impacted on the internal politics of the school, where total outsiders were brought in as advanced skills teachers, creating excess current staff. I represented some form of stability. Most staff believed the school was going to close down, enrollments were going down and spi-

raling, the building had not been looked at for twenty years. The grounds had grass up to your knees, rubbish everywhere, very messy. Kids were in rodent-infested buildings in a disheveled state. There was gang violence in the school and in the district, even at the girls' school. So I came in very firmly on behavior. I always backed staff in supporting acceptable behavior and conferred intensively with parents and the police. . . . On arriving, I immediately cleared up the violence, bad language, and hugely disrespectful behavior towards teachers. I think people started to feel fairly good. Within three months we achieved a grant of thirty thousand dollars to upgrade the diseased staff area, a truly sick space. So that made a bit of a difference. Since then I've been pushing futures in the honeymoon period. I think staff are very hopeful, but we're in a demographic trough still.

Barbara's resilience and endurance, clear focus, and a capacity to manage the symbolic, cultural and material dimensions simultaneously were key factors in her (short-term) achievements. Her success in revitalizing the school lay in her ability to identify key issues and priorities, to communicate these to all stakeholders, and to mobilize a range of resources.

One secondary school principal (Bev) identified three strategies by which she maneuvered change. The first was to extend people's knowledge of whole school management, so they had a more informed dialogue. "I try to keep people up to scratch with those particularly interested in gaining promotion . . . I expand their bases to make decisions." Paula, head of school in a Utech likewise emphasized the need to "be able to have some clear directions of where you would like to see the school going but also to involve your staff so that it's owned by them, to be both approachable and supportive." For Bev, a second strategy was to restructure the school organization creating new positions, exploiting diversity through utilizing the intergenerational and cultural strengths of the teaching staff through teams, and creating transparency in selection and appointments.

> The school was academically and behaviorally out of control. I folded the system and made thee levels: junior, middle, and senior. I set up teams of three people. We had six people from the old system, so with teams of three that meant that they had to reapply. The selection panels appointed the best three who could be trained up with partners. It was an injection of new blood that actually brought on three women, one who had been named in excess. (Bev)

This redistribution of leadership responsibilities and knowledge was enhanced by institutionalizing mentoring of staff, democratic processes of decision making, and dialogical modes of communication. The force of ideas won the necessary authority, as Fran argued: "True leadership does not come from wearing jack boots. If you believe strongly enough in something then it's possible to gain support in a school situation through the staff, parents, and the students. I like to share ideas with people, sow seeds, have people take ideas on board . . . from the entire school community" (assistant principal, rural secondary school). Bev's third strategy was to focus on teacher professional learning through organizing the school to provide time and space for discussion, planning, reflecting, and teamwork. "We deliberately set funds aside for the development of leadership skills and organized the timetable so that those groups can get together in class time to discuss plans or to review the program." She judged the effectiveness of these actions by the fact that staff now competed for jobs "with an 80 percent turnaround with more women. It's changed the personality of the whole place. Increasing the numbers of positions and reducing the fear of failure encouraged them to try."

In a university, one dean was implementing multiple reforms: a possible merger with another faculty member at another university to teach a common course; restructuring a law research center; and internationalizing the curriculum in economics and commerce requiring restructuring administration to meet academic needs. To do so, she had to "harness a hundred thousand dollars, fifty from me, and fifty from somewhere else." Dianne's strategy in a large sandstone university was to first get ownership among key change agents, that is, the academic leaders,

> to work first with the people in the faculty who are sympathetic to the ideas, not necessarily the head. You identify these people, build up working parties and teams. Then once something has started, take it back to the full faculty to approve. This gets enough of a critical mass to move stuff forward, though people resist all the way. So, it was academic planning first, then the budget stuff later. It's helped by a very strong ethos of university-wide redevelopment and a better combination of academic and administrative work.

A professor, Kim, at a Utech university worked with and against the managerial game:

> You put people who are carefully picked together and provide them with an opportunity to grow, be fostered and challenged, sometimes pushing harder than they think they can cope with. We work very hard on personal styles and skills . . . create an environment that takes off. I've studied adult learning. I've studied groups and how to work with groups: you operate in a participatory manner and strategically. I had a two-day planning workshop before I began with people from the clinical field and university colleagues, put in an external facilitator to set goals, objectives, and philosophy, a business plan taken to faculty review team, detailed down to what we're doing for service for education, for research, for administration, strategies for goals, what we didn't achieve and why.

Evelyn, an assistant director of a regional TAFE, focused more on

> networking with the community. I'm an equal player and a participant in a
> group. Participatory management encourages emancipation: the team func-
> tions in the style I've encouraged without me necessarily being here. Anyone
> can raise anything; anyone can have a different opinion to mine. I empower
> them with the resources that it's necessary for them to do the job. If I'm imple-
> menting a major change I liaise, consult, and advise and hold hands but be firm
> when I need to be. I think if change is imposed that's not good for anyone . . .
> I'm also the first person to let go of what I can't change. I prioritize.

Producing change also meant ongoing change of self, constantly meeting
the demands of the new organizational environment, being in touch, and
assuming an educative responsibility. Jane, general manager in a small, progressive, suburban TAFE, believed change required self-development:

> I must provide staff with a reasonable workplace and rationale. So I need to
> be able to be up to date so that I can work with them and negotiate their
> work plans . . . so that they can come back to me and say, "What do you mean
> by this," and I can give them anecdotally based experience. Also, if your
> organization doesn't have a vision for five years' time, then you have to have
> clear view. In this organization, we don't have a clear, marketable vision.
> We're workshopping again what the college will look like as we are being
> restructured. We've set strategies and core values without having a longer
> picture. If I don't know where I'm heading, how can I expect to help my
> team? So I spend a lot of time making sure that I'm up to date with federal
> and state policies and business trends.

Dilemma Work

The managers in this study constantly negotiated dilemmas. In particular, the
discursive shift to team work was particularly appealing for those who sought
to impart ownership through process, yet the organizational imperatives and
rewards were individualized and outcome driven. Jane recognized new opportunities in a restructured progressive TAFE that focused on process as well as
outcomes. She observed: "I think we're trying to achieve improvement in
strengthening teamwork, but we also have responsibility for facilitating the
processes. We don't sit down and say to them, 'You need to get there.' So we
use review processes and progress reports against the strategic plans. We have
a job to make sure that those who are sceptical embark with the rest of the
department."

As Jane, others sought to change practices by mobilizing dominant managerial discourses to produce the outcomes they valued. Felicity, a senior

TAFE quality assurance manager, mobilized quality discourses in order to change practice. The quality audits had indicated to her that in the male-dominated departments, administrative strategies and the record keeping were poor and new programs were initiated, dropped, and reinstated without evaluation in a "she'll be OK" attitude. These staff were "not open to a more proactive way of bringing teaching and education to the client, refusing to make us more flexible by training apprentices on site, expressing a negativity that says 'go away and leave us' . . . people who refuse to play the game when you rely on people to work together. So you look for the block and spend time with them to achieve desirable outcomes."

In invoking quality discourses, Felicity was both compliant to managerial and performative requirements yet initiated pedagogical reform among particularly nonprogressive departments. Likewise, Margaret, in the same TAFE, mobilized the managerial discourse of quality to gain external funds to develop internal programs of reform, meeting short-term management requirements but with a long-term purpose of improving professional learning.

> Quality assurance and measurement is intelligent copying essentially. We got the money, met their guidelines, did a bit of research, internally. Then we supported professional learning, so staff could adapt to the new environment. There was a huge change in roles and responsibilities of teachers away from being in a classroom, to being a facilitator of learning, because of the pendulum swing towards economic rationalism. But there are fruitful aspects. If we don't, we will go down the gurgler. We have to learn to play the game to be viable. So we are working creatively within the current context, much of which is sinister.

Margaret linked quality less to the discourse of assurance (recording and evidence of process) than Felicity and more to a discourse of improvement (production of new courses and knowledge). The former was more an exercise in organizational performativity and compliance; the latter was more about substantive change and organizational learning. But the discursive power of quality had another spin other than to justify improved learning; it also appealed to women's sense of improvement for perfection within a gendered division of labor. Female middle managers tend to do the quality "housekeeping" in producing the detailed textual evidence (audit), and executive masculinities did the performance of quality at the final show (e.g., Morley 2003). Quality assurance was likened to "cleaning up the house for visitors." Thus there were discursive associations between resistance to quality assurance by traditional masculinities (blue collar in TAFE, white collar in universities) and its promotion by new managerial masculinities, with the repositioning of womanagers as being "good at quality."

Notions of compliance, collusion, accommodation, and resistance are complex, as compliance at one moment can have resistant effects in the long term. Often the logic embedded in planning is internally contradictory and self-destructs as it becomes apparent in its operationalization or peters out through lack of will or resources. Often giving up on short-term issues gains more by strategizing for long-term effects. But being compliant in the short term meant individual women were considered as "traitors" or "puppets of the government" by some of their colleagues, as was Barbara, a principal of an inner-city, working-class, high cultural mix secondary school. She elected to pilot the Schools of the Future program. "I guess there was the trauma of closure and absorption of transferred staff after the school amalgamation, then the decision to pilot Schools of the Future. It was partly me saying, well sooner or later, we are going to have to do this. So we might as well get on with it rather than drive energy into opposition. Schools in the later intake now deal with more complexities." Her focus was less on the politics of Schools of the Future, although she opposed its principles of marketization and managerialism and the practices they encouraged, and more on delivering an effective program for a group of severely disadvantaged students.

Organizational change has both an ethical and a political dimension to it that taps into and produces particular "emotional responses" (Evans 1996; Blackmore 1996; Fullan 1998; Sachs and Blackmore 1998; Boler 1999; Hargreaves 1998). Strategically, womanagers were expected to advocate and implement reforms with which they fundamentally disagreed ethically, politically, and educationally. Some were pragmatic. "Change is going to continue. You either embrace it and make the best of it, or you can sit there and grizzle and grump. Otherwise, our whole school will fall to bits" (Paula, head of school, Utech). As did women managers in the postcompulsory sector in Alexiadou's (2001) study, Paula tried to "link their work to very different discourses of purpose that impact on how they relate to each other and their students" (432). She was consultative, using her academic leadership in research and overseas teaching to model her expectations, balancing staffing and the budget fairly, using her colleague's strengths and thus valuing them. Another head of school felt, "I'm good at growing people. I keep staff informed, challenge them, push them, while supportive, to develop a shared value base" (Francesca, Utech).

The leadership habitus of our womanagers was unconsciously accommodating managerial logics and practices, incorporated merely through their organizational participation as much a consequence of role rather than intent. While they mobilized the managerial discourses to more educational objectives, by default they reified the managerial and market discourses to the neglect of any publically well-articulated normative dimension or alternatives other than in their daily encounters. Their subordinates recognized how they sought to be more democratic and collegial; the reality was that it was often superficial. Ironically, it was mutual recognition and respect for their leadership practices that silenced oppositional voices, another affective and effective trap of the performative organization.

Alexiadou (2001), in her study of managers in the further education system in the United Kingdom, spoke of responsive, proactive, and entrepreneurial managers. Responsive managers took a position of "pragmatic accommodation" underpinned by a sense of inevitability, as did Barbara. They sought to retain pedagogic discourses based on educational values by meeting the needs of students and community. There was a clear separation, if not opposition, maintained between business and educational values. Their desire was to adjust market demands to meet educational criteria as much as was possible within the real constraints of budget. These managers sought to protect their staff and facilitate their core educational work, shielding them from the pressures and changes, providing professional development and opportunities, and thereby absorbing the crisis. This was the most typical response of women leaders of institutions where educational reforms had the most severe effect and where ethical dilemmas were difficult to ignore, the poorer schools, newer universities, and community TAFEs.

The proactive discourse was more accepting of change and active engagement with management and market values. Their aim was to tailor pedagogic discourses to the market and in so doing, redefine their work. That is, there was a "temporal and qualitative distancing from the function of teaching" that then became evident in the ways they viewed their staff (Alexidaou 2001, 433). They acknowledged the different and important expertise of lecturers and teachers, but with significant tensions emerging. By mobilizing discourses of technical/managerial professionalism, such as quality, they maintained institutional credibility but also generated a "theory of use" (drawing on discourses of practice relevance) that meant staff should teach what was in demand. The overarching aim was institutional survival. Management was, on the one hand, about encouraging staff to change their attitudes and was achieved by devolving minor decision making to staff so they could realize (and own) the constraints; and it was, on the other hand, about welcoming performance-based approaches as providing some rationale. This was more typical in the male-dominated cultures of the large, metropolitan TAFEs, but increasingly common in universities.

Then there was the entrepreneurial discourse in which winning the game at all costs was the key to success. Few women in our study assumed this discourse unquestioningly, although the "exposure to risks and costs of their activities is constructed as enabling them to better create opportunities, signifying a form of 'empowerment and success' within the organization" (Edwards 1997, 163). Collectively, these codified management knowledge practices "emphasise women's suitability for more intensive 'people' work of the managerialized post compulsory sector," constructing a new managerialist "feminized" subject (Prichard and Deem 1999, 328).

RESISTANCE, INVESTMENT, AND IDENTITY

Managing and leading change meant providing a language, structures, and processes that facilitated change. But it also meant providing conditions that were conducive to people changing sedimented practices. Margaret, a manager in a small, progressive, suburban TAFE expresses some of the dimensions of this:

> I think with change people by and large self-select. I've got to put all the structural things in place, do all the encouraging and communicating: it's not really about power, it's about empowerment—a very female perspective—guiding the way, but not actually necessarily enforcing it. Women want to see change; they want to be let out of some of the boxes they are in; they want opportunities for everyone, not just some.

Her focus was on providing opportunities for voice by all stakeholders, participation, and inclusivity. This feminist discourse of change was informed often by their own marginalization and exclusion as informal leaders working in multiple arenas. But establishing conducive conditions was not enough if there was little understanding of what motivated people to change or resist change. This was a key aspect of change many womanagers learned from gender equity reform during the 1980s. It meant "acknowledging that you can't change other people; you can only change yourself and your reaction to them. . . . [M]en want to change everybody else. Just look at the women's movement. We can't change the men, but we can change the way we react to what they do to us" (Cathy, working-class secondary school with high cultural mix). Deep-seated change is about identity work. Radical change such as antisexism and antiracism challenged professional and traditional gender identities (Blackmore 1998), just as a shift from trade to service work in TAFE challenged traditional masculinist cultures. To change practice meant working positively by recognizing such investments and identifying gains, not negatively by implying poor behavior or highlighting loss. Renata, a director of a TAFE, argued that "when people come to you with problems, you basically try to draw out their best. Obviously you don't want to frighten people. And it's got to be positive . . . a very delicate task."

Womanagers, as the transmitters and enactors of the organizational messages and corporate values, threatened subordinates' professional and personal identity. "There is resistance to change because they don't want to get away from what they're doing. People sometimes resent the fact that you're telling them they're not doing a good job, which is not the case. But again that's lack of understanding about what we're trying to do" (Felicity, large, community-oriented, suburban TAFE). Resistance to change is part of any change process, not always bad and sometimes an important modifying influence. Individual resistance to particular changes is not just a humanistic deep loyalty to the familiar and the need for predicability, or a particular individual predisposition, or professional pathology, but is often based on commitment to certain values and certain types of social relationships, as well as individual and collective investments in professional identity. Women managers also resisted reforms they were expected to implement. But as change managers, they also categorized staff according to their level of "opportunism, compliance or resistance" (Brown et al. 1996). Karin saw resistance as against their femaleness as much as reform itself.

> There is an element of resistance if you're talking to a male-oriented or male-dominated department of a trade area. They don't see you as a barrier. Initially its "Oh here's a female. She's probably nothing much more than just you know an ex secretary with no expertise," until you can build up rapport, match them intellectually, become knowledgeable in the area. . . . [Y]ou just need to make sure that they understand what you're asking them to do. (Metropolitan TAFE)

Deep-seated change means shifting loyalties and allegiances within a specific network of relationships of power, friendship, and professional activity (often gendered); it is also about "the defeat of hopes" and emerging opportunities (Evans 1996, 28). Deep-seated change also requires a level of spontaneity, intuition, and even "emotional intimacy" that some see as being a feminized practice arising from societal norms and women's experiences. "Whereas for the masculine subject the experience of spontaneity is as threatening as it is precarious and destabilizing. . . . Masculinity gives the appearance of providing masculine subjects with the knowledge of how to respond, and of how to manage, rather than experience, intimate situations" (Kerfoot 1999, 184–86). Therefore many, but not all, men resort to "instrumental intimacy . . . instrumental in its desire to capture the subtleties and nuances of social relations for organizational ends, discounting or displacing other forms of intimacy," while maintaining a distance from the messiness of everyday social relations (Kerfoot 1999, 186).

The paradox of the neobureaucratic corporate organization was its undermining of the very culture of creativity and learning that it claimed to value. The everexpanding field of change theory informs us that radical change is about conflict and unpredictability. Yet policy makers still presume a rational, instrumental perspective based on the view that change will occur if it is centrally imposed, then explained, justified, and accompanied by training sessions and/or mandates, what some would argue typifies old bureaucratic masculinities (Evans 1996). Yet "the fallacy of rationalism is the assumption that 'social' work can be altered by logical argument or 'brute sanity.' Arrangements cannot be altered by rational explanation alone in some 'impersonal utilitarian calculation of the common good'" (Fullan 1999, 3). Changing organizational practice is about meaning making. Meaning is about *understanding* (I see what you mean) and *attachment* to people and ideas (you or this means so much to me), both with cognitive and emotional dimensions (Evans 1996, 28).

"JUST GETTING THINGS DONE": THE DANGERS OF PRACTICAL RATIONALITY

The final danger for women positioned "in the buffer zone" of middle management was their apparent "practical" disposition of getting things done and their passion for change. "Men are threatened by change, whereas women tend to take it on board. Men are very single focused. Women do so many tasks: okay I'll do it, and then I'll go and do something else. I think women say, well, that's it, it has to be, and accept it, whereas men tend to, well why does it have to be, why can't it be?" (Denise, advanced skills teacher, rural secondary school).

The popular discourse of women being good change agents, which implied that women were predisposed to, and had the emotional energy for, change, was readily appropriated by organizations. But any practical action is not in the conditions of our own making, and it is without a capacity to control effects. In getting things done to meet institutional agendas, the danger was that the wider view of education as a force for social change was readily forgotten. Being a change agent in the 1980s as a femocrat or feminist educator was about bringing in a subversive voice to undermine hegemonic views, utilizing allegiances outside the field to change the field internally (Yeatman 1998b). Being a change agent in the 1990s was now about mobilizing resources to meet predetermined organizational ends. Change agency, as leadership, was coopted during the 1990s into the corporate logic of the field. It left less space for subversive play within the disciplining discourses of mission statements and constantly reworked strategic plans, triennial reviews, and accountabilities. As Ozga and Walker (1999) argue:

> Managerialism reflects a particular formation of masculinity that is competitive, ritualistic, unreflective and false. . . . [B]oth "first-wave" and "second wave" public sector managerialism are gendered in ways that work against women. By this, we mean that both the thrusting, competitive, cost cutting entrepreneurialism of the early 1990s and the team building, empowering and envisioning of the late 1990s are interdependent and represent two "performances" of the same managerialist text. The insecurity created by the first wave created the necessary conditions for the contrived collegiality of the second. (107)

But the isolation of management from the daily core work, and the increasing government and organizational disparagement of collective activism, meant that there was a tendency toward individual and defensive action strategies rather than collective commitment and action to a feminist and/or emancipatory politics.

> The link between the view taken of the underlying purposes of education and specific institutional vision is evident. The latter, however, has to translate ideals into specific activities, taking into account external prospects and internal capacities. The task requires more than pragmatism wrapped up as values, and unless the vision is congruent with the beliefs, values and goals shared widely among the staff, it is unlikely to stand the test of translation into action. Deep and widespread differences of conviction within an institution, or between institutional leadership and the wider community are a recipe for dispute and ethical conflict. (Bone 1997, 21)

So while these women leaders produced quite coherent narratives imparting a sense of purpose and agency, this coherence was not as evident in their daily work. The issue of course is when the paradoxical, ambiguous, or contradictory nature of that work is no longer considered to be so; and if so have we accommodated the "managerial habitus" as part of a new work order?

DOING WELL AND DOING GOOD

Performativity exploits the desire of educational workers to "do well" according to predetermined external parameters, while at the same time the performative transforms the very practices, values, and processes from which educational workers derived their passion and pleasure, the motivating force for many in education being to "do good" in terms of social justice (Acker and Feuerverger 1996). This is what Arlie Hochschild (1983) refers to as the difference between "surface" and "deep" emotion. Surface emotion is about the superficial roles we play as teachers, researchers, and institutional actors, where we call upon different language games to run an argument or win a point. Deep emotion is about an emotional commitment to what we value, closely tied to our personal and professional identity and our politics (See also Boler 1999). Hopfl and Linsted (2000) talk about passion, performance, and suffering as three aspects of people's emotional involvement with organizations. With managerialism, performance was measured against predetermined attributes based on externally imposed standards, suffering was treated as occupational stress, and power was exerted to "govern the soul" as well as hearts and minds (Rose 1990). New wave management theory portrays managers as "cultural practitioners"; but visionary leadership comes from the "soul and the market simultaneously" (Clarke and Newman 1997, 431).

Social theorists perceive postmodern identities as being characterized by reflexivity, suggesting increased autonomous action and reflection on action. Yet the response of the state and organizations has been to intensify control over that for which they are responsible. The intellectual and human capital, and increasingly, emotional capital, of educational workers are prime sites of productivity. The power of performativity in this context lies in the "fabrication of new languages and techniques to bind the worker into productive life" and new identities (Rose 1999, 60). The individual educator in the performative organization, we have argued, is more managed, but also manages him- or herself better. Academics and trainers working in more volatile and competitive markets constantly repackage themselves in a multiplicity of ways to meet the demands of diverse niche markets, research priorities, and institutional strategic initiatives. The commodification of image is now core management work, yet the maintenance of the image relies upon the educational workers' self-management; that is, it relies on recording, promoting and managing themselves in ways that also promote the institution through self-promotion, winning grants and awards, annual reports, performance appraisals, and quality assurance processes. These activities require individuals to be compliant, at least superficially, to school, departmental, and university strategy plans, otherwise one's use-value was diminished. The persistence and pervasiveness of these regulated and regulating practices produced more compliant rather than creative habitus. Academics and teachers had to negotiate between

DOING WELL AND DOING GOOD

Performativity exploits the desire of educational workers to "do well" according to predetermined external parameters, while at the same time the performative transforms the very practices, values, and processes from which educational workers derived their passion and pleasure, the motivating force for many in education being to "do good" in terms of social justice (Acker and Feuerverger 1996). This is what Arlie Hochschild (1983) refers to as the difference between "surface" and "deep" emotion. Surface emotion is about the superficial roles we play as teachers, researchers, and institutional actors, where we call upon different language games to run an argument or win a point. Deep emotion is about an emotional commitment to what we value, closely tied to our personal and professional identity and our politics (See also Boler 1999). Hopfl and Linsted (2000) talk about passion, performance, and suffering as three aspects of people's emotional involvement with organizations. With managerialism, performance was measured against predetermined attributes based on externally imposed standards, suffering was treated as occupational stress, and power was exerted to "govern the soul" as well as hearts and minds (Rose 1990). New wave management theory portrays managers as "cultural practitioners"; but visionary leadership comes from the "soul and the market simultaneously" (Clarke and Newman 1997, 431).

Social theorists perceive postmodern identities as being characterized by reflexivity, suggesting increased autonomous action and reflection on action. Yet the response of the state and organizations has been to intensify control over that for which they are responsible. The intellectual and human capital, and increasingly, emotional capital, of educational workers are prime sites of productivity. The power of performativity in this context lies in the "fabrication of new languages and techniques to bind the worker into productive life" and new identities (Rose 1999, 60). The individual educator in the performative organization, we have argued, is more managed, but also manages him- or herself better. Academics and trainers working in more volatile and competitive markets constantly repackage themselves in a multiplicity of ways to meet the demands of diverse niche markets, research priorities, and institutional strategic initiatives. The commodification of image is now core management work, yet the maintenance of the image relies upon the educational workers' self-management; that is, it relies on recording, promoting and managing themselves in ways that also promote the institution through self-promotion, winning grants and awards, annual reports, performance appraisals, and quality assurance processes. These activities require individuals to be compliant, at least superficially, to school, departmental, and university strategy plans, otherwise one's use-value was diminished. The persistence and pervasiveness of these regulated and regulating practices produced more compliant rather than creative habitus. Academics and teachers had to negotiate between becoming "managed" professionals and being reflexive, critical, self-managing professionals (Rhoades 1996). The extent to which individuals engage with these discourses of the managed self is personal and ethical in terms of the "sort of relationship you should have with yourself, as the means by which individuals come to act upon themselves in relation to the true and the false, the desirable and undesirable" (du Gay 1996, 55).

Paradoxically, performativity emphasizes a conformist and "managed self" at a time when organizational productivity relies more upon increased creativity and reflexivity and the passionate work of education (Dadds 1995). The effect of performative regimes has been productivism (a focus on work itself) and not productivity (substantive work for a desired end, valuable educational experience). Thus, "work becomes a standard bearer of moral meaning to the extent that it defines whether or not individuals feel worthwhile or socially valued. Why one wishes, or feels compelled, to work is defined in terms of what work itself is—the need to work has its own inner dynamic" (Giddens 1994, 175). One academic commented about "how the commitment to work has become an all consuming passion." In this way, the new performativity regimes tapped into the emotional dimensions of organizational cultures and work identities; and the passion for educational work, doing well, and a desire for change. But, we suggest from our study, this exploitation of "unbridled passion" undermined its own mission as it was channeled toward organizational ends. Previously, passion was undesirable because it was uncontrollable. Now, "being a passionate manager, is given salience, as a new discursively produced response, it is now viewed as desirable rather than as a dangerous excess" (Hatcher 2003, 399). Academics, teachers, and trainers are now expected to be advocates and working emissaries for their institutions with a "naive zealousness" (Edwards 1997, 28). "I have enormous amounts of energy, almost a missionary zeal. I think that one of my most important roles in this institution has been to show that teacher education is an intellectual activity and that I have a view of education that can be articulated [and] is based upon what we know about teaching and learning and social justice" (Peta, dean, redbrick). Many of the women in our study grew up with second-wave feminism and professional activism during the 1970s and saw themselves as committed professionals, social activists, and equity workers. Protecting the public sphere against the macropolitical agendas of privatization and managerialism was central to their professional habitus in which their passion was purposeful and strategic.

THE SOCIOPSYCHIC ECONOMY

De Groot (1997) suggests that for women academics there were three themes during the 1990s: alienation, anxiety and accountability. This was echoed in

Victorian public schools, and community based TAFE, where there was a collective grieving over recent reforms that many opposed for educational reasons (Down, Hogan, and Chadbourne 1999; Demspter 2000; Bishop and Mulford 1999; Blackmore et al. 1996). Teresa, principal of a disadvantaged, regional secondary school commented: "I would love to have seen a return to the 70s. Then we were empowered, not controlled: we had control of curriculum, we had resources, the stuff we were doing with kids was just so exciting. It was a wonderful time in teaching. We're here because we believe in the kids."

This nostalgia was symptomatic of the anger felt as reform challenged practices and principals' and teachers' sense of purpose and doing good. Teresa, principal, regional secondary college, believed, "If I can influence something that is going to help one kid succeed that's what you are on about. That little red head has been here now for two terms. She was expelled at the nearby school but has lasted here. If you can save one child it is worth it." Her professionalism was premised upon her moral responsibility to all children, a motivating factor for many to become teachers and principals (Nias 1999). When such values were compromised, there were high levels of stress arising from anger. As Colleen, principal of a working-class secondary school put it, "I have been working as a principal in the western, working-class suburbs most of my career. I think that education has a point. It isn't just to reinforce the prevailing set of comforts and lies. I have a very crude, simple view that some people don't have a fair go, and if I'm going to put my energy somewhere I'd rather put it there than to enhance the privileges of the privileged."

Education as a field of social practice is historically marked by a collective political commitment to make a difference. Colleen was upset that the new expectations and responsibilities imposed on them by restructuring had reduced her capacity as a principal to ensure a fair go for all students. Her school, with its high cultural mix in a low socioeconomic suburb, was under the challenge of closure because of its size, regardless of its program's effectiveness and the community's need. Likewise in a similar inner-city school, Barbara felt angry at the abrogation of responsibility by government with regard to disadvantage "At the philosophical or value level, what I have found most difficult is the lack of acknowledgment by this government that students who have traditionally been seen as disadvantaged probably don't deserve anything different. The special needs staffing was slashed. I couldn't have morally made the decision, but it was put upon me."

Charlotte, a primary principal in an inner-city, progressive, middle-class primary school stated that

> the reason I get as angry as I do is that I actually worked for four years in the English system that regarded Australian teachers, in particular teachers trained in Victoria, as the "crème de la crème." And now this government has alienated our system. We are talking about deprofessionalizing in terms of

teacher skills, curriculum development, a whole lot of things in which we were seen world wide as the model. Suddenly we are told they're no good any more. That is the rationale being used to force change.

Teresa, Colleen, Barbara, and Charlotte were from a generation of teachers immersed in professional discourses of responsibility to "the public" and social change through education. They had experienced active participation in school-based decision making and parental participation in Victorian public schools during the 1980s. To be angry or feel grief, one has to value what is lost, as emotions embody how an individual sees her commitment as part of her place in the scheme of things. One university EO practitioner commented about a PVC: "He doesn't understand what gender equity is about at all. He does understand economics." She commented on how public-sector reform had leached out the humanity so critical to educational work. "But you can't underestimate the symbolic or the type of emotion, the emotional realm. Public-sector reform is almost removing the human element from all that we do: it's as if power is not an issue, that interpersonal relationships are not an issue, yet organizations are only about power and personal relationships."

Anger, despair, anxiety, and fear echoed throughout the interviews. Anger was expressed about the value shift away from a collective sense of education for the public good to that of a positional or consumer "good"; about media-generated perceptions about the failure of public schooling that increased as funding decreased; and about how "cultures of compliance and competition bec[a]me endemic to the system driven by whatever economic rationalism means—devaluing what these children are and can be" (Dempster 2000, 9). A primary school principal, Colleen, describes how systemic dispositions focusing on the rational and economic impacted on her own behavior, attitude, relationships, and psyche:

> I found that I'd been angry now in my own mind. People are not performing to the standard that I now require . . . I'm becoming more and more impatient. The rate of imposition of change and the imposition of accountability without necessarily knowing the direction has meant often decisions are made without sound reasonable and democratic decision-making processes. I've had to dictate things more. I think that collaboration is over. . . . [I]n fact we're lucky to consult, least of all collaborate. Staff are in a state of disbelief. They can't believe it's happening so quickly. None of us want to take it on board. You can easily ostrich away.

This principal was angry about the reforms themselves, her incapacity to resist them, her staff's resistance to her having to mandate them, and the ineffectiveness of her attempts to protect her staff. She learned to practice subterfuge as the system discouraged, and in some instances forbade, her from being open and honest with her staff, thus infusing her staff relationships with distrust; yet she shared their commitment to particular political and ethical positions now under threat. Deem and Ozga (2000, 204) comment on similar reforms in the United Kingdom: "Values about markets, business, enterprise, efficient management, individualism, and competition sit uneasily with those which emphasise public service on the basis of need, social justice, collective ideas, human development of the aesthetic and the emotional as well as the cognitive."

Nias (1999) comments about how the "enactment of values" through teaching and pedagogical work requires a commitment to the work itself, the prerogative to make decisions, and the need to control the process. Emotions are forms of resistance and of transformation: resistance in the sense that teachers displayed frustration as well as guilt in that they were unable to do what they felt was educationally best for their students, producing an inner fragmentation within teacher identities (Nias 1999). The effect was physiological as well as emotional and intellectual, referred to by one principal in our study as "the niggling behind the left shoulder blade" and by another manifested as frequent migraines. The struggle was also about basic democratic principles. According to Colleen (principal, working-class secondary college)

> I've always believed, whether it be false or not, that we are all equal. But I don't think we are anymore. Every staff member does too. But the point is they've got to account to me, whereas in the past if one had to account to anyone it was to an external body. The bogeyman who said we had [to] reduce jobs or funding tended to be the ministry: now it's me. So I find myself making some fairly harsh decisions sometimes, out of necessity. I think my basic morality and my ethics are there, but I think I'm losing a bit of my humanity. I don't like that. It's one thing I value most of all about myself and about female administrators. But the pace of change and the huge expansion of the job without support for administrative staff has meant that I collaborate very little, consult a fair bit, but decide solo.

Matters of trust, values, and ethics emerged in the interviews, tinged with cynicism and disillusionment. Carmel, a professor in a sandstone university, commented, "I'm very passionate about human rights because my research is in the area of prejudice and intergroup relationships. I guess I'm probably not more passionate about gender issues than other intergroup issues, as there are a lot of similarities across the game for men and women. But I am very passionate about how students are treated."

Organizational theory now sees emotions as critical to understanding change (Fineman 2000). In times of radical restructuring, emotions are simultaneously binding and fragmenting: there is a sense of solidarity between workers who all undergo the stress of the intensification of postmodern work

life, the guilt they have at being employed while others lose their jobs, and isolation produced by the fear of being named redundant. Emotional responses
to change arise from different ways of seeing and embody beliefs about the
object of change. On the transformative side is the passion that teachers and
researchers invest in their work. Resistance arises often from particular value
stances about educational work. Thus Peta, a dean in a redbrick university,
commented on "doing well" ethically: "I'd rather do the things that I thought
were right, philosophically. I feel guilty because I don't do the job as well as I
really want to do it."

In addressing emotions in organizations, new wave management theory
refers to emotional intelligence, human resource management theory to stress,
and critical organizational theory to power. Emotional intelligence has, as did
culture in the 1980s, become the contemporary site in which to explore discourses of social control rather than politics. As constructed, emotional literacy pretends to be morally neutral, another "attribute" of the good leader (e.g.,
Goleman 1995). Human resource management domesticates emotions by
reducing it to conflict management or occupational stress. Mainstream educational management theory and managerial and market logics of practice
retain the unhealthy rationality/emotionality binary (male/female split) that
denies the emotional and the political.

> Rationality surfaces as the positive while emotionality is viewed as a nega-
> tive. The prevalence of these dualities contributes to treating emotion as a
> form of labor or as a tool of exerting influence in organizational settings. In
> organizations, emotions are consistently devalued and marginalized while
> rationality is privileged as an ideal of organizational life. Moreover, the
> devaluing of emotions and the elevating of rationality results in a particular
> moral order, one that reflects the politics of the social interaction rather than
> a universal norm for behavior. . . . [R]ationality is typically seen as objective,
> orderly, and mental while emotionality reflects the chaotic and bodily drives.
> (Putnam and Mumby 2000, 39–40)

Yet as we have shown, consuming organizations tap into physical as well
as psychological being on the basis of rationality, while exploiting individual
and group emotions. Emotions are embedded in culture and ideology; they
are "embodied and situated, sensational and physiological, cognitive and conceptual in terms of shaping our perceptions, and there is an additional linguistic dimension to our emotional awareness, attributions and interpretations" (Boler 1999, xix).

We have argued elsewhere (Sachs and Blackmore 1998) that emotions
(e.g., anger and stress) are often the surface response to deeper issues around
organizational malaise, political conflict, and values dissonance. These phenomena are experienced and felt by individuals but often expressed collectively,

as part of what we call the "sociopsychic economy" of education. The notion of sociopsychic economy makes links among social intimacy, the emotional, and the political economy in organizational life. As a concept, we suggest, it is more complex than notions of organizational morale, usually measured in terms of satisfaction surveys, occupational climate questionnaires, or levels of occupational stress. It is more than role ambiguity or "burnout," defined as arising from "emotional exhaustion, depersonalization and reduced personal accomplishment resulting from conflicts between professional caregivers' values in enhancing the lives of their recipients and the limitations in the structures and processes of their service organizations" (Huberman and Vanderberghe 1999, 1). The paradigmatic shift in academic and teacher habitus, and the value shift based on contractualism, competition, and compliance, along with the emergence of the performative organization and nation state has led to a collective sense of anomie, alienation, and disengagement, a shift in the sociopsychic economy of the field of education.

THE EMOTIONAL MANAGEMENT WORK OF CHANGE

Leadership is also emotional work as emotions involve judgments that are salient to one's sense of self-identity and how one feels, sees, and thinks about the world. Politics, emotions, and values are inextricably intertwined, as are emotions and cognition. Yet any rebellion against the instrumental logic of the practices of restructuring or the drive for improved performance was readily typified as being irrational or emotional, illogical, and to be ignored. Of this, women, who are stereotypically portrayed as the bearers of emotion, are highly aware. Nevertheless, it was womanagers who undertook the emotional management work of cultivating social relationships in organizations in crisis. Emotions, care, and responsibility have been discursively related to female attributes. Women are seen to be the "keepers, so to speak, of much of the moral fabric of social life once woven so more closely into wider traditional forms . . . as men lost touch with the emotional origins of society in which work was the icon. . . . [R]elegated to the private sphere, now women's 'labor or love' becomes as important to productivism as the autonomy of work itself" (Casey 1995, 176–77).

This emotional maintenance work is like housework; never ending but essential to sustain the processes of labor commodification. Francesca (Utech) referred to the "lack of time, sheer workload, being tired, the huge amount of time taken up with emotional energy. You get to the point when you think, if another person comes through the door with a complaint, I'm going to scream." 'Mending the social fabric" was an extension of the "emotion work" women tend to undertake in their more "traditional" familial roles. Women were expected to relate to colleagues as "mothers" rather than colleagues, as

Gabriella (head of school, Utech) ironically commented that "getting bogged down in all the procedures, I get impatient having to be nice to people all the time. I find it tiring to sort of mother all the time [in] meetings where all the people around the table are in competition with each other [and] having to contain conflict." Leesa, an associate dean, agreed that "you are always expected to be the mother. My loss of time is a huge cost of this mothering role." Similarly, one VC commented that the psychology of leadership is actually like a form of good parenting with the associated aspects of nurturance, authority, and dependability that it implies. "They look at you and need to be reassured—not as some mummy or daddy—but to get a sense that you are competent. [There is] a strong parental element in leadership." Working at the executive level with senior male colleagues was also a matter of negotiating emotions, keeping a distance, making collegial moves, but being forever wary. Renate, director of a TAFE institute, saw gender politics as a form of maternalism: "Removed yes, they don't know me as well. A lot of men are very frightened of me. My heart bleeds for them. I actually feel that, with women, the mettle is tested, and the boundaries are pushed just a little bit further. If they catch me out, that's fine, and I appreciate that. If they behave like children, well they're going to get treated like kids."

Then there was the labor in controlling one's own emotions as "roles and tasks exert overt and covert control over emotional displays. Through recruitment, selection, socialization and performance evaluations, organizations develop a social reality in which feelings become a commodity for achieving instrumental goals" (Putnam and Mumby 2000, 37). Particular emotional displays were allowable for men and not women, as emotional displays are read differently. Raffaella, a senior coordinator in a disadvantaged secondary school believed: "Yes, a man doesn't have to prove himself that much. A woman has to doubly prove herself, triply prove herself. Also you learn from any early age to try not to be emotional; not to be hysterical about things; don't show tears. You can get angry, and you can fly off the handle, but you don't show tears, as that is weakness."

Eve, a dean in a redbrick university, reflected on how "people come in my office and cry a lot. I rarely find myself moved to tears. Work stuff I don't get emotional about . . . except maybe once or twice out of sheer frustration. But I don't, no matter how rough it gets, burst into tears. It does affect me badly. I don't sleep at night." Others claimed the right to be angry or tearful:

> I have sometimes been very close to tears. I have never resiled from the fact that I have the right to because people need to see that you can be hurt, distressed, and that's how the job impacts on you. But I'm also very articulate when I'm angry. I think people find it uncomfortable, but I am going to continue to do that because I think that we just closed up people's emotional lives in the name of so-called objectivity. (Peta, head of school, redbrick)

Emotional management work became critical in times of radical restructuring. Middle managers were aware how intense emotions emerged out of frequent restructurings, redundancies, and retirements. A dean reflected on how "there's been a lot of anger around—'why us, why not someone else in the faculty?'" In a university where redundancy letters had been issued, Paula (dean, Utech) expected considerable anger and resentment: "It's perfectly reasonable to make the Dean an object of anger and grief. So I would plan to make myself very available, as I have done in the past, in the process, both to people who wish to see me but also to my heads of schools, as well and to staff members. We are the only faculty required to increase our efforts at the same time as having cuts."

The emotional management work was fraught because restructuring decisions were largely made elsewhere, intervening in longstanding social relations, as Jill recalled:

> I liked talking to people, and that was very nice. Then they talk about restructuring . . . a lot of them were quite depressed, critical, and angry, [saying] it's all the fault of somebody in the school. I found that a bit hard to handle. As head of school I've had everybody in this negotiation phase wanting things from me, people putting in stress leave plans for example, then not giving students back their marks. We get complaints. Then someone's always going on sick leave, stress leave, or getting very upset.

Anne Marie (dean, redbrick) was highly "conscious of doing organizational housework. I just came and did it before. Now, it's got out of hand, because the restructure has totally shaken up the whole system, and all power is up for grabs."

Across all sectors there was a strong discourse about women's different experiences as being othered, yet being held (and feeling) responsible for relationships in the organization, underpinned by the expectation that as women they were expected to be communicative, collaborative, consensual, and caring, although the organization expected them to restructure efficiently. Some women also undertook the emotional labor to support other women in an often hostile climate, which involved representational work in committees, mentoring female colleagues, and "networking with the powerful." Melanie Walker (1997, 3) refers to how women are expected to nurture students (and indeed other male academics), but "the qualities welcomed in this nurturing identity are not what is required to survive and advance in the cut and thrust of male dominated committees and other public spaces." Self-protection was the key to survival, a point made succinctly by Anne Marie, a dean of engineering (redbrick): "Avoid the love and student support crap, and get on with the research. Now that sounds very ruthless. But there are bottom lines, and, quite frankly, young and female academics make a very real mistake if they allow the students to eat them alive . . . open door policy, twenty four hours a day . . . the eternal maternal breast."

Such discourses of care and collaboration upon which many of our participants drew derived from their experience as women and also from a body of cultural feminist research identifying women leaders' preferences for care, cooperation, and communication. But to be too caring was dangerous because it heightened expectations from other women, ignored difference among women, and cultivated false hope in the capacity of women leaders to transform organizations singlehandedly. Elle, a DVC, warned about

> an expectation amongst younger women that we go into leadership and display a nice, nurturing, and cooperative leadership style and transform the institutions. But life on the top is very hard if you try and do that only. You will not get there. There is a limit to the nurturing stuff, or we wear ourselves out. As a woman at the top, you have to put a bit of fence around yourself for self-protection. You can't just go on forever looking after others.

Leadership was about emotional as well as intellectual toughness. Our womanagers' emotional capital was readily appropriated by the organization's gendered division of labor. Rima (senior lecturer, sandstone) commented that "people are always muttering and mumbling, and there is a general air of disaffection about the place. The VC sees his main task as making money for the institution and not academic leadership." The emotion rules that dominated thus upheld the "gendered division and roles," "focusing on women's association as the virtuous mother/school teachers, and the simultaneous absence of emotion in the 'masculinized' representations" (Boler 1999, xxii).

These discourses effectively mean that "the 'postmodern,' emotionally intelligent person reflects a paradigm of hard wired morality combined with the neo-liberal autonomous 'chooser'" (Boler 1999, 60). Thus many highly successful women are now seen to be out of touch with their feelings (de Groot 1997). For womanagers more overtly committed to social justice, emotional displays were about being disorderly, disruptive, and transgressive. The tension lay for most in the seductiveness of practicing tough love required by management, and compassionate leadership that was informed by their professional and personal ethics. Male managers increasingly confront this tension as they too are expected to practice emotional awareness, management, and control (Lingard and Douglas 1999). But the danger is that this new managerial masculinity instrumentalizes passion in ways that glamorize management, manage conflict, and recognize the emotional turmoil of downsizing, while always delineating what one cannot feel, "such as guilt over lay offs, bullying and demands for increased productivity and demand of constant monitoring, testing and improving and transforming the individual" (Hatcher 2003, 408). So in effect, there is an ongoing distinction between compassion for others as exercised though ethical leadership (women's emotional management work) and a passion for work expressed as an uncomfortable integration of instrumental emotion and rationality (men's emotional management work).

But this is not depicting women "doing deference" and men "doing dominance" (Aschraft and Mumby 2004, 5). While some of our participants called upon discourses of women having a "superior moral position" relative to their male colleagues because of their "pre-disposition" towards care, they saw caring work as an essential part of good management, as did many men. The difference was that mobilizing emotional capital is a positive attribute for male managers but "natural" for women and devalued (Aschraft and Mumby 2004, 5; Lingard and Douglas 1999; Avis 2002; Keamy 2004). Consequently, women's emotional management work went unrecognized and unsupported and therefore was "tiring work, incorporating caring and service, with responsibilities that are often not regarded as demanding high skill or rewarded. . . . [T]hus many women . . . even in positions of leadership are 'doing good and feeling bad'" (Acker and Feuerverger 1996).

Alienation and Disengagement

The psychotherapeutic territory charted above was the site of struggle between performative and professional dispositions within the leadership habitus. The sense of a shifting professional psyche was a commonly expressed sentiment in all sectors, as if caught between the subjective sense of professional identity and the objective sense of professionals as bearers of rationality. Each responded differently. As in other caring professions, some "dislocated their interest from the profession and the technical qualification" (Olesen 2001, 291). Others integrated their sense of professional responsibility in other ways, through political and civil involvement, for example, by becoming active in unions (Olesen 2001). Many respondents spent considerable energy grieving the demise of collegiality, care, and cooperation. While our participants remained committed to teaching and research, many no longer felt any attachment to their institution. This loss of organizational commitment and self-estrangement was producing a "crisis of professional self-identity" which led to disengagement (Winter, Taylor, and Sarros 2000, 283; Gronn and Rawlings Sanaei 2003). In the past, according to a principal of a large secondary school, "teachers used to withdraw to the classroom at times when there were changes they did not like or when they've got a lot of disappointments under their belt. But now they no longer find that withdrawal into the classroom the source of joy that it used to be. The classroom has changed so much—they are under closer scrutiny there than ever before." Carol, aspirant principal in a working-class secondary school, lacked the language to express her alienation until "someone at a conference was talking about corporate managerialism and why we now have outcomes-based education in terms of the political and social changes that have led to this being accepted as the right way in education. She articulated explicitly that the dominant attitude was that you teach technique and content doesn't matter. This is how I feel as a teacher now."

De Groot (1997) defines alienation as "the growing sense of separation between work and personal identity" and the experience of "loss of control or even influence over many aspects of their work" (134). Alienation was articulated in numerous ways. One state education bureaucrat commented about how she actually got the job that was "the peak of my career. But what I really disliked is the idea of selling myself. I got a real 'distance' feeling" (Charlotte). Another university manager of EO commented: "I don't feel attached to the job any more but do feel attached to issues." Implementing mandated change with which they disagreed led to some disengagement but also produced a form of "sociopsychological splitting" so that they could do "what they had to do" for the survival of the organization, although always ambivalent. To succeed required being seen to be competent but also behaving according to the organizational scripts for success. Margaret, a newly appointed senior manager in a small, progressive TAFE, was conscious of the demand for productivity savings and the escalation in sessional staff. Her resolution was "deciding that you actually don't own all the problems. . . . So even though I would like to do certain things, I can't: I would blow the budget, and I would be out of job, and they wouldn't have jobs either. I can't own the problem of solving the Australian economy by employing some people here: it's a matter of being realistic." Her response to norm-governed behavior was to distance herself from the difficult decisions in many committees. Barbara, a secondary school principal, viewed distancing as a "coping mechanism, because if you get angry about this you lose your effectiveness, and it is not good for the kids, and that's bad for all of us."

The extent of institutional "fabrication" required by the new performative regimes hit hardest for middle managers (heads of school and departments and principals) who were presented with images and strategic plans that did not represent the experiences, needs, or desires of those at the interface. The madness of performativity requirements produced "inauthentic practice and relationships" where "authenticity is replaced by plasticity" (Ball 2000, 17). Lesley, a middle manager at a TAFE institute reflected:

> I've had rolling existential crises about the integration of my corporate and personal soul. When I moved from the adult community education sector . . . to the commercial environment here . . . I had a crisis for about six months. I felt that my soul was in jeopardy. How was I going to keep my values so important to my reason for living and being in this job? How was I going to maintain the learning that I got from working with people who are dying in an environment that is now essentially profit driven? And I worried for

myself. And I would hear things coming out of my mouth that shocked me. Bottom line stuff. Then the crises stopped. Then I had another huge crisis because it stopped! I wondered about the implications. There is another letting go . . . of what I value.

This constant accommodation of contrary beliefs was felt by Bev, principal of a rural secondary school. She was "discussing the possibility of throwing in my job because I believe that my ethics and morality are now under question. The problem was that I had to name someone 'in excess' for instance. While I have done this before, for the first time in my life, it didn't particularly bother me." We are all social actors; but when there is a strong sense of alienation of the actor from the performance, there is need for considerable "repair work" (Hopfl and Linstead 2000, 77).

This sense of alienation and disengagement is illustrative of the paradoxical relations of neobureaucratic corporate organizations. Managers were encouraged to use team building, renewal days, consultation, and focus groups to build a sense of purpose (Sinclair 1995a). But "the system says it wants teamwork but I don't think it really does" (Jane, TAFE). The reality was

> competitive individualism. People become flavor of the month, and you get rewarded if you say the right thing. It is double think and double speak: everybody knows it is meaningless. But everybody is participating. . . . Why? I get to work at 7:15 AM and rarely leave before dark. I try to cut down, but there is more work. I am one of these people who believes in the idea of being a public servant. (Charlotte, school bureaucrat, Queensland)

Productivism did not bring the same satisfaction as effecting meaningful change. Any sense of the collective was fragmented, if not dissipated. There was a disconnectedness with organizations, a reduced sense of belonging, but not to education as a field of practice.

MANAGING THE SOCIOPSYCHIC ECONOMY

Our cohort of leaders managed and mediated the sociopsychic economy. "The different groupings in organizations, and their relative hierarchical and status positions, must be held in place by feelings—such as belonging, respect, diffidence, fear, awe and love. As social glue, feelings will make or break organizational structures and gatherings" (Fineman 2000, 14–15). The focus on competitive social relations, performativity, and self-regulation undermined old allegiances, loyalties, and relations of trust and cooperation with the emphasis now on compliance and rituals of verification .

Trust and Respect

Critical incidents indicated moments of hope as well as despair. With wo-managers as the new players in a small, progressive TAFE, Lesley spoke of "an extraordinary and general feeling of great hope. Not just because they are women, but because they are seen as being very capable. And for me, the last year of restructuring was frozen, very painful, and very, very bloody. . . . [T]his is my honeymoon time. It won't last. We need some successes soon to see that the pain and the blood has been worthwhile." This hope was premised upon the trust many women had earned "on the shop floor" and now was put to the test by management and being in management. For other women, trust had to be earned, as for a female VC:

> She is pragmatic to a fault, and she makes things happen. She is very strongly directed and very decisive. She does contradictory things like any complex influential person. She is also enormously supportive on a range of things, such as talking to women in promotion workshops. . . . [S]he knows them all individually. She espouses a set of values and actually works them. She knows the stuff about getting close to people and knowing about them and the power of actually personalizing what she says. But then she can turn around and do something really shitty, and you think, that was awful, how could you do that? Our school budget is going to lose $1.4 million, and staff will go. (Deana, senior lecturer).

In large institutions such as universities, institutional trust was built on perceptions arising from discourses, symbols, actions, and policies, which in turn fed into institutional narratives of hope or despair. Most educators were conscious, particularly in large institutions, that decisions would often impact detrimentally unintentionally and that collegiality and collaboration were not always possible. Many of our middle managers' capacity to lead and manage well was based on trust that built on past behaviors, practices, and relation-ships. Their decisions, while difficult and unpleasant, when based on princi-ples of fairness, openness, and collegiality, were more palatable because staff realized the pressures they personally felt.

At the same time, Bishop and Mulford (1999) argued that in restructur-ing Victorian schools "teacher trust in principals is undermined by perceptions of principal cooption to change initiatives which are unsupported by teachers. In turn, qualified trust of the principal fuels teacher anxiety" (180). Academics as teachers were antagonistic and resistant when there were no transparent processes or evident rationale, lack of fairness, or maltreatment of colleagues, more typical of workplaces under restructuring (see chapter 3). In systems and organizations, particular incidents and stories fueled distrust. A TAFE man-ager recalled vividly how a female colleague went on leave after a meeting in which a male manager left in distress because he was losing his position and no one went to comfort him. This lack of compassion and respect for others was, she considered, becoming the norm. Many middle managers themselves expressed how in relations with other managers they felt "a sense of betrayal, of not being wanted, whereas I like honesty and hate silence" (Janis, large, metropolitan TAFE). Collegial relationships of trust are critical for "professional and emotional sustenance" (Nias 1999, 2).

Trust was also linked to issues of respect. Even when committed to achieving organizational goals, there was little sense of mutual respect as "you never feel as though you get it right before the goals have changed. I'm sick of it. You never actually get to the point where you are told that you have done a good job" (Leanne, community-oriented, suburban TAFE). In Victoria, the changed sociopsychic economy of the system was described by Barbara, principal in a working-class secondary college: "It is difficult to watch some of the interrelations within the department, and the lack of respect in the way they deal with people within their own organization, both principals and other senior officers . . . the rules they are imposing on the schools for staff selection they are not imposing on themselves. There is a moral dilemma there."

Despite being highly trained teachers and/or researchers, there was a lack of recognition of their expertise and professional work by organizations and systems. Recognition was largely derived either from students, professional "communities of practice," or networks. "The reward (and sense of respect) comes from people who actually use my work, buy your books, and keep asking you to go back to work with them—not from the university" (Chee Wah, senior lecturer, redbrick).

Loyalty and Belonging

Yet corporate educational organizations expected higher levels of loyalty than ever before, loyalty most often mobilized on the grounds of survival rather than in building organizational cultures conducive to employee satisfaction. There was little reciprocity of loyalty, as multiple restructurings were marked by a lack of consultation and consensus; a readiness to "offload" staff, "slim down" or "hive off" parts; shifting responsibility down the line without the resources and capacity to improve outcomes; sporadic attempts to induce greater worker commitment through reward systems for some and a punitive culture for most; and a superficial concern for employee health and well-being at a time when work has intensified by a factor of three. "You get really angry, and people are very demoralized. . . . [T]here are signals about the university being uncaring. . . . [Y]ou are expected to commit to a job and your institution, but it is not repaid in kind. So you let that commitment slip—they lose you" (Fay, senior lecturer, redbrick). In a university facing restructuring after the appointment of a new VC, one associate professor commented: "I love the faculty, but I find the university at large much more problematic. There is an obsession with managing its image rather than its substance. There is an atmosphere of great uncertainty and anxiety about the future. There is a pressure of trying to generate a sense of future and positivity, which is not easy. I find the future depressing" (Brenda, associate professor, redbrick).

Loyalty was increasingly to immediate colleagues, to a field of practice, but not to the institution.

> The problem about this restructuring is that the reason I [felt] more loyal to my university in the past was because it was into disciplinary excellence. But now it is becoming a regular straight-jacket type of university. And I think that as a lot becomes centralized, there will be very little variety. But I think less of loyalty to the university and loyalty to being an academic. We have to attract the new young bright ones, but the quality of life is not there anymore. It is not so much about money; it's about the time, that quality of life that you get, but I don't think we will be about excellence any more. (Sue, sandstone)

There were similar comments at a sandstone university with a relatively new VC that indicated a shift in loyalties: "[W]e have a pretty supportive departmental head. I have some wonderful colleagues who are very supportive.... But not at the institutional level: I don't think the institution has done a lot for its staff" (Helen, lecturer, sandstone). Such sentiments were echoed in each sector, the localization of loyalty exacerbated by structural and cultural divisions forcing competitive relations, encouraging social fragmentation rather than cohesion. These weak ties are because "fleeting forms of association are more useful to people now than long term associations" (Sennett 1998, 24), as part of the wider "disengagement of labor with capital." There is "no reciprocal dependency" with the increased autonomy of capital, despite the "nuisance factor" of even the most compliant local government (Bauman 2001, 25).

Agency and Disempowerment

Restructuring produced both new opportunities and new constraints. For some, there was newfound agency in the entrepreneurial culture that was enticing, "reinventing systems . . . changing strategies, policies" (Jane, small, progressive, suburban TAFE). Tricia actively subverted the dominant agendas of a large, metropolitan TAFE:

> [T]he corporate is enormously present in the culture, and it has huge implications in terms of pedagogy and day-to-day practice, the shape of the service we offer. And it's got a very ugly side, dehumanizing. But there are also

enormous potentials to work creatively within a fairly heartless environment and find ways to score the dollars without losing your soul, and to ensure social capital is on the agenda, and equity issues, sometimes seen as being marginal and flaky. It's challenging to be overt about them, in some contexts. But if you learn the language of the economic rationalists, you can ensure that those other deeper values are embedded in your own perspective, and you can access the funding and then do something good with it. It's one of our covert briefs. You bring in the money, and then we do what we want to do with it as much as possible. Clearly there are accountabilities. But wherever possible, you manipulate and turn these to your own objectives.

By contrast, others in less flexible (often less wealthy) institutions had little sense of agency. The seeming inevitability of further restructuring also produced a feeling of disempowerment in terms of these women managers' own capacity to produce change in the ways they felt were worthwhile.

The changes that are occurring at TAFE due to the amalgamations are having a bad effect on people's morale. For people who have been in the system a long time, there is a form of grieving and a sense of loss. TAFE is changing so quickly you can't guarantee that you will have a job even in the next few years, producing fear. Teaching is no longer given the importance due to time constraints. I try to keep morale up and help people to feel in control of their future. (Sheila, large, metropolitan TAFE)

As Janis in the same large, metropolitan TAFE commented, "change wasn't too rapid, but the system fell down here because it didn't explain the changes to people." TAFE institutes in particular were confronting another round of restructuring at the time of this study. "The workplace is hard here. The pressure is on. We are always under the threat of amalgamation, the threat of being taken over, the threat of going out of business" (Sandra, small, rural TAFE). A large, metropolitan TAFE relied heavily on competitive tendering for income and therefore contractual casualized labor. Alice, a middle manager in the literacy area, expressed anger and frustration as she described how the loss of a competitive tender exacerbated division, fear, and insecurity:

We've just been told we will lose at least another twelve teachers and a sixth of our students as a result of losing the tender. The new providers will be using abandoned factories and warehouses, and highly qualified students will be misplaced. It is undoing an enormous amount of work. It's very difficult and stressful with industrial conflict. People are tense about losing jobs. Teachers are a commodity and being sold down the drain.

Alice went on to say, "I feel quite powerless in the workplace." Joanna, manager in a large, outer suburban, community-oriented TAFE, was quite depressed about her job, the TAFE, and life in general. She felt defeated, depicting the coordinator's position as a "fairly thankless position" and not seen as a promotion. She had some aspirations of bringing about change in the department but framed by a "them and us" approach—management versus workers. "I've had to play it both ways. I've had to play different games at different times." The enterprising character of this new work order was typified as being about self-reliance, assuming personal responsibility, and being bold in action and risk taking. Yet agency was significantly constrained by organizational parameters, for some more than others, in which individuals took on all the risk.

COMPLIANCE AND COMPROMISE

The discursive effects of education's corporatization have been to increase self-regulation as the performative exercises required of educational workers are internalized and indeed, as Butler (1999) would suggest, become part of the everyday. Repeated performances "naturalize" what was initially a construct. There was the constant drive to get another grant, present another conference paper, produce another article in a refereed journal, win another contract, or improve student performances on another standardized test. The irony was that the gross aggregating exercises embedded in the disciplinary technologies of accountability had universalizing and normalizing effects that valued quantity over quality, image over substance, money over intellectual work. The focus on the performative led to a shift in behaviors: "They now feel disenfranchised after restructuring and have disengaged. Academics feel bitter. Seventy percent of the faculty are just here for the money now" (Jill, head of school, Utech).

Promotion also required new levels of compliance. One TAFE manager did not get a job because "I don't like to compromise my values for a job . . . I don't know whether I'm disillusioned or burned out or it's a phase I'm going through. I do know I am pretty pissed off" (Leanne, large, metropolitan TAFE). Refusal to compromise an ethical position meant one did not "fit" organizational expectations. Compliance, as Roya, manager in a large, outer suburban, community-oriented TAFE, explained, was, on the one hand, a product of fear and, on the other, a product of guilt.

> Restructuring generates fear and inwardness—not being able to think creatively about what's best for the organization. Rather it's about what's going to help you survive personally—the incredible waste of time and energy that goes into people holding onto their jobs in a restructuring.

Temporary staff are really discriminated against—women in lower positions. The restructure has collapsed two jobs into one, for me, and that's too much.

Heather (large, metropolitan TAFE) attested to how in TAFE as schools and universities, the climate of fear meant "people are a bit frightened to take industrial action." Managers often excused their seeming complicity with actions they disagreed with. "If someone else does it, it could be worse, so better that I do it" or "we have no choice." This apparent decline in the "quality of the self" is the result of the "tyranny of inner compulsions and anxieties" that are socially produced (Casey 1995, 24).

In the good times, organizations gained productivity through work satisfaction; in the bad times, corporate culture and productivity is closely linked to fear. Clearly, the connection between fear and loyalty, compliance and compromise, is close. As Clarke (1998, 180) puts it—there were the converts to the new managerialism; there were those who used the discourse "conditionally and calculatingly in performing compliance," and those who "do not believe a word of it; but whose behaviors are necessarily constrained and constructed by its institutional embeddedness." This indicates "the ability to produce behavioral compliance at the same time as inducing scepticism, cynicism, and disbelief. There is a difference between being subjected to a discourse and becoming a subject through it" (Clarke 1998, 180). The effect, according to Calabrese and Roberts (2001), is a "fragmented organization [where] there is little structure and members work together on temporary alliances, consolidating power and isolating potential threats to the illusion of stability" (270).

A CRISIS IN MEANING

This cult of performativity therefore leads to the production of symbolic capital for some and not others in these contexts. "Prestige and a glowing reputation . . . operate as symbolic capital because they mean nothing in themselves, but depend on people believing that someone possesses these qualities" (Webb, Schirato, and Danaher 2002, xvi). Those who benefit from the cult of performativity in education tend to have the attributes of the postmodern elite who flourish in dislocation, without familial responsibilities, have mobility and a capacity to shift and change, the "very attributes of character (exuberance and spontaneity) that are self destructive for those lower down in the flexible regime" (Bauman 2001, 39). Performativity encourages change to be superficial and not deep-seated or owned throughout the organization, with knee jerk short-term reactions to problems rather than informed and creative responses that question the assumptions underpinning how the organization works: that is, first-loop and not second-loop learning.

Our study points to a crisis in meaning. Organizations now see motivation is something that can be "tapped" into and "translated into achievement in terms of actual performance or levels of emotional, psychological or spiritual satisfaction" (Middlehurst 1993, 43). But the motivation to become teachers or academics for this generation was more for the "psychic rewards of teaching—different from extrinsic rewards of pay, bonuses and promotion to the ancillary rewards of work hours, vacation etc. . . . but to the classroom and school events, relationships with students and colleagues" (Lortie 1975, 101). Our cohort of educators had political and emotional investments in educational work. As performative institutions exploit this investment, they undermine the motivation for being educators, their sense of purpose, producing deep social and moral dilemmas outside the scope of the new management calculus. Individuals accommodate and internalize the normative codes of various practical settings, provided they were not overly dissonant with primary dispositional patterns. These are the self-conserving tendencies of habitus, to have a sense of identity that is ethical and egoistic. But when there is significant dissonance due to a radical change in the rules of the game, then "habitus tends to shun the practices that inculcate such secondary dispositions, perceiving them as alien and 'other' to any comfortable coherence of 'Oneself'" (Zipin and Brennan 2003, 358). Many of our women participants experienced dissonant rather than accommodative habitus, producing significant distress because "it requires considerable courage to acknowledge the potentially damaging effect of lack of congruence between beliefs and behavior, values and action, and decide that there may be other ways of achieving goals" (Brooks 2001, 25).

The issue here is not between "bounded rationality" (normalizing masculinist stereotypes of distance, objectivity, decision-making, logic) or "bounded emotionality" (normalizing feminine styles of nurturance, caring community, supportiveness), but one that recognized that emotionality and rationality are integrated and integral to organizational life. While a focus on bounded emotionality provides an "alternative mode of organizing based on the construction of inter-subjective meanings, an integration of mind and body, work as community, tolerance of ambiguity and non-hierarchical goals and values" (Ashcraft and Mumby 2004, 99), it also fails to ask "how particular emotions are expressed, perceived and interpreted within organizations." This is where gender becomes the issue; how gender performance is enacted and interpreted. There is, we suggest, more of unity among thinking, feeling, and morality than often depicted.

Norms regulating feelings have a high moral content, and feelings are aroused when particular normative dimensions are lost, infringed, or rejected. On the one hand, the type of organizational purposing assumed in corporate management loses out because it lacks that normative dimension. On the other hand, performativity carries with it its own "ethical logic" as the notions of enterprise and excellence are increasingly central to new forms of governmentality accompanying the "progressive enlargement of the territory of the market" that "defines the sort of relation an individual should have with him or herself and the 'habits of action' he or she should acquire and exhibit" (du Gay 1996, 56). Clearly then the sociopsychic psychic economy and emotional health of an organization are important indicators of the "well-being" at the individual and institutional level. Issues of performativity now stand at the core of how women experience this and negotiate their place in an organization.

TEN

Progression and Regression: Managing Diversity, Equity, and Equal Opportunity

GLOBALIZATION HAS PROVIDED the conditions through which national, organizational, and individual identities are being reconstructed by raising questions about who we are and where we belong. But what do we mean by "we" (Prasad and Prasad 2002, 58)? The Karpin report (1995) on management education predicted cultural, linguistic, racial, and gender diversity in leadership by 2010 that would reflect the cultural diversity of the Australian workforce and global clients. However, in 2005 in Australia, while there is increased contact with different cultural groups within organizations, it is often without any change in hierarchical relations. The cultural homogeneity, the whiteness and maleness of executive and middle management in Australia (including education) (Sinclair and Wilson 2002), stands out starkly against the multicultural nature of the Australian workforce, one of the most culturally and linguistically diverse in the world (Wilkinson 2005). This lack of the presence of the "other" has become a significant problem for management—symbolically and practically—with changing demographics locally and the internationalization of education.

This chapter explores the emergence of discourses of equity (gender, multiculturalism, and antiracism) during the 1980s through the distinctive work of the femocrats (feminist bureaucrats installed within the state) (Yeatman 1998b), professional groups, and unions (Franzway 2001; Taylor 2001), as well as grassroots activism by teachers, academics, and EO practitioners in universities, TAFE, and schools (Kenway et al. 1998). It considers how these equity discourses came to be marginalized or dismissed in the 1990s under neoliberal and socially conservative governments and at the same time appropriated by discourses of diversity and management strategies of mainstreaming and devolution. Of particular concern is how did this impact on the work of women leaders and gender equity practitioners in education? Despite the possibilities raised by equal opportunity policies and discourses of diversity, and the opportunities to shift the cultures, change structures, and remove biases at a moment of radical restructuring and "reculturing" of education, the underrepresentation of women and non-Anglo groups in executive management and leadership positions is enduring.

RESTRUCTURING EQUAL OPPORTUNITY: THE LEGACIES OF GENDER EQUITY REFORM

During the 1970s and 1980s, Australia was seen to model gender equity policy development. Indeed, Australia's international reputation in gender equity reform was often credited with having greater effects than actually occurred. Why then is it that Australia in 2004 is seen by international bodies such as UNESCO as no longer exemplifying good practices in human rights and equity and commentators gender equity initiatives as stalled? Three phases of gender equity reform in Australian education mark the shifting conceptualization of equity, each phase indicative of the shifting terrain of gender politics nationally with educational restructuring.

Phase 1: In the Age of the "Femocrats" (1973–86)

In Australia, there was "a fortuitous coming together of the second wave of the women's movement and the election of a socially progressive Keynsian Labor government in 1972" (Lingard 2003, 34). The political agendas and interests of the state and of feminism as a social movement converged, even if temporarily, on a common equity agenda. This period was marked by the development of a legalistically based equity infrastructure and policy machinery resulting from the positioning of feminist bureaucrats, women's advisors, and policy units within the state (femocrats) with direct access to the prime minister. This was achieved through central policy coordination agencies, ministerial portfolio responsibility, a separation of women's policy and equal employment opportunity, bureaucratic monitoring, the funding of women's advocacy groups and services, and community representation on policy advisory committees (Sawer 2003, 40). Gender issues informed public policy formation through the mechanisms of women's budgets, statistical databases, and audits. The federal approach of incorporation was replicated in some version in each state, Victoria, South Australia, and Queensland in particular.

The femocrats were expected to be strong policy activists outside the state and advocates for gender equity within the state (Yeatman 1998b). Educational policy activism involved a dialogue with grassroots women's movements in schools, community and further education, and universities. The combination of top down equity policies and bottom up feminist activism and networking (e.g., unions) was most successful in schools during the 1980s. Reform was most marked in Victoria, where for example, gender equity was institutionalized with the appointment of EO coordinators in all schools with an ongoing policy dialogue among state policy bodies, local practitioners, and activists; networking across government and nongovernment organizations and community groups in each sector and across sectors; newsletters and conferences; and representative policy bodies (Kenway et al. 1998; Taylor 2001). The dominant approaches during this time can be characterized as promoting equal access to employment opportunities (assimilationist) with a proceduralist approach to gender equity for women in terms of removing obstacles to their advancement. This particular model of "institutionalized feminism" was participatory, and the policy process was dialogical until the late 1980s as Labor had at least rhetorically sought to balance equity issues against those of efficiency and effectiveness (Blackmore 1995; Lake 1999). The women's budget process has since been taken up in the Philippines and South Africa, and gender audits are considered best practice in equity reform by the United Nations and the Commonwealth (Sawer 1999).

Phase 2: Labor's Corporate Governance (1987–95)

In 1987, Australia stood out internationally as an example of a strategic but contested alliance between the women's movement and the state (Hancock 1999). After 1987 Labor's federal corporatism began with the tripartite agreement among business, unions, and government to restructure in response to international monetary pressures to undertake structural adjustment (see chapter 2). The femocrats, educational policy activists, and feminist unionists were considerably weakened due to their exclusion from negotiations that set the agenda for workplace restructuring, devolved industrial relations, and corporate managerialism. They saw award restructuring and devolution as a "dangerous opportunity" to redefine skill and career to be more inclusive of women's experience (van Gramberg 1999). Many opposed decentralization because, historically, any successes in equity had been delivered through central federal and state policies, reinforcing not reducing local activism (Yeatman 1998a). Enterprise bargaining also was seen to weaken union capacity, with the shift from a centralized wage-fixing system that had "been more successful in reducing differentials between men's and women's earnings than countries with relatively decentralized wage fixing systems" (Affirmative Action Agency 1995, 4; Sawer 1999). During workplace restructuring, feminist bureaucrats, unionists, and academics maintained pressure from the margins, with some symbolic policy wins that sought to improve access, participation in employment, education, and training in all sectors (e.g., National Agenda for Women 1988; Australian Women's Employment Strategy 1988). In 1991, all higher education institutions (and industries) with more than one hundred employees were expected to develop equity plans and programs. However, any gains, such as increased numbers of women academics, after 1989 were more the result of amalgamations of universities with female-dominated colleges of advanced education rather than equity policies. While the decentralized enterprise bargaining approach maintained the disadvantage test (not certifying agreements that discriminated on grounds of marital status, family responsibilities, and pregnancy), women in feminized occupations tended to bargain off child care flexibility with wages. Importantly, enterprise bargaining did not extend to casual or contract work, which were rapidly increasing in the education sector.

A key aspect of the new public administration was the mainstreaming and downstreaming of EO. The rationale was to develop an institution-wide commitment to equity "through devolving responsibilities for equity down to institutions, and in turn individual managers and units" (Bacchi 2001, 123). A positive interpretation of mainstreaming was that it embedded equal opportunity policies into daily practice, encouraging a type of gender audit as to how decisions were made, by whom, and with what effect on women. Indeed, the European Union now sees mainstreaming of gender equity as a strength and necessary for "unity" and economic growth (Mazey 2000). In Australia, mainstreaming in the 1990s (while a long-term aim of gender equity reform) weakened the capacities of the specialist EO units as they were often integrated into human relations management. EO was devolved before the substantive principles, policies, and practices had been firmly implanted into the structures, processes, and mindsets of managers (predominantly men) and practitioners on the ground. Equity was everybody's and nobody's responsibility. "It was like pouring a bottle of ink into a fast-flowing river" (EO manager). EO was still seen by most to be an imposition, an afterthought, rather than central to management practice or good leadership. As in the United Kingdom, the managerial gender agenda regressed to merely monitoring the patterns of women's distribution within institutions, with little follow-up action in the form of rewards or sanctions (Salisbury and Riddell 2000).

With the rise of economic rationalism in government in the late 1980s, the women's advisers moved out of their central location in federal government. This led to a lack of gender input into intergovernmental arrangements as Treasury took control; the disappearance of women's subcommittees in areas of health, education, and housing; increased volatility of structures of governance with frequently changing ministerial portfolios; the devaluing of policy expertise (e.g., of academics) required for authentic accountability; reduced funding of women's community organizations; and the marginalization of feminist activists in the policy process. Devolution, with its focus on outcomes and not process, and NPA, with the imposition of private-sector practices, also meant accountability for the fair application of HRM procedures was loosened with less emphasis on procedural fairness, and financial accountability was tightened. The new multiskilled bureaucrats in HR where EO units were now integrated lacked substantive knowledge of, and commitment to, equity. Merit was less equated with "suitability" and more with "acceptability" within a still largely male culture (Burton 1999). Thus "the conception of social justice which underpinned the policies of [earlier] Labor governments was distorted, reconstituted, and weakened through its coupling with, or subordination to, the meta-policy status granted to the broader economic restructuring agenda" (Lingard and Garrick 1997, 158). Despite this, universities, school departments of education, and TAFE maintained aspects of EO as part of "good HR" and for its symbolic power of being seen as an "equal opportunity employer."

Phase 3: Neoconservative Backlash (1996–)

Feminists' engagement with the state and progress toward gender equality "stalled" (Probert 2001b) and indeed became confrontational with Howard's election in 1996, midway through our study. Many EO managers experienced this change with trepidation, among them Joan, EO manager in a sandstone university, who captures this: "There is a perpetual shortage of resources in EO. But will this government dismantle EO? We sense that legislation will stay in place, but resources will be cut back." The combination of neoconservative governments federally and in some states (Queensland after 1995, Victoria after 1993) meant socially conservative policies promoting self-help and pronuclear family policies were fuelled by antifeminist discourses that "Men are victims of feminism" and "feminism gone too far." This was matched by a "cultural backlash" as coalition federal and state conservative governments fed on populist fears against refugees, indigenous people, and multiculturalism in a form of wedge politics that also "disciplined feminism" (Blackmore 1997).

There was also a structural backlash with the extension of new public administration, deregulation of the labor market, disinvestment in the public sector, a watering down of equity policies, a reduction of funding in childcare, and marginalization of equity as a policy issue. Prime Minister Howard, always strategically astute, retained equity legislation and statutory bodies such as the Affirmative Action Agency but reduced their access to power, money, and infrastructure. After 1996 the Office of Status of Women had budget cuts of 40 percent; the women's statistics unit in the Australian Bureau of Statistics as well as the *Women and Work* publication were abolished, as was the women's budget process; the Office of Indigenous Women and its various functions were "mainstreamed"; and the Office of Status of Women no longer coordinated women's policy (Sawer 2003). Adherence to EO requirements was largely restricted to large companies and then only voluntarily. The capacity of feminists to work within and through the postwelfare managerialist state in Australia, as in New Zealand, Canada, and the United Kingdom, was now severely curtailed (Coulter 1997; Arnot, David, and Weiner 1999). Similar patterns emerged in state education bureaucracies, as summed up by one teacher unionist:

> Because there is such a culture in the head office, the women who have worked as feminists have all been completely bought off and now stopped talking to all the other networks. They have either lost their jobs or moved somewhere else. They have cut off communications that created the network that allowed us to operate in the system. Now it is much easier for the system to get rid of feminists. Any left are concerned about keeping their jobs.

As Ozga and Walker (1999, 109) argued for the United Kingdom, 'the stripping of the old public service cultures of education has gender specific consequences, because, first, those cultures included the use of formal procedures and processes to support gender equality in education; and secondly, those cultures also encompassed values other than the rational a selfish calculation of benefit."

POLICY SHIFT: FROM EQUAL OPPORTUNITY TO MANAGING DIVERSITY

During the 1990s conceptualizations of equity were under transformation as part of metapolicy shifts transforming relations among education, the state, and the individual with the move to postwelfarism. Throughout the period of this study (1995–98), we identified a discursive shift away from the concept of 'equal opportunity' and 'equity' to that of 'managing diversity' in national bodies such as the Committee for Economic Development and Office of Multicultural Affairs, policy texts (*Working Nation* white paper), and reports such as the Karpin report (1995) on management education. After 1987 social democratic and liberal democratic equity discourses within the Labor Party were also increasingly subjugated to neoliberal economic rationalism.

The discourse of managing diversity has distinctly different origins and trajectories. One discursive strand arises out of the demands for equity and the rise of social movements making claims upon the state, pressures that have intensified with changing demographics. This discourse has its origins in the identity politics of the 1970s and early 1980s that promoted cultural pluralism. Diversity was seen to be a force for cultural change in and through organizations with recognition of the benefits of a diverse workplace or student population. Workforces as classrooms were no longer homogenous and united, and there was a struggle over identity, as gender, race, class, and ethnicity informed organizational loyalties and social relations. The rise of the multiculturalist movement during the 1980s and indigenous rights in the 1990s became evident in the discourse of diversity in school and community education but failed to impact in the educational leadership and administrative literature and policies (Wilkinson 2005). Multiculturalism and diversity were emancipatory notions based on democratic theories of social inclusion. Diversity was understood as recognizing cultural pluralism, what Benhabib (2002, 7–8) refers to as "mosaic multiculturalism." The theme was "cohesion in diversity . . . where identity was both hybrid and unitary" (Cope and Kalantzis 1997, 275; Prasad and Prasad 1997, 4). In the European Union, discourses of diversity have been linked more overtly to notions of citizenship, where education was about the "creation of a cultural community," an aide in the process of identity formation (Stoer and Cortesao 2000, 261). In Australia, the links between student cultural diversity, the lack of cultural diversity in educational management, and citizenship have not been made.

Another strand in the discourse of diversity was more in alignment with global managerialism. It was now realized that organizational survival was dependent on "managing diversity" better (Karpin 1995). Here diversity was perceived as a problem. Educational institutions as providers required their services to be responsive to more culturally diverse populations. With the rise of national and international market regimes, diversity came to mean offering programs, awards, pathways, and so on that enabled individual purchasers to exercise choice that suited their personal preferences. Diversity was thus reduced to be a celebration of the full range of individual differences of "age or generation, ethnicity, life experiences, educational experiences, language, ways of speaking, ways of thinking, skills interests and aspirations" (Cope and Kalantzis 1997, 267). This discourse of managing diversity was readily taken up in universities and TAFEs, then school systems, as the internationalization of education required improved customer service for more culturally diverse student populations. This imperative has been less about inclusivity and cultural exchange and more about gaining and maintaining international market share, more a colonization of diversity than an "act of strategic optimism" favoring multiculturalism (Cope and Kalantzis 1997, 268; Butler, E. 1997).

This managerial discourse of managing diversity reconceptualized equity in ways that symbolically legitimated the individualization of equity by organizations. The official discourse cast diversity as more fluid and positive, whereas EO was constructed as being inflexible and punitive. It was the "metaphoricity" of diversity conceptualized as a rich tapestry and its fluidity of meaning that made the notion of diversity so amenable to management. This could be seen as a search for legitimacy and stability by organizations, while management seeks security through range of rules, representations, and symbols. The issue of cultural pluralism is problematic because it raises uncertainty. The managing diversity discourse provides a way of reestablishing managerial competence without conflict. The effect is a form of "practical tolerance" in which "the Other is accepted insofar as he or she enriches the center" (Cavanagh 1997, 45; Hage 1994).

Managing diversity has become a useful rhetorical ploy that focuses on the superficial and surface manifestations, neither underpinned by serious research or managerial action. Diversity training has become a major industry in the United States and Australia, encouraging "sensitivity" to, and appreciation of, difference and the acquisition of cross-cultural skills in order to do business. The following example of diversity training in a rural TAFE is indicative of how diversity policies were readily incorporated by management.

> Sally aimed at supporting women as a target group but also changing the culture. She commented, "No matter what sorts of skills and abilities you have got, you can't show them off if the culture, and structures hold you back.' She developed an audit of skills in a leadership team so that everyone valued what each other did. She promoted the idea that diversity is good. She encouraged team members to look at each other's skills as complementary and the importance of interdependence within a team. "It helps women (and men) recognize their skills. It acknowledges the skills of men rather than put them on the defensive. It instils a culture of acknowledging the skills women bring and the skills men bring—not saying that they have to be the same."

Diversity here is conceptualized both as gendered difference and also as a set of skills that could be mobilized in team building. Often discrimination was reduced to conflict resolution. There was no discussion about the gendered nature of organizations, the dangerous territory of male advantage, or indeed the lack of cultural diversity that questioned the naturalized whiteness of the participants (Sinclair 2000a). Such sessions often actively constitute ethnic minorities, women, and Asians as "the exotic other" or "deficit," and therefore needing development, "practical tolerance," and acceptance, thus reproducing old notions of domination and difference. There is no reflexivity here in terms of investigating the manager's privilege and whiteness. Because of their conceptual and strategic weakness, diversity training programs could be "insidious because they attempted to harness the very identities that could, from a critical perspective, be the basis for resistance, and recast them as the basis of compliance" . The discourse of managing diversity as acted upon above does not disrupt managerialist or masculinist hegemony. It is about complementarity, by bringing "feminine qualities," on management and male terms, into leadership. Meanwhile men also are expected, as progressive managers, to develop a wider repertoire of management skills, including a more sensitive approach to people management to capture both the hearts and minds of workers. Thus the close relationship between masculinity, although "new and softer," and management, is left intact (Lingard and Douglas 1999).

The discourse of diversity as currently mobilized in management and education policy also tends to ignore group difference (Clarke, Cochrane, and McLaughlin 1994). There is no recognition of a hierarchy of difference, as second-order differences (individual preferences and attributes) were equated to first-order differences (race, class, gender, and ethnicity) meaning that all differences could be managed according to equivalent processes (Sinclair 2000b). This effectively severed the discourse of diversity from any histories or legacies of wider structural and cultural inequalities premised upon "race," gender, ethnicity, and class. "Whereas the concepts of equity and equal opportunities imply an underlying concept of social justice for all and actively endeavour to achieve this, the notion of diversity invokes the existence of difference and variety without any necessary commitment to action or redistributive social justice" (Deem and Ozga 1997, 33). In contrast, the concepts of equal opportunity, equity and social justice have implicit legalistic and normative elements recognizing legacies of structural inequality and focus on access, process, and outcomes. Diversity is a soft option that fits well within the managerial functionalist frame as it lacks any moral or political claims or a legalistic and procedural frame (Woodall, Edwards, and Welchman 1997).

In the uncertain deregulated times of the 1990s, the discourse of managing diversity, in drawing from a liberal pluralist and assimilationist tradition, reflected the "successful" mainstreaming of liberal feminist theory and equal opportunity police into new managerialist discourses (as best practice in human resource management) and liberal market theory (as best practice in service to international students) (Bacchi 2001). Thus more radical notions of difference identified by postcolonial, feminist, critical pedagogy, and neo-Marxist theory are ignored. For example, a politics of difference sees not only difference as positive social capital, but that recognition requires new political frameworks and transformed power relations, as well as some form of redistribution of resources to provide the material conditions to exercise "choice." The liberal discourse tends to assume diversity is about beliefs, opinions, and goals, a form of intellectual diversity (Phillips 1996). Thus liberal strategies focus on composition (e.g., the representativeness of committees) rather than action (i.e., who has the capacity to influence) as this would require a more complex understanding of the relationship between ideas and experience (Phillips 1996, 140). As token women have found, "presence" is insufficient if there is little recognition of ideas and capacity to influence change.

It is not surprising that connections between increased student "diversity" and inclusivity and lack of "diversity" in leadership are never made in corporate missions, plans, or outcomes (Mirza 1995). To do so would mean changing management practices, cultures, and power relations. Linguistic, cultural, racial, and gender inclusion in leadership would require a fundamental rethinking of who is in management, changing management cultures and practices to develop more inclusive processes and deliberations. It would also require addressing the complexity of subject positions within the category of woman. Colonialism, economic imperialism, the dominance of English, and institutional pressures of corporatization and democratization work together to pseudoinclude white women, but they exclude women who are not white (Prasad and Prasad 2002; Ahnee-Benham and Copper 1998). This is an issue for white women leaders as well as men.

PROMOTING WOMEN

During the 1980s equity infrastructure developed in each state consisting of a framework of EO and antidiscrimination policies, institutional policies with strategies, and professional development for women and managers. EO policies were, in most states, reviewed triennially, with targets set. While the language was of affirmative action, there was never positive discrimination for women (e.g., quotas) in Australia as in the United States. By the 1990s, institutional policies and strategies encouraged women to apply and set criteria for managers to meet with regard to recruitment and promotion. Joan, EO manager in a sandstone university, recognized that

> in a positive way, at this university, amalgamation helped rethink promotion, and restructuring produced new positions. Women are coming through the deputy head route, and early retirement takes out more men than women, freeing up positions. Also, increased professional development means that some men have picked up on concepts of EO as part of the changing world. It is common practice to do searches for women for the senior posts.

Numerous programs developed across the three education sectors to encourage individual women to move into leadership focusing on mentoring, skills development, networking, and shadowing senior staff.

Some universities ran public lectures and residential workshops on "how to do well as an academic." A national network between the Utechs was developed for senior academic women, Women's Executive Development. The new corporate work order was conducive to women according to one VC because of frequent opportunities in "acting positions, and moving people around has given women a taste of things, putting people in and letting them have a go. Also the team approach of management enables nonmanagement women and gives women the whole picture of the institution. Women are unduly disadvantaged for promotion from lecturer B to C as a result of the structure of committees" (vice-chancellor, sandstone). Mentoring programs in some institutions aimed to "build networks at the grass roots" (Monica, sandstone). One sandstone university's Women and Leadership program sought to develop a "more gender neutral concept of leadership, improve the overall quality of leadership through increased participation of a pool of skilled women leaders, more representative decision-making processes, a greater understanding of gender differences and equity issues in the working environment, a network of women leaders, emergent models of best leadership practice etc." (UWA 1996, 1). But such programs, while seeking to emulate the masculine practices by providing opportunities for upskilling and learning the institutional game, "raised expectations when leadership opportunities were limited in the streamlined organization" (UWA 1996, 31).

In schools, EEO programs ranged from shadowing principals and mentoring through to training in writing of CVs and being interviewed (e.g., the Eleanor Davis program in Victoria; the Leadership Center, South Australia). But in the mainstream professional development of principals, gender was ignored, as "the training programs for principals do not teach them how to do it differently" (Colleen, principal, working-class secondary school). One unionist argued that "you should never allow principal associations to control their own professional development: they never put equity in there. I think the type of people who are being appointed, even the guys, have come out of that period of time. The point is they don't know how to do it." The impact of equity programs was variable, depending on regional directors' and superintendents' support and more successful in urban than rural areas (Blackmore 1999b).

The TAFE sector was informed, particularly during this period, by the Karpin report on management training (1995), focusing on managing diversity. A few more progressive and community-based TAFE institutions wrote well-developed and integrated EEO plans supported by structures close to the executive that elaborated on strategies, resources, performance measures, and time lines around the themes of managing diversity, women in management, creating a culture of fairness, individual rights, and having a sex-based, harassment free workplace and learning environment. Senior women initiated and supported networking. In a small and progressive TAFE, women leveraged into leadership by the director felt committed to others, as did Jane, executive manager in a small, progressive, suburban TAFE: "I'm given opportunities for those women who've identified that they wanted to work with management, and worked very hard to promote themselves. The director has given them the opportunity to take the next step and become managers. But it did have a lot to do with their homework in the previous months with me deliberately picking projects to get experience."

However, not all women took up such opportunities. Sara, a senior teacher in a working-class secondary school, argued, "I've got other things I want to do—I'd rather do additional study about the literacy issue rather than

going to the seminars on women in leadership or shadowing a principal." The
message from EO practitioners was that women have to be more political and
understand the ways in which institutions work and not be too reliant on others. Justine (Utech) said: "The system can only be what we make the system.
The structure revolves around the personalities. Women have got to see the
opportunities, and they've got to take them. So, if there is an election for a
university committee, women have to nominate. But be clever and not field
five candidates against five men. I believe we really need to be strategic."

EQUITY DISCOURSES: STRATEGIC, SYMBOLIC, AND INTERVENTIONIST

Despite "premature" mainstreaming of EO in Australia and the weaker managing diversity approach, the executive women felt that the EO legislation and
equity policies since 1975 had produced a cultural change. The legislation was
seen to empower women leaders, particularly at the executive level, to set the
ground rules. And as one VC commented: "The boys know what they cannot
say . . . I went to a meeting the other day with all this racism debate going on
and said, if any manager wanted to be racist or sexist in this institution they
were out." Positional authority combined here with legal and moral authority.
EO policy was important because it named the problem, provided a language
to talk about the problem, imparted legitimacy for local action, and suggested
strategies. It made gender an organizational and not just a women's concern
because, as Jim, director of a small, progressive, suburban TAFE conceded,
"men are blind to EEO issues." Policies also provide a legal framework and a
set of behavioral expectations. According to Gabriella, an EO manager in a
large, metropolitan TAFE, "without EEO there are some men that may have
been more open about blocking women. An equity manager in a Utech, Justine, argued that:

> EO allows us to have the authority for what we do. It allows the notion of
> equity groups to be named. EO policy and legislation allows you to be the
> social conscience, to be the moral voice, and to say that, in my experience, if
> you go down this path this could happen . . . often not only loss of face but
> also dollars. It allows you to get them to say the words and adapt behaviors.
> Maybe you can change their attitudes.

Importantly, EO discourses were utilized strategically by managers and
EO practitioners to inform policy.

Our participants were sometimes ambivalent about EO depending upon
their experiences and political perspective. "I think it is probably redundant
having affirmative action and action plans here. Except when I look at the

spread of where the managers are, so far as women in nontraditional roles, we haven't really shifted that much" (Felicity, large, suburban, community-oriented TAFE). "EEO made people conscious, you know, on selection panels, that they really have to have some equity about it. Now you start getting into the insidious forms of sexism, which are the more hideous ones to deal with" (Maria, advanced skills teacher, working-class secondary school). One assistant principal in a rural college, Natalie, considered EEO policies were still necessary because

> equal opportunity policies are as good as people make them: it is easy to mouth things. Merit and equity policies were necessary because women were never going to get into any position to be able to prove they could do it until someone forced it to happen. There are good women around in decision making now, but we should not throw merit and equity away, just not be as heavy-handed, because I think that men are beginning to realize that they benefit as well.

Sally, a manager in a small, rural TAFE commented how "EEO legislation has heightened awareness of women and provided a mentoring program. It gives time to reflect, and [you] look at yourself. It provides time to analyze your skills, look at other styles, and gives greater insight into the dimensions of jobs and time for self-reflection."

While equity was a marginal discourse in many schools, TAFE, and universities, it was more central in those institutions where, because of their location, student composition, history, and often leadership, integrated equity in, and through, their planning as a strategic priority. Community-based TAFE institutes, working-class, culturally diverse schools, or newer universities were instances where this was the case. One Utech, for example, saw itself as quite different from other universities:

> We're a different university for a number of reasons: one's our history; second is our student group (they come from equity categories); and third, I think, is our leadership, our current leadership; fourth, a very strong history of strength in affirmative action planning; and finally an aboriginal faculty [and] even legislation that set the university up. We talk about needing to be a university that addresses the needs of aboriginal/Islander people and disadvantaged groups: we've got to be different. Equity and social justice are stated in its mission statement. There is a pro vice-chancellor equity: a very strong statement about the commitment to equity and targets for equity growth. EO and equity issues are being mainstreamed, rather than having them as side issues. We are constantly educating people about being inclusive, so equity and EO are central in policy making. (Justine, EO manager, Utech)

In another Utech, also with equity in its profile, Jodie argued that "the procedures for grievances are very good—informal and formal networks exist. The university is supportive of women. It's a terrific place for women. There are workshops for people who are thinking of promotion and workshops on preparing a CV and interviews and acting positions." These institutional differences shaped reception to gender equity reform more broadly. For example, in universities committed to equity, there was a more comprehensive understanding of the ways in which equity and difference could be met. Sarah, an associate professor (Utech), referred to "forward thinking policy. I went for promotion on a totally nontraditional platform. I argued my case within each of the categories, basing it on twenty-three or twenty-four years of very nontraditional academic work (fourteen of those years part-time lecturer while the children were growing up)."

By contrast, high-status institutions (schools in particular) without the complex issues of disadvantage, because market-oriented systems encouraged policies of exclusion, were attractive to their clients *because* of their cultural homogeneity arising from specialist programs and capacity to select. Cynthia, an EO manager at a sandstone university, commented that despite evidence that universities outside the Group of Eight (sandstones) had innovative EO policies, "we assume we have the best EO policies. This uni perceives itself as the leading uni and therefore will not take on another's successful equity programs (a shadowing program). It has the culture that they have to have the best practice to attract the best people; the others can have second best. New unis have a whole different culture and look at a different market."

This perspective was confirmed by another EO manager at a sandstone university, who summed it up by saying that "if a uni judges itself as a research institution, they are not going to care if they are good at affirmative action. We are our own authority."

Instead, in school systems, as in universities and TAFE, there was little intrusion of equity issues or even the presence of equity officers in the powerful central decision-making bodies where the policy and "hard" financial decisions were made. This is most evident with the institutionalization (and domestication?) of equity through management training of principals, managers, heads of schools, and selection panels, as well as the oft mobilized discourse of "gender balance" (i.e., one token woman "balances" ten men in a committee). Equity was treated in these contexts as a technical and legal problem rather than a substantive moral principle upon which to operate across a range of management practices. The emphasis in grievance matters, as well as recruitment and promotion procedures, was on procedural justice and not equitable outcomes.

BACKLASH POLITICS

Despite the popularity of discourses in education about women's styles of leadership and the apparent "successes" of individual women, there remained significant resistance to the gender equity agenda. The takeup was partial, fragmented across systems and within schools, with significant opposition in some sites (Kenway et al. 1998; Burton 1999; Butler, E. 1996). While all universities claimed to be equal opportunity employers, EO was not embedded into the cultural practices of universities. Likewise, in TAFE, feminist activism tended to be lower down the organization, in the community education sector where there were strong feminist networks with a focus on students not teachers (Sanguinetti 1998; Angwin 1994). In most institutions, there were pockets of resistance, largely "a backlash against EO from a group of men who have been disenfranchised by tighter EO legislation. They tend to be senior lecturers who aren't going any further. They have the most to lose" (Dianne, dean, sandstone). Resistance to EO comes from that "group of males outraged that they are losing their advantage, who know the words and who know the rhetoric and do what they do from a well-thought-out position" (Justine, EO manager, Utech). This backlash derived from a sense of loss (of assumed advantage) and also "fear" of being managed by women. Renata, director of a TAFE commented about many men's attitude to women: "Hatred is probably a bit strong: fear, yes. There are a lot of Australian men who just don't like women in equitable positions. We are talking power relations. They can only handle women in subordinate roles. . . . Most of them are clever enough to disguise it, but it is still there, insidious stuff. They won't sit down while they talk to me. They're uncomfortable, having trouble making eye contact."

According to a pro vice-chancellor (equity), there is a "deep sexism in universities, an intellectual arrogance, a civilized veneer with deep levels of arrogance, and many intellectual bullies." Resistance often went underground but in many instances was up front. Likewise, in one rural secondary school, Barbara recalled that "an older fellow on staff . . . was resistant to me because I was a woman principal, and he resisted the other women in leadership roles. His way of coping was to make unpleasant remarks about the 'sheilas.' He modified his behavior in twelve months because he was never allowed to get away with it. He obviously found it difficult relating to me."

Embedded in this resistance was a level of denial by men of the nature and extent of systemic or structural disadvantage experienced by women (Currie and Thiele 2001). Men also had a significant personal and emotional investment in maintaining the existing social relations of gender that naturalized male advantage as the norm. These systemic advantages for men were largely invisible, embedded in organizational practices and values (e.g., networks, informal mentoring, unpaid work). Prue, EO manager in a gumtree, felt that for many men "gender equity is the worst for any of them to deal with because it's about personal identity and relationships: there is a deep misogyny." Geraldine, manager in a community-oriented, suburban TAFE observed that "some men feel that EO policy is discriminating against them. They expected to get the jobs that went to women; they resent the fact that they are now competing against women. There is a perception that senior management is loaded with women."

But the apparent successes of gender equity reform were often superficial—changing behaviors not attitudes. In Victorian schools, where EO was institutionalized through industrial relations agreements, inclusive curriculum strategies, and a range of EO activities for girls and women, awareness of EO was made a criterion for promotion. "In job interviews, the last two questions were about equal opportunity and social justice. How do you make sure that the girls in your class are treated fairly? How have you supported women in your workplace? Men would come to me as EO coordinator, I've got a job interview, what do I say?" (Cathy, working-class, culturally diverse secondary school).

But fundamental attitudes went unchanged and unchallenged: "[M]any think women brought sexual harassment on themselves" (Ingrid, large, metropolitan TAFE). Furthermore, the capacity of EO policies to produce radical change were hindered by the wider structural changes in educational work (intensification of labor) and the lack of change in the gender division of labor at home. "Well, things haven't changed at home. . . . Are we really any better off?" (Helen, Utech). Some women were ambivalent about EO, in part because both men and women understood it (incorrectly) as positive discrimination in favor of women, rather than recognition of women's disadvantages and rectifying systemic inequalities (Burton 1997).

Lingard (2003) refers to how women's disadvantage, the reason for EO, was quickly forgotten, reinforced by "structural amnesia" in the fields of education and media representations of educational issues facilitated by a conjuncture of events (Bourdieu 1996). Restructuring, with the quick turnover of multiskilled managers without substantive knowledge of equity or education, the flight of the femocrats from bureaucracies, together with the rise of social conservatism and a vocal "men's movement" in the media and the academy, were fertile ground nurturing the public and political amnesia underpinning the policy shift during the 1990s from a focus on the social relations of gender (and male advantage) to "boy friendly schooling" and "men as victims of feminism." And equity for women in educational management, more than girls, challenged the "naturalized" advantage of men in everyday organizational life. With the Victorian government's removal of the equity requirement in promotion, as observed by a teacher unionist, "there was relief that there are no longer these EO objectives in job descriptions. . . . [N]ow the focus is on a very narrowly defined form of management and on individuals."

The respondents in our study emphasized how the structural (devolution) and cultural (antifeminist discourses) backlash was subtle and subversive. There was no single oppositional moment that allowed for collective action against this reconfiguration of the social relations of gender, just a gradual erosion of benefits and sidelining of concerns about the impact of restructuring and a refocusing on managerialism. As outlined by Elle, senior executive manager in the university sector (Utech),

> those factors which have stimulated equity planning and equity initiatives in higher education institutions have also produced some theoretical dilemmas and operational issues. In particular, structural and staffing matters, particularly with the expected mainstreaming of equity funding and responsibility, the lack of institutional coordination and leadership, an emphasis on short-term and identifiable outcomes of managerialism, and the absence of any serious or consistent attempts to analyze the causes and extent of the current inequalities. . . . Indeed, the equity planning processes currently in place avoid interrogation of these matters by discouraging analysis of the causes of the inequities and disadvantages it aims to remedy.

UNDERSTANDING GENDER REFORM

Gender equity practitioners were both insiders and outsiders. Often they were structurally positioned as senior academics or staff managers overseeing others. Being an EO manager was dangerous and often personally and professionally damaging work, leading to marginalization and reduced career opportunities. Trish, an EO coordinator in a rural secondary college recalled how "the principal was very old fashioned, and he just tolerated me. I did not get an advanced skills teacher position because of EEO: it branded me as too confrontationalist." Equity practitioners in universities, for example, had a wide brief, working across the institutional structures (academic and administrative) and decision-making processes (industrial relations, promotions committees, selection panels), as well as all levels; undertaking both developmental and policy work; monitoring as well as receiving complaints; and undertaking grievance procedures. As such, these women had an understanding of what it was like to work in the "belly of the beast" as well as organizational gender politics.

Gender equity practitioners adopted an "ethics of pragmatism" (Yeatman 1998b) about how organizational change was affected and were necessarily strategic. A number of assumptions about the nature of gender reform emerged from our study. First, while equity practitioners disagreed about what motivated people to change attitudes and about strategies (e.g., mainstreaming versus specialization, Bacchi 2001), a common theme was recognition that gender equity challenged individual and collective identities. Individuals had significant emotional, physical, and intellectual investment in their gender identities as mothers or fathers, partners, and professionals—"[I]f their daughters are being discriminated against they understand the situation better" (Joan, sandstone). A

TAFE manager, Geraldine, agreed that "men see their own daughters grow up and be discriminated against. And if men don't have a relationship with a strong, assertive woman in the home, they find it very difficult to deal with women in power in the workplace."

It was not enough for men to experience discrimination, even if vicariously, or to provide a rationale to change (e.g., statistical evidence). It was equally important to tap into emotional investments. As Francesca, EO in a Utech put it, "people will change when they see something in it for them, an immediate benefit. It has to make sense to them. By getting them to understand the effect of their actions you've got some chance of changing their attitudes." The problem about individualizing the emotional and personal aspect of equity reform (antiracism, antisexism, etc.) was articulated by Nadia an EO manager (Utech):

> The thing about equity is that people somehow feel that it's only about personal values. If it is so defined people can go with it or not as a personal preference. If I don't believe in it then I don't have to subscribe to it or do anything. There is no notion that it is an intrinsic part of organizational structure. A dean can't say, "I don't believe in research and therefore won't do any," [but] they do get away with saying they don't believe in gender equity.

There were also organizational investments to be considered. Sinclair (2000b) identifies four responses to gender equity issues that coexist in most large organizations: that women just "don't fit; some incremental adjustment occurs; institutions realize the costs as highly experienced women exit because they have no place; and finally, recognition that the lack of women is indicative of deeper organizational problems requiring a change in culture" (143).

Consequently, gender equity managers worked simultaneously at multiple levels. Monica, EO manager in a sandstone, stated that "I like to work from the bottom as well as the top. Working from the top means getting gender equity into key policy areas. Working from the bottom means developing a grassroots base, allowing women to see the kinds of things that we are doing and their relevance to them." Recognition of gender inequality as a problem was the first step to "confront people with the data and information that says it is not a level playing field then educate people about why and what are the benefits of having a more level playing field" (Karin, TAFE). But the second issue was to get engagement with, and ownership of, the problem. Justine, an EO manager in a Utech, cited a number of strategies she had learned, recognizing how her own history informed and changed her practices over time.

> In the beginning we used to do seminars on EO. Now we go into work areas and say, "Look, we'd like to do something with you around these issues. Can we design and do a workshop for you?" Talk through legislation and

approaches . . . explain how it works, so they don't feel threatened. We are educative, not punitive: here's some scenarios, some ideas, how it impacts on you to know what's okay for indigenous people, international students . . . make it relevant, make them actually think, engage with issues.

These strategies were possible because her cross-disciplinary connections meant "influential men know me, and they trust me . . . knowing that my whole philosophy is educative, educative, educative: we've got workshops, collegial groups, projects, public lectures, and mentoring . . . and a smack, finally, if it is not done." For her, the "keywords were *informing, challenging, supporting,* and *saving.*" Open communication and trust were central in her own management "within the EO unit. You need to be driven by values; otherwise you really don't belong . . . I think institutions that are successful have a value base, and that's my leadership style." EO practitioners concurred with most senior and middle managers that widespread institutional change with regard to gender equity required investment in equity infrastructure, as well as the symbolic and practical necessity of an integrated policy framework that worked across all aspects of the institution. Monica (sandstone) concluded that "a good place for women is an institution which not only has rules, regulations, statements, and policies about equal opportunity but that actually tries to see it carried out."

Our case studies identified what worked for gender equity reform. One feature was systemic and structural recognition, support and resources, and the managerial and moral authority to intervene. Alan, a regional manager in the Victorian school system, encouraged women into leadership. Yet "his capacity to have it influenced and implemented is severely curtailed by the absence of structure (for gender equity) at the school level, which was so heavily dominated and empowered by the principal." The second feature of women-friendly organizations was the political will of executive leadership to initiate and enforce equity policies throughout the organization (Sinclair 1998), " to have a commitment to EO" (Monica). Bob Meyenn (1996, 10) concluded in his study of senior academic women:

> The most critical factor in the degree of gender-based difficulty was whether a Vice Chancellor supports women and other issues of equity and social justice. . . . [U]nless universities have Vice Chancellors' and other powerful males with a commitment to equity . . . legislation will be applied selectively, and the bands of elderly male misogynists will revert to notions of merit or expertise in order to legitimate the continuation of discrimination.

Ironically, men's commitment meant it was not seen to be "just another feminist looking after her own." That is, "senior men need to take EO more seriously and mentor women" (Cynthia, EO manager, sandstone). Third,

managerial tools such as budget incentives and "gender audits" were mobilized to leverage EO and embed it throughout the institutional decision
making (Hancock 1999). Constant surveillance was required as even those
institutions ahead in equity indicators easily dropped equity off in budgets,
market strategies, and planning. Sustainability of reform therefore required
an equity impact analysis of decisions and regular reviews of HR and decision making in terms of fairness and equity principles. Finally, EO managers
had to be a constant presence on the ground, acting as the institution's conscience, "to work in the departments because as soon as I leave the whole
thing will fall apart: senior men will not say EO is a heap of rubbish but will
passively resist by not finding time to resolve issues. It is not a priority"
(Claudia, TAFE manager). In all instances, equity reform was "too dependent
on individuals whether something gets pushed or something doesn't get
pushed" (EO coordinator, rural secondary college). Equity was not part of
the responsibilization of the managerial self in the corporate neobureaucratic
educational organization.

BEYOND THE "BODY COUNT"

EO for women was a "management issue" from its inception because of its
legalistic frame, consolidated as a management issue by the devolution of
responsibility (mainstreaming) for equity. Liberal feminism that underpinned
EO, with its emphasis on access and its limited critique of the power structure, failed to challenge patriarchal or capitalist formations. Our study indicated a failure to alter dominant representations of leadership, to significantly
shift organizational cultures, and, in particular, to change the structural and
cultural gendered division of labor that limited most women's possibilities.
Equity policy in that sense was often more "symbolic" than "real," another
aspect of performativity signaled by superficial performance indicators, where
the discourse was not matched by flow on effects in terms of resources, evaluation, and professional development. Thus equity initiatives such as EO and
managing diversity, through their incorporation into new managerialism as
just another aspect of public relations, had little regard for any oppositional
roots or emancipatory intentions. This appropriation of gender equity discourses by management under such ambiguous conditions was a means by
which to keep women in their place and thus another form of symbolic violence perpetrated on women.

Notably absent during the 1990s public discourses over women and
leadership was any concern about racial or ethnic representation, uninformed
by the identity politics of the 1980s (Ang 1995). Despite the debates over
reconciliation with indigenous people and the politics of multiculturalism,
racial and ethnic difference continue to be unrecognized in Australian

research and policy on educational leadership (Wilkinson 2005). It was understandable that gender was foregrounded as the few white women "broke" into the male domain of management and " found themselves to be in such an inhospitable environment that one of their survival strategies is to make their private experience part of a public debate, by putting gender on the organizational agenda" (Goode 2000, 244). It was around these white women that new patterns and relations were worked out. But on the ground, despite the hostile external political environment after 1996 to reconciliation and multiculturalism, equity workers in universities, schools, and TAFE institutes sought to integrate policies for indigenous and non-English-speaking background students into their agenda as a logical extension of the equity agenda. Dianne, dean at a sandstone university, said that she was "having an increasing amount to do with aboriginal issues because I have also got the aboriginal studies unit in my section. But, nevertheless, you clearly find attitudes around the university hostile to aboriginal people and also aboriginal perspectives in doing things differently."

This highlights the central problem of category politics that arose out of the claims for recognition from various groups during the 1980s to produce "mosaic multiculturalism" based on the assumption that the aggregate of cultural groups through equal representation and recognition will produce a cohesive political entity (Benhabib 2002). Carol Bacchi (1996) suggests that category politics has two aspects: on the one hand, the politics of how different meanings are constructed and acted upon through terms such as *equal opportunity, affirmative action,* and *merit,* and, on the other, the politics of identity, which is about how particular social groups such as women, blacks, Greeks, and so on make claims for equity. With regard to the former, as the language was neutered with the supplanting of equal opportunity by diversity, the notion of merit, a product of patriarchal bureaucracies, provided less leverage for women under the new regime of accountability and performance than in the old procedurally based bureaucracies. Anna, senior lecturer in a sandstone, considers that "it's worse for women in this environment as the merit principle has been hijacked. It is not individual merit anymore, but fitness for purpose, and based on pure competition." Clare, a teacher, felt "that what constitutes merit is now a very narrow definition that excludes the bulk of the female population." Recognition of diversity would require recognition of difference and "comparability between difference" in terms of performance and communication, rather than "presentability" and presentation. (Cope and Kalantzis 1997, 271)

In terms of identity, category politics during the 1980s arose out of a search for group identity and the desire to gain recognition on the assumption that cultural groups were homogenous, had common interests, and that culture is static and not hybrid. In defining a policy category as women or indigenous, it also produces a sense of immutability and homogeneity about the category (either black or female); and a blindness, for that which is not categorized or named in this manner goes unrecognized (Bacchi 2000b). Gender as a dominant category in itself is problematic, as its intersections with race, class, and linguistic difference are ignored, a point made by postcolonial, indigenous, and black feminists (Ang 1995; Moreton-Robinson 2000). One does not find white, middle-class women leaders talking about their "whiteness" or about their class position, whereas black women leaders are inevitably positioned as black and working-class women leaders and thus feel the need to deal with their blackness and working classness as a priority. Yet whiteness is also a color, and a category of privilege, as is masculinity, both unnamed in policy (Moreton-Robinson 2000).

Category politics therefore creates significant policy dilemmas that do not always facilitate reform, although it does provide recognition through representation. For example, the naming of the problem as "women's underrepresentation" and "individual deficiencies" makes women the problem rather than the structure and culture of organizations. Or the category can be removed from policy, as is the case in universities as women's participation rate exceeds 50 percent. Women are no longer categorized as an equity group, rendering gender again as invisible. Here the numerical performance indicator of the category is an inadequate measure of success as it ignores other modes of exclusion. For example, when the policy problem of gender is redefined, as is the case with the perceived underachievement of working-class men and boys, masculinity is now named as yet another homogenous category of disadvantage. In each instance, because gender is treated as fixed and homogenous, there is no analysis of how unequal relations of power work with the social relations of gender to structure and organize work in ways that advantage particular masculinities (e.g., new entrepreneurial and transnational masculinities) to the detriment of other, "weaker" masculinities (working-class, trade masculinities) and all femininities (caring and strong women) (Kerfoot, Pritchard, and Whitehead 2000; Kerfoot and Knights 1999; Connell 1998). By failing to address the social relations of gender within a framework of social justice and an analysis of inequality, and by maintaining the homogeneity of gender as a category, differences arising from race, class, and sexuality within the category of gender are rendered invisible. Categories reduce equity politics as one of representation of each category, who is present, and not what is done or how it was done, and with what effect. The "body count" strategy has taken us so far in terms of reforming organizations. We need to consider not just the numbers of women and minority groups at each level, but also the diversity within groups, the image associated with particular tasks, the values and ideas that dominate the activities and the form in which the activity is undertaken, whether more protected or exposed, public or private, and with what benefits to the holder (Alvesson and du Billing 2002, 72).

The new managerialism has incorporated the changing social (and gender) relations of education through new structures (centralized decentralization), new modes of communication (decisional), and a new language (privileging efficiency not equity). But these new modes of educational governance informed by managerialist and market philosophies lack a moral and ethical commitment to equity and indeed democratic modes of governance, thus removing a basis for claims women make upon the state and organizations. A teacher unionist pointed out the irony of the recruitment drive for women leaders at the same time that "They imposed a change agenda without any regard to the appalling impact on women. . . . [T]he new positions are described in a way that does not accommodate women's skills, knowledge, and experience. Their form of liberalism does commit to fairness and natural justice . . . but now there is none of the infrastructure to support it—i.e., affirmative action and EO written into job descriptions for principals, action plans for them to follow."

Our study indicates that equity is most likely to have effect with multiple strategies, and a combination of top down interventions by the state and organizational leadership together with bottom up activism by networks of practitioners and social movements. One EEO manager in a university summed up the position of equity reform: "If you talk to people in EO in the public sector, they feel less not more empowered. So at one level it is rational and makes sense. At another level, it fails to address culture, the values, and the symbolic side." Devolution, markets, and managerialism collectively reduced, and indeed undermined, the capacity of the collective to act, while promoting a form of individual responsibilization that does not include equity or address difference or impart either agency or legitimacy to act for social justice.

ELEVEN

Conclusion:
Separation, Transition,
and Incorporation?

THIS TEXT HAS SOUGHT to problematize discourses about gender and leadership in the context of the restructuring of educational governance and educational labor in Australia during the 1990s. We have tracked how educational redesign in the 1990s was marked by moves toward market-based systems of provision based on choice, managerial professionalism, strong external systems of accountability, performance management, increased federal intervention in state domains of curriculum and assessment, and a shift in policy to focus on outcomes. At the institutional level, the progressive blurring of boundaries between the subfields of the education sectors and between public and private provision with competitive tendering in an open training market was reflected in moves to redesign educational provision and governance.

Our metanarrative of educational restructuring in Australia has provided a retrospective analysis of a new educational settlement similar to that undertaken earlier in the United Kingdom and New Zealand (Gewirtz, Ball, and Bowe 1995; Whitty, Halpin, and Power 1998; Wylie 1999). Woods (1999) argues that macroshifts in UK education policy from the 1970s were like "status passages" from "separation" to "transition" through to "re-incorporation." Although one mapped onto and interpenetrated the other, there is no "transition" per se, but various "moves" over time in structural, cultural, and social relations between individuals and the state, some progressive, others regressive. We have mapped similar "passages" in the macronarratives of the field and subfields (universities, TAFE institutes and schools) of education in

Australia and micronarratives of organizational life. As in the United King-dom and New Zealand earlier (Lauder and Hughers 1999), the reforms of corporate Labor after 1987 marked an increasing "separation" from the post-1945 education settlement based on child-centered philosophy, partnerships with parents, professional autonomy, and equality premised upon democratic notions of participation toward more contractual relations (Blackmore 1990). Australian education was not only "reshaped" but also "renormed" in terms of its "relations, practices and centers of power" and how they articulate, with government as the "re designer" embarking on "purposive strategies for edu-cational change" (Angus and Seddon 2000, 151). While transnational policy metanarratives have "renormed" education toward competition and contrac-tualism, policy metanarratives are also mediated locally. The macroshift toward postwelfarism in Australia emulated earlier moves in the United Kingdom and New Zealand, changing the relation of the state to individuals (from dependence to independence), to social groups (and how they made claims on the state based on needs, rights, or interests), and particular policy communities or fields (with the subordination of education to the economic). There was a "rationalization and wholesale redistribution of functions between center and periphery such that the center maintains overall strategic control through fewer policy levers including the operationalization of crite-ria relating to output quality. . . . [S]o rather than a withering away of the state, the state withdraws from the "murky plain" of overwhelming detail, the better to take refuge in the clear and commanding heights of "profiling" (Whitty 2001, 161–62).

Policy discourses emphasizing choice and competition, when articulating with the common grammar of education (certification, credentialing mecha-nisms) and a shared English legacy, fed into local systemic predispositions toward selectivity, ranking, and sorting, with similar effects exacerbating edu-cational inequalities. The new public administrative reform reconfigured structures, relationships, and norms, with the individualization of responsibil-ity and risk (Bauman 2000). The public and private lives of educational work-ers in all three sectors blended with the commodification of the self—physi-cally, intellectually, and emotionally.

Australian responses to global pressures were shaped by our marginal global location, our federal system of governance that moderated any extreme tendencies toward centralization or decentralization. Federalism has led equity groups to argue for more centralized exertion of power within the social liberal tradition, as did the femocrats with regard to gender equity and union-ists with regard to centralized wage fixing. The vocationalization of education revitalized old instrumentalist attitudes to education. This could pessimisti-cally be viewed as the result of increased precarity in both "core" and "periph-eral" labor markets, job and training scarcity, and the privatization of educa-tional costs. Optimistically, it could signify an epistemological shift toward "new knowledge work" in postindustrial economies collapsing old Enlightenment theory/practice and disciplinary divides.

Educational restructuring at the macrolevel led to "institutional redesign" of internal organizational structures, cultures, and practices in gender-inflected ways (Goode 2000). The assumption of neoliberal policy frames by both Labor and Coalition governments during the 1990s and informed by transnational global policy communities such as the OECD meant equity discourses competed with, were subverted by, and in some instances appropriated by discourses of merit, diversity, quality, excellence, efficiency, service, competition, and choice (Henry et al. 2001). "Ironically, neo-liberal policies for quality assurance and the audit culture have been successfully globalized while policies for gender equity have not" (Morley 2003, 2).

We have tracked the cumulative effects of reform on the gender micropolitics experienced by a particular cohort of nonaspirant, aspirant, and successful women leaders. The leadership habitus of this cohort of women was (in)formed by their educational, professional, community, and familial experiences from a time of social and educational progressivism marked by state feminism and teacher professionals being coparticipants in education reform. The key struggle for them with radical educational restructuring was between their passion for education, its potential for social justice and change, and how education "contributes to the social polity, the economy and the social fabric of society" (Angus and Seddon 2000, 168) and the drive to perform well and manage themselves better according to numerous externally imposed performative measures (Day 2004). Inwardly, many perceived the performative aspects of reform as subverting not improving student learning, staff well-being and more equitable outcomes. Outwardly, they maintained appearances by being in a constant state of improvement and performativity as their personal (and institutional) survival depended on such performances.

This chapter has three tasks. The first task is to review the state of play of gender politics in Australian education in 2005. The second is to identify and explore what we have learned about gender equity, educational restructuring, and organizational change. The last task is to bring together feminist normative political theory and critical social science and policy to yet again argue that equity should be the benchmark against which individual and institutional success should be judged, not just efficiency and performativity (Gewirtz 1998; Lynch and Lodge 2002).

EQUITY AS THE TOUCHSTONE: WHAT "STATE" ARE WE IN NOW?

Schools, universities, and TAFE institutes are at the localized intersections of social, economic, and political forces but also of local, state, national, and global relations. But Whitty, Halpin, and Power (1998) caution that "to regard current espousals of heterogeneity, pluralism and local narrative as indicative of a new social order may be to mistake phenomenal forms for structural relations" (42). Educational restructuring has reproduced an unequal distribution of power based on gender, class, and race, but in new forms, confirming Ball's (1994) warning about the difference between changes in structures systemically and locally (first order effects) and the impact these changes have on "patterns of social access, opportunity and social justice" (second-order effects) (25–26).

Feminists (Summers 2003) and profeminists (Lingard 2003) have referred to the rise of neoliberal ideologies in social and education policy as witnessing "an end to equality" with the rise of "recuperative masculinity" and corporate governmentalities. The early 1990s in Australia was a period marked by debates over republicanism, reconciliation, indigenous land rights, immigration, population, and supportive family policies within a framework of "mosaic multiculturalism" (Benhabib 2002, 8). A decade later, defensive discourses circulate about protection where "difference is left outside" (Prasad and Prasad 2002). These discourses are implicitly antagonistic to reconciliation, feminism, and multiculturalism, as the Australian nation-state struggles between unifying around national identity and recognition of difference. This tension is highlighted in debates over inclusion of female, immigrant, indigenous, and refugee populations. Discourses of "political correctness" now discipline those who speak up about equity. Wedge politics is mobilized to exclude "the other" within an assimilationist policy frame of neoconservative liberalism. At the same time, the "masculinist" image of strong public leadership has been in crisis (although temporarily revived by the post-September 11 Iraq war), marked by massive global corporate collapses due to institutional and individual corporate greed and moral crises in the church and government over cover-ups of impropriety and fabricated justifications to go to war. Corporate, political, religious, and public service governance in terms of ethical accountability are now seen to be lacking. Public servants feel "dispirited, fearful and lacking in self confidence" (Currie, Thiele, and Harris 2002, 19).

We have argued that gender restructuring in education occurred in the context of a post traditional order that still worked in traditional frames, and an emerging "global cosmopolitan order" (Giddens 1994, 83–85). The detraditionalization of modern society was motivated by capitalism, democratization, and the rise of new social movements that, for example, put femininity and, more recently, masculinity under scrutiny, and that promote a discourse of women in leadership. The social relations of gender in the family have been transformed with the "feminization'" of the workforce imparting greater economic independence to some women but increased dependence on the state for others (e.g., single parents), although with a widening wage gap between women and men due to reduced protection by the state and weaker unions. Precarious employment is now the norm, with an expanding casual labor market (of women and youth) and public- and private-sector contractualism (of middle-class professionals) (Pusey 2003). Good workplace policies supporting women are being "undermined by longer working hours, increased childcare costs, loss of award protection, and the failure of enterprise bargaining and individual contracts to give women's needs and interests high priority" (Probert 2001a, 2). Within families, there have been few readjustments of domestic arrangements, with women still largely doing the familial work (Summers 2003). Howard's reelection in 2004 promises further radical labor market reforms, and education will be a site of contestation.

Neoconservative social policies have also promoted retraditionalization through a new gender fundamentalism and social reregulation that assert purist forms of tradition in gender, class, ethnic, and religious relations, referencing back to idealized middle-class notions of the nuclear family headed by a male breadwinner. The 1990s, Lingard (2003, 34) argues, marked the "endgame" for gender equity for women in Australian education, with a backlash exacerbated by the "evacuation of centralized approaches to gender equity with the move to school [local] based management and accountabilities that do not include more qualitative measures of equity."[8] EO reports signal a decade later that the growth of women in academic leadership, such as professors, is slow if not stalled,[9] although there has been a rapid increase from three to nine of the thirty-eight Australian vice-chancellors, but far less advancement at the TAFE executive level. The number of women in the school principalship is rising slowly, though unevenly distributed across regions and systems, with women concentrated in pockets of urban poverty arising from globalization, but less so in rural areas (Brooking 2005). As leaders, these women are positioned within competing managerial discourses of "flexibility, diversity and the conservation of scarce resources on the one hand, and . . . productivity and accountability on the other" (Glazer-Raymo 2000, 203),[10] at a time when "the motivational climate produced by contractual arrangements—the norms and values that they produce—is hierarchical and rule based" (Glazer-Raymo 2000, 61–62). Our cohort operated in an increasingly flexible, volatile, and differentiated education labor market (tenured, part time, fixed contract and casual), with rights and wages being negotiated away in contracts and enterprise bargaining to gain family friendly conditions (Probert 2001).

The neoconservatism of the federal coalition also changed the basis upon which women can make claims upon the state. Whereas previously EO policies in Australia have been based on needs and rights, women's claims under current federal policy discourses are now overtly subsumed by the national (economic) interest, responded to only if everyone benefits, producing weak policies with regard to women's rights, access to work, and individual merit in the workplace. Voluntaristic EO accountability for the largest institutions (e.g., universities and TAFEs) requires employers to "take reasonably practicable actions to eliminate discrimination and promote equity." The rights orientation of EO has been expunged from federal policies but less so in practice (Bacchi 2000a, 65). Conservative social policies equate women's interests to family interests, and not as separate identities, defining female identity economistically. Women, however, bear the brunt of postwelfare social policies that reprivatize care arising from increased reliance upon the civil (community, family, and NGOs), with Australian voluntarism peaking. An *Age* editorial (10 March 2005) stated a need for "dedicated women's policies" nationally if women are to receive "a fair deal" in work, questioning the abolition of the equity infrastructure on the assumption that "gender equity is no longer an issue."

Against this, one has to read with some cynicism federal government and media discourses that portray men as victims of feminism and boys disadvantaged in education, due to feminized school cultures and curriculum and female-headed households (Mills, Martino, and Lingard 2004a). The narrow focus on male academic underachievement has been possible because "equity has been rearticulated in respect of performance conceived in a particular fashion; that is, performance is measured by standards, tests and university entrance scores" (Lingard 2003a, 36). Yet the federal government is seeking to amend sex discrimination legislation to facilitate the first instance of positive discrimination for a "men only" teaching scholarship against the spirit of the act, a move manifested by a fear of the replaceability of men. "The basic question is not so much whether men will be able to hold on indefinitely to their economic privileges, but as to whether they will be able to break with ideals of masculinity based on performance in the public sphere, in the domain of work and other activities" (Giddens 1994, 173).

Ironically, the focus on masculinity allows government to sidestep the real problems facing educational managers of a more deeply entrenched educational inequality among girls *and* boys based on socioeconomic disadvantage, ethnicity, and indigeneity (Teese and Polesel 2003; Vinson 2002; Collins et al. 2000) resulting from policies of marketization. Historically, social liberal traditions in Australia have been premised upon some redistributive mechanism (e.g., taxes) and a willingness by the "nanny state" to intervene to protect individuals and disadvantaged groups (e.g., Disadvantaged Schools program; Blackmore 1999a; Sawer 2003). Now welfarism is depicted by neoliberal discourses as creating dependency and disincentives in market-driven systems, adeptly ignoring how dependency is structural and systemically raced, classed, and gendered in its conceptualization and practice. "Whereas social liberalism conveyed the promise of more autonomy within the private sphere and more caring values in the public sphere, neo liberalism depicts the results of social liberalism as a loss of masculinity—through over protection by the state in the public sphere and the usurpation of male roles in the private sphere" (Sawer 2003, 24). The issue now for educational and social progressivists is how to work within a logic of practice of increasingly centralized federal/state policy

frames and new governmentalities that ignore, marginalize and oppose intervention for social justice unless it is politically advantageous. "Postpatrimonial
governance" witnesses the demise of the ethical model of policy and administration but can take on either a democratic form in which government ensures
the conditions of participation (citizen choice and voice) or a neoliberal market form where ownership is sovereign (consumer choice), a nonegalitarian
model based on survival of the fittest (Yeatman 2000, 171–2).

PARADOXICAL RESTRUCTURING
YET AGAIN IN THE "NEW MILLENIUM"

Seddon and Angus (2000, 186) considered that neoliberal politics of globalization in education during the 1990s produced a three-way crisis of public educational provision: declining funding symbolizing a declining commitment to the "nation building role of education"; a crisis in identity as to
the role and function of education; and a crisis of global strategy in terms of
the globalizing learning environment. In response, the focus of the late
twentieth century to the early twenty-first century has shifted from structural to cultural reform in an ongoing search for improved performance.
"The less organizations are able to rely upon a framework of stable social
and political relations, the more they are forced to engage in a project of
'hegemonic construction.' . . . Thus 'new wave management' is concerned
with changing people's values, norms and attitudes so that they make the
'right' and necessary contribution to the success of the organization for
which they work" (du Gay 1996, 57–58). This is the struggle for the soul,
not just the mind and the body, producing new paradoxes to confront educational managers and leaders.

Knowledge Society or Knowledge Economy?

Education is arguably central to a knowledge-based society seeking to promote economic growth through vocationalism and the formation of individual and collective identity through diversity of experience and knowledge in a
time of cultural pluralism and hybridity. Undisputably in 2005, education is
also an industry, producing significant export income ($4.6 billion), employ-
ing the largest workforce nationally, and sustaining local economies. But is
education to be a driver of social and economic change or the "handmaiden to
global capitalism"? (Slaughter and Leslie 1998, v).

Despite policy discourses about life-long learning and knowledge
economies, there has been a continuing disinvestment by the federal government
in public education (government schools, higher education, and TAFE) and
infrastructure (research and training), in stark contrast to increased educational

investment in the European Union, the United States, the United Kingdom, and the Asian Tiger states. The funding per student in universities has decreased in real terms from just over $10,000 to $9,400, while student contributions have increased from 3 percent to 30 percent of costs from 1991 through 2004 after the introduction of the Higher Education Contribution Scheme (HECS). Commonwealth funding in 2004 contributes only to 30 percent of total operating revenue of universities (cf., 90 percent in 1991 and 46.7 percent in 2001). Student-staff ratios increased from 12.9 in 1990 to 18.8 in 2000 to over 24 in 2004 at the same time casualization of academic staff trebled from 8 percent in 1984 to 24 percent in 2004. The massification of tertiary education (including TAFE) is contingent on a regime of domestic and international fees and, ironically, reduced proportional participation of equity groups. In 2003, indigenous are 1.3 percent (cf., 3.5 percent population), NESB 3.8 percent, rural 18.6 percent and lower socioeconomic 15.3 percent (Australian Vice Chancellors' Committee 2004). Deferred student loans disadvantage women (only 20 percent of whom compared to 60% of men repay HECS in full by thirty-four).

Likewise in schools, Howard's federal government funding formula, which is based on choice, not need, means federal funds to private schools are now greater than to universities, with 70 percent of federal funds going to 30 percent of students in the private sector. Federal policies on new schools have facilitated the greatest increase in small religious schools, Christian and Muslim). Extremely wealthy schools (due to student fees. property assets, benefactors, and sponsors) are receiving more government funds than poorer schools in both the systemic Catholic and government sectors (Australian Bureau of Statistics 2004). Evidence in Australia now clearly indicates the effects of 1990s restructuring based on markets and devolution. The expanding poverty gap between rich and poor during the 1990s (risen from 11 percent to 19 percent of children in poverty) directly impacts on public schools in high-welfare and high-unemployment locations (Vinson 2002; Collins et al. 2000), while benefiting the "aspirational" and mobile middle class with the economic and cultural capital located in urban pockets. Lamb and colleagues (2004, 56) conclude that

> social and cultural factors are strong influences on school performance. Schools that serve largely middle class populations do better on a range of scholastic and student outcomes measures. The high level of segregation of students in Australia, due in large part to residential segregation and the sector organization of schools, tends to reinforce patterns of inequality and strengthen differences in school performance. It means that students from disadvantaged SES backgrounds tend to do worse because of the extent of segregation. One upshot, according to a recent OECD study of PISA results, is that much talent remains unused and human resources are wasted.

Schooling is increasingly being organized and institutionalized along class, racial, gender, and ethnic demarcations mobilized through policies of choice emphasizing cultural/socioeconomic homogeneity not heterogeneity. These trends are evident in other devolved systems in marketized environments (e.g., for England and Ireland see Whitty 1996; Gillborn and Youdell 2000; Lynch and Lodge 2002; Power et al. 2003b; Levavic and Woods 2000; for the United States see Freeman 1999; Wells et al. 1998; for New Zealand see Fiske and Ladd 2000; Thrupp 1999; and Wylie and Matthews 2003; for Canada see Bosetti 1999; Mitchell 2001).

Despite discourses about market responsiveness to diversity, the market norm of a "good school" is an elite private school. There has been a decline in comprehensiveness in favour of increased selectivity, specialization and reprivileging of the academic/liberal education as the curriculum of distinction, a trend exemplified in a recent restructure of public schools in inner Sydney (Gulson 2004; Campbell 2003). Vocational education remains the education for the marginalized (nonacademic) student. Selectivity—whether through social mix, specialization, selection, or discipline policies, curriculum and assessment practices, fees, residential ghettos—is the key determinant of school outcomes, *the* measure of success of the performative state and markets (Campbell and Sherington 2003; Gillborn and Youdell 2000). Public schools are increasingly being "made over" to look more corporate, to categorize, track, and test, often excluding their traditional clientele in order to perform (Meadmore and Meadmore 2004, 386). They have thus "abandoned any claim to an alternative rationale . . . grounded in their own history and purposes as comprehensive institutions with a broad social mission" (Marginson 1997, 202).

This socioeconomic polarization of educational provision impacts on leadership practices and possibilities in all sectors. Women in Australia, as elsewhere, tend to be leaders, through preference and selection, in more challenging institutions: schools with the highest cultural/linguistic mix and lowest socioeconomic communities, community-based TAFEs, and newer, regional, and Utech universities that under current policies will be teaching rather than research intensive (Limerick and Anderson 1999b, see Brooking 2005 and Strachan 1999a for New Zealand). They will bear the brunt of "managing" the educational inequalities of increasingly stratified education systems. This has flow on effects. Numerous reports and surveys in Australia, the United Kingdom, the United States, Canada, and New Zealand identify a crisis in attracting and retaining teachers, and in turn principals, particularly in "challenging" public schools and rural/regional areas (e.g., Lacey 2002; d'Arbon et al. 2001; Preston, Blackmore, and Thomson 2004). Indeed, the principalship is now seen by many women (and men) as being too demanding on family life, a health risk, and lacking opportunities to "make a difference" (Thomson et al. 2003; DET 2004).

Professional Learning Networks Building
Communities/Performance-Based Centralism

Recent policy discourses in all education sectors, in response to rising awareness of educational inequality, now promote discourses about interagency support, networking, life-long learning, community capacity building, clusters, university/school/TAFE/industry partnerships, and learning communities as new institutional formations for re-forming education (Blackmore 2002c). In Victoria, Local Learning and Employment Networks are expected to improve coordination between agencies assisting young people's transition from school to work or training, as were Education Action Zones and Cities of Excellence in England, and New Communities in Scotland (Power et al. 2003a; Lieberman and Grolnick 1997). These reform initiatives tend to be imposed, underfunded, or unfunded, exploiting teacher and academic good will, overlying extant competitive funding models and centrally managed through even tighter accountability regimes (Kamp 2003). Significant energy is dispersed in individual institutions networking to gain short-term funding to achieve minimal flexibility.

Similarly in universities and further education, the discourse is about innovation and creativity to be gleaned through university/TAFE/industry partnerships. Yet such arrangements are impeded by contractualism and enhanced performative regimes that shape winners and losers between research-intensive and teaching-intensive universities and active researchers and teachers. Performance-based models even more tightly link retention and graduation rates to funding (e.g., research funding in universities. Federal funding of schools is now tightly linked to standardized tests of functional literacy and numeracy. The Victorian Labor *Blueprint for Government Schools* (2003) flagship strategies have a twofold even contradictory focus: on the one hand, the policy focuses on leadership (mentoring, attracting and retaining principals), and on the other, it seeks to promote a "performance culture" in schools through the strategies of a "balanced scorecard" by linking principal performance assessment to overall school performance (i.e., failing principals = failing schools). Such accountability measures are very blunt, focusing on the means but not on student knowledge and understanding. Strathern (2000b, 309) argues that "when a measure becomes a target, it ceases to be a good measure. The more an examination performance becomes an expectation, the poorer it becomes as a discriminator of individual performances. . . . However, targets that seem measurable becoming enticing tools of improvement."

These localized standardizing and universalizing tendencies are exacerbated by intensified global pressures toward international standards in student outcomes and professional standards. These testing regimes are themselves not being "tested" for their validity, value, and effects, but they do impact on what and how people lead and teach. This is indicative of the "tension between competing narratives of diversity and heteroglossism with the proliferation of knowledges and experiences and the favouring of knowledge of an instrumental and operational kind" (Whitty 2001, 163). So while policy responses to inequality (learning networks, seamlessness) mobilize discourses of teacher leadership, innovation, and partnerships, they are undermined by the systemic globalizing disposition for centralized control and performativity that in turn lacks any substantive focus (e.g., equity, active participation, and inclusion) or normative dimension (e.g., discourses of citizenship). "The preoccupation with specifying goals and tasks distorts the practice of public services as quantifiable models of quality and evaluation increasingly displaces concern for the internal goods of excellence. Moreover, the regimes of regulation designed to enhance public accountability paradoxically strengthen corporate power at the expense of the public sphere" (Ransom 2003, 460).

These challenges face the public sector over issues of coordination and control, the key roles of middle management. Contemporary educational discourses position "the authentic" as the remedy to disengagement and alienation from education. We have argued that teacher, leader, and indeed student disengagement is a by-product of the emphasis by the state, and markets and management on "the performative" that acts as a simulcarum in which the original is lost in multiple images and fabrications. Educators are more likely to provide an authentic account of their practices that will enhance professional and organizational accountability when there is strong internal accountability premised upon deliberative planning, multiple modes of professional knowledge, and processes that value professional judgment, supported by a rich appreciation of ethical and social consequences and knowledge bases within the professional field (Newmann et al. 1997). This means recognizing the diverse and often conflicting aims of universities, schools, or TAFE institutes because of their unique educational role.

> Diverse social arrangements allow one to move in many directions at once, to allow persons to go off in different directions. Contradiction is the engine of the intellect. But turn aims into objectives, turn multiple possibilities into plans of action, and contradiction is banished. The institution becomes judged by acts that presume unity—by the degree of consensus by which it will achieve its aims and this by the effectiveness with which it has actually eliminated contradictions. . . . Here the loop gets to throttling tautness. (Strathern, 2000b, 313)

LIFELONG LEARNING OR A REVITALIZED VOCATIONAL/ACADEMIC DIVIDE?

The ongoing desire for seamlessness among TAFE, universities, and schools is in the context of vocational education and training (VET) being reinvented to address youth disengagement and unemployment, with increased privileging of industry voice. Multiple initiatives have been imposed on schools and TAFE, competing for attention and funds: VET in schools, the Victorian Certificate of Applied Learning, workplace training (new apprenticeships), and innovative school-industry models. But these initiatives are at significant cost to the poorer public schools with the most diverse and disadvantaged student populations (Smith and Keating 2003). "Too many vocational education in schools programs have been developed by educators and politicians driven by the need to be seen to be 'doing something' about the disconnection between the worlds of education and work" (Ryan 2002, 11). VET in schools, Ryan (2002) argues, has "problems of organizational complexity, cost and academic bias," is unsustainable financially, subtly excludes the high achievers and least advantaged, and lacks employer cooperation. Furthermore, the TAFE sector, a provider of VET, has been grossly underfunded to the point of bankruptcy for some institutes at the same time a national skill shortage in the traditional trades has become headlines. It is now evident that the market has been an ineffective distributive mechanism by which to optimize training or address youth disengagement.

For educational workers in TAFE, largely "ignored in official policies during the 1990s" (Smith and Keating 2003, 228), conditions have worsened. An Australian Education Union *Review of TAFE Teachers* in 2001 found that "a pernicious effect of under-funding has been the growth of casualization in employment . . . with teachers 'forced to work 200% percent harder,' living in a 'dislocated and lonely existence on the periphery of the colleges'" (AEU 2001, vi). Increased unpaid work is the norm, due to increased "preparation and administration (reporting and accountability requirements), correction/assessment, coordination and meetings, customization and development of curriculum, funding cuts in teaching staff, constant change and restructure, changes in delivery and curriculum, reduced job security and greater casualization" (Kronemann 2001, viii). Significantly, most respondents perceived the "current management culture as having turned away from a prime focus on education as a result of current financial and cultural pressures, a failure of management to value and recognize teachers' work . . . and the lack of an effective open and competent management structure" (Kronemann 2001, ix–x). Furthermore, the review cited half the women respondents stating child care as central to their participation (Kronemmann 2001), yet childcare has become more costly and scarce (Summers 2003). Women more than men saw a change in workplace culture as necessary and the need to get more women in management. Men tended to oppose women-only strategies, seeing them as unnecessary, with 10 percent considering "women already advantaged" (Kronemann 2001, xiii). So there is an ongoing discrepancy between the experience of women and how women are perceived when it comes to equity in a more volatile education market with even harsher, less supportive institutional cultures.

What Wins: Quality or Comparability?

The last decade has seen an intensified interest by government in outcomes and quality assurance. In the context of more volatile international education markets, reputations associated with quality will be the primary comparative advantage, particularly for universities and TAFE institutes, but also schools. Quality audits provide a capacity for government to direct and control and markets to rank and compare. Audits can also work for equity, such as gender audits, and, some argue, the standards-based movement in the United States (Skrla and Scheurich 2004). But audits can produce more complex patterns of differentiation premised upon who you are and not what you do (Morley 2003). Thus university research assessment exercises categorise the same research done by a female contract researcher as "low level status" and that done by tenured (usually male) academics as "high level status" (Reay 2000, 15). In the United Kingdom and New Zealand, the narrow parameters (efficiency) and assumptions (privileging scientific fields) of research assessment means male academics and particular models of research are overrepresented, further marginalizing oppositional (feminist, postcolonial) and interdisciplinary fields (e.g., education). Yet it is the female academics who do the quality "management" work as middle managers (Morley 2003). So "both men and careerist masculinities, are reinforced by the bureaucratic bullying of a managerialist rather than an intellectual elite" (Harley 2003, 387).

The quality movement's desire for comparability has aligned with the competency movement's search for consistency and the evaluative state's emphasis on outcomes. This is evident in how concepts such as 'competency' and 'generic and employability skills' now permeate strategic plans and performance indicators of schools, universities, and TAFE in the form of "graduate attribute outcomes" and leadership competencies for principals. Yet there is no evidence that, for example, "graduate skills assessment measures anything relevant to higher education or indeed anything at all outside performance on that test" (Moodie 2004, 39) or whether "employability skills" are of any more value to employers than a general liberal education. But new authorities governing credentialing, certification, and quality are emerging, such as the National Institute for Teacher Quality and School Leadership similar to the National College of School Leadership in the United Kingdom, to administer these performative regimes nationally and increasingly internationally. The emergence of an international professional standards movement also increases the influence of professional associations and "the market" on curriculum and pedagogy (Middlehurst and Campbell 2001). Paradoxically, the search for comparability encourages the narrowly normative and standardising tendencies of quality assurance, reducing responsiveness to diversity/inclusivity (and one could suggest quality) while often encouraging antipedagogical and antitheoretical reductionist approaches to teaching and learning (Morley 2003).

Similarly, tighter links are being made among quality assurance, teacher performance, and student satisfaction with the rise of regulative and standardized evaluations applied across institutions and systems. Such evaluations usually fail to inform academics or teachers actually how to *improve* curriculum and pedagogies as quality assurance (as opposed to quality improvement) assumes process ensures quality (Rowley 1995; Blackmore 2003). QA not only intensifies labor, but it also disperses managerial tasks of surveillance: appropriating student, parent, academic, and teacher voice by making quality everyone's responsibility. Student charters, service and care centers in universities, TAFE or school councils position student or parent voice in a customer-service and not partnership or pedagogical relationship, their involvement being on the grounds of improving service rather than representativeness. Even as "representatives" on decision-making bodies, students and parents are also caught up in the internal logics of auditing, evaluation, and planning that "make compliance with them, at the very least in some dramaturgical way, extremely difficult to avoid" (Prichard and Deem 1999, 328). Student evaluations and customer surveys inform this logic, in which students are assumed to know what they wish to learn and how to learn it so as to be prepared to arbitrarily reject knowledge that does not fit with current experience, also act as another form of control by executive management over academics and teachers (Alexiadou 2000, 13). And those teachers and academics who articulate the conflict between customer-service contractualism and student-teacher pedagogical relations are depicted as political and resistant. Student and parental voice is not about participation of an active corporate citizen or as an educative process. QA is now the primary role of academic boards, TAFE curriculum boards, and school councils (Moodie 2004). It is therefore the key task of middle managers. But because they lack the necessary resources to nurture substantive improvements in quality more broadly, quality assurance becomes another performative exercise encouraging managers to produce "'fabrications' of performance manufactured for their effect as 'accountability'" (Ransom 2003, 462). QA does not "extinguish culture" but is "at one with culture" (du Gay 1996, 58).

Furthermore, these regulative discourses jostle up against empowering discourses in schools, universities, and TAFE institutions, extolling transformational and distributed leadership, forging partnerships, and building networks locally and globally. Teachers are expected to be facilitators, communicators, and strategists of learning, focusing on student difference. School systems are reviewing curriculum, assessment, and pedagogy, stripping down the curriculum to core/generic elements utilizing notions of essential learning and productive pedagogies, working to integrate theory and practice and make learning more relevant through authentic assessment while engaging in interdisciplinary rich tasks and community-based education (Cope and Kalantzis 1997: Lingard et al. 2003). In TAFE, there is an ongoing struggle over the capacity of competencies to do the necessary work in the formation of skilled worker identities or to deliver "authentic" learning (Smith and Keating 2003). New fields of academic activity such as online pedagogy offer promising possibilities for women as researchers and as managers of teaching and learning. But academics struggle to encourage critical professionalism (Brabazon 2002).

Such discourses, as we have indicated, excite leaders, academics and teachers and open up new spaces for more participatory modes of leadership organized around student learning, teams, horizontal structures, and research that makes a difference (Whitty 2001). But the "conflation of power (managerial relationships) and empowerment (leadership relationships)" (Hatcher 2003, 255), and the refusal to recognize social inequalities, means notions of transformational leadership are politically neutralized. Change is constrained within parameters set by organizational strategic plans. Distributed leadership becomes the delegation of tasks. There is little recognition of the democratic and ethical underpinnings of such concepts and their intent to redistribute power, flatten hierarchies, value professional judgement, or promote democratic governance (Hatcher 2003; Gunter 2004; Blackmore 2002a; Woods 2004).

Calibrating Difference, Craving Consistency

But as these four paradoxes indicate, what was paradoxical is now increasingly less so. Systemic dispositions toward standardization have facilitated finer calibrations of differentiation in terms of ranking, benchmarking, and sorting between individuals and institutions. Institutional "fluidity" facilitating student pathways and choice between sectors has produced a craving for "consistency" and "coherence" producing a tightening of control over process, content, and outcomes in education by management and government through contractualism, certification, and accreditation (Gleeson and Husbands 2001). These new governmentalities are mobilized by a "negative logic" of risk and "tight-loose" control (du Gay 1996, 60). These trends have significant effects. The rise of performance cultures and processes of commodification of knowledge has harnessed the psychological and intellectual striving of individuals for autonomy and creativity through the practices of "audit, funding and planning that produce forms of self surveillance but not reflexivity" (Prichard and Deem 1999, 327). These "rational actor theories" of neoliberal educational redesign fail to consider how actors are located in "thick environments that have histories and cultures, patterns of affiliation and difference, relations of advantage-disadvantage, and possession-dispossession" (Seddon and Angus 2000, 205). While not entirely "governed," educators have become more self-managing, individualized, and competitive. The question is whether discourses of social capital, partnerships, networks, workplace and lifelong learning, and community capacity building have the capacity to rework localized relations more democratically.

Somehow the balance must be struck between respect for colleagues, freedom of action (the ethics of subsidiarity) and the organizational need to manage hard choices and to ensure the maintenance of standards in a context of innovation and rapid and substantial change. Bureaucracy in a true sense of the word is not necessarily a repressive instrument. The maintenance of quality assurance procedures, for example, frequently viewed as an intrusion into the proper territory of individual [academic] judgement, may be a support to impartial and consistent judgement within an institution, and the best defence against innovation of questionable standards in pursuit of short term gain. The converse obligation is that senior staff should resist the temptation to use such procedures as a form of control which diverts legitimate challenge, to allow them to become layers of process which obscure or weaken the [university's] aims and organizational objectives. (Bone 1997, 22).

We therefore see a rearticulation of old problems such as social justice emerging in new forms and changing contexts for the next generation of women leaders. Our women participants were not reluctant, as Grace's (1995) United Kingdom woman principals were, to foreground gender. Their leadership habitus was informed by their experiences and observations of injustice, marginalization, and subordination that had produced more generally a "reflexive awareness of the potential damage of power imbalances that, just as much as gender, influences whether individuals conform to, or challenge, orthodox 'masculine' ways of managing in the contemporary market place" (Reay and Ball 2000, 149). But in the new millenium, women manage in the context of a more fully corporatized mode of educational governance and conservative gender politics. Discourses of social justice and equity in education have been displaced by discourses of individual choice and self-promotion. The state has become more interventionist on managing performance outcomes other than for equity. The feminist theoretical movement has disengaged with the feminist political movement. Past alliances among educators, unions, and the women's movement are in jeopardy, as "the universal worker on which trade unionism is premised has become a rapidly diminishing figure; the universal woman in feminism has become an insult" (Franzway 2001, 15). The current generation of women educators, with similar aspirations to our cohort to make a difference, do well, and succeed, have been educated in the more individualistic and competitive education systems of the 1990s. Knowing the rules of the game better, the question is whether the next generation of women is prepared to be the major source of new leaders to remedy systemic deficiencies as the costs emotionally, personally, and intellectually are high, and alternative, more lucrative, and family friendly work is readily available in the private sector.

RESTRUCTURING, ORGANIZATIONAL CHANGE, AND THE RENORMING OF EDUCATION

We are currently seeing a further intensification, consolidation, and institutionalization of the emerging trends we identified during the 1990s. "Now management, marketing and public relations, have gained equal, if not privileged, status with the 'old' professional concerns of teaching, learning, assessment and professional support" (Leonard 1998, 72). The hybrid corporate neobureaucratic organization has a reduced capacity for democratic governance and yet is unable to work freely in economic markets as a private organization. The professional habitus of the late twentieth-century education worker, for whom education was part of an democratic imaginary, was informed by loyalties outside managerial control derived from political activism in social movements, notions of public service, and a collective commitment to the profession. Now education professionalism is framed by customer sovereignity and discourses of client responsiveness. Issues of social justice are more difficult to raise in practice because the emphasis is on rights, contractual relations, and entitlements, not fairness, inclusivity, and responsibilities.

Governments' and management's capacity for control was initially through both structural reform (devolution, corporate management, marketization) that radically changed the nature and conditions of educational work. But it was the new technologies of performativity that ultimately recultured and renormed the education field by fundamentally changing educational relationships among educator, student, parent, industry, and community. Though contractualism, competition, and accountability played out by "self-managing" better, professional identities were transformed within a "regulated autonomy" in which there was no "professional mandate" as there had been in the twentieth century (Whitty 2001, 161). The professional norm has moved "from a progressive educator and participant in educational politics to one of a competent performer of relatively neutral tasks related to efficient and profitable delivery of pre-specified curriculum and of being a responsible manager of learning contexts" (Seddon and Angus 1999, 497).

At the same time, there continues to be contestation at all levels over government aims and stakeholder expectations. Executive managers of educational organizations (principals, vice-chancellors and directors) in particular are expected to be the gatekeepers of reform, resisting externally imposed changes to keep their institutions happy (Dempster and Logan 1998; Blackmore et al. 1996). Individual institutions seek to consolidate and patrol boundaries, to identify the self from the imaginary "other," the competitor, "creating a forced unit out of diversity, coherence out of inconsistencies and homogeneity out of narrative dissonance" (Benhabib 2002, 8). Universities, TAFE institutes, and schools "represent themselves as unified, continuous, accumulative, in an ongoing pedagogical process of organizational change, while they utilized the 'repititious recursive strategy of the performative,' as a representational strategy by which the organizations 'self regeneration' was reenacted" (Benhabib 2002, 9). Paradoxically, in so doing, institutions managed themselves better in at least partial alignment with government priorities; just as individuals in rejecting the performative as inappropriate to govern educational work simultaneously internalize performativity's demands, managing themselves better for the organization. Yet as active agents, they also appropriate, subvert, and resist managerial and market discourses whenever possible, "by not feeling compelled to play games by the 'blokey rules' and subverting bureaucratic structures" (Limerick and Anderson 1999b, 412). This agency is possible, then and now, because of the "situated" complexities of educational practice, as the overlayering of multiple reform imperatives provide space to play. Past practices can be modified, adjusted, renamed; structures and lines of responsibility altered; and jobs/subjects/schools disappear or are redefined. Shared memories and narratives bind people together as sites of sociality are nurtured whenever possible (Strachan 1999b).

From this perspective, resistance to reform cannot be viewed as a pathology or property invested in some individuals or groups and not others ("teachers are conservative" or "academics just want to do their own thing"). Rather resistance is temporal and situated, a form of social action (or nonaction) at particular moments, a discourse mobilized to be oppositional one moment and hegemonic the next. Our women leader/managers saw resistance as a rational-emotional response, for example, to those reforms that did not improve the educational outcomes of students, that subverted collegiality, that threatened one's professional or personal identity, or that led to loss of power, status, or expertise. A key aspect of their success as leaders (and therefore change managers) was understanding their own and other people's investments in the status quo, in their institutional and professional identities, and therefore how some individuals are, due to their habitus and location, more open to change on some things, though resistant on others. Accordingly, as managers they sought to moderate the worst aspects of the reform imperatives. In this endeavor some mobilized practical discourses of organizational change based on "moral discourses about universal norms of justice, ethical discourse about forms of the good life, and political-pragmatic discourses about the feasible" (Benhabib 2002, 12). Others sought to create deliberative democratic practices to negotiate "situationally shared understandings" out of competing discourses (Benhabib 2002, 16). Most mobilized internal discourses (often about survival) and external discourses (accountability and quality) to shift local practices, with the intention to improve student outcomes, although not necessarily with that effect.

While reform discourses were arbitrarily and partially taken up, many institutional practices were retained and modified, accommodating where possible new policies and practices. The logic embedded in the discourses and practices of equity reform institutionalized during the 1980s did not disappear with the dismantling of the national equity infrastructure after 1996. Rather they were retained and indeed promoted within institutions as part of local collective and individual memories, perpetuated through organizational narratives, structures, and individual dispositions that had become habitual. At the same time, equity was also increasingly mobilized to gain market credibility, and out of necessity to recruit women as the new pool of talent. This was possible in part because the logic of gender equity policy was itself "managerial" with its focus on transparent processes, targets, and centralized monitoring and therefore readily incorporated into the managerial logics of new public administration and institutional performativities. Even the weaker discursive frame of managing diversity enabled equity practitioners and managers to retain practices embedded by past equity reforms to draw on "best HR management practice" and market "responsiveness to diversity" discourses. At the same time, the embeddedness of equity practice was highly variable, dependent on location and contingent on the political will of the executive, institutional image (whether equity accrued positive capital in the market) and resourcing (Sinclair 1998). Significantly, under conservative governments, the delivery of equity will be increasingly reliant upon individual institutions. Ironically, equity reform will be contingent on feminists' collective capacity to pressure reluctant governments and institutions through a public shaming of their inability to perform against international measures of democratic governance and economic progress (Blackmore 1999a).

Signficantly the renorming of education has more generally, we have argued, shifted the sociopsychic economy of the field. There has been an ongoing redistribution down of administrative activities to lower cost workers (women) mobilized through new management discourses of team-based activity, with retention of central control; a labor process that is both individualizing and alienating. The counterproductive effect of the performative is leadership disengagement (Gronn and Rawlings-Sanaei 2003) because of a crisis in meaning manifest in a sense of (declining) optimism that education can improve individual and collective futures, a grief over the loss of professional solidarity and collegiality, and a professional logic of practice that focused on fairness. Underlying the contestation over the reform agenda during the 1990s was disputation about core educational values, public service professionalism, and democratic governance.

GENDER AS A USEFUL ANALYTIC FOCUS

Gender was therefore a useful lens through which to analyse leadership, educational restructuring, and organizational change. A feminist analysis allowed us to track, map, and illuminate the networks of power and influence. Gender and equity were not foregrounded in educational restructuring. Indeed, equity policies, central intervention, and political will were weakened at the moment when internal arrangements were in disarray, facilitating well-institutionalized networks of power to "articulate themselves in ways that are specifically gendered" producing a structural backlash (Leonard 1998, 73). Managerial masculinity reemerged in organizational life in new/old forms of "traditional authoritarianism (bullying and fear), a gentleman's club (protective paternalism), entrepreneurialism (task focused workaholism), informalism (larrikin-like cultures, sports, and sex), and careerism (expert and detached)" (Sinclair 1998, 61). While a particular "hard form of masculinity was still associated with success" (Leonard 1998, 72), there is now increasing recognition that "traditional and narrow constructions of acceptable masculinities [in leadership and management] have become a prison for both women and men" (Sinclair 1998, 57) because of the expectations of heroism, physical and emotional toughness, and self-reliance.

Womanagers get caught up in this web of interlocked and seamless performativities stretching across all education sectors. Women as managers are the subjects and objects of managerial and market reform as managers and leaders, agents of the "psychosocial management of 'obligatory achievement'" embedded in performative systems and self-audit (Hey and Bradford 2004, 691). This has been achieved, first, by neoconservative governments and corporate organizations exploiting women's desire for reform and agency to undercut old masculinist alliances between the professions and government welfarism.

> Women are being increasingly drawn into such positions both to subvert resistance to management practices and to challenge embedded bureau-professional inefficiencies . . . bureau professionalism being the old alliance between administrative and professional knowledge practices, accountability to politicians, the promise of best treatment for those in need, legitimated by professional criteria of judgement . . . [but based on] strong gender divisions. (Prichard and Deem 1999, 328)

Thus the "new bourgeois masculine self" is open to "increased vulnerability to the loss of gender competitive advantage—the potential erosion of the patriarchal dividend" (Hey and Bradford 2004, 700). But women have become willing/unwilling subjects/objects in managing processes that ultimately undermine the very professional status, image, and power they sought to acquire. These new arrangements, ironically, reposition the feminized education professions outside the political center, reasserting an older but managerial policy/execution dichotomy.

Second, while some masculinist alliances have disintegrated, new ones have been forged. Women now mediate and negotiate work cultures that have been reconstituted yet again as a masculinist project characterized by "overly rational, disembodied and instrumental pursuits" (Kerfoot and Knights 1996, 37). For men in education, particularly those in universities where masculinity is premised upon reason, autonomy, and "muscular intellectualism," the audit, for example, is the mechanism for the "retooling" of global masculinities (Connell 2000) to give it a sharper edge. Other masculinities experience "anxiety" with the loss of power due to the hotter competition from women. Yet women continue to do the emotional and quality housekeeping (Hey and Bradford 2004, 701). Within this frame, other men and women who do not "fit" into the performative culture and representations of leadership are excluded (Reay and Ball 2000; Gleesons and Husbands 2001). The difference is that women exist in "regimes of representation" (Hall 1997, 259), where power is mobilized by men, by the media, and by organizations to represent women in particular ways, producing contradiction and ambivalence for women in leadership in terms of normative femininities (caring, collaborative, consensual) (Blackmore 1999b). Women leaders realize the traps of such normative femininities yet still believe that organizations premised upon care, collaboration, and communication are better for both educators and students alike.

Third, central to this appropriation of women's capacities for management to feed new local/global relays of power is the sociopsychic dimension of corporatizing public labor. Whereas the human relations schools perceived the worker as a social creature desiring to belong to a group, the entrepreneurial worker is perceived to be an "individual in search of meaning in work, and wanting to achieve fulfilment through work" (Seddon and Angus 1999, 504). Women in middle management are critical in this cultural movement to produce new work subjectivities, both their own and those of others, to link changing political rationalities and objectives. As we and Morley (2001a, 4–6) argue, "women's gendered socialization makes them particularly well schooled players" in handling the performative technologies, familiar as they are with the gaze, self-management, organizing others, and sociopsychic splitting of identity. Thus the performative (e.g., the audit) taps into the "gendered habitus" of "good behavior" (McNay 2000), suggesting

> a new gender conjuncture—an articulation between the opportunities for reflexive forms of gendered practices taken up by women (detraditionalization) with the structural and strategic requirement to micro-manage the conditions of uncertainty signalled by such shifts. Could it be that aspects of reflexive modernization read through a more psycho-social/analytical take suggest why there might be a fit between new times demands for "feminine" positions of flexibility and revivified masculine capacities for extorting this capacity in the service of greater masculinist/managerialist intractability? (Hey and Bradford 2004, 704)

Fourth, while the white, middle-class women in our study were privileged in comparison to most women, as educators they also struggled with managing the impact of wider social and economic change, such as poverty. Leader disengagement also resulted from the "unanticipated outcomes of new government modes which have reconstituted leadership aspirations, career trajectories, and professional identities" (Gronn and Rawlings-Sanaei 2003, 172). This alienation arose from contestation over the moral purpose and ethical practices of education. "The question remains whether women who move into positions of power in the new context of [performativity's] disciplines and incentives and its 'debased' moral environment are able to resist its influences and maintain their existing values" (Reay and Ball 2000, 150).

Finally, we see this push for an enterprise or performance culture in education is perhaps part of "a wider attempt by the state to re-design civil society" through work reorganization and educational governance (Alexiadou 2000, 12). The 1990s was a period in which discourses of "reengineering" dominated restructuring through new modes of governmentality that shifted relations between the civic and civil society. The new voluntarism has meant women's private lives are appropriated through extended unpaid work hours, increased caring and voluntarism, taking up the slack of the state with its disinvestment in civil society. Governance here is underpinned by a way of thinking about democratic life, not as a collective, public, collaborative expression but from a more individualized, representative view (Woods 2004). Organizationally, the neoliberal frame allows the token offer by predominantly white, middle-class men to share leadership activities with white, middle-class women without any significant loss of power, and on the assumption that white, middle-class women "represent" all women, while pseudoincluding "the other" through discourses of diversity. But representativeness does not equate to agency. It is not good enough for successful women to simply take their place alongside successful men; the mark of achievement would be more equitable outcomes in education generally.

LEADING AND MANAGING FOR SOCIAL JUSTICE, NOT JUST WORKING HARDER AND SMARTER

While we have focused on shifting leadership habitus, on the multiple identities of leaders, on being in a constant state of being and becoming leaders, our study indicates that leadership is a contextualized social practice in which people are jointly engaged. Leadership is a set of performances and representations that are both familiar and that also distinguish the activities of some individuals from others in particular contexts. Managers do leadership, and leaders manage. But in our study, the discourse of leadership was most often mobilized when referring to ethical ways of managing social and political relationships. Discourses of management were most often mobilized to gain strategic advantage and resources to create the social *and* material conditions in classrooms, lecture theaters, workshops, and meeting rooms that were conducive to teaching, learning, and research, about organizing how to get things done. But planning was also infused with the notions of distributing resources fairly and considering outcomes with regard to equity. Making quick and dirty decisions caused significant distress up and down the decision-making chain. There was a clear preference among our womanagers for establishing deliberative democratic processes integrating a practical ethics into planning at all levels: ethical inquiry through deliberation. "Deciding to 'do the right thing' is only a small part of 'doing the right thing'" informed by principles of care, trust, respect, collegiality, and a sense of equity (Forester 1999, 221), although some were more prone to assume the managerial habitus than others. Nussbaum (1990, 79) argues that "good deliberation" requires a form of "perceptive moral improvization" that requires greater attention to relationships with others, "provisional agreements, temporary accommodations, working with contingency, enjoying surprise, but always with particular principles in mind as reference points . . . attention to both principle and detail, both to encompassing norms and commitments and to specific circumstantial particulars."

Leadership, therefore, was seen to be about articulating and sharing ideas; taking the initiative at particular moments and responsibility for planning and action; working outside/against/within the dominant way of thinking; nurturing, mentoring, and caring for others; communicating often about decisions; and developing collaborative and collegial relations based on trust, ethics, reciprocity, and mutual recognition (Day 2004). Leaders took into account the "thick context" of interpersonal relations, habits, and customs that determine the meanings and associated expectations of formal rules. As relational work, leadership was about building social capital and drawing on the "networks, associations and shared habits that enable individuals to act collectively" (Warren 1999, 9). These connections most often came from outside their organizations (unions, social movements, professional organizations, community networks, etc.) given the moral anorexia within. Leadership required "ethical judgement to be brought to bear, sometimes in an acute form. For anyone in such a position, the formation of good thinking requires reflection on experience, resolution for oneself of the consequences of failure to sustain values and standards, accommodation of new insights and above all the ability to see the role in its proper and limited perspective" (Bone 1997, 26).

For many of the women in this study, leadership in and of itself was not the issue, as they had been teacher and academic leaders throughout their lives, although more often in the mode of democratic (participatory) rather than distributed (delegated) leadership. However, formal positions of management were more problematic. This was because such positions imparted institutional legitimacy, often unwelcome, that changed their relationships with colleagues, students, management, and communities. Their systemic position in line management was premised upon authority rather than trust as in more participatory modes of governance and more reliant upon a negative use of power to change practice ("I have been instructed to . . ."). While previous bureaucratic modes of governance had required adjustments, the performative organization not only altered social relations in creating new hierarchies, utilizing new systems of reward and punishment, and mobilizing new forms of soft and hard surveillance but also demanded new norms that challenged many women's leadership habitus. They were caught, therefore, between new wave managerial theory that sought to control costs through soft regulations of norms and mutual engagement and reengineering that assumed hard rules of instrumental reciprocity and contractualism.

Whereas they had moved into formal administrative positions on the basis of their leadership based on collegial trust, now they found "[T]rust has been made more difficult by the problems of scale, complexity and interdependency that often work to limit democratic ways of decision making and create functional pressures for trust" (Warren 1999, 2). Yet trust remains critical in democratic societies and is equally important in organizations capable of responding to society's complexities. Our study also indicated how greater interdependence had previously meant individuals trusted others, institutions, and systems to "expand their opportunities for action" (Warren 1999, 4) on the assumption that organizations will "work towards stated cultural norms of fairness, truth telling and solidarity. . . . [But] organizations are now suspect" . It was the "deficit of trust" in organizations that became evident in our study. Now trust in interpersonal relationships was becoming more important than trust in democratic institutions. This "particularized trust" encourages specific groups to solidify against outsiders and leads to "factionalization." Generalized trust is about large-scale, complex, interdependent social networks, a key to developing social capital that underwrites democratic culture, including pluralism and criticism (Warren 1999). And this is where the neobureaucratic corporate educational organization and the performative state were "failing."

Educational restructuring based on economic rationalism, making education just another arm of national productivity and global capitalism, has produced a moral vacuum and confusion with regard to the purpose of education other than just "working smarter." While leaders were positioned as the linchpin in educational reform, we illustrated the counterproductive effects of performativity (doing more with less, image rather than substance, embodied performance) producing disengagement and alienation among educational leaders and educational professionals more generally. Educators, we would argue, need to refocus on the purpose of education and therefore of educational leadership and management. This requires us to reopen debate about educational governance, inequality, and social justice that addresses long-term issues of education inequality but with different manifestations than those confronted in the twentieth century.

First, we need to develop and invest in critical professionalism. "The expression of critical thought calls for emotion, (if only emotional control), commitment and courage. Criticality therefore embraces action and the self, just as much as it embraces thinking" (Barnett 1997, 48). Such a position gets beyond the notions of the reflective practitioner, which is often reduced to the therapeutic, knowing oneself better, labeling leadership styles through superficial psychological tests, and "feel good, do nothing" professional development. Critical professionalism is more than the instrumental approach of evidence-based policy and practice, in that it recognizes the underpinning political and ethical assumptions, the "fusing of moral will with the grasping of evidence" (Christie and Limerick 2004, 2). Critical professionalism is about examining one's privilege, breaking "inscribed habits of (in)attention," moving beyond passive empathy as a means to develop the social imagination that rids us of fear of "the other," while "questioning cherished beliefs and assumptions" and "learning to see differently" (Boler 1999, 176). Thus, women and men in management would consider "concealed white race privilege" (Weedon 1999, 161). Masculinist discourses of managerialism and markets that exclude women are the "unspoken counterparts to the qualities attributed to people of colour—for example, rationality, enterprise and suppression of emotion—are also assumed to be quintessentially white. . . . Whiteness as 'masculinity' functions as 'unmarked categories of neutrality'" (Weedon 1999, 154). White women have to bypass the guilt of white advantage to consider how racism distorts and lessens our lives as white women and how to work for mutual respect and reciprocity (Moreton-Robinson 2000). Critical professionalism would also require leader/managers to "profess" about education within and outside the field, to become advocates for the less advantaged and activists within a range of policy communities, forming strategic alliances between groups and with other professions, in a wider educational alliance for collective action to improve all aspects of education at the macrolevel and student learning outcomes and teacher status at the microlevel. Lynch and Lodge (2002, 13) comment that "while there has been substantive critique, there have been few serious attempts to develop 'counterfactuals,' serious and systemic outlines of alternative structures and systems."

Second, extraorganizational networks, bodies, and movements may become increasingly more important with the deinstitutionalization of education and career. Professional networks, local and international, may be more relevant than organizations or government to promote status, professional learning, and activism, but from a critical rather than a standards-driven perspective. Similarly, as any social movements that are sites of international and national bottom up activism, feminism cannot assume that it is the "natural" political destination for all women, no matter how "multicultural" and that a "self conscious politics of partiality" may be necessary where feminism becomes a "limited political home which does not absorb difference" (Ang 1995, 58).

Third, our study indicated how the sense of ethical and moral purpose (e.g., redressing inequality and promoting social justice) provides meaning to educational work (Newmann 1996; Nias 1999). Sinclair (2000b) suggests that the new managerialism and markets have disallowed notions of public commitment and moral practice to be foregrounded. While educators are no more ethical than other occupations, a primary task for leadership in education is "a recovery of concern with the ethical basis of [higher] education and the reassertion on the foundation of the scope and breadth of its purposes" (Bone 1997, 19). Discourses of self-management and choice, framed by the organizing principles of contractualism and competition, for example, tapped into desires for more responsive democratic governance, particularly for those who felt excluded, but also localized discontent, fears, and loyalties around dogmatized racial, ethnic, gender, and class identities (Phillips 1996, 144). While recognizing difference and diversity in a pluralistic society, self-management did not reduce inequality because governance was not framed by social justice principles of redistribution as well as recognition (Wells et al. 1997). Fraser (1997) argues that cultural and economic injustices are imbricated with each other, and any struggle for a theory of justice demands both dealing with redistribution (e.g., theories of exploitation, fairness, and capabilities) and recognition (theories of representation, interpretation, and communication). The former requires a change in distribution of income, division of labor and democratic decision-making structures; the latter cultural and symbolic change in the form of valorizing cultural diversity. Most injustices derive from both the political and economic structures and the cultural valuational structure of society, producing the bivalent collectivities of gender and "race." Educational reform that meaningfully focuses on broad definitions of student outcomes for all has to be in conjunction with other redistributive policies that address social and economic inequality through taxation, social welfare, employment, health, and housing policies (Thrupp 1999, 184). To do so requires deliberate interventions by the state, the moral use of power that cannot be left up to leaders or schools alone, and a reinvention of the public that encompasses human values and social ideas, and education as again a site of generativity (Sinclair 2000b).

Fourth, this book has not just been about women leaders, although it is their voices you have heard. The ongoing whiteness and maleness of educational, political, business, and community leadership is not about gender, but is a problem for democracy. This issue has been defused by focusing on leaders rather than leadership, and leadership rather than democratic practice, as central to organizational life. The lack of women in leadership has been constructed as only an issue of representativeness, a limited understanding of democracy assumed in neoliberalism, when indeed the issue is about collective agency and social action as understood in more participatory models of democracy and associational or relational justice (Phillips 1996).

We can apply the four elements of social justice—redistribution, recognition, association, and agency—outlined above to enable women to become full corporate citizens beyond doing the emotional management work. Redistribution would require a new division of labor and resource redistribution within work and the home, while the principle of recognition would mean that the devaluation of the feminine in language and other cultural representations of organizations would be rectified. The associational principle would require reflexivity by individuals and organizations not just on who is represented (e.g., cultural and linguistic difference) but also on deliberative democratic processes of decision making that encourage debate over principles and outcomes (e.g., equity audits). And finally, agency would be imparted by determining that the minimal conditions for full participation in organizational life are guaranteed through freedom from discrimination on the one hand and the capacity for voice and action on the other.

So the marketization and managerialization of education during the 1990s have made education central to the processes of global capital accumulation in knowledge-based economies. Capital may have won in terms of its global pervasiveness and interpenetration, but it may lose in other ways because of its incapacity to deal with issues of respect, recognition, and redistribution, the social covenant that forms the glue for binding, even if temporarily, relationships within organizational and everyday life. Education, policy makers need to be reminded, is central to a knowledge-based and democratic society, not only for its vocational content, but increasingly for the formation of individual and collective identity, social capital formation, and social cohesion in both the civic and civil domains. The issue is whether educational leadership and management provide the space for the transgressive practices necessary to do this democratic work.

Notes

1. "Living at the crossroads" is from Bauman 2001, 127.

2. Jill Blackmore was deputy chair of the academic board at Deakin University, and Judyth Sachs was chair of the academic board at the University of Sydney. At both institutions the academic boards are independent of the management structures of the university but provide advice to the vice-chancellor and the governing body on issues relating to teaching, research, and quality assurance.

3. During the period of this project the proportion of women in universities was 45.0 percent of level A (tutor), 41.0 percent level B (lecturer), 23.2 percent level C (senior lecturer), 13.3 percent of level D (associate professor) and 9.8 percent of level E (professor). Women constituted 26.5 percent of continuing staff, 46.1 percent fixed term contracts and 46 percent sessional, totaling 38.9 percent of academic staff in all. Of female academics 36.1 percent had continuing positions, 23.7 percent had fixed terms, and 40.2 percent had sessional positions (Castleman et al. 1995). Between 1995 and 1997 the number of female vice-chancellors rose from one to three out of thirty-eight. In 1984 women constituted 70.3 percent of Australian primary teachers, 47 percent of secondary. By 1995, the figures were 74.7 percent and 51.3 percent, respectively.

4. Women in the labor force from 1985 through 1995 rose from 45.7 percent to 53.2 percent, 36.5 percent part time in and 42.5 percent respectively (Australian Bureau of Statistics 1995, Canberra, 76–77).

5. The desire for coherence is evident in the ways in which women leaders self-presented in constructing the biographical narrative of the interview. "Narrative is the privileged medium of this process of self-formation. The process of active appropriation immanent in the construction of narrative identity suggests a more autonomous model of agency that is offered by the negative paradigm of subjectivity. . . . [T]he self has a unity but it is a dynamic unity of change through time" (McNay 2000: 27).

6. Australia, along with the Netherlands and Ireland, has a historically high proportion (app. 30 percent school population) in church and independent schools, a colo-

nial legacy. In 1974 the federal Labor Party introduced state aid to improve the basic conditions of all students as the Catholic sector was in severe decline and free tertiary education. This radical policy shift removed the split between church and state. This expedited middle-class flight into private schooling in a deregulated market, a trend exacerbated after 1996 as new private schools could claim federal funds with changes in federal funding policies encouraging these moves.

7. During the period 1995–97 the number of female vice-chancellors increased from one to three of the thirty-eight universities. There were only two female TAFE directors, one in New South Whales and Victoria in 1996. There were 13 women out of 359 Further Education principals in the United Kingdom (Whitehead 1999, 63).

8. In New Zealand, school boards select principals without any central account-ability, training in merit, and equity, resulting in high levels of gender discrimination (Brooking 2005).

9. Globally, in 2000, the proportion of women CEOs and chairs of corporations was 2.4 percent in the United States, 1 percent in Great Britain, and 1–2 percent in Australia. Women senior executives are 4 percent and decreasing in the United States, 8 percent and declining in the United Kingdom, 3 percent and plateauing in Australia, and almost invisible in Asia (EO 2004). In a sandstone university women have moved, between 1995 and 2002, from 10 percent to 14.5 percent of professors, 6 percent to 23.13 percent of reader/associate professors, 27 percent to 34.3 percent of senior lec-turers, 42 percent to 47.4 percent of lecturers, and 55.4 percent tutors. Research only women (research assistants) are 61.6 percent with no female professors in positions of research only (University of Melbourne 2003).

10. Australia had a lower workforce participation of women than other OECD countries. But women took up 75 percent of all new low-paying jobs from 1985 as casual work rose from 16 percent in 1984 to 27 percent in 2002, part-time work from 18 percent to 29 percent, and permanent full-time work fell from 74 percent in 1988 to 61 percent in 2002 (ABS 2004).

References

Aaltio, I. and Mills, A. (Eds.) 2002. *Gender, Identity and Culture in Organisations.* Routledge, London.

Acker, S. and Feuerverger, G. 1996. "Enough Is Never Enough: Women's Work in Academe." In C. Marshall (Ed.), *Feminist Critical Policy Analysis: A Perspective from Post-Secondary Education.* Falmer, London, pp. 122–40.

———. 1997. "Doing Good and Feeling Bad: The Work of Women University Teachers." *Cambridge Journal of Education,* vol. 26, pp. 401–22.

Affirmative Action Agency. 1995. *Negotiating Equity: Affirmative Action in Enterprise.* Affirmative Action Agency, Canberra.

Ahnee-Benham, M. 2003. "In Our Mother's Voice: A Native Woman's Knowing of Leadership." In M. D. Young and L. Surla (Eds.), *Reconsidering Feminist Research in Leadership.* State University of New York Press, Albany, N.Y.

Alexiadou, N. 1999. "Situating Further Education within a Changing Public Sector in England." In N. Alexiadou and C. Brock (Eds.), *Education as a Commodity.* John Catt Educational, London.

———. 2000. "The Authority of the Customer: Some Reflections on Relations and Identities within Further Education." *Education and Social Justice,* vol. 2, no. 3, pp. 12–18.

———. 2001. "Management Identities in Transition: A Case Study of Further Education." *The Sociological Review,* vol. 49, no. 3, pp. 411–34.

Alvesson, M. and Due Billing, Y. 1996. *Understanding Gender and Organisation.* Sage, London.

———. 2002. "Beyond Body-counting: A Discussion of the Social Construction of Gender at Work." In I. Aaltio and A. Mills (Eds.), *Gender, Identity and Culture in Organisations.* Routledge, London, pp. 72–91.

Anderson, D. 1994. *Private and Public Providers in the Open Training Market,* Masters of Education Thesis, Center for Higher Education, University of Melbourne, Melbourne.

275

Andrews, D. and Crowther, F. 2003. "3-Dimensional Pedagogy: The Image of 21st Teacher Professionalism." *Teachers as Leaders.* Teachers College Press, New York, pp. ??.

Ang, I. 1995. "I'm a Feminist but . . . 'Other' Women and Postnational Feminism." In B. Caine and R. Pringle (Eds.), *Transitions: New Australian Feminisms.* Allen and Unwin, Sydney. pp. 57–73.

Angus, L. 1994. "Sociological Analysis and Educational Management: The Social Context of the Self Managing Schools." *British Journal of Sociology of Education,* vol. 15, no. 1, pp. 79–91.

Angus, L. and Brown, L. 1997. *Becoming a School of the Future: A Case Study of the Practical Interpretation of Education Policy in Victoria.* Monash University.

Angus, L. and Seddon, T. 1998. *Visions of the Future: Marketisation and Decentralisation of Vocational Education and Training: Implications for TAFE and Schools.* Monash University.

———. 2000. "The Social and Organisational Renorming of Education." In T. Seddon and L. Angus (Eds.), *Beyond Nostalgia: Reshaping Australian Education.* ACER Press, Camberwell, pp. 151–69.

Angwin, J. 1994. "The Reconstruction of Women's Work in Adult Education." In Deakin Center for Education and Change (Ed.), *Schooling: What Future?* Deakin, Geelong, pp. 35–44.

Appadurai, A. 1996. *Modernity at Large.* University of Minneapolis Press, Minneapolis.

Arnot, M. 2002. *Reproducing Gender: Essays on Educational Theory and Gender Politics.* RoutledgeFalmer, London.

Arnot, M., David, M., and Weiner, B. G. 1999. *Closing the Gender Gap: Post War Education and Social Change.* Polity, Cambridge.

Aronowitz, S. and de Fazio, W. 1997. "The New Knowledge Work." In H. Halsey, P. Lauder, P. Brown, and A. S. Wells (Eds.), *Education, Culture, Economy, Society.* Oxford University Press, Oxford, pp. 193–206.

Ashcraft, K. and Mumby, D. 2004. *Reworking Gender: A Feminist Communicology of Organisation.* Sage, Thousand Oaks.

Atkinson, E. 2000. "Critical Dissonance and Critical Schizophrenia: The Struggle between Policy Delivery and Policy Critique." *Research Intelligence,* vol. 73, pp. 14–16.

Australian Bureau of Statistics. 1995. *Australian Women's Year Book.* Australian Government Publishing Service, Canberra.

———. 2004. *Higher Education.* Australian Government Printing Services, Canberra.

Australian Teaching Council. 1994. "Newsletter." *The Council,* vol. 3, Nov. pp. 3–6.

Australian Vice Chancellors Committee. 2004. *Higher Education Statistics,* Canberra.

Avis, J. 2002. "Imaginary Friends: Managerialisn, Globalisation and Post-compulsory Education and Training in England." *Discourse,* vol. 23, no. 1, pp. 75–90.

Bacchi, C. 1999. "Managing Diversity: A Contested Concept." *International Review of Women and Leadership,* vol. 5, no, 2, pp. 1–8.

———. 2000a. "The See-Saw Effect: Down Goes Affirmative Action, Up Comes Workplace Diversity." *Journal of Interdisciplinary Gender Studies*, vol. 5, no. 2, pp. 65–83.

———. 2000b. "Policy as Discourse: What Does It Mean? Where Does It Get Us?" *Discourse*, vol. 21, no. 1, pp. 45–56.

———. 2001. "Managing Equity: Mainstreaming and Diversity in Australian Universities." In A. McKinnon and A. Brooks (Eds.), *Gender and the Restructured University: Changing Management and Cultures in Higher Education*. Open University Press, Buckingham, pp. 119–35.

Ball, S. 1994. *Education Reform: A Critical and Post-Structuralist Perspective*. Open University Press, Buckingham.

———. 1998a. "Performativity and Fragmentation in Postmodern Schooling." In J. Carter (Ed.), *Postmodernity and the Fragmentation of Welfare*. Routledge, London; New York, pp. 187–203.

———. 1998b. "Big Policies/Small World: An Introduction to International Perspectives in Education Policy." *Comparative Education*, vol. 34, no. 2, pp. 119–30.

———. 1999. "Labour, Learning and the Economy: A 'Policy Sociology' Perspective." *Cambridge Journal of Education*, vol. 29, no. 2, pp. 195–206.

———. 2000. "Performativities and Fabrications in the Education Economy: Towards a Performative Society?" *Australian Educational Researcher*, vol. 27, no. 2, pp. 1–25.

Barnetson, B. and Cutright, M. 2000. "Performance Indicators as Conceptual Technologies." *Higher Education*, vol. 40, no. 3, pp. 277–92.

Barnett, R. 1997. *Higher Education: A Critical Business*. Open University Press, Buckingham.

Barrett, F. 1995. "Leadership for the 21st Century." In the Karpin report, *Enterprising Nation: Renewing Australia's Managers to Meet the Challenges of the Asia-Pacific Century*, vol 2, pp. 1289–1342.

Bascia, N. and Young, B. 2001. "Women's Careers beyond the Classroom: Changing Roles in a Changing World." *Curriculum Inquiry*, vol. 31, no. 3, pp. 271–302.

Bauman, Z. 1993. *Postmodern Ethics*. Blackwell, Oxford

———. 2000. *The Individualized Society*. Polity, Oxford.

———. 2001. *The Individualised Society*. Polity, Cambridge.

Beck, U. 1992. *A Risk Society*. Polity, Cambridge.

Benhabib, S. 2002. *The Claims of Culture: Equality and Diversity in the Global Era*. Princeton University Press, Princeton.

Bensimon, E. 1995. "TQM in the Academy: A Rebellious Reading." *Harvard Educational Review*, vol. 4, pp. 593–611.

Bishop, P. 1999. "School Based Trust in Victoria: Some Telling Lessons." *Australian Journal of Education*, vol. 43, no. 3, pp. 273–84.

Bishop, P. and Mulford, B. 1999. "When Will They Ever Learn? Another Failure of Centrally-Imposed Change." *School Leadership and Management*, vol. 19, no. 2, pp. 179–87.

Bishop, P. and Mulford, W. 1996. "Empowerment in Four Australian Primary Schools: They Don't Really Care." *International Journal of Educational Reform*, vol. 5, no. 2, pp. 193–203.

Blackmore, J. 1991. "Corporatism, Democracy and Teacher Unions." In D. Dawkins (Ed.), *Power and Politics in Australian Education*. Falmer, Sussex, pp. 53–86.

————. 1992. "More Power to the Powerful: Mergers, Corporate Management and Their Implications for Women in the Reshaping of Higher Education." *Australian Feminist Studies*, vol. 15, Autumn, pp. 65–98.

————. 1995. "Policy as Dialogue: Feminist Administrators Working for Educational Change." *Gender and Education*, vol. 7, no. 3, pp. 293–313.

————. 1997. "Disciplining Feminism? Australian Perspectives on Feminism and the Backlash in Tertiary Education." In L. Eyre and L. Roman (Eds.), *Dangerous Territories: Struggles for Equality and Difference in Education*. Routledge, New York, pp. 75–98.

————. 1996. "Gender and the Politics of Change: Managing Gender or Changing Gender Relations?" In A. Hargreaves (Ed.), *International Handbook of Educational Change*, vol. 1, Kluwer, pp. 460–81.

————. 1996. "Doing Emotional Labor in the Educational Market Place: Stories from the Field of Women in Management." *Discourse*, vol. 17, no. 3, pp. 337–50.

————. 1999a. "Localization/Globalization and the Midwife State: Strategic Dilemmas for State Feminism in Education?" *Journal of Education Policy*, vol. 14, no. 1, pp. 33–54.

————. 1999b. *Troubling Women: Feminism, Leadership and Educational Change*. Open University Press, Buckingham.

————. 1999c. "Shifts in Governance: Schools of the Future." In L. Hancock (Ed.), *Women, Public Policy and the State*. MacMillan, London, pp. 178–92.

————. 2002a. "Is It Only 'What Works' That 'Counts' in New Knowledge Economies? The Trend Towards Evidence Based Practice and Its Implications for Educational Research and Teacher Education in Australia." *Social Theory and Policy*, vol. 1, no. 3, pp. 257–66.

————. 2002b. "Learning Networks as Strategies of Educational Reform and Community Renewal in Response to Risk and Interdependence." Symposium, New Institutional Formations. European Educational Research Association Conference, Lisbon, Sept. 11–14.

————. 2002c. "'Silly Us! Of Course the Grid Doesn't Work': Reading Methodologies and Policy Texts on Principals." Work AARE Annual Conference, Brisbane http://www.aare.conference/papers02/.

————. 2003a. "Tracking the Nomadic Life of the Educational Researcher: What Future for Feminist Public Intellectuals and the Performative University?" *Australian Educational Researcher*, vol. 30, no. 3, pp. 1–24.

————. 2003b. "'What Students Want': An Exploration of Teacher Evaluation in Performative Universities," NZARE/AARE Joint Conference, Auckland http://www.aare.conference/papers03/.

Blackmore, J. and Angwin, J. 1998. "Educational Outworkers: The Impact of Restructuring upon Women Educators." Work in Post-compulsory Education, *Forum of Education*, vol. 52, no. 2, pp. 1–23.

Blackmore, J., Barty, K., and Thomson, P. (in press). "Principal Selection: Homosociability, the Search for Security and the Production of Normalised Principal Identities." *Educational Management, Administration and Leadership*.

Blackmore, J., Bigum, C., Hodgens, J., and Laskey, L. 1996. "Managed Change and Self Management in Victorian Schools of the Future." *Leading and Managing*, vol. 2, no. 3, pp. 195–226.

Blackmore, J. and Hutchison, K. 2001. "Changing Relations: Parental Involvement, Literacy Practices and Home School Relations," http://www.aare.conference/papers01/.

Blackmore, J. and Sachs, J. 2003. "Managing Equity Work in the Performative University." *Australian Feminist Studies*, vol. 18, no. 41, pp. 141–62.

Blackmore, J. and Thomson, P. 2004. "Just 'Good News'? Disciplinary Imaginaries of 'Star' School Heads." *Journal of Education Policy*, vol. 19, no. 3, pp. 301–20.

Blackmore, J. and Thorpe, S. 2003. "Media/ting Change: The Print Media's Role in Mediating Education Policy in a Period of Radical Reform in Victoria, Australia." *Journal of Education Policy*, vol. 18, no. 6, pp. 577–96.

Bloland, H. 1995. "Postmodernism and Higher Education." *Journal of Higher Education*, vol. 66, no. 5, pp. 521–70.

Bohman, J. 1999. "Practical Reason and Cultural Constraint: Agency in Bourdieu's Theory of Practice." In R. Shusterman (Ed.), *Bourdieu: A Critical Reader*. Blackwell, Oxford, Malden Massachessetts, pp. 125–92.

Bohman, J. and Rehg, W. 1997. *Deliberative Democracy: Essays on Reason and Politics*. MIT Press, Cambridge, Mass.

Boler, M. 1999. *Feeling Power: Emotions and Education*. Routledge, London and New York.

Bone, J. 1997. "Women and the Ethics of Leadership in Higher Education." In H. Eggins (Ed.), *Women as Leaders and Managers in Higher Education*. Open University Press, Buckingham, pp. 17–27.

Bourdieu, P. 1990. *The Logic of Practice*. Polity, Cambridge.

——— . 1993. *Sociology in Question*. Sage, London, Thousand Oaks.

——— . 1996. *On Television*. New Press, New York.

——— . 1998. *Practical Reason: On the Theory of Action*. Polity, Cambridge.

Bourdieu, P. and Wacquant, L. 1992. *An Invitation to Reflexive Sociology*. University of Chicago Press, Chicago.

Bowman, K. (Ed.) 2004. *Equity in Vocational Education and Training: Research Readings*. National Council of Vocational Education Research, Brisbane.

Brabazon, T. 2002. *Digital Hemlock: Internet Education and the Poisoning of Teaching*. University of New South Wales Press, Sydney.

Brennan, M. 1996. "Multiple Professionalisms for Australian Teachers in the Information Age?" Paper presented at AERA Annual Conference, New York.

Brint, S. 1994. *In an Age of Experts: The Changing Role of Professionals in Politics and Public Life.* Princeton University Press, Princeton.

———. 2001. "Professionals and the 'Knowledge Economy': Rethinking the Theory of Post Industrial Society." *Current Sociology*, vol. 49, no. 4, pp. 101–32.

Broadfoot, P. 1998. "Quality Standards and Control in Higher Education: What Price Lifelong Learning." *International Studies in Sociology of Education*, vol. 8, no. 2, pp. 155–80.

Brooking, K. 2005. *Principals and School Boards in New Zealand.* Unpublished PhD, Deakin University, Geelong.

Brooks, A. 2001. "Restructuring Bodies of Knowledge." In A. Brooks and A. MacKinnon (Eds.), *2001 Gender and the Restructured University: Changing Management and Culture in Higher Education.* Open University Press, Buckingham, pp. 15–44.

Brooks, A. and MacKinnon, A. (Eds.). 2001. *Gender and the Restructured University: Changing Management and Culture in Higher Education.* Open University Press, Buckingham.

Brown, L., Seddon, T., Angus, L., and Rushbrook, P. 1996. "Professional Practice in Education in an Era of Contractualism: Possibilities, Problems and Paradoxes." *Australian Journal of Education*, vol. 40, no. 3, pp. 311–27.

Burbules, N. and Torres, C. (Eds.). 2000. *Globalization and Education: Critical Perspectives.* Routledge, New York, London.

Burton, C. 1995. *An Equity Review at the University of South Australia.* University of South Australia, Adelaide.

———. 1997. *Gender Equity in Australian University Staffing.* Department of Employment, Education, Training, and Youth Affairs.

———. 1999. "Merit, Gender and Corporate Governance." In L. Hancock (Ed.), *Women, Public Policy and the State.* Macmillan, South Yarra, pp. 20–35.

Butler, E. 1996. "Equity and Workplace Learning: Emerging Discourses and Conditions of Possibility." *National Colloquium on Research Directions for Workplace Learning and Assessment*, University of Technology, Sydney.

———. 1997. *Beyond Political Housework: Gender Equity in the Post-School Environment.* University of Adelaide.

Butler, J. 1993. *Bodies That Matter: On Discursive Limits of "Sex."* Routledge, New York.

———. 1997. *Excitable Speech: A Politics of the Performative.* Routledge, New York.

———. 1999. "Performativity's Social Magic." In R. Schusterman (Ed.), *Bourdieu. A Critical Reader.* Blackwell, Oxford, pp. 113–28.

Calabrese, R. and Roberts, B. 2001. "The Promise Foresaken: Neglecting the Ethical Implications of Leadership." *The International Journal of Educational Management*, vol. 15, no. 6, pp. 267–75.

Caldwell, B. and Hayward, D. 1998. *The Future of Schools: Lessons from the Reform of Public Education.* Falmer, London.

Campbell, C. and Sherington, G. 2003. "Residualisation and Regionalism in the Recent History of the Comprehensive School." Paper presented at AERA Annual Conference, Chicago.

Carnoy, M. 1998. "Globalisation and Education Reform." *Melbourne Studies in Education*, vol. 39, no. 2, pp. 221–40.

Casey, C. 1995. *Work Self and Society after Industrialism.* Routledge, London, New York.

Castleman, T., Allen, M., Bastalich, W., and Wright, P. 1995. *Limited Access: Women's Disadvantage in Higher Education Employment.* National Teacher Education Union.

Cavanagh, J. 1997. "(In)corporating the Other? Managing the Politics of Workplace Difference." In P. Prasad, A. Mills, M. Elmes, and A. Prasad (Eds.), *Managing the Organisational Melting Pot: Dilemmas of Workplace Diversity.* Sage, Thousand Oaks, pp. 31–53.

Chadbourne, R. and Ingvarson, L. 1998. "Self-Managing Schools and Professional Community: The Professional Recognition Program in Victoria's Schools of the Future." *Australian Educational Researcher*, vol. 25, no. 2, pp. 61–93.

Chapman, J. (Ed.). 1990. *School-Based Decision-making and Management.* Falmer, London.

Chase, S. 1995. *Ambiguous Empowerment: The Work Narratives of Women School Superintendents.* Massachussetts University Press, Massachussetts.

Choo, C. W. 2001. "The Knowing Organisation as a Learning Organisation." *Education and Training*, vol. 43, no. 4/5, pp. 197–205.

Christie, P. and Limerick, B. 2004. "Leadership as a Field of Study." *Discourse*, vol. 25, no. 1, pp. 1–3.

Christie, P. and Lingard, B. 2001. "Capturing the Complexity of Leadership." Paper presented to the AERA Annual Conference, Seattle.

Clarke, J. 1998. "Thriving on Chaos? Managerialisation and Social Welfare." In J. Carter (Ed.), *Postmodernity and the Fragmentation of Welfare.* Routledge, London and New York, pp. 171–86.

Clarke, J., Cochrane, A., and McLaughlin, E. (Eds.). 1994. *Managing Social Policy.* Sage, London.

Clarke, J. and Newman, J. 1993. "The Right to Manage: A Second Managerial Revolution." *Cultural Studies*, vol. 7, no. 3, pp. 427–44.

———. 1997. *The Managerial State.* Sage, New Delhi.

Clegg, S. 1999. "Professional Education, Reflective Practice, and Feminism." *International Journal of Inclusive Education*, vol. 3, no. 2., pp. 167–79.

Collins, C., Kenway, J., and McLeod, J. 2000. *Factors Influencing the Educational Performance of Males and Females in School and Their Initial Destinations on Leaving School.* Department of Education, Training and Youth Affairs, Canberra.

Coates, G. 1996. "Organisation Man: Women and Organisational Culture," <<http://www.socresonline.org.uk/socresonlilne/2/3/7.html>.

Connell, B. 1998. "Masculinity and Globalization." *Men and Masculinity*, vol. 1, no. 1, pp. 3–23.

Connell, R. 1995. *Masculinities.* Polity, Cambridge.

———. 2000. *The Men and the Boys.* Allen and Unwin, Sydney.

Cooper, J. and Heck, R. 1995. "Using Narrative in the Study of School Administration." *Qualitative Studies in Education*, vol. 8., no. 2, pp. 195–210.

Cope, B. and Kalantzis, M. 1997. *Productive Diversity: A New, Australian Model for Work and Management*. Pluto, Sydney.

Coulter, R. 1997. *Equity Lost: Neo-liberal Conservatives and Educational Restructuring*. Educators for Gender Equity, London, Ontario.

Court, M. 1998. "Women Challenging Managerialism: Devolution Dilemmas in the Establishment of Co-principalships in Primary Schools in Aotearoa/New Zealand." *School Leadership and Management*, vol. 18, no. 1, pp. 35–57.

———. 2003. *Different Approaches to Sharing Leadership*. National College of School Leadership, Nottingham.

———. 2004. "Talking Back to the New Public Administration's Version of Accountability in Education: A Co Principal's Practice of Mutual Responsibility." *Educational Administration and Management*, vol. 32, no. 3, pp. ???.

Cowen, R. 1996. "Performativity: Postmodernity and the University." *Comparative Education*, vol. 21, no. 2, pp. 245–57.

Crozier, G. and Ray, D. 2005. *Activating Participation: Parents and Teachers Working Towards Partnership*. Trentham Books, Stoke-on-Trent.

Currie, J. and Thiele, B. 2001. "Globalisation and Gendered Work Cultures in Universities." In A. McKinnon and A. Grant (Eds.), *Gender and the Restructured University: Changing Management and Cultures in Higher Education*. Open University Press, Buckingham, pp. 90–116.

Currie, J., Thiele, B., and Harris, P. (Eds.). 2002. *Gendered Universities in Globalized Economies: Power, Careers and Sacrifices*. Lexington Books, Lexington.

Currie, J. and Woock, R. 1995. "Deck Chairs on the Titanic: Award Restructuring for Academics in the Age of Economic Rationalism." In J. Smyth (Ed.), *Academic Work*. Falmer, Sussex, pp. 144–59.

Czarniawska, B. 1998. *A Narrative Approach to Organisation Studies*. Sage, Thousand Oaks.

Czarniawaska, B. and Hopfl, H. 2002. *Casting the Other: The Production and Maintenance of Inequalities in Work Organisations*. Routledge, London.

Dadds, M. 1995. *Passionate Enquiry and School Development: A Story about Teacher Action Research*. Falmer, London.

d'Arbon, T., Duignan, P., Dwyer, J., and Goodwin, K. 2001. *Leadership Succession in Catholic Schools in New South Wales: A Research Project on Behalf of the Catholic Education Commission, New South Wales. Phase Two. Final Report*. Australian Catholic University, School of Educational Leadership.

David, M. 2003. *Personal and Political: Feminisms, Sociology and Family Lives*. Trentham Books, Stoke, Trent.

Davies, C. and Holloway, P. 1995. "Troubling Transformations: Gender Regimes and Organizational Culture in the Academy." In L. Morley and V. Walsh (Eds.), *Feminist Academics: Creative Agents for Change*. Taylor and Francis, London, pp. 7–21.

Day, C. 2004. "The Passion of Successful Leadership." *School Leadership and Management*, vol. 24, no. 4, pp. 425–38.

Deane, E. 1996. *Women, Research and Research Productivity in Post–1987 Universities: Opportunities and Constraints.* Higher Education Division, Australian Department of Education, Training and Youth Affairs.

Deem, R. 2001. "Gender Processes under New Managerialism and the Practices of Manager-Academics in UK Universities." Rethinking Gender, Work and Organization Conference, University of Keele, Keele.

Deem, R. and Ozga, J. 1997. "Woman Managing for Diversity in a Postmodern World." In C. Marshall (Ed.), *Feminist Critical Policy Analysis*, vol. 2, Falmer, London, pp. 25–40.

———. 2000. "Transforming Post-Compulsory Education? Feminists at Work in the Academy." *Women's International Studies Review*, vol. 23, no. 2, pp. 153–66.

Deetz, S. 1992. *Democracy in the Age of Corporate Colonisation.* State University of New York Press, Albany, N.Y.

De Groot, J., 1997. "After the Ivory Tower: Gender, Commodification and the 'Academic.'" *Feminist Review*, vol. 55, Spring, pp. 130–42.

Dempster, N. 2000. "Guilty or Not: The Impact and Effects of Site-based Management on Schools." *Journal of Educational Administration*, vol. 38, no. 1, pp. 47–63.

Dempster, N. and Logan, L. 1998. "Expectation of School Leaders: An Australian Picture." In J. McBeath (Ed.), *Effective School Leadership*. Chapman, London, pp. 85–101.

Dempster, N. and Mahoney, P. 1998. "Ethical Challenges in School Leadership." In J. Macbeath (Ed.), *Effective School Leadership: Responding to Change*. Chapman, London and Sage, California, pp. 125–39.

Department of Education and Training, Victoria. 2004. *The Privilege and the Price: A Study of Principal Class Workload and Its Impact on Health and Wellbeing.* DET, Melbourne.

Department of Employment Education and Training, Australia. 1995. *The Position of Women in the National Training Reform Agenda and Enterprise Bargaining.* Women's Research and Employment Initiatives Program, Canberra.

Dillabough, J. and Arnot, M. 2001. "Gender Theory and Research in Education: Some Contemporary Themes." In B. Francis and C. Skelton (Eds.), *Investigating Gender: Contemporary Perspectives in Education*. Open University Press, Buckingham, pp. 11–26.

Down, B., Hogan, D., and Chadbourne, R. 1999. "Making Sense of Performance Management: Official Rhetoric and Teachers' Reality." *Asia-Pacific Journal of Teacher Education*, vol. 27, no. 1, pp. 11–24.

du Gay, P. 1996. *Consumption and Identity at Work.* Sage, London.

Edwards, R. 1997. *Changing Place: Flexibility, Lifelong Learning, and a Learning Society.* Routledge, London.

Elliott, J. 2001. "Characteristics of Performance Cultures: Their Central Paradoxes and Limitations as Resources for Educational Reform." In D. Gleeson and C. Husbands (Eds.), *The Performing School: Managing, Teaching and Learning in a Performance Culture*. RoutledgeFalmer, London, pp. 192–209.

Elmore, R. 2000. *Building a New Structure for School Leadership.* Shanker Institute, Washington.

Evans, R. 1996. *The Human Side of School Change: Reform, Resistance, and the Real-life Problems of Innovation.* Jossey-Bass, San Francisco.

Eveline, J. 1998. "Heavy, Dirty, and Limp Stories: Male Advantage at Work." In M. Gatens and A. Mackinnon (Eds.), *Gender and Institutions.* Cambridge, Melbourne, pp. 90–106.

Ferrier, F. 1995. "Two Steps Forward, One Step Backward? Equity and Vocational Education and Training." In F. Ferrier and C. Selby-Smith (Eds.), *The Economics of Education and Training.* Center for the Economics of Education and Training, Monash, Clayton, pp. 49–59.

Ferrier, F. and Anderson, D. (Eds.). 1998. *Different Drums: One Beat? Economic and Social Goals in Education and Training,* NCVER/CEET Monash, Melbourne.

Ferrier, F. and Selby-Smith, C. 1995. *The Economics of Education and Training.* Center for Economics of Education and Training, Monash University, Clayton.

Fineman, S. 2000. *Emotions and Organisations,* 2nd ed. Sage, New York.

Fiske, J. and Ladd, H. 2000. *When Schools Compete: A Cautionary Tale.* Brookings Institute Press, Washington.

Foldy, G. 2002. "Managing Diversity: Identity and Power in Organisations." In I. Aaltio and A. Mills (Eds.), *Gender, Identity and Culture in Organisations.* Routledge, London, pp. 92–112.

Forester, J. 1999. *The Deliberative Practitioner: Encouraging Participatory Planning Processes.* MIT Press, Cambridge, Mass.

Franzway, S. 2001. *Sexual Politics and Greedy Institutions.* Pluto, Annandale.

Fraser, N. 1997. *Justice Interruptus: Critical Reflections on the "Postsocialist" Condition.* Routledge, New York.

Freeman, E. 1999. *Community as Incentive in the Formation of Charter Schools.* Paper presented to AERA Conference, Montreal.

Fullan, M. 1997. "Emotion and Hope: Constructive Concepts for Complex Times." In A. Hargreaves (Ed.), *Rethinking Educational Change with Heart and Mind.* Association for Supervision and Curriculum Development, Alexandria, Va., pp. 216–32.

———. 1999. "The Return of Large-Scale Reform." *Journal of Educational Change,* vol. 1, no. 1, pp. 1–6.

Gee, J., Hull, G., and Lankshear, C. 1996. *The New Work Order: Behind the Language of the New Capitalism.* Allen and Unwin, Sydney.

Gewirtz, S. 1997. "Post-welfarism and the Reconstruction of Teachers' Work in the UK." *Journal of Education Policy,* vol. 12, no. 4, pp. 217–31.

———. 1998. "Conceptualising Social Justice in Education: Mapping the Territory." *Journal of Education Policy,* vol. 13, no. 4, pp. 469–84.

Gewirtz, S. and Ball, S. 2000. "From 'Welfarism' to 'New Managerialism': Shifting Discourses of School Headship in the Education Marketplace." *Discourse,* vol. 21, no. 3, pp. 253–68.

Gewirtz, S., Ball, S., and Bowe, R. 1995. *Markets, Choice, and Equity in Education.* Open University Press, Buckingham.

Gherardi, S. 1995. *Gender, Symbolism, and Organisational Cultures.* Sage, Thousand Oaks.

Giddens, A. 1991. *Modernity and Self-identity: Self and Society in the Late Modern Age.* Polity, Cambridge

———. 1994. *Beyond Left and Right.* Polity, Cambridge.

Gillborn, D. and Youdell, D. 2000. *Rationing Education: Policy, Practice, Reform, and Equity.* Open University Press, Buckingham, Philadelphia.

Glazer-Raymo, J. 1999. *Shattering the Myths: Women in Academe.* John Hopkins University Press, Baltimore.

———. 2000. *Women in Higher Education: A Feminist Perspective.* Pearson Custom Publishing, United States.

Gleeson, D. and Gunter, H. 2001. "The Performing School and the Modernisation of Teachers." In D. Gleeson and C. Husbands (Eds.), *The Performing School: Managing, Teaching, and Learning in a Performance Culture.* RoutledgeFalmer, London, pp. 139–58.

Gleeson, D. and Husbands, C. (Eds.). 2001. *The Performing School: Managing, Teaching, and Learning in a Performance Culture.* RoutledgeFalmer, London.

Gleeson, D. and Shain. F. 1999. "Managing Ambiguity: Between Markets and Managerialism—A Case Study of 'Middle Managers' in Further Education." *The Sociological Review,* vol. 47, no. 3, pp. 461–91.

Gold, A., Evans, J., Earley, P., Halpin, D., and Collarbone, P. 2003. "Principled Principles? Values Driven Leadership: Evidence from Ten Case Studies of 'Outstanding School Leaders.'" *Educational Management and Administration,* vol. 31, no. 2, pp. 125–36.

Goode, J. 2000. "Is the Position of Women in Higher Education Changing?" *International Perspectives on Higher Education Research,* vol. 1, pp. 243–84.

Grace, G. 1995. *School Leadership: Beyond Educational Management.* Falmer, London.

Grogan, M. 1999. "Equity/Equality Issues of Gender, Race, and Class." *Education Administration Quarterly,* vol. 35, no. 4, pp. 518–36.

Gronn, P. 2000. "Distributed Properties: A New Architecture of Leadership." *Educational Management and Administration,* vol. 28, no. 3, pp. 317–37.

———. 2003. *The New Work of Educational Leaders: Changing Leadership Practice in an Era of School Reform.* Sage, Thousand Oaks.

Gronn, P. and Lacey, K. 2004. "Positioning Oneself for Leadership: Feelings of Vulnerability among Aspirant School Principals." *School Leadership and Management,* vol. 24, no. 4, pp. 405–24.

Gronn, P. and Rawlings-Sanaei, F. 2003. "Principal Recruitment in a Climate of Leadership Disengagement." *Australian Journal of Education,* vol. 47, no. 2, pp. 172–84.

Groundwater-Smith, S. and Sachs, J. 2002. "The Activist Professional and the Reinstatement of Trust." *Cambridge Journal of Education,* vol. 32, no. 3, pp. 341–58.

Grundy, S. and Bonser, S. 1997. "In Whose Interests? Competing Discourses in the Policy and Practice of School Restructuring." *Australian Journal of Education,* vol. 41, no. 2, pp. 150–68.

Gulson, K. 2004. "Education Policy, Urban Renewal, and Identity: A Spatial Analysis of Global Change." Unpublished PhD thesis, Education, Macquarie University, Sydney.

Gunter, H. 2004. "Labels and Labelling in the Field of Educational Leadership." *Discourse*, vol. 25, no. 1, pp. 21–42.

———. 2000. "Thinking Theory: The Field of Education Management in England and Wales." *British Journal of Sociology of Education*, vol. 21, no. 4, pp. 623–35.

———. 2004. "From Sedition to Sedation: The Growth of Teacher Leadership." Paper presented to BELMAS conference, Oxford University, Oxford.

Gunter, H., Smith, P., and Tomlinson, H. 1999. "Introduction: Constructing Headship Today and Yesterday." In H. Tomlinson, H. Gunter, and P. Smith, P. (Eds.), *Living Headship: Voices, Values and Vision*. Paul Chapman/Sage pp: xi–xxxv.

Hage, G. 1994. "Locating Multiculturalism's Other: A Critique of Practical Tolerance." *New Formations*, vol. 24, pp. 19–34.

Halford, S., Savage, M., and Witz, A. 1997. *Gender, Careers, and Organisations*. Macmillan, London.

Hall, S. 1992. "The Question of Cultural Identity." In S. Hall, D. Held, and T. McGrew (Eds.), *Modernity and its Futures*. Polity, Cambridge, pp. 327–76.

———. 1997. "Who Needs Identity." In S. Hall and P. du Guy (Eds.), *Questions of Cultural Identity*. Sage, London, Thousand Oaks, pp. 1–17.

Halsey, A. 1995. *The Decline of Donnish Dominion*. Clarendon, Oxford.

Hancock, L. (Ed.) 1999. *Women, Public Policy, and the State*. Macmillan, South Yarra.

Hargreaves, A. 1998. "The Emotions of Teaching and Educational Change." In A. Hargreaves, A. Lieberman, M. Fullan, and D. Hopkins (Eds.), *International Handbook of Educational Change*, vol. 1, Kluwer, Dordrecht, London.

———. 2003. *Teaching in the Knowledge Society: Education in the Age of Insecurity*. Open University Press, Buckingham.

———. 2004. "Distinction and Disgust: The Emotional Politics of School Failure." *International Journal of Leadership in Education*, vol. 7, no. 1, pp. 27–42.

Harley, S. 2003. "Research Selectivity and Female Academics in UK Universities: From a Gentleman's Club and Barrack Yard to Smart Macho?" *Gender and Education*, vol. 15, no. 4, pp. 377–92.

Hartley, D. 1997. "The New Managerialism in Education: A Mission Impossible?" *Cambridge Journal of Education*, vol. 27, no. 1, p. 47.

———. 1998. "In Search of Structure: Theory and Practice in the Management of Education." *Journal of Education Policy*, vol. 13, no. 1, pp. 153–62.

Hatcher, C. 2003. "Refashioning a Passionate Manager: Gender at Work." *Gender Work and Organisation*, vol. 10, no. 4, pp. 391–412.

Hearn, J. 1998. "On Ambiguity, Contradiction, and Paradox in Gendered Organisations." *Gender, Work and Organisation*, vol. 5, no. 1, pp. 1–5.

———. 2002. "Alternative Conceptualisations and Theoretical Perspectives on Identities and Organisational Cultures: A Personal Review of Research on Men in Organisations." In I. Aaltio and A. Mills (Eds.), *Gender, Identity, and Culture in Organisations*. Routledge, London, pp. 39–56.

Henry, M., Lingard, B., Rizvi, F., and Taylor, S. 2001. *The OECD, Globalisation, and Education Policy.* Pergamon, Amsterdam, London, New York.

Hey, V. and Bradford, S. 2004. "The Return of the Repressed? The Gender Politics of Emergent Forms of Professionalism in Education." *Journal of Education Policy*, vol. 19, no. 6, pp. 691–714.

Huchschild, A. 1983. *The Managed Heart: The Commercialization of Human Feeling.* University of California Press, Berkeley.

Hood, C. 1995b. "The 'New Public Management' in the 1980s: Variations on a Theme." *Accounting, Organisations and Society*, vol. 20, no. 3, pp. 93–109.

Hopfl, H. and Linsted, L. 2000. "Passion and Performance: Suffering and Carrying Out Organisational Roles." In S. Fineman (Ed.), *Emotions in Organisations.* Sage, London, pp. 76–93.

Institute, Barton, 1995. *Best Management Practice: Strategic Plan 1995–97.* Melbourne.

Johnson, J. 2002. *Poverty in Australia: Developing Community Dialogue.* Report of a Qualitative Study, Botherhood of Saint Lawrence.

Johnson, S. M. 2004. *New Generation of Teachers Project.* Harvard University, Harvard.

Kamp, A. 2003. "Reactions and Responses: The Concepts of Learning Networks." ANZARE/AARE Joint Annual Conference, Auckland.

Kaplan, G. 1995. *The Meagre Harvest: The Australian Women's Movement 1950s–1960s.* Allen and Unwin, Sydney.

Karpin, D. 1995. *Enterprising Nation: Renewing Australia's Managers to Meet the Challenges of the Asia-Pacific Century*, vols. 1–3. Australian Government Printing Service.

Keamy, K. 2004. *Masculinity and Leadership in Universities.* Unpublished PhD thesis, Deakin University, Geelong.

Kell, P., Balatti, J., and Muspratt, S. 1997. "The Private, Public, and Open Training Markets: A Study of Private Training Providers in Regional North Queensland." *Australian Educational Researcher*, vol. 24, no. 2, pp. 43–58.

Kell, P. and Blakeley, J. 1997. *Impact of the Open Training Market on TAFE Teachers' Work at the Institute Level.* National Council Vocational Education Research, Melbourne.

Kenway, J., Willis, S., with Blackmore, J. and Rennie, L. 1998. *Answering Back: Girls, Boys, and Feminism in Schools.* Routledge, London.

Kerfoot, D. 1999. "The Organisation of Intimacy: Managerialism, Masculinity, and the Masculine Subject." In S. Whitehead and R. Moodley (Eds.), *Transforming Managers: Gendering Change in the Public Sector.* UCL Press, London, pp. 184–99.

Kerfoot, D. and Knights, D. 1996. "The Best Is Yet to Come? The Quest for Embodiment in Managerial Work." In D. Collinson and J. Hearn (Eds.), *Men as Managers, Managers as Men: Critical Perspectives on Men, Masculinities and Management.* Sage, London, pp. 78–98.

———. 1999. "Man Management: Ironies of Modern Management in an Old University." In S. Whitehead and R. Moodley (Eds.), *Transforming Managers: Gendering Change in the Public Sector.* UCL Press, London, pp. 74–91.

Kerfoot, D., Pritchard, C., and Whitehead, S. 2000. "(En)Gendering Management: Work, Organisation, and Further Education." *Journal of Further and Higher Education*, vol. 24, no. 2, Special Issue, pp. 157–61.

Kronemann, M. 2001. *TAFE Teachers: Facing the Challenge*. Australian Education Union Research Report, AEU, Melbourne.

Lacey, K. 2002. *Understanding Principal Class Leadership Aspirations: Policy and Planning Implications*. Department of Education and Training Victoria.

Lake, M. 1999. *Getting Equal: A History of Australian Feminism*. Allen and Unwin, Sydney.

Lamb, S., Rumberger, R., Jesson, P., and Teese, R. 2004. *School Performance in Australia: Results from Analyses of School Effectiveness*. Department of Premier and Cabinet, Victoria.

Lauder, H. 1994. *The Creation of Market Competition in New Zealand*. Smithfield Project.

Lauder, H. and Hughers, D. 1999. *Trading Away Our Futures: Why Markets in Education Don't Work*. Open University Press, Buckingham.

Leonard, P. 1998. "Gendering Change? Management, Masculinity and the Dynamics of Incorporation." *Gender and Education*, vol. 10, no. 1, pp. 71–84.

Levavic, R. and Woods, P. 2000. *The Impact of Quasi Markets and Performance Regulation on Socially Disadvantaged Schools*, AERA Annual Meeting, New Orleans.

Levavic, R., Woods, P., Hardman, J., and Woods, G. 1998. *Responses to Competitive Pressures on Secondary Schools: Headteachers' Perceptions in English Secondary Schools*. Open University.

Levin. B. 2001. *Reforming Education: From Origins to Outcomes*. Routledge, London.

Lieberman, A. and Grolnick, S. 1997. "Educational Reform Networks: Changes in the Form of Reform." In A. Hargreaves, A. Lieberman, M. Fullan, and D. Hopkins (Eds.), *International Handbook of Educational Change*, part 2, 710–29.

Limerick, B. and Anderson, C. 1999a. "'Go Out There and Go for Broke': Senior Women and Promotion in Education Queensland, Australia." *Women in Management Review*, vol. 13, no. 1/2, pp, 13–17.

———. 1999b. "Female Administrators and School-Based Management: New Models in an Era of Change?" *Educational Management and Administration*, vol. 27, no. 4, pp. 401–14.

Limerick, D., Cunnington, B., and Crowther, F. 1998. *Managing the New Organisation*, Business and Professional Publishing, Brisbane.

Lingard, B. 2000. "It Is and It Isn't: Vernacular Globalisation, Educational Policy and Restructuring." In N. Burbules and C. Torres (Eds.), *Globalisation and Education: Critical Perspectives*. Routledge, London.

———. 2003. "Where to in Gender Policy in Education after Recuperative Masculinity Politics?" *International Journal of Inclusive Education*, vol. 7, no. 1, pp. 33–56.

Lingard, B. and Douglas, P. 1999. *Men Engaging Feminisms: Pro-feminism, Backlashes and Schooling*. Open University Press, Buckingham.

Lingard, B. and Garrick, B. 1997. "Producing and Practising Social Justice Policy in Education: A Policy Trajectory Study from Queensland, Australia." *International Studies in Sociology of Education*, vol. 7, no. 2, pp. 157–79.

Lingard, B., Hayes, D., Mills, M., and Christie, P. 2003. *Leading Learning*. Open University Press, Buckingham.

Lingard, B., Knight, J., and Porter, P. (Eds.). 1993. *Schooling Reform in Hard Times*, Falmer, Sussex.

Lortie, D. 1975. *School Teacher: A Sociological Study*. University of Chicago Press, Chicago.

Louis, K., 1998. "Effects of Teacher Quality of Work Life in Secondary School on Commitment and Sense of Efficacy." *School Effectiveness and School Improvement*, vol. 9, no. 1, pp. 1–27.

Luke, A. 1997. "New Narratives of Human Capital: Recent Redirections in Australian Educational Policy." *Australian Educational Researcher*, vol. 24, no. 2, pp. 1–22.

Luke, A. and van Kraayenoord, C. 1998. "Babies, Bathwater, and Benchmarks: Literacy Assessment and Curriculum Reform." *Curriculum Perspectives*, vol. 18, no. 3, pp. 55–62.

Luke, C. 1997. "Feminist Pedagogy Theory in Higher Education: Reflections on Power and Authority." In C. Marshall (Ed.), *Feminist Critical Policy Analysis: A Perspective from Post-Secondary Education*. Falmer, London, pp. 189–210.

Lynch, C. and Lodge, A. 2002. *Equality and Power in Schools: Redistribution, Recognition and Representation*. RoutledgeFalmer, London.

Lyotard, J. 1984. *The Postmodern Condition: A Report on Knowledge*. Manchester University Press, Manchester.

MacBeath, J. 1998. "I Didn't Know He Was Ill: The Role and Value of a Critical Friend." In L. Stoll and K. Myers (Eds.), *No Quick Fixes*. Falmer, London.

MacBeath, J. and MacDonald, A. 2000. "Four Dilemmas, Three Heresies and a Matrix." In K. Riley and K. Louis (Eds.), *Leadership for Change and School Reform*. Routledge, London, New York, pp. 13–29.

MacMillan, K. 2002. "Narratives of Social Disruption: Education News in the British Tabloid Press." *Discourse*, vol. 23, no. 1, pp. 27–38.

Mahony, P. 1997. "Talking Heads: A Feminist Perspective on Public Sector Reform in Teacher Education." *Discourse*, vol. 18, no. 1, pp. 87–102.

Mahony, P. and Hextall, I. 2001. "Performing and Conforming." In D. Gleeson and C. Husbands (Eds.), *The Performing School: Managing, Teaching and Learning in a Performance Culture*. RoutledgeFalmer, London, pp. 174–91.

Mahony, P., Menter, I., and Hextall, I. 2004. "The Emotional Impact of Performance-Related Pay on Teachers in England." *British Educational Research Journal*, vol. 30, no. 3, pp. 435–56.

Marginson, S. 1997. *Markets and Education, Melbourne University Press*. Melbourne.

———. 2004. "Can High Status Universities Provide Equal Access? Global Reflections on the University of Melbourne, Social Competition and Equity in Higher Education." Centre for Public Policy, University of Melbourne.

Marginson, S. and Consindine, M. 2001. *The Enterprise University: Power, Governance and Reinvention in Australia.* Cambridge University Press, Melbourne.

Marshall, C. 1996. "Implementing Equity in Universities: Possibilities for Pro-feminist Men." Paper presented to Special Interest Group of AERA, Women in Education Conference, San Jose California.

Massey, D. 1994. *Space, Place and Gender.* Polity, Oxford.

Matthews, J. 2001. "Internationalising State High Schools: If It's Such a Good Idea Why Don't More Schools Do It?" Paper presented at the Australian Association of Research in Education Conference, Freemantle.

Mazey, S. 2000. "Integrating Gender: Intellectual and 'Real World' Mainstreaming." *Journal of European Public Policy*, vol. 7, no. 3, Special Issue, pp. 333–45.

McCollow, J. and Graham, J. 1997. "Not Quite the National Curriculum: Accommodation and Resistance to Curriculum Change." In B. Lingard and P. Porter (Eds.), *A National Approach to Schooling in Australia?* ACER, Melbourne.

McInnes, C. 2000. "Changing Academic Work Roles." *Quality in Higher Education*, vol. 6, no. 2, pp. 143–52.

McNay, L. 2000. *Gender and Agency: Reconfiguring the Subject in Feminist and Social Theory.* Polity, Oxford.

Meadmore, D. and Meadmore, P. 2004. "The Boundlessness of Performativity in Elite Australian Schools." *Discourse*, vol. 25, no. 3, pp. 375–88.

Meadmore, D. and Symes, C. 1997. "Keeping Up Appearances: Uniform Policy for School Diversity?" *British Journal of Educational Studies*, vol. 45, no. 2, pp. 174–86.

Menter, I., Muschamp, Y., Nicholls, P., Ozga, J., and Pollard, A. 1997. *Work and Identity in the Primary School: A Post Fordist Analysis.* Open University Press.

Meyenn, B. 1996. "Recipes for Avoiding Limpness: An Exploration of Women in Senior Management Positions in Australian Universities." AERA, New York.

Middlehurst, R. 1993. *Leading Academics.* Society for Research into Higher Education, Open University Press, Buckingham/Bristol.

———. 1997. "Leadership, Women and Higher Education." In H. Eggins (Ed.), *Women and Leaders and Managers in Higher Education.* Open University Press, Buckingham, pp. 3–16.

Middlehurst, R. and Campbell, C. 2001. *Quality Assurance and Borderless Higher Education: Finding Pathways through the Maze.* Observatory on Borderless Education.

Miller, H. 1995. "State Economies and the Changing Labour Process of Academics: Australia, Canada and the United Kingdom." In J. Smyth (Ed.), *Academic Work.* Falmer, Sussex, pp. 40–59.

Mills, M., Martino, W., and Lingard, B. 2004a. "Attracting, Recruiting, and Retaining Male Teachers: Policy Issues in a Male Teacher Debate." *British Journal of Sociology of Education*, vol. 25, no. 3, pp. 355–71.

Mills, M. and Martino, W. 2004. "The Media, Marketing and Single Sex Schools." *Journal of Education Policy*, vol. 19, no. 3, pp. 335–52.

Mirza, H. 1995. "Black Women In Higher Education: Defining a Space, Defining a Place." In L. Morley and V. Walsh (Eds.), *Feminist Academics: Creative Agents for Change.* Taylor and Francis, London, pp. 145–55.

Mitchell, K. 2001. "Education for Democratic Citizenship: Trans-nationalism, Multi-culturalism and the Limits of Liberalism." *Harvard Educational Review*, vol. 71, no. 1, pp. 51–78.

Moodie, G. 2004. "The Neglected Role of the Neglected Body: Academic Board's Role in Assuring Standards." *Australian Universities Review*, vol. 47, no. 1, pp. 35–41.

Moreton-Robinson, A. 2000. *Talkin' Up to the White Woman: Indigenous Women and Feminism.* University of Queensland Press, St Lucia.

Morley, L. 2004. 1999. *Organising Feminisms: The Micropolitics of the Academy.* Macmillan, London.

———. 2001. "Subjected to Review: Engendering Quality and Power in Higher Education." *Journal of Education Policy*, vol. 16, no. 5, pp. 465–80.

———. 2003. *Quality and Power in Higher Education.* Open University Press, Buckingham.

———. "Sounds, Silences and Contradictions: Gender Equity in Commonwealth Higher Education." Clare Burton Memorial Lecture, RMIT, Melbourne.

Morley, L. and Walsh, V. (Eds.). 1996. *Breaking Boundaries: Women in Higher Education.* Taylor and Francis, London.

Mulford, B. 2003. *School Leaders: Changing Roles and Impact on Teacher and School Effectiveness.* OECD, Paris.

Mulford, B. and Silins, H. 2001. "Leadership for Organisational Learning and Improved Student Outcomes—What Do We Know?" *NSIN Research Matters*, vol. 15, Aug., pp. 1–8.

Murphy, J. 1997. "Restructuring through School-based Management." In T. Townsend (Ed.), *Restructuring and Quality.* Routledge, London, pp. 35–54.

Myers, K and Goldstein, H. 1997. "Failing Schools or Failing Systems." In A. Hargeaves (Ed.), *Rethinking Educational Change with Heart and Mind.* ASCD Yearbook, pp. 113–27.

Newmann, F. and Associates. 1996. *Authentic Achievement: Restructuring Schools for Intellectual Quality.* San Francisco, Jossey-Bass.

Newmann, F., King, B., and Rigdon, M. 1997. "Accountability and School Performance: Implications from Restructuring Schools." *Harvard Educational Review*, vol. 67, no. 1, pp. 41–74.

Newmann, F. and Wehlage, G. 1995. *Successful School Restructuring: A Report to the Public Educators.* Center on Organization and Restructuring of Schools, Madison.

Nias, J. 1999. "Teachers' Moral Purposes: Stress, Vulnerability and Strength." In A. M. Huberman and R. Vandenberghe (Eds.), *Understanding and Preventing Teacher Burnout.* Cambridge University Press, New York, pp. 223–37.

Nussbaum, M. 1990. "Nature, Function and Capability." In R. Douglass, G. Mara, and H. Richardson (Eds.), *Liberalism and the Good.* Routledge, New York.

Olesen, H. 2001. "Professional Identity as Learning Processes in Life Histories." *Journal of Workplace Learning*, vol. 137, no. 7/8, pp. 290–97.

Ozga, J. and Deem, R. 2000. "Carrying the Burden of Transformation: The Experiences of Women Managers in UK Higher and Further Education." *Discourse*, vol. 21, no. 2, pp. 141–53.

Ozga, J. and Walker, L. 1999. "In the Company of Men." In S. Whitehead and R. Moodley (Eds.), *Transforming Managers: Gendering Change in the Public Sector*. UCL Press, London, pp. 107–20.

Parker, L. 2000. *Organizational Culture and Identity*. Sage, London.

Pascoe, S. and Pascoe, R. 1998. *Education Reform in Victoria Australia*. World Bank, Washington.

Peters, M., Marshall, J., and Fitzsimons, P. 2002. "Managerialism and Educational Policy in a Global Context: Foucault, Neo-liberalism and the Doctrine of Self Management." In N. Burbules and C. Torrres (Eds.), *Globalisation and Education: Critical Perspectives*. Routledge, London and New York, pp. 109–32.

Phillips, A. 1996. "Equality, Difference and Public Representation." In S. Benhabib (Ed.), *Democracy and Difference*. Princeton University Press, Princeton, pp. 139–52.

Pocock, B. 1998. *Demanding Skills: Women and Technical Education in Australia*. Allen and Unwin, Sydney.

Poole, D. 2001. "Strategically Managing Entrepreneurialism: The Australian University." *Higher Education Quarterly*, vol. 55, no. 3, pp. 306–40.

Pounder, D., Galvin, P., and Shepherd, P. 2004. "United States Educational Administrator Shortage." *Australian Journal of Education*, vol. 47, no. 2, pp. 133–45.

Power, M. 1999. *The Audit Society: Rituals of Verification*. Oxford University Press, Oxford.

Power, S., Gewirtz, S., Halpin, D., and Whitty, G. 2003a. *Paving a "Third Way"? A Policy Trajectory Analysis of Education Action Zones*. ERSC.

Power, S. T. E., Whitty, G., and Wigfall, V. 2003b. *Education and the Middle Class*. Open University Press, Buckingham.

Powles, M. and Anderson, D. 1994. *Participation and Access in TAFE: Economic Utility or Social Service?* Center for the Study of Higher Education, University of Melbourne.

Prasad, A. and Prasad, P. 2002. "Otherness at Large: Identity and Difference in the New Globalised Organisational Landscape." In I. Aaltio and A. Mills (Eds.), *Gender, Identity, and Culture in Organisations*. Routledge, London, pp. 57–71.

Preston, B., Blackmore, J., and Thomson, P. 2004. "Lifelong Work, Inter-generational Shifts, and the Future of School Leadership: Principal and Teacher Demand and Supply." Conference proceedings AARE Annual Conference, Melbourne.

Prichard, C. and Deem, R. 1999. "Wo-managing Further Education: Gender and the Constuction of the Manager in the Corporate Colleges of England." *Gender and Education*, vol. 11, no. 3, pp. 323–42.

Probert, B. 1998. "Working in Australian Universities: Pay Equity for Men and Women?" *Australian Universities Review*, vol. 42, no. 2., pp. 33–42.

———. 2001a. "Researching Australia's Gender Culture: From Shared Expectations to Profound Ambivalence." *Dialogue*, vol. 20, no. 2, pp. 21–27.

———. 2001b. *"Grateful Slaves" or "Self-made Women": A Matter of Choice or Policy?* Clare Burton Lectures, RMIT, Melbourne.

Pusey, M. 2003. *The Experience of Middle Australia: The Dark Side of Economic Reform.* Cambridge University Press, Sydney.

Putnam, R. Mumby, 2000. "Organisations, Emotion and the Myth of Rationality." In S. Fineman (Ed.), *Emotions and Organisations.* Sage, London, pp. 36–57.

Randle, K. and Brady, N. 1997. "Managerialism and Professionalism in the 'Cinderella Service.'" *Journal of Vocational Education and Training*, vol. 49, no. 1, pp. 121–39.

Ransom, S. 2003. "Public Accountability in the Age of Neo-liberal Governance." *Journal of Education Policy*, vol. 18, no. 5, pp. 59–80.

Reay, D. 2000. "Dim Dross? Marginalised Voices Both Inside and Outside the Academy." *Women's Studies International Forum*, vol. 23, no. 1, pp. 13–21.

———. (2004). "Cultural Capitalists and Academic Habitus: Classed and Gendered Labour in UK Higher Education." *Women's Studies International Forum*, vol. 27, no. 1, pp. 31–39.

Reay, D. and Ball, S. 2000. "Essentials of Female Management: Women's Ways of Working in the Education Market Place?" *Educational Management and Administration*, vol. 28, no. 2, pp. 145–59.

Reed, R. 1995. "Entrepreneurialism and Paternalism in Australian Management: A Critique of the Self Made Man." In D. Collinson and J. Hearn (Eds.), *Men as Managers, Managers as Men: Critical Perspectives on Men, Masculinities and Management.* Sage, London, pp. 99–122.

Rees, S. and Radley, G. (Eds.). 1995. *The Human Costs of Managerialism: Advocating the Recovery of Humanity.* Pluto Press, Australia.

Reich, R. 1997. "Why the Rich are Getting Richer and the Poor Poorer." In A. Halsey, H. Lauder, P. Brown, and A. S. Wells (Eds.), *Education: Culture, Economy and Society.* Oxford University Press, Oxford, pp. 163–71.

Rhoades, G. 1996. *Managed Professionals: Unionised Faculty and Restructuring Academic Labour.* State University of New York Press, Albany, N.Y.

Rose, N. 1989. *Governing of the Soul: The Shaping of the Private Self.* Routledge, London.

———. 1999. *Powers of Freedom: Reframing Political Thought.* Cambridge University Press, Cambridge, New York.

Rosenau, P. 1992. *Post-Modernism and the Social Sciences: Insights, Inroads and Intrusions.* Princeton University Press, Princeton.

Rowley, J. 1995. "Student Feedback: A Shaky Foundation for Quality Assurance Innovation and Learning." *Education*, vol. 1, no. 3, pp. 14–22.

Ryan, R. 2002. "Making VET in Schools Work: A Review of Policy and Practice in the Implementation of Vocational Education and Training in Australian Schools." *Journal of Educational Enquiry*, vol. 3, no. 1, pp. 1–16.

Sachs, J. 1999. "The Activist Professional." *The Journal of Educational Change*, vol. 1, no. 1, pp. 77–95.

——— . 2003. *The Activist Teaching Profession.* Open University Press, Buckingham.

Sachs, J. and Blackmore, J. 1998. "You Never Show You Can't Cope: Women in School Leadership Roles Managing Their Emotions." *Gender and Education*, vol. 19, no. 3, pp. 265–79.

Salisbury, J. and Riddell, S. (Eds.). 2000. *Gender, Policy and Educational Change: Shifting Agendas in the UK and Europe.* Routledge, London.

Sanguinetti, J. 1998. *Within and against Performativity: Discursive Engagement in Adult Literacy and Basic Education.* Unpublished PhD thesis, Deakin University, Geelong.

Saul, J. R. 1995a. *The Unconscious Civilisation.* Anansi Press, Toronto.

Saunderson, W. 2002. "Women, Academia and Identity: Constructions of Equal Opportunities in the "New Managerialism"—A Case of Lipstick on the Gorilla?" *Higher Education Quarterly*, vol. 56, no. 4, pp. 376–406.

Sawer, M. 1999. "The Watchers Within: Women and the Australian State." In L. Hancock (Ed.), *Women, Public Policy and the State.* Macmillan, South Yarra, pp. 36–53.

——— . 2003. *The Ethical State? Social Liberalism in Australia.* Melbourne University Press, Melbourne.

Schmuck, P., Hollingsworth, S., and Lock, R. 2002. "Women Administrators and the Point of Exit: Collision between the Person and the Institution." In C. Reynolds (Ed.), *Women and School Leadership: International Perspectives.* State University of New York Press, Albany, N.Y.

——— . Scott, S. 1999. "The Academic as a Service Provider: Is the Customer Always Right?" *Journal of Higher Education Policy and Management*, vol. 21, no. 2, pp. 193–202.

Seddon, T. 1994. "Changing Contexts: New Debates ALBE in the 1990s." *Open Letter*, vol. 5, no. 1. pp. 1–5.

——— . 1997. "Education Deprofessionalised? Or Reregulated, Reorganised and Reauthorised?" *Australian Journal of Education*, vol. 41, no. 3, pp. 228–46.

Seddon, T. and Angus, L. 1999. "Steering Futures: Practices and Possibilities of Institutional Redesign in Australian Education and Training." *Journal of Education Policy*, vol. 14, no. 5, pp. 491–506.

——— . 2000. "Beyond Nostalgia: Institutional Design and Alternative Futures." In T. Seddon and L. Angus (Eds.), *Beyond Nostalgia: Reshaping Australian Education.* ACER, Camberwell.

Sennett, R. 2004. *Respect: The Formation of Character in the Global Era.* Penguin, St. Ives.

Sergiovanni, T. J. 1999. "Conflicting Mindscapes and the Inevitability of Stress in Teaching." In R. Vanderberghe and A. M. Huberman (Eds.), *Understanding and Preventing Teacher Burnout.* Cambridge University, Cambridge, pp. 256–68.

——— . 2001. *Leadership: What's in It for Schools?* RoutledgeFalmer, London.

Shacklock, G. 1998. "Professionalism and Intensification in Teaching: A Case Study of 'Care' in Teachers' Work." *Asia-Pacific Journal of Teacher Education*, vol. 26, no. 3, pp. 177–89.

Shain, F. 1999. "Managing to Lead: Female Managers in the Post-incorporated Further Education Sector." British Educational Research Association Annual Conference Sussex University, Brighton.

Shore, C. and Wright, S. 2000. "Coercive Accountability." In M. Strathern (Ed.), *Audit Cultures: Anthropological Studies in Accountability, Ethics and the Academy.* Routledge, London, pp. 57–89.

Silins, H. and Mulford, B. 2002. "Schools as Learning Organisations: The Case for System, Teachers and Student Learning." *Journal of Education Administration*, vol. 40, no. 5, pp. 425–46.

Sinclair, A. 1994. *Trials at the Top.* Australian Management Center, University of Melbourne, Melbourne.

———. 1995a. "The Seduction of the Self Managed Team." *Leading and Managing*, vol. 1, no. 1, pp. 44–62.

———. 1995b. "The Chameleon of Accountability: Forms and Discourses." *Accounting, Organisations and Society*, vol. 19, no. 2, pp. 219–37.

———. 1998. *Doing Leadership Differently: Gender, Power and Sexuality in a Changing Business Culture.* Melbourne University Press, Melbourne.

———. 2000. "Leadership in Administration: Rediscovering a Lost Discourse." In G. Davis and P. Weller (Eds.), *New Ideas, Better Government.* Allen and Unwin, St. Leonards, pp. 229–44.

———. 2000a. "Teaching Managers about Masculinities: Are You Kidding?" *Management Learning*, vol. 31, no. 1, pp. 83–101.

———. 2000b. "Women within Diversity: Risks and Possibilities." *Women in Management Review*, vol. 15, no. 5/6, pp. 137–45.

Sinclair, A. and Wilson, V. 2002. *New Faces of Leadership.* Melbourne University Press, Melbourne.

Sklra, L. 2003. "Mourning Silence: Women Superintendents (and a Researcher) Speaking Up and Speaking Out." In M. Young and L. Sklra (Eds.), *Reconsidering: Feminist Research in Educational Leadership.* State University of New York Press, Albany, N.Y., pp. 103–38.

Skrla, L. and Scheurich, J. 2004. *Educational Equity and Accountability: Paradigms, Policies and Politics.* RoutledgeFalmer, London.

Slaughter, S. and Leslie, L. 1998. *Academic Capitalism: Politics, Policy and the Entrepreneurial University.* John Hopkins University Press, Baltimore.

Smith, E. and Keating, J. 2003. *From Training Reform to Training Packages.* Social Science Press, Australia.

Smulyan, L. 2000. *Balancing Acts: Women Principals at Work.* State University of New York Press, Albany, N.Y.

Smylie, M. 1999. "Teacher Stress in a Time of Reform." In R. Vanderberghe and A. M. Huberman, *Understanding and Preventing Teacher Burnout.* Cambridge University Press, Cambridge, pp. 55–84.

Smyth, S. 1995. *Academic Work.* Falmer, London.

Spillane, J., Havelson, R., and Diamond, J. 2001. "Investigating School Leadership Practice: A Distributed Perspective." *Educational Researcher*, April, pp. 23–28.

Spillane, J. 2004. "Towards a Theory of Leadership Practice: A Distributed Perspective." *Journal of Curriculum Studies*, vol. 36, no. 1, pp. 3–35.

Spivak, G. 1988. *In Other Worlds: Essays in Cultural Politics.* Routledge, New York.

Spurling, A. 1997. "Women and Change in Higher Education." In H. Eggins (Ed.), *Women and Leaders and Managers in Higher Education.* Open University Press, Buckingham, pp. 47–58.

Stake, B. 1995. *The Art of Case Study Research.* Sage, Thousand Oaks.

Starr, K. 1997. *The Roar Which Lies on the Other Side of Silence: The Responses of Women Principals to the Structural Reform Agenda in South Australian Education.* AARE, Brisbane.

Stoer, S. and Magalhaes, A. 2004. "Education, Knowledge and the Network Society." *Globalization, Societies and Education*, vol. 2, no. 3, pp. 319–36.

Strachan, J. 1999a. "Feminist Educational Leadership in a New Zealand Neo-Liberal Context." *Journal of Educational Administration*, vol. 37, no. 2, pp. 121–38.

———. 1999b. "Feminist Educational Leadership: Locating the Concepts in Practice." *Gender and Education*, vol. 11, no. 3, pp. 309–22.

Strathern, M. (Ed.). 2000a. *Audit Cultures: Anthropological Studies in Accountability, Ethics and the Academy.* Routledge, London.

———. 2000b. "The Tyranny of Transparency." *British Educational Research Journal*, vol. 26, no. 3, pp. 309–21.

Summers, A. 2003. *The End of Equality: Work, Babies and Women's Choices in 21st Century Australia.* Random House, Melbourne.

Taylor, S. 2001. "Teacher Union Activism for Gender Equity." *Australian Educational Researcher*, vol. 28, no. 1, pp. 47–80.

Taylor, S., Rizvi, F., Lingard, B., and Henry, M. 1997. *Educational Policy and the Politics of Change.* Routledge, London.

Teese, R. 2002. *The Cultural Benefits of Vocational Education and Training for Early School Teachers.* Australian National Training Authority, Melbourne University.

Teese, R. and Polesel, J. 2003. *Undemocratic Schooling: Equity and Quality in Mass Secondary Education in Australia.* Allen and Unwin, Sydney.

Thomson, P. 1998. "Thoroughly Modern Management and Cruel Accounting: The Effect of Public Sector Reform on Public Education." In A. Reid (Ed.), *Going Public: Education Policy and Public Education in Australia.* Australian Curriculum Studies Association, Canberra.

———. 1999. "How Doing Justice Got Boxed In: A Cautionary Curriculum Tale for Policy Activists." In A. Reid and and B. Johnson (Eds.), *Contesting the Curriculum.* Social Science Press, Katoomba, pp. 24–32.

———. 2000. "Like Schools," Educational "Disadvantage" and "Thisness." *Australian Educational Researcher*, vol. 27, no. 3, pp. 157–71.

———. 2001. "How Principals Lose 'Face': A Disciplinary Tale of Educational Administration and Modern Managerialism." *Discourse*, vol. 22, no. 1, pp. 1–30.

Thomson, P. and Blackmore, J. 2006. "Beyond the Power of One: Redesigning the Work of School Principals." *Journal of Educational Change*, vol. 7, pp. 161–77.

Thomson, P., Blackmore, J., Sachs, J., and Tregenza, K. 2003. "High Stake Principalship: Sleepless Nights, Heart Attacks and Sudden Death Accountabilities: Reading Media Representations of the United States Principal Shortage." *Australian Journal of Education*, vol. 47, no. 2, pp. 118–32.

Thrupp, M. 1999. *Schools Making a Difference: Let's be Realistic.* Open University Press, Buckingham.

Thrupp, M. and Willmott, R. 2003. *Education Management in Managerialist Times: Beyond the Textual Apologists.* Open University Press.

Townley, B. 1997. "The Institutional Logic of Performance Appraisal." *Organisation Studies*, vol. 18, no. 2, pp. 261–85.

Townsend, T. 1994. "Community Involvement: The Hidden Factor in Devolution." *Journal of Educational Management*, vol. 8, no. 4, pp. 24–29.

———. 1997. "Schools of the Future: A Case Study of Systemic Educational Development." In T. Townsend (Ed.), *Restructuring and Quality: Issues for Tomorrow's Schools.* Routledge, London, pp. 199–212.

Troman, G. 1997. "Selfmanagement and School Inspection: Complimentary Forms of Surveillance and Control in the Primary School." *Oxford Review of Education*, vol. 23, no. 3, pp. 345–64.

———. 2000. "Teacher Stress in the Low-trust Society." *British Journal of Sociology of Education*, vol. 21, no. 3, pp. 331–52.

University of Western Australia. 1996. *Evaluation of the Women and Leadership Program.* UWA, Perth.

Vanderberghe, R. and Huberman, A. M. 1999. *Understanding and Preventing Teacher Burnout.* Cambridge University Press, Cambridge.

van Gramberg, B. 1999. "Women, Industrial Relations and Public Policy." In L. Hancock (Ed.), *Women, Public Policy and the State.* Macmillan, South Yarra, pp. 99–113.

Victoria, Department of Education. 2003. *Blueprint for Government Schools.* Victorian Government Printing Service, Melbourne.

Vidovich, L. and Currie, J. 1998. *Universities and Globalisation: Critical Perspectives.* Sage, Thousand Oaks.

Vidovich, L. and Slee, R. 2001. "Bringing Universities to Account? Exploring Some Global and Local Policy Tensions." *Journal of Education Policy*, vol. 16, no. 5, pp. 431–53.

Vincent, C. (Ed.). 2003. *Social Justice, Education and Identity.* RoutledgeFalmer, London.

Vinson, T. 1999. *Unequal in Life: The Distribution of Social Disadvantage in Victoria and New South Wales.* Ignatious Center, Melbourne.

———. 2002. *Inquiry into the Provision of Public Education in NSW: Report of the Vinson Inquiry.* Ignatious Center, Melbourne.

Wacjman, J. 1998. *Managing Like a Man.* Allen and Unwin, Sydney.

———. 1999. *Managing Like a Man: Women and Men in Corporate Management*. Allen and Unwin, Sydney.

Walby, S. 2000. "Beyond the Politics of Location: The Power of Argument in a Global Era." *Feminist Theory*, vol. 1, no. 2, pp. 189–206.

Walkerdine, V. 1989. "Femininity as Performance." *Oxford Review of Education*, vol. 15, no. 3. pp. 267–79.

Warren, J. 1999. *Democracy and Trust*. Cambridge University Press, Cambridge.

Waslander, S. 1995. "Choice, Competition and Segregation: An Analysis of a New Zealand Secondary School Market." *Journal of Education Policy*, vol. 16, no. 1, pp. 1–26.

Webb, J., Schirato, T., and Danaher, T. (Eds.). 2002. *Understanding Bourdieu*. Allen and Unwin, Sydney.

Weedon. C. 1999. *Feminism, Theory and the Politics of Difference*. Blackwell, Oxford.

Wells, A., Carnochan, S., and Allen, R. 1998. "Globalisation and Educational Change." In A. Hargreaves, A. Lieberman, M. Fullan, and D. Hopkins (Eds.), *International Handbook of Educational Change*, vol. 1, Kluwer, Dordrecht, pp. 322–48.

Wells, A. S., Lopez, A., Scott, J., and Holme, J. 1999. "Charter Schools as Post Modern Paradox: Rethinking Social Stratification in the Age of Deregulated School Choice." *Harvard Educational Review*, vol. 69, no. 2, pp. 172–219.

Wenger, E. 1998. *Communities of Practice: Learning, Meaning and Identity*. Cambridge University Press, Cambridge.

Whitehead, S. 1999. "From Paternalism to Entrepreneurialism: The Experience of Men Managers in UK Postcompulsory Education." *Discourse*, vol. 20, no. 1, pp. 57–71.

Whitehead, S. and Moodley, R. (Eds.). 1999. *Transforming Managers: Gendering Change in the Public Sector*. UCL Press, London.

Whitty, G. 1996. "Creating Quasi-Markets in Education: A Review of Recent Research on Parental Choice and School Autonomy in Three Countries." *Review of Research in Education*, vol. 22, pp. 3–48.

———. 2001. "Teacher Professionalism in New Times." In D. Gleeson and C. Husbands (Eds.), *The Performing School: Managing, Teaching and Learning in a Performance Culture*. RoutledgeFalmer, London, pp. 159–74f.

Whitty, G., Halpin, D., and Power, S. 1998. *Choice and Devolution in Education: The School, the State and the Market*. ACER, Melbourne.

Wilkinson, J. 2005. "Dead, White (Fe)males? Examining Representations of Women's Leadership in the Media and Australian Universities," unpublished PhD thesis, Deakin University, Geelong.

Williams, R., Harold, B., Robertson, J., and Southworth, G. 1997. "Sweeping Decentralisation of Educational Decisionmaking Authority: Lessons from England and New Zealand." *PhiDeltaKappan*, vol. 78, no. 8, pp. 626–31.

Willmott, H. 1995. "The Odd Couple? Re-engineering, Busines Processes, Managing Human Relations." *New Technology, Work and Employment*, vol. 10, no. 2, pp. 89–98.

Winter, R., Taylor, T., and Sarros, J. 2000. "Trouble at the Mill: Quality of Academic Worklife." *Studies in Higher Education*, vol. 25, no. 3. pp. 279–94.

Wong, K. 1999. "Chicago School Reform: From Decentralisation to Integrated Governance." *Journal of Educational Change*, vol. 1, no. 1, pp. 97–105.

Woodall, J., Edwards, C., and Welchman, R. 1997. "Organisational Restructuring and the Achievement of Equal Opportunity." *Gender, Work and Organisation*, vol. 4, no. 1, pp. 2–12.

Woods, P. 1999. "Competition Cooperation and the Public Market: Themes and Variations in Producer Engagement." Paper presented to the Eighth Conference on Quasi-markets, Bath.

———. 2004. "Democratic Leadership: Drawing Distinctions with Distributed Leadership." *International Journal of Leadership in Education*, vol. 7, no. 1, pp. 3–26.

Woods, P. and Bagley, P. 1996. "Market Elements in a Public Service: An Analytical Model for Studying Educational Policy." *Journal of Education Policy*, vol. 11, no. 6, pp. 641–53.

Woods, P., Levacic, R., and Hardman, J. 1998. *Better Education? The Impact of School Performance of Choice and Competition between Schools.* Annual Conference of the American Educational Research Association, Montreal.

Wylie, C. 1995. "Contrary Currents: The Application of the Public Sector Reform Framework in Education." *New Zealand Journal of Educational Studies*, vol. 30, no. 2, pp. 54–59.

———. 1997. *At the Centre of the Web: The Role of the New Zealand Primary School Principal with a Decentralised Education System.* New Zealand Council of Educational Research, Wellington.

———. 1999. "Choice, Responsiveness and Constraint after a Decade of Self Managing Schools in New Zealand." Paper presented to Australian/New Zealand Associations of Research in Education Conference, Melbourne.

Wylie, C. and Mitchell, L. 2003. "Sustaining School Development in a Decentralised System: Lessons from New Zealand." International Congress for School Effectiveness and Improvement Conference, Sydney.

Yeatman, A. 1992. "Women's Citizenship Claims, Labour Market Policy and Globalisation." *Australian Journal of Political Science*, vol. 27, Dec., pp. 449–61.

———. 1994. *Postmodern Revisionings of the Political.* Routledge, New York.

———. 1998a. "Interpreting Contemporary Contractualism." In M. Dea and B. Hindess (Eds.), *Governing Australia.* Cambridge University Press, Cambridge.

———. 1998b. *Activism in the Policy Process.* Allen and Unwin, Sydney.

———. 2000. "The Politics of Postpatrimonial Governance." In T. Seddon and L. Angus (Eds.), *Beyond Nostalgia: Reshaping Australian Education.* ACER, Camberwell.

Young, B. 1998. "'The Alberta Advantage': DeKleining Career Prospects for Alberta's Women Educators?" Paper presented to AERA Annual Conference, San Diego.

Zipin, L. and Brennan, M. 2003. "The Suppression of Ethical Disposition through Managerial Governmentality: A Habitus Crisis in Australian Higher Education." *International Journal of Leadership in Education*, vol. 6, no. 4, pp. 351–70.

About the Authors

JILL BLACKMORE is a Professor of Education in the Faculty of Education, Deakin University. Her research interests include feminist approaches to globalization and education policy, administrative and organizational theory, educational leadership and reform, organizational change and innovation, teachers' and academics' work, and all their policy implications. She previously published *Troubling Women: Feminism, Leadership and Educational Change* (1999, Open University Press). She is on several editorial boards of international journals, including the *British Educational Research Journal*, and is regional editor of the *International Journal of Leadership in Education*. She undertakes professional development with teachers, principals, and parents as well as policy consultancies to government.

JUDYTH SACHS is Professor and Deputy Vice Chancellor (Academic) at Macquarie University. Her research interests have focused particularly on school and higher education reform, leadership, teachers' work and professionalism, and quality assurance and university governance. Her current research projects have been on school principalship and how schools manage risk. Her most recent book is *The Activist Teacher Professional* (Open University Press, 2003). She is on several editorial boards.

Index